The Eighteenth Century 1714–1815

A HISTORY OF ENGLAND

General Editors

CHRISTOPHER BROOKE, M.A.,. Litt.D., F.B.A., F.S.A., F.R.Hist.S.
Professor of History, Westfield College, University of London

DENIS MACK SMITH, M.A.
Fellow of All Souls College, Oxford

Volumes in the series

1 ROMAN BRITAIN AND EARLY ENGLAND, 55 B.C.–A.D. 871
Peter Hunter Blair

2 FROM ALFRED TO HENRY III, 871–1272
Christopher Brooke

3 THE LATER MIDDLE AGES, 1272–1485
George Holmes

4 THE TUDOR AGE, 1485–1603
Mervyn James

5 THE CENTURY OF REVOLUTION, 1603–1714
Christopher Hill

6 THE EIGHTEENTH CENTURY, 1714–1815
John B. Owen

7 FROM CASTLEREAGH TO GLADSTONE, 1815–1885
Derek Beales

8 MODERN BRITAIN, 1885–1955
Henry Pelling

The Eighteenth Century 1714–1815

JOHN B. OWEN

ROWMAN and LITTLEFIELD
Totowa, New Jersey

First published in the United States, 1975
by Rowman and Littlefield, Totowa, N. J.

ISBN 0-87471-622-5

Printed in Great Britain by A. Wheaton & Company, Exeter

GENERAL EDITORS' PREFACE

KNOWLEDGE and understanding of English history change and develop so rapidly that a new series needs little apology. The present series was planned in the conviction that a fresh survey of English history was needed and that the time was ripe for it. It will cover the whole span from Caesar's first invasion in 55 B.C. to 1955, and be completed in eight volumes. The precise scope and scale of each book will inevitably vary according to the special circumstances of its period; but each will combine a clear narrative with an analysis of many aspects of history—social, economic, religious, cultural and so forth—such as is essential in any approach to English history today.

The special aim of this series is to provide serious and yet challenging books, not buried under a mountain of detail. Each volume is intended to provide a picture and an appreciation of its age, as well as a lucid outline, written by an expert who is keen to make available and alive the findings of modern research. They are intended to be reasonably short—long enough that the reader may feel he has really been shown the ingredients of a period, not so long that he loses appetite for anything further. The series is intended to be a stimulus to wider reading rather than a substitute for it; and yet to comprise a set of volumes, each, within its limits, complete in itself. Our hope is to provide an introduction to English history which is lively and illuminating, and which makes it at once exciting and more intelligible.

C. N. L. B.
D. M. S.

To my wife, Phyllis

CONTENTS

PREFACE

THE origin of this volume lies in the provocative remark of an erstwhile colleague in an Oxford common-room that no 'Namierite' would ever dare to write a text-book. That was many years ago, and the relentless passage of time testifies as much to my foolhardiness in accepting the challenge as to the many changes in personal circumstances that have wrought delays. I began writing at Lincoln College, Oxford, when I was still primarily a teacher of history; but soon administrative responsibilities came to consume more and more of my time, and eventually most of the chapters had to be written in Canada where, for better or worse, I have become at least temporarily a full-time administrator. Since in modern universities scholarship and administration are increasingly difficult to reconcile, my translation may help to explain, although it can scarcely excuse, the many defects in the following pages. These would have been significantly greater had it not been for the helpful advice and encouragement of the two editors, Christopher Brooke and Denis Mack Smith. Without the almost saintly patience of the publishers, the book would not be appearing at all. Only the reader can judge whether that patience has been justified.

Any author of a general historical survey must pick the brains and pillage the writings of his fellow-historians, and much that follows has been shamelessly lifted from the works which appear in the bibliography. My unacknowledged debt is beyond calculation, and I deeply regret that pressure of time has prevented me from submitting my conclusions for criticism to those many friends whose expertise is so much greater than mine. But it would be churlish not to record that my limited knowledge of the eighteenth-century scene has been greatly augmented across the years by many happy and stimulating discussions with the late Sir Lewis Namier, the late Romney Sedgwick, Dame Lucy Sutherland, Steven Watson, Jack Plumb, John Brooke and Ian Christie—not to mention several generations of pupils, undergraduate and graduate, whose searching comments forced me to defend, and sometimes change, my views.

My deepest obligation, no less for the subtle methods by which she cajoled me into finishing the book than for her patient typing and stylistic polishing of an indecipherable manuscript, is acknowledged on another page.

Saint Mary's University JBO
Halifax NS
Canada
September 1974

INTRODUCTION

THE eighteenth century saw England advance, despite many uncertainties and some reverses, from a tentative threshold of greatness to a position of unrivalled political and economic supremacy in Europe. But in 1714 even the most acute and optimistic observer would scarcely have dared to predict that a nation just emerged from a 'century of revolution' would so quickly achieve so much. She had admittedly thwarted the ambitions of Louis XIV, but, in the process, had alienated her allies without gaining any very clear idea of her role in Europe, still less in the rest of the world; she had acquired an Empire more by accident than by design, but had scarcely yet begun to think about the problem of governing it efficiently; she had rejected absolute monarchy, but had not yet learnt how to reconcile the paradoxes inherent in the system of 'mixed' government which she had half-consciously accepted in its place, and seemed to many to have committed herself to violent party conflict and near political anarchy; she had abandoned the idea of a single persecuting State Church, but her politics were not yet sufficiently secularized to allow true religious toleration; she was on uneasy terms with Scotland, and the durability of the recent Act of Union had still to be demonstrated; she barely comprehended the complexity of the Irish problem, and had not even learnt that coercion could solve nothing.

If her political future was open to conjecture, her economic prospects—notwithstanding the significant progress of the late seventeenth century—were equally uncertain. Still overwhelmingly agricultural and rural in character, she had only recently begun to think in terms of global rather than purely European commerce and, despite the growing importance of colonial re-exports, was still largely dependent upon the cloth trade with Europe, which had been the major basis of her prosperity for over two centuries but was beginning to reach saturation point. As yet manufacturing was small-scale and organized on a purely domestic basis, and the new interest in science which had found expression in the foundation of the Royal Society in 1660 had provided little in the way of technological advance. If she had already outstripped her chief economic rivals, the Dutch, it was far from clear that her pre-eminence, like theirs, would not prove short-lived. Although the creation of the Bank of England and the funding of the national debt had facilitated the harnessing of national wealth for the purposes of foreign aggrandizement and imperial expansion, the new organization of public credit aroused widespread suspicion, and the conflict between the landed and monied interests was bitter and prolonged. The previous century had established the political supremacy of the landed classes, with the merchant and monied classes still very much the junior partners. Political stability, economic progress and the spread of empire were all dependent upon their ability to work together in the pursuit of common aims. Meanwhile, like her arch-enemy France, Britain was exhausted by the long wars of the two previous decades, bedevilled by an insecure dynasty, and a prey to financial and political instability.

The following pages attempt to explain the highly complex manner in which the men of eighteenth-century Britain sought to meet the various challenges which faced them. For the most part their efforts were strikingly successful; sometimes—most notably with the problem of imperial government—they had to accept temporary failure; but invariably they showed a vigour and a resilience that enabled them ultimately to turn to full advantage the gains which they had inherited from the previous century.

I have departed, perhaps unwisely, from the format adopted by the authors of the preceding and subsequent volumes in this series by including much more narrative and placing significantly greater emphasis upon political history than is currently fashionable. I have correspondingly devoted rather less space to those social and intellectual developments which are nowadays seen by wiser and more enlightened historians to be the real stuff of history. In part this reflects my own prejudices and limitations, in part my convictions that history is primarily a story, that a superabundance of analysis can bewilder rather than clarify, and that to interpret the eighteenth century in terms of present-day preoccupations is merely to follow in the footsteps of Whig historians. It was an oligarchic and pragmatic age, in which—except perhaps during the closing decades—ideas had little influence upon either political or economic life, and the working classes were expected to remain in that decent obscurity to which they were believed rightly to belong. This was the century neither of tiresome ideologies nor of the common man, and if we are to understand its remarkable achievements it seems not unreasonable to accept contemporary criteria and priorities, which gave pride of place to the practical politics of the ruling classes.

The format which I have adopted may pose problems for those with no previous knowledge of eighteenth-century English history. For example, the political situation in 1714 was highly complex and in a state of flux, but the reader will have to wait until chapter 5 for a general analysis. To avoid too much interim confusion, I have indicated appropriate subsequent page references for a few key topics and have included occasional explanatory notes, even at the risk of some repetition. It may also help at this point to emphasize that during the reign of Queen Anne (1702–14) England had been involved in war on a scale hitherto unknown, from which she had unilaterally managed to extract herself in 1713 by the Treaty of Utrecht—a peace stigmatized by her allies as flagrant desertion, and criticized at home as providing inadequate recognition of the great victories of the Duke of Marlborough. During the war Parliament and the nation had been bitterly divided over many issues and on a predominantly party basis. Broadly speaking, the Whigs were the war party, sympathizing with the claims of Protestant Dissenters, having significant links with the new monied interest in the City, and strongly supporting the succession on the Queen's death of the House of Hanover, as envisaged in the Act of Settlement of 1701. The Tories were the peace party, staunch supporters of the Established Church, spokesmen of the landed (and especially the squirearchical) interest, and believed by many to favour the restoration of the Stuart monarchy in the person of the Old Pretender, son of James II.[1]

Although the Tories had been solidly entrenched in power since 1710, they were a far from united party. For some years the leadership of the moderate but devious and widely distrusted Robert Harley, Earl of Oxford, had been challenged by the brilliant but erratic and irresponsible Henry St John, Viscount Bolingbroke, who had not hesitated to play upon the anti-war prejudices of the Tory squirearchy or to revive their zeal for persecuting nonconformists. Moreover, the increasing tendency of Bolingbroke, Francis Atterbury (Bishop of Rochester) and James Butler, Duke of Ormonde, to flirt with Jacobitism alarmed not only Whigs but a significant number of Hanoverian Tories whose chief spokesman was Daniel Finch, Earl of Nottingham. The Whigs displayed greater unity of outlook and action, but of the original great lords of the so-called Whig junto (Somers, Halifax, Wharton, Orford and Sunderland) all save Sunderland were past their prime; and, apart from him, the future belonged to younger men such as Viscount Townshend, James Stanhope and Robert Walpole. With scarcely concealed impatience, the Whigs assiduously cultivated the Elector of Hanover and prepared for the change of dynasty which, they hoped, would see their return from the political wilderness. Between 1713 and 1715 the advent of peace, the death of the Queen, the succession of George I, the failure of the Jacobite

---

[1]For a fuller discussion of Whigs and Tories see pp 112–14.

rebellion and the erosion of the ranks of the Tory party all combined to usher in a new age.

Few aspects of eighteenth-century English history are uncontroversial. There is much in the following chapters that is gravely oversimplified, and much that may seem to many people perverse. In politics, the orthodox interpretation until the 1920s was that of the great Whig historians, such as Lord Macaulay, Thomas Erskine May, W. E. H. Lecky, and both G. O. and G. M. Trevelyan, who tended to see the revolution of 1688 as a Whig triumph, making possible the emergence of the two-party system, constitutional monarchy and the basic elements of modern Cabinet Government—all of which progressive developments were believed to have been threatened after 1760 by the sinister determination of George III to turn back the political clock and revert to the arbitrary practices of his Stuart predecessors. In 1929 and 1930 the late Sir Lewis Namier published *The Structure of Politics at the Accession of George III* and *England in the Age of the American Revolution*, which challenged virtually every aspect of the Whig interpretation, but at the same time so atomized the politics of the eighteenth century that they became almost incomprehensible except to the discerning few. For over twenty years, if only from fear of Namier's devastating criticism, most historians avoided the period, while he himself turned to nineteenth-century European history and to the diplomacy of the 1930s. In the 1950s he returned to his first love, and in a few brief essays began to supplement his earlier work of demolition by postulating a more positive alternative to the over-simplified Whig picture. At the same time, other younger historians attempted, with varying degrees of success, to use Namier's approach for periods of the century other than the 1760s, with which he had been chiefly concerned. Their work, and the criticism which it provoked—most notably in Sir Herbert Butterfield's *George III and the Historians*—has sometimes clarified, sometimes confused the issue. Although a self-confessed member of the so-called 'Namier school', I have attempted here to provide a post-Namier synthesis, which may well satisfy neither those who have accepted as articles of faith their own, sometimes misconceived, notions of Sir Lewis's findings, nor those Whig critics who were strangely silent during his life-time but have become increasingly vocal since his death. But I hope that my idiosyncratic views have not wholly concealed the conciliatory role which I have endeavoured to play.

In economic developments I have tried to assess the present state of knowledge in such controversial areas as those of the industrial and agricultural revolutions. In religious, intellectual and cultural history I have confined myself to a few subjective, and doubtless superficial, comments. But perhaps above all I have sought to give due weight to personalities in an age when personal loves and hatreds were more significant in determining political actions, and even the fate of the nation, than any ideas or principles. The best introduction to the history of the period must remain the lines from Aeschylus with which Namier prefaced his first great work:

> I took pains to determine the flight of crook-taloned birds, marking which were of the right by nature, and which of the left, and what were their ways of living, each after his kind, and the enmities and affections that were between them, and how they consorted together.

PART ONE
1714–1760

I

THE PRELUDE TO STABILITY: 1714–21

DURING the sixteen months between the conclusion of the War of the Spanish Succession and the death of Queen Anne, the strength of the great Tory Ministry which had been appointed in 1710 was steadily undermined. However widespread had been the desire for peace, the terms were considered insufficiently favourable to win lasting gratitude for its authors, as was evident from the defeat of the proposed commercial treaty with France. Nor, especially after the passage of the Occasional Conformity and Schism Acts,[1] could it seriously be contended that Anglicanism was any longer threatened by Protestant nonconformists. Finally, as Bolingbroke, Atterbury, Ormonde and other prominent Tory leaders adopted an increasingly Jacobite position, the succession question came to dominate political life. The old Tory battle-cry of 'Peace and the Church in Danger' could not rival in popular appeal the Whig slogan of 'Trade and the Protestant Succession', to which Hanoverian Tories no less than Whigs could be expected to rally. Rent by internal dissent, the Tory Ministry staggered on, while Bolingbroke indulged in fantasy by planning a wholly Jacobite Administration and trying to gain control of the army and of strategic points in the kingdom. He even managed to secure the dismissal of his old rival, Oxford, from the Lord Treasurership, but neither Hanoverian Tories nor Oxford's friends would participate in schemes that ran counter to the manifest disposition of the country. Even hot-headed Tory squires, who viewed the prospect of a Hanoverian king with scant enthusiasm, were unlikely to fight for a Stuart claimant who had only recently reaffirmed his Roman Catholic faith. Bolingbroke was already doomed when on 30 July 1714 it became obvious that the Queen was on her death-bed and a meeting of the Privy Council was hastily summoned.

[1]Tory measures which prevented nonconformists from qualifying for office by occasionally taking communion and sought to destroy the Dissenting Academies, which were the major nonconformist educational institutions.

Of the twenty-three members who attended, some were avowed Jacobites, some staunch Hanoverians, and some still uncommitted. Everything would depend on who took the initiative, and at the crucial moment Bolingbroke and his supporters baulked at challenging the Act of Settlement. But the Whigs were ready. Early that morning the Dukes of Argyle and Somerset had decided to exercise their rights as Privy Councillors and attend. Their voices were thus added to that of the Duke of Shrewsbury, then Lord-Lieutenant of Ireland and Lord Chamberlain, and the waverers appear to have been swayed by the presence of three great moderate Whigs. The immediate appointment of a Lord Treasurer had become vital; Shrewsbury was the unanimous choice, and his nomination was accepted a few hours later by the dying Queen.

From then until midnight the Council worked incessantly to secure the peaceful succession of the Hanoverian dynasty. Orders were issued to Judges, Lords-Lieutenant, Mayors, and the army and navy; fortresses were revictualled and garrisons increased; troops were recalled from abroad; the London militia was called out and Roman Catholics everywhere were disarmed. The next day the Whig element on the Council was strengthened by the re-appearance of Sunderland, Somers and Cowper—junto lords who had wisely left the initiative on the crucial day to their more moderate associates. Measures were taken to warn the Elector of Hanover of the impending crisis, and to seek armed assistance from Holland if the need arose. On 1 August the Queen died.

The leading Jacobites met immediately to consider their course of action, but in the face of the Council's decisive measures only Atterbury was in favour of proclaiming James. Meanwhile the Whig triumph continued. King George was proclaimed with enthusiasm, not only in London, York and the leading English cities, but in Dublin and Edinburgh as well; and when the names of the Lords Justices (who were to govern the Kingdom until the arrival of the King) were announced, George's eighteen nominees included only four Tories, all of whom were avowed Hanoverians, to serve with the three Whigs and four Tories who were *ex officio* members under the Regency Act of 1707. Both Houses of Parliament unanimously voted loyal addresses to the new King and granted him a Civil List of £700,000 per annum. From France, too, came comforting news. Louis XIV rejected the advances of the Pretender and assured the Lords Justices of his support for the Hanoverian Succession, and the Pretender himself did his cause scant service by issuing a manifesto in which he reasserted both his right to the Crown and his Roman Catholicism. Meanwhile Bolingbroke lurked apprehensively in the background until on 31 August, in accordance with instructions from

George I, Shrewsbury, Somerset and Cowper requested the Secretary's seals from his reluctant hands and locked the doors of his office. Though his dismissal was far from unexpected he confessed mournfully to Atterbury: '. . . the manner of my removal shocked me for at least two minutes . . . I see plainly that the Tory party is gone.'

Not until 18 September did the new King arrive at Greenwich, accompanied by his private secretary Robethon and his chief Hanoverian ministers, Bernstorff and Goertz. Amid the vast concourse of nobility and gentry which greeted him, he had eyes only for the Whigs. The new King, then fifty-four years of age, was an unattractive character, possessing neither personal charm nor regal bearing. Honest, dull and diffident, he had little liking for domestic politics or public appearances, preferring instead the company of his ugly and elderly mistresses, his Hanoverian servants and a small coterie of personal friends. Lady Mary Wortley Montague remarked of him:

> He could speak no English, and was past the age of learning it. Our customs and laws were all mysteries to him, which he neither tried to understand, nor was capable of understanding if he had endeavoured it. He was passively good-natured, and wished all mankind enjoyed quiet, if they would let him do so.

And Chesterfield described the King with his usual penetration:

> Importunity alone could make him act, and then only to get rid of it. His views and affections were singly confined to the narrow compass of his Electorate; England was too big for him. If he had nothing great as a King, he had nothing bad as a man; and if he does not adorn, at least he will not stain the annals of this country. In private life he would have been loved and esteemed as a good citizen, a good friend, and a good neighbour.

During September and October the composition of the new Ministry was determined. Nottingham as Lord President of the Council was the only Tory member. The Lord Treasurership was suppressed, the Treasury being put into commission with Halifax as First Lord; Townshend, Stanhope and Montrose became Secretaries of State, Cowper Lord Chancellor, Wharton Lord Privy Seal, and Sunderland Lord-Lieutenant of Ireland; Pulteney was made Secretary at War, Walpole Paymaster of the Forces, and places were found for many leading Whig Commoners at the Boards of Treasury, Admiralty, and Trade and Plantations; Somers, whose age and ill-health precluded him from responsible office, was given a seat in the Cabinet, and the Privy Council was completely remodelled on a Whig basis and reduced to thirty-three members. From the beginning the chief influence rested with Townshend and Stanhope. Charles,

2nd Viscount Townshend, was the intimate friend and brother-in-law of Robert Walpole and an acknowledged expert in foreign affairs. Of unimpeachable integrity and with an enormous capacity for hard work, he proved an excellent man of business; but he was an inelegant speaker, abrasive in manner, tenacious of his own opinions and impatient of all opposition. General James Stanhope, despite his defeat and capture at Brihuega, had won renown as a soldier, and was already showing marked signs of political and administrative ability. His frankness and boyish sincerity won him many friends, and his instinctive understanding of foreigners gave him an influence in Europe unequalled among his English contemporaries. But his bluntness sometimes offended, and like Townshend he could be violent, precipitate and even ruthless in pursuit of his ends. Originally, as the only Commoner in the Cabinet, he was acknowledged leader of the lower House, but his tactlessness and overbearing temper made it expedient to promote Walpole to the leadership in 1715.

Meanwhile, loyal addresses poured in from most of the counties, cities and towns in the Kingdom; and, with the coronation of the new King on 20 October the dynasty seemed firmly established. Yet there were spasmodic flashes of Tory resentment and outbursts of Jacobite sympathy. Riots broke out in many places, the Tory University of Oxford chose Coronation Day to confer an honorary degree on the Jacobite ex-Chancellor of Ireland, and the rejuventated *Examiner* virulently attacked the Whig ministry. To quell this rising spirit of opposition, three proclamations were issued during November and December—for suppressing riots, for enforcing laws against Papists and for banning clergy from discussing political matters from their pulpits. Parliament was dissolved at the end of the year, and a further royal proclamation exhorted voters in the coming general election 'to have a particular regard to such as showed a firmness to the Protestant Succession when it was in danger'. Tory Lords-Lieutenant were replaced by Whigs and favourable sheriffs were appointed. The Whigs were determined to leave nothing to chance in the last election of the century that was to be fought primarily on a Whig-Tory basis. The Tories could only attempt to revive religious passions, but the cry of 'the Church in Danger' came ill from the mouths of those whose leaders had recently intrigued to bring in a Roman Catholic sovereign. The Whigs made the most of the national and merchant resentment at the Peace of Utrecht and with the added advantage of Crown patronage[1] their victory was a foregone conclusion. Early success in the City of London (always of great prestige value) was repeated throughout the

---

[1]On electoral patronage see pp 100–3.

country, and the Whigs even doubled their number of seats in the English counties, normally strongholds of Toryism. All told, the Tories lost 141 seats and the Whig majority in the new Parliament was 124. Well might a Tory versifier lament the passing of 1714:

Farewell Old Year, for thou with Broomstick hard
Hast drove poor Tory from St James's Yard.
Farewell Old Year, Old Monarch, and Old Tory
Farewell Old England, thou hast lost thy Glory.

Secure in the knowledge of a comfortable majority in the new House of Commons, the Whig ministers leapt to the attack. On the Address-in-Reply Walpole declared:

> His [the Pretender's] hopes were built upon the measures that had been taken for some time past in Great Britain. It shall be our business to trace out those measures whereon he placed his hopes, and to bring the authors of them to condign punishment.

A majority of 106 endorsed his sentiments. Faced by this threat of impeachment, the three chief Tory leaders—Oxford, Bolingbroke and Ormonde—reacted quite differently. Oxford, with his usual phlegmatic temper, determined calmly to face the storm; Bolingbroke, falsely informed that Prior, his erstwhile companion in Jacobitism, was turning King's evidence, lost his nerve and fled to France; the popular Ormonde openly consorted with the most ardent Jacobites, set about provoking riots and made himself the idol of the mob.

A Whig-dominated secret committee of twenty-one, under Walpole's chairmanship, was elected by the Commons to investigate the activities of the former ministers, with special reference to the Peace of Utrecht. Walpole's report, presented on 9 June 1715, was a masterly document, but though it brilliantly illuminated the war blunders of the Tories, it was weak and inconclusive on their intrigues with the Pretender. Nonetheless Bolingbroke and Oxford were impeached without a division, Ormonde only after a debate of nine hours and by a majority of a mere forty-seven votes. The ministers were inclined to abandon proceedings against him, but in a moment of panic he fled to join Bolingbroke in France. With little opposition, Acts of Attainder were then passed against the two Tory exiles, declaring them traitors and forfeiting their estates and civil rights. Strafford, one of the plenipotentiaries at Utrecht, was impeached of high crimes and misdemeanours; Atterbury's episcopal rank appears to have saved him from a similar fate; and Oxford was left in the Tower for two years before he was finally acquitted by his peers in

July 1717. Thus was the political power of the Tory leaders finally shattered.

These proceedings did not pass without protest in the country, where riots broke out and Dissenters and their meeting-houses proved popular objects of attack. The powerlessness of the local authorities in the face of these disturbances provoked the Riot Act of 1714, whereby refusal to disperse by an unlawful assembly of twelve or more persons, after the reading of a proclamation by a justice of the peace, was made a felony. In the absence of an adequate police force this was still insufficient to maintain law and order in times of popular excitement, as was later demonstrated by the violent reactions against the Excise Bill of 1733 and the Jew Bill of 1753. But the efficiency of the Government was soon tested by a challenge more serious than that of spasmodic disturbances—the ill-starred Jacobite Rebellion.

Encouraged by these minor signs of Government and Hanoverian unpopularity, and stung by the vindictive activities of the Whig Ministry, both English and Scottish Jacobites urged the Pretender to attempt the overthrow of the new dynasty. The Scots were optimistic and eager for immediate action, but Ormonde had always urged the need for French assistance in men, money, arms and ammunition. In order to sound the French Court, Bolingbroke was made Secretary of State by James and sent to Paris in late July. Here he found his fellow-conspirators full of enthusiasm, but with 'no subordination, no order, no concert'; and they talked so openly of their schemes that Lord Stair (the British Ambassador to France) had little difficulty in discovering and reporting their activities. Furthermore, Bolingbroke's hopes were severely shaken by Ormonde's flight from England, and by the death in September of Louis XIV. The accession of a five-year-old king removed all possibility of French support, for the Regent Orleans, fearful of Spanish pretensions to the French throne in the event of the death of the sickly boy, could not afford to antagonize England. The unloading of arms from French ships in Le Havre, where they had been equipped for the Pretender, made it clear that James must look to his own resources. Bolingbroke sent immediate advice of this development to England, but it was already too late. The Earl of Mar—'Bobbing John', as he was known to contemporaries from his frequent changes of political allegiance—had made a final and decisive *volte-face*. On 1 August he had attended King George's levee, only to be snubbed, and on the following day he set out to raise the Highlands for King James. Jacobite peers and gentry flocked to the Pretender's standard, all Scotland north of the Tay was in rebel hands by the middle of September, and Mar entered Perth with some four thousand men at the end of the month.

In the face of this sudden threat, the British Government had to act promptly, especially as the total force at its disposal amounted to no more than about eight thousand men. Stanhope immediately assumed control and wisely decided to send no more troops to Scotland, but to concentrate instead on the south-west, where invasion was daily expected. The King was empowered to seize suspected persons and warrants were issued for the arrest of six prominent Jacobite Commoners. Troops were sent to guard Bristol and Plymouth, while Oxford (which had shown its defiance by conferring its vacant Chancellorship on Ormonde's brother) was visited with a squadron of dragoons. Thus the Government retained the initiative in vital areas. In addition, Argyle was sent to command in Scotland, the Earl of Sutherland despatched to raise the loyal clans, and old Horace Walpole[1] set off for The Hague to seek Dutch aid. Parliament voted loyal addresses, the Habeas Corpus Amendment Act was suspended, all half-pay officers were recalled, twenty-one regiments (some seven thousand men) were ordered to be raised, and a reward of £100,000 was placed on the head of the Pretender, dead or alive.

After these strenuous preparations the course of the rebellion came as something of an anti-climax, and may be quickly passed over. Though Argyle's position at Stirling was initially highly vulnerable, the various bands of Scottish rebels could not sufficiently co-ordinate their efforts to mount a united campaign against him before he received reinforcements from Ireland. Nor could the rebel troops of south-west Scotland combine effectively with those raised by Thomas Forster from the Roman Catholic populations of Lancashire and Northumberland in order to make a stand against the English army advancing from the south. The only military engagement of any consequence was the indecisive battle of Sheriffmuir in November between the armies of Argyle and Mar, and before the Pretender arrived in Scotland in mid-December his cause was already doomed. Lacking the aura of romance that was later to surround the Forty-Five, and notwithstanding individual instances of gallantry and chivalry among the Highlanders, the story of the Fifteen makes sorry reading. Hampered by clan rivalry in Scotland and by hatred of Catholicism in England, the rebels lacked unity, organization, supplies and—above all—leadership. Mar and Forster both had their chances but neither seized them. The English Government, despite its vigorous actions, was in no position to face a large-scale rebellion, and Argyle certainly showed little enthusiasm for a major assault upon his fellow-countrymen. A

[1]The brother of Robert Walpole, so described to distinguish him from his namesake, Robert's son.

daring military leader might have transformed the Jacobite cause; none of even modest ability was forthcoming. But the collapse of the rebellion was chiefly due to the lack of a significant English rising (especially in the south-west) to synchronize with the Scottish one and split the Government's forces, to the failure of the Pretender to arrive early and inspire his followers, and to the absence of any assistance from France. So pathetic did it seem in retrospect that in the end only two peers and fewer than thirty commoners were executed for their part in the rising.

Although the Rebellion never seriously endangered the new dynasty, its political repercussions profoundly changed the course of British politics. Before 1715 the bitter animosity between Whig and Tory had been a constant factor in political life. The more basic division into Court and Country[1] was concealed by the persistence of religious antagonisms inherited from the previous century and by the force of traditional loyalties in individual families and particular localities. General elections were still regarded predominantly as conflicts between the two rival parties, even if changes of circumstance frequently wrought surprising reversals of principle in each of them. But the Fifteen dramatically altered the existing political alignments, for it confirmed George I in his belief that only Whigs could be entrusted with office. The Tories were virtually condemned to the political wilderness.

Basking in the credit of having crushed the rebellion, the Whigs hastened to consolidate their victory. Their predominance in the localities was ensured by a widespread purge of Tory JPs, sixty-eight being replaced in Middlesex alone; and with the dismissal of Nottingham and his relations, the Ministry became for the first time exclusively Whig. The life of the existing Whig Parliament was prolonged for a further four years by the passage of the Septennial Act in May 1716, which also extended the maximum duration of subsequent Parliaments to seven years. Triennial Parliaments had indeed increased the political instability of the previous two reigns, and many members were unenthusiastic at having to undergo the expense of elections every three years. But the Septennial Act would have smacked less of Whig factiousness had it applied only to subsequent Parliaments, and the readiness of members to prolong their own security did not pass without pungent comment. Having consolidated Whig power in local government and in the House of Commons, Stanhope confirmed the Protestant Dissenters in their support of Whiggery by the repeal, in December 1718, of the Occasional Conformity and Schism Acts. This was not mere political opportunism, for George I had

---

[1]See pp 105–14.

already promised his protection to the Dissenters, and Stanhope was a genuine believer in religious toleration. He would indeed have been happy to go further by repealing the Test Act and granting concessions to Roman Catholics, but popular prejudice was too strong for him.

Stanhope and Sunderland, who had now become his closest associate, proposed further to ensure Whig domination by establishing governmental control over Oxford and Cambridge, repealing the Septennial Act and indefinitely prolonging the life of the present Parliament, and limiting the royal prerogative of creating peers. The opposition of the young Earl of Newcastle persuaded them to abandon the first two plans, but they determined to persist with the Peerage Bill. By its provisions the number of new peerages which could be granted by the King was limited to six, apart from Princes of the Blood and replacement of extinct titles; and the sixteen elective Scottish peers were to be replaced by twenty-five hereditary ones. The Whigs had not forgotten Anne's creation of twelve Tory peers in order to get the Peace of Utrecht through the House of Lords and, not without reason, regarded her use of the prerogative as endangering the balance of the constitution. Ostensibly, the Peerage Bill was meant to guard against a repetition of this practice, but it did not require much intelligence to see that the principal aim of Sunderland and Stanhope was to ensure a permanent majority for themselves in the House of Lords. They need fear little opposition to the measure in the existing Upper House, and the King was even prepared to accept this limitation of his prerogative in order to restrict the future freedom of his hated son, who had already become the patron of the parliamentary Opposition.[1] But in the Commons and in the country the outcry against the Bill was so vociferous that the first attempt to carry it, in February 1719, was quietly abandoned. Nevertheless, strengthened by successes abroad in the course of the year, the ministers returned to the attack in November, hoping to rush the measure through the Commons before many of the independent members came up to town. They were frustrated by Walpole, Townshend and a group of dissident Whigs who had left the Ministry in 1717 and had since been a constant thorn in the Government's side. These malcontents seized the opportunity to rally the country gentlemen,[2] and by the time of the debate on the second reading of the Peerage Bill the numbers in the Commons had grown to over four hundred. One such country gentleman voiced the sentiments of the

---

[1]On the relationship between successive Princes of Wales and the parliamentary Opposition see pp 109–12.

[2]On the importance of the country gentlemen in the House of Commons see pp 107–8 and 112–15.

great majority: 'What, shall I consent to the shutting the door upon my family ever coming into the House of Lords?' On 8 December the Bill was rejected by 269 votes to 177.

The defeat of this measure was the most dramatic manifestation of the Whig schism. The security bred in Whig ranks by the collapse and disgrace of the Tories in 1714–15 had allowed full rein to the factious rivalries inherent in a body of men who were not a united party and who in victory lost any principles that might have acted as a cohesive force. Walpole and Townshend were jealous of the superior influence of Stanhope; Argyle hated Cadogan, who was his leading rival in the army; and Sunderland (who had been made Lord Privy Seal on Wharton's death) resented Walpole and Townshend, whom he regarded as upstarts, but who occupied the important offices of First Lord of the Treasury[1] and Secretary of State. Moreover, Townshend had offended one of the King's mistresses, von Schulenberg, by fobbing her off with the Irish title of Duchess of Munster when she wanted an English one; and she co-operated with the King's German advisers in working for his downfall. But it was not merely personal animosities that bedevilled the Whigs. While the King was in Hanover with Stanhope in the summer of 1716, and especially when they were later joined by Sunderland, matters were bound to get worse. Ministers at home always feared that their colleagues in Hanover were engrossing the ear of the King to their detriment, and their apprehensions were heightened on this occasion by the hatred between the King and the Prince of Wales and by genuine differences of opinion over foreign policy. George I had indeed been loath to leave his son as Regent during his absence abroad, and was only too ready to listen to the tales of Robethon and Sunderland, who reported that the Prince was courting popularity in the country, and was being encouraged by Walpole and Townshend to challenge his father's authority. Nor were matters improved when Townshend showed little enthusiasm for the Hanoverian emphasis of the King's Baltic policy and threw delays in the way of the treaty then pending with France. The final outcome was Townshend's relegation to the Lord-Lieutenancy of Ireland in December 1716; and when he had the temerity to vote against the Mutiny Bill in the following April he was dismissed entirely from the King's service. As a protest against this treatment of their colleague, Walpole, Pulteney, Methuen, Orford and Devonshire gave up their offices and a number of lesser men either resigned or were dismissed. The Whig schism was an

---

[1]Robert Walpole had been elevated to the headship of the Treasury in October 1715.

accomplished fact, and Stanhope's reorganized Ministry was bereft of some of its ablest members. Stanhope himself was no adequate substitute for Walpole at the Treasury, and Addison, however gifted a writer, proved a dismal failure as Secretary of State and had to be replaced by the younger James Craggs in March 1718.

The new Opposition leaders soon showed that their sole object was to embarrass their erstwhile colleagues, and that they would not be hampered in the pursuit of that object by any 'Whig' principles. To win Tory favour they opposed the repeal of the Occasional Conformity and Schism Acts, the repressive character of which they had roundly denounced in the previous reign, and used obstructionist tactics to ensure that the delayed impeachment of their former arch-enemy Oxford should go by default. To satisfy Argyle's jealousy they accused Cadogan of peculation over payment of the Dutch forces used during the Jacobite rebellion and failed to carry their attack by only ten votes. The presence of 124 Whigs (including thirty-two actual office-holders) in the minority was a crisp warning to Stanhope and Sunderland. To win independent Country support Walpole and his friends attempted to reduce the small standing army, the existence of which they had formerly defended as essential to the preservation of the Hanoverian succession, and attacked placemen and pensioners with a vehemence that ill became men who had so recently quitted office and whose sole desire was to force their way back into it. They condemned the Spanish war, which the merchant community deplored as disruptive of trade with Spain and her colonies, and denounced the Baltic policy of the Ministry, which they depicted as subordinating the interests of England to those of Hanover. Finally, over the Peerage Bill they used independent opinion to inflict a resounding defeat on the Government and render problematic its ability to survive in the existing House of Commons.

As if this were not enough, Stanhope had to face the unpalatable fact that this new and formidable Opposition enjoyed the patronage and encouragement of the heir to the throne. Relations between the King and the Prince, always unhappy and raised to a new height of tension during the King's absence in Hanover, reached an open rupture at the end of 1717. A trivial incident over the choice of god-parents for the Prince's newly-born son, in which the excitable Newcastle mistakenly believed that he had been challenged to a duel by the Prince, led the King to confine his son and later drive him from St James's. At the same time George I deprived the Prince of his Guards, his Beefeaters and the care of his children. Determined to get his revenge, the Prince set up a rival Court at Leicester House, and the readiness of Walpole and his friends to use this new establishment as a focal point for Opposition created a precedent that was to be followed at various times throughout the century.

The final discordant element with which Stanhope had to cope was the ever-growing influence of the King's German advisers. It was not unnatural that George I should attach great weight to the advice of Bernstorff and Bothmer, who spoke the same language and approached continental problems from the same viewpoint as the King himself. Nor were Hanoverian and English interests as antipathetic as contemporaries believed. But memories of William III's Dutch favourites and expensive European entanglements were too fresh to allow Englishmen to view without misgiving a recrudescence of foreign influence. From the time of George I's accession Bernstorff and Bothmer had acted as intermediaries between the King and his English ministers. While the emphasis was on domestic affairs this mattered little, but when foreign policy became the principal concern of the Government there were bound to be suspicion and and friction. This situation reached a peak when Stanhope was in Hanover with the King in 1719 and found himself virtually superseded by Bernstorff in the conduct of foreign policy. He made it plain to George I that he must choose between Bernstorff and himself. As a result both Bothmer and Bernstorff were told bluntly by the King that they must not meddle further with English business, but this ultimatum merely determined the Germans to make a final bid for power. In April 1720 they negotiated with the dissident Whigs for the overthrow of the Ministry and a reorientation of foreign policy.

The situation of Stanhope and Sunderland had now become desperate. Defeated over the Peerage Bill, opposed by the heir to the throne and undermined by a German cabal, they could no longer stand alone. Negotiations with the Tories proved abortive and they were compelled to come to terms with the dissident Whigs. Walpole, Townshend and their associates were readmitted to office and the King was reluctantly persuaded to effect a reconciliation with his son. Finally, the influence of the Hanoverian ministers was irrevocably broken; Bernstorff travelled with the King to Hanover in 1720 but never returned, and Bothmer was relegated to obscurity. London celebrated the reunion of the royal family, and Stanhope was heartened to find himself with a majority of nearly three to one in the House of Commons.

If Stanhope's domestic policy was an odd blend of liberalism and authoritarianism, in foreign affairs his influence was decisive and his achievements of permanent value. In the years after 1714 Britain above all needed peace and allies. These Stanhope acquired by grafting the Tory notion of friendship with France on to the traditional Whig policy of alliance with the Empire and the United Provinces—an unorthodox but effective combination.

The importance attached to the preservation of the old ties with the Dutch and the Austrians was demonstrated by Stanhope's mission to Vienna and The Hague immediately on George I's accession. The United Provinces still placed great faith in the Anglo-Imperial connection as the best guarantee of their own security, but their Protestantism made them suspicious of the Emperor. In the past, their commercial ambitions had also caused friction with their British allies, but by 1714 they had become financiers rather than traders, and their large-scale investment in the national debt gave them a vested interest in Britain's stability. The Emperor Charles VI required more careful handling, for he had not the same motives for peace as Britain and the Dutch. He refused to recognize Philip V as King of Spain, denounced as intolerable the conditions on which the Netherlands had been ceded to him, manoeurved for more extensive power in Italy in order to check Spanish ambitions there, and in particular wanted the Duke of Savoy to exchange Sardinia for Sicily. Yet he could not afford a breach with Britain. In the face of Ottoman advances in the Danube basin and the threat of Spanish aggression in Italy, the aid of the British fleet could be an important, even decisive, factor. Thus Stanhope's mission paved the way for a reconciliation. In February 1716 the Dutch renewed their treaty of alliance and guarantee with Britain, and by the Treaty of Westminster of the following May the Emperor and George I guaranteed each other's possessions. Finally, after a year of haggling, a revised Barrier Treaty between the Emperor and the Dutch completed the tripartite alliance in November. The old system had been revived even if former resentments still smouldered, and relations between the allies remained lukewarm.

Meanwhile, Spain too had been making overtures to Britain. There had been widespread national irritation at the Italian cessions to Charles VI, and Philip V's astute chief minister, Cardinal Alberoni, was determined to reconquer them. But first he needed time to rescue Spain from exhaustion and economic stagnation, and since he was afraid that the Emperor might use the danger of possible Turkish attack as an excuse to pour troops into Italy, he was looking for allies. Philip's continued designs on the French throne made impossible any agreement between him and Orleans, and the possibility of British naval support encouraged Alberoni to make commercial concessions in an attempt to win British friendship. Stanhope was only too ready to enlarge his support in the City, and a commercial treaty with Spain was signed in December 1715; but further progress was checked by Spain's desire to recover Gibraltar and by the growing friendship between Britain and France.

The idea of alliance with the traditional enemy was anathema to many Englishmen, and had indeed been previously denounced by the Whigs. But there were cogent arguments in its favour. Both countries were impoverished and exhausted by the recent wars, and both had rival claimants to their thrones. George I had the additional incentive of wishing to prevent an alliance between France and Russia to the detriment of Hanover. The first overtures came from the abbé Dubois, the Regent's secretary, but because of the ambiguous attitude of France towards the Pretender, his advances were at first treated with caution, and even his secret meetings with Stanhope at the Hague in July 1716 produced little more than mutual expressions of good-will. But before the conclusion of the next discussions at Hanover in September George I's fears for the safety of his Electorate were greatly increased by the Russian occupation of Mecklenburg; and Stanhope did not wish to see the Tsar threatening the Empire or cooling in his antagonism to Sweden at a time when Charles XII was secretly encouraging Jacobite schemes. The support of France, always one of the most influential Powers in the north, therefore acquired a fresh significance. On 28 November France and Britain signed the Dual Alliance, and the adherence of the United Provinces converted it into the Triple Alliance on 4 January 1717. All three Powers agreed to uphold the Utrecht settlement, especially the Hanoverian succession, and France promised to dismantle Dunkirk, destroy the works at Mardyck and permanently expel the Pretender from French territory. Stanhope had achieved a revolution in foreign policy, and the Anglo-French alliance was to last nominally until 1744 and profoundly affect European politics until 1731. It had its critics on both sides of the Channel, but it gave both Powers much-needed security and helped to localize conflicts in northern and southern Europe that might otherwise have led to a general conflagration.

The Triple Alliance was concluded none too soon, for in the following May the uneasy relations between Philip V and Charles VI were brought to a sudden rupture by the unfortunate arrest of the Spanish Grand Inquisitor while travelling through the Milanese. Philip, ever sensitive where the Emperor was concerned and only too happy to force a breach while his enemy was still hard pressed by the Turks, overruled Alberoni's desire for peace and insisted on the dispatch of a Spanish fleet to Sardinia, which, as he well knew, the Emperor was proposing to exchange for Savoy. The island was quickly overrun and the immediate mediation of France and Britain became essential if open war was to be avoided.

Despite the belligerence of both parties and the belated attempts of Alberoni to stir up trouble in Britain and France, Stanhope and Orleans were able on 2 August 1718 to persuade the Emperor to agree to the Quadruple Alliance, so called because it was misguidedly believed that the Dutch would subsequently concur. By this treaty Charles VI renounced the Spanish throne and recognized Philip V, in return for which he was to be allowed to exchange Sardinia for Sicily. Spain was to be mollified by the guarantee of the reversions of Parma, Piacenza and Tuscany to a Spanish prince. This was a praiseworthy attempt to preserve peace, but Philip V was adamant, his morale boosted by the Spanish conquest of Sicily at the beginning of July. Stanhope had already dispatched a British fleet under Admiral Byng to the Mediterranean, ostensibly to guard British interests there but actually to repel any Spanish aggression; and in August he visited Madrid in a final attempt to persuade Spain to accept the Quadruple Alliance. He was even prepared the surrender Gibraltar in the cause of peace, but Philip V would not listen. Meanwhile, Byng had routed the Spanish fleet off Cape Passaro and the declaration of war by France and Great Britain in December was a mere formality.

The naval defeat virtually ended Spanish hopes of Mediterranean conquest, especially when English mediation secured the Peace of Passarowitz between the Emperor and the Turks, and left Charles VI free to pour troops into Italy. Byng's command of the Mediterranean enabled the Austrians to recapture Sicily, French forces under Berwick took San Sebastian and Fuentarabia, a French fleet broke Spanish naval power in the Bay of Biscay, and a somewhat desultory British expedition under Cobham captured Vigo. Spain had nothing to gain by prolonging a senseless conflict and, as a preliminary to peace, Alberoni was dismissed on 5 January 1720, scapegoat for a war which was not of his making. Three weeks later Philip agreed to accept the terms of the Quadruple Alliance. Since the defeat of Spain left Charles VI in a strong position, it was not unnatural that France, Britain and Spain should draw more closely together and in 1721 they signed the defensive Treaty of Madrid.

While Stanhope was struggling to maintain general peace in southern Europe he was forced at the same time to cope with the intricate situation which had developed out of the dying stages of the Great Northern War. Here Charles XII was fighting a losing battle against Russia, Prussia, Poland and Denmark in an attempt to maintain Swedish power in the Baltic and along the north German coast. England's position in this northern conflict was highly ambiguous. As Elector of Hanover George I was committed by treaty to fight the Swedes, as King of England to support them. At first both British and Hanoverian interests suggested hostility to Sweden; Hanover wanted to retain Bremen and Verden, and Britain resented Swedish interference with Baltic commerce and support for the Pretender's cause. But in the course of 1716 the situation changed. The Jacobite plots of Gortz and Gyllenborg were exposed, the rebellion had been crushed, and the Russian occupation of Mecklenburg made Peter the Great a more immediate menace to Hanover than Charles XII. It only required the death of the Swedish king in December 1718 to convince Stanhope that the prevention of Russian domination of the Baltic must become the principal object of British policy, but it was no easy matter to achieve this object. In the first place, France was not prepared actively to support Britain; secondly, Stanhope badly needed the assistance of Prussia against the Tsar, but was hampered at every turn by the traditional hostility between Prussia and Hanover; finally, he could never be quite sure that George's activities as Elector would not place him in an impossible situation. A hint of this danger was given when Bernstorff, who had personal reasons for hating Frederick William of Prussia, promoted the Treaty of Vienna in January 1719 between the Emperor, Hanover and Saxony. This defensive alliance against Russia and Prussia even bound George I to repel any attack on Polish ports by the use of a British fleet! As no English minister would counter-sign the treaty, and its clauses were never invoked, no harm was done. But it gave Stanhope an additional reason for seeking to destroy the German influence in England.

As his mediating agents Stanhope chose Whitworth for Berlin and Carteret for Stockholm, both men of considerable gifts in the sphere of diplomacy. Whitworth succeeded in winning over Frederick William and treaties were concluded which promised Bremen and Verden to Hanover, Stettin to Prussia, and mutual co-operation to secure peace in the north and freedom of trade in the Baltic. Carteret's personal charm soon endeared him to the young Queen Eleanora of Sweden who, with Russian forces advancing on the capital, was only too eager for British support. In return for a subsidy and naval assistance she agreed to the terms of the Anglo-Prussian agreement, and formal treaties were signed between Britain, Prussia, Hanover and Sweden at the end of 1719 and the beginning of 1720. Carteret's final diplomatic triumphs came when he managed to persuade both Poland and Denmark to make peace with Sweden, leaving Russia alone of the original league still in arms against her. But Sweden's days of greatness were over. Neither monetary aid nor Admiral Norris's efforts in the Baltic could prevail against the vastly superior power of Russia. Stanhope did not live to see the ultimate humiliation of Sweden at the Peace of Nystadt in 1721, when she lost all her Baltic provinces except Finland. But if he failed in his final object his efforts had been decisive in ending the northern war and bringing peace to the whole of the European Continent. Not until the days of the elder Pitt was England's voice again so dominant in European affairs.

Important as were Stanhope's achievements in foreign affairs, they were soon overshadowed by the chaos of the South Sea Bubble, which was to shatter his Ministry and threaten the financial stability of the nation. This disruptive episode was the product of the Government's natural and commendable desire to reduce the interest on the national debt, the unscrupulous determination of the South Sea directors and a few politicians to make some easy money, and a passion for speculation that was sweeping through Western Europe. The South Sea Company, which had been founded in 1711 by Robert Harley, was primarily not a trading venture but an institution for the administration of part of the national debt, and one which Harley hoped would give him an interest in the City which would help to offset the Whig connection with the Bank of England. The holders of over £9,000,000 of public debt were incorporated into the South Sea Company, which received a perpetual annuity of 6 per cent and a monopoly of trade with South America. In 1714 by the addition of arrears of interest and a new loan, the Company's capital was increased to £10,000,000; two years later the interest rate was reduced to 5 per cent; and in 1719 the assumption of a portion of the 1710 lottery annuities brought its total share of the debt up to nearly £11,750,000. Commercially its activities had been negligible, for the South American trade, despite public belief in its lucrative nature, was dependent on privileges granted by Spain in 1716 but scantily respected when relations between the two countries became strained. It was thus in public finance that the directors hoped to make their fortunes, and here they were greatly influenced, as was the Government, by the apparent success in France of the Scotsman, John Law, whose radical experiments seemed to be converting economic stagnation into widespread and vigorous prosperity. Stanhope and Sunderland, deploring the flow of capital across the Channel, and hoping to emulate Law's success, opened secret negotiations with the Company in November 1718. At first the directors offered to take over the entire national debt, including even those portions held by the Bank of England and the East India Company. But the ministers knew that the Bank in particular was unlikely to surrender its privileged position without a struggle, and the scheme presented to the Commons in January 1720 excluded that part of the debt held by the two other corporations. At Walpole's suggestion the Bank was invited to submit alternative proposals, but it was promptly out-bid by the South Sea Company, whose final scheme was accepted by the Commons on 1 February.

The essence of his scheme was simple enough. The Company was to take over the whole of the remaining debt, redeemable and irredeemable, estimated at £30,981,712 6s. 6d. On this amount, and on its existing share of the debt, it would receive 5 per cent interest up to 1727, and 4 per cent thereafter. In return for this privilege it was prepared to pay £7,000,000 to the Government, which would also benefit by a total reduction in annual debt charge that would amount after 1727 to over £700,000. Indeed, the Chancellor of the Exchequer confidently prophesied that this reduction would enable the total debt to be extinguished in twenty-five years. The advantages to the Government were obvious, the aims of the directors and the attitudes of the debt-holders perhaps less so. Yet there was much in the scheme to appeal to the gambling spirit of the age. The South American trade continued to lure investors and a company with a 'fund of credit' of over £40,000,000 and which was intimately associated with the State seemed to contemporaries capable of almost any economic enterprise. In case this was insufficient attraction the directors bribed their prospective victims by offering them stock at appreciably below the market price. Not unnaturally the overwhelming majority of debt-holders hastened to convert to South Sea stock, only to find themselves facing disaster. The Government, with almost criminal neglect, had failed to fix the amount of stock to be given for each unit of the public debt. This meant that the directors had a vested interest in a rising market, for the higher the stock the less need be exchanged for Government securities, and the greater would be the surplus which would constitute a clear profit to the Company. The directors, by creating fictitious stock, distributed over £1,200,000 in bribes to royal favourites, ministers and members of Parliament. They also lent some £11,000,000 on the unsound security of their own stock, issued new stock for subscription without legal authority, and took various other illicit measures in order to create a bull market. As the stock soared, men rushed to buy simply in the hope of rapid capital appreciation. At the beginning of April the stock stood at 300, by the end of May it was 700, and on 24 June it reached the record level of 1,050.

This fantastic inflation soon affected other securities and led to a spate of mushroom companies which sought to profit from the speculative mania that was sweeping the country. One such company was for trading in hair, another for purchasing tracts of bog in Ireland, another was confined to female subscribers dressed in calico! A temporary check was applied when the Government passed the 'Bubble' Act on 24 June, threatening the prosecution of any company which acted without a charter. But great ingenuity was used to stretch existing charters to the utmost, and the South Sea directors deplored the continuing loss of capital that might have been used to further their schemes. Consequently, on 18 August, they applied for writs against four rival companies. Ironically enough this proved their undoing, though nemesis could not in any case have been long delayed. The stock of those who had speculated in these four companies dropped steeply in value, and they had to sell other stock—including that of the South Sea Company—to meet their liabilities. The general price of shares fell severely, that of South Sea stock disastrously. On 17 August it stood at 900, by the end of the month it had dropped to 775. Desperately the directors pledged the capital resources of the company for the payment of dividends, but as the market crumbled panic spread and the directors were no longer trusted. By the middle of September the stock had fallen further to 450, and when the Company's bankers were forced to suspend payments a week later, it plummeted to 190. Fortunes had been lost and the stock now stood at a level below which almost all holders of the public debt had converted. Government intervention had become essential.

Parliament re-assembled on 8 December, amidst widespread, almost hysterical, cries for vengeance. With many of the Ministry seriously implicated in the Bubble, Walpole was given the opportunity of a political lifetime. His own hands were clean, he had something of a reputation for financial ability, his relations with the Bank of England (whose co-operation was bound to be necessary) were excellent, he had dissociated himself from the disaster by discreetly withdrawing to Norfolk at the height of the crisis, and he was ready with a remedial scheme devised by his banker, Robert Jacombe. A month before Parliament was due to meet, Walpole set out to restore public credit and to turn the chaotic situation to his own political advantage. He began by persuading the Bank of England and the East India Company to accept Jacombe's proposal that each of them should take over £9,000,000 of South Sea stock. This 'engraftment' scheme passed through an unenthusiastic House of Commons on 21 December, but it was merely permissive and was in fact never acted upon. Nonetheless it promoted the first signs of returning confidence, and the stock—which had reached its lowest point at 124 on 14 December—rose to 200 by the end of the year. But this did nothing to diminish the desire for vengeance. Despite Walpole's warnings that investigation and recrimination would only heighten passions and increase existing tensions, the Commons insisted on demanding the punishment of the 'creators of our present misfortunes', ordered the accounts of the Company to be presented to the House, restrained the directors from leaving the kingdom, compelled them to declare the value of their estates, and elected a secret committee to investigate the Company's affairs. Though hindered by the flight of the Company's cashier, Robert Knight, to the Netherlands the Committee (according to one of its members) 'discovered a train of the deepest villainy and fraud that Hell ever contrived to ruin a nation'. Those directors who were members of the Commons—Janssen, Sawbridge, Eyles and Chaplin—were expelled from the House and imprisoned, to be followed shortly by Sir George Caswell, a highly influential ex-director who was deeply implicated in the scandal. The directors as a whole were found guilty of a gross breach of trust, and sequestration of their estates was ordered for the benefit of their victims. Then the wrath of the Commons turned against those members of the Government who were suspected of involvement. Aislabie, the Chancellor of the Exchequer, against whom the evidence was particularly strong, was sent to the Tower; but Walpole's strenuous efforts to lower the political temperature, together with a growing uneasiness at recurrent outbursts of mob violence, gradually turned the tide against the quest for unlimited vengeance. Charles Stanhope, Secretary to the Treasury, escaped conviction of corrupt practices by three votes, Sunderland was acquitted by a majority of sixty-one. James Craggs the younger, Secretary of State, died of smallpox before he could be examined by the Committee; and his father, the Postmaster-General, died in circumstances suggestive of suicide on the very eve of his trial. Walpole, for his continued efforts to protect his colleagues and thus prevent the complete disintegration of the Ministry, was execrated as the 'Skreen', a nickname that was confirmed by his gaining reasonable allowances for all save one of the directors when the sequestration of their estates was approved in detail by Parliament, and when he very sensibly carried the remission of the £7,000,000 which the Company had undertaken to pay the Government. All that remained was to settle the terms for those debt-holders who had agreed to convert to South Sea stock. Even though the credit of the State was at stake, it was inevitable that they should suffer loss of income. Some faced a diminution of little more than a fifth, others nearly 40 per cent. It was not surprising that an angry mob invaded the lobbies, or that, when induced to disperse by the reading of the Riot Act, they protested that: 'You first pick our pockets and then send us to gaol for complaining.'

The economy of the nation was essentially sound, public confidence quick to recover, and soon there remained of the crisis little but an abiding distrust of 'stock-jobbing'. In a sense the political results of the Bubble were more important than the economic ones. Stanhope, an innocent victim of the crisis, had died of an apoplexy, induced by the strain of defending himself. Sunderland's faction was badly shaken by the death of the two Craggses and the disgrace of Aislabie, and the leader himself was temporarily in eclipse. It was Walpole's broad shoulders that had borne the burden of staving off anarchy and restoring the credit of the nation; and to the victor went the spoils. Already in February his brother-in-law, Lord Townshend, had succeeded Stanhope as Secretary of State; in April Walpole himself took over the seals of the Treasury from Sunderland, who could scarcely with decency remain at the head of the country's finances, but who was nevertheless determined to challenge Walpole's growing ascendancy. He still enjoyed the confidence of the King, controlled the Secret Service money, and was strong enough to secure the appointment of his associate Carteret as the second Secretary of State. But Walpole was firmly entrenched at the head of the Commons, his ambition was great and his tenacity unlimited. It is difficult to believe that he could not finally have thwarted the constant intrigues of his rival, but in the event he was relieved of the necessity. On 19 April 1722 Sunderland died of pleurisy, and the way was open for Walpole to assert his supremacy. The Robinocracy had begun.

2

THE ROBINOCRACY: 1721–42

ROBERT WALPOLE was forty-four years of age when in April 1721 he was for the second time appointed First Lord of the Treasury and Chancellor of the Exchequer. He was sixty-four when in February 1742 he was driven from power by the furious attacks of his political enemies. No man, before or since, has dominated British politics for so long, yet few have been challenged across the years by an Opposition so talented or so well served by propagandists of near genius. To modern premiers royal confidence is irrelevant, to Walpole it was essential; and he had to convince two sovereigns, both of whom initially detested him, that he was indispensable to them. The modern prime minister has a well-disciplined, highly-organized party behind him; Walpole had to create his own majority, one that would stand by him in the face of back-stairs intrigues and the ringing denunciations of disappointed rivals. Yet so successful was he that all soon acknowledged him, whether admiringly or grudgingly, as 'The Great Man', whose domination the Opposition had almost despaired of breaking before forces that he little understood and could ill control swept him at last from office.

In Opposition eyes Walpole's success was easily explained. He was a monster of corruption who defiled everything he touched and who lived by the cynical maxim that 'every man has his price'. Utilizing to the maximum the considerable resources of royal patronage,[1] he bound to him by a complex network of obligations a sufficient majority of the limited electorate and of both Houses of Parliament to ensure his continuing predominance. Thus, to his supporters, with their friends and relatives, went offices, pensions, preferment in the Church and the armed services; to his opponents, political and professional oblivion. There is a small element of truth in this Opposition picture, even if those who protested most loudly only wished themselves in Walpole's place. Yet his triumph was essentially one of personality, character, ability and shrewd common

[1]See pp 100–3.

sense; he was a master of the art of politics. He himself declared that he was 'no saint, no Spartan, no reformer', and Chesterfield did him justice when he remarked: 'He was very able as a minister, but without a certain elevation of mind necessary for great good or great mischief . . . He was both the best Parliament-man and the ablest manager of Parliament that I believe ever lived.' His policy might be unadventurous, his methods unspectacular; but, as a hard-headed Norfolk squire he understood the problems and prejudices of the class to which he belonged. The seventeenth century had seen the gentry emerge as the ruling caste in English politics, with the merchants still very junior partners. They were weary of revolutions, party violence, and expensive foreign wars; they wanted time to consolidate their gains; they asked only for peace, stability and prosperity, and these were Walpole's watchwords.

In retrospect there seems something almost inevitable about Walpole's consolidation of his power and his repeated successes in thwarting challenges to his supremacy. Yet there were many obstacles to be overcome before his authority was firmly established and many subsequent occasions when he seemed in imminent danger of defeat. He had first to win the confidence of George I, who had not forgiven him for allying with the Prince of Wales in 1717-20 and harrying the Ministry in a factious and irresponsible manner. The King's natural sympathies had lain with Stanhope and Sunderland, and after their deaths he gravitated towards their leading disciple, Carteret, whose personal charm, command of the German language, and comprehensive knowledge of continental politics endeared him as readily to George I as they were later to endear him to George II. As Secretary of State Carteret had a substantial voice in foreign affairs; after 1723 his friend Cadogan was in command of the army, the other sphere closest to the King's heart; he had several allies in the Cabinet and an influential voice in Irish affairs; and at Court he had the ear of the King's favourite mistress, the Duchess of Kendall. Against this formidable rival Walpole could at first depend only on his brother-in-law Townshend, his brother Horace Walpole, the young Duke of Newcastle (whom he won over from Carteret in the course of 1723), and the Duke's brother Henry Pelham, who rapidly became Walpole's most trusted lieutenant in the Commons.

Yet Walpole had only to bide his time. Carteret might lead at Court; Walpole had the Commons to command. Moreover, he had already earned the gratitude of the King for the skill with which he had extricated the nation from the chaos of the South Sea Bubble, and in 1722 the exposure of Atterbury's plot gave him a further opportunity to prove his mettle. The more extreme Jacobites, undeterred by the failure of the

Fifteen, still hoped to overthrow the Hanoverian dynasty, and were heartened by the birth of a son to the Pretender on 31 December 1720 and by the financial and political confusion engendered by the Bubble. Yet, as always, their timing and strategy were hopelessly inept. Just as they had been too late to synchronize their earlier challenge with the death of Queen Anne, so they failed to strike in 1721 when the country was still in an uproar. They also foolishly entrusted much of their intricate correspondence to the general mails, which ministers had no hesitation in opening and examining, and which confirmed the plot, the existence of which they had already been warned of by Dubois, whom the Jacobites had naïvely approached for aid. Their cypher was broken with little difficulty and the details of the conspiracy revealed to the nation on 8 May. This was Walpole's chance and he acted with ruthless efficiency. A large body of troops was encamped in Hyde Park, several arrests made, including Francis Atterbury (Bishop of Rochester, Dean of Westminster and the Pretender's principal agent in Britain), the Duke of Norfolk, the Earl of Orrery, Lord North and Grey, and a number of lesser figures. When Parliament met in October Habeas Corpus was suspended for a year instead of the six months that was usual in time of crisis, and a tax of five shillings in the pound levied on all Roman Catholics and non-jurors,[1] which, it was calculated, would provide £100,000 to reimburse the Government for its expenses in crushing the conspiracy. These were stern measures which met with considerable opposition in the Commons; but Walpole was determined to exaggerate the crisis in order to strengthen himself at Court and drive the lingering memories of the Bubble from the minds of his countrymen. Though Atterbury was merely banished and there was only one execution, the upsurge of loyalty to the dynasty and confidence in the Government had served Walpole's purpose.

If Sir Robert's standing at Court was now greatly enhanced, the King's refusal to countenance a premature attempt to secure Carteret's dismissal reminded him that he was not yet supreme. When Carteret accompanied Townshend and the King to Hanover in the summer of 1723 Walpole experienced the usual fears of a minister who remained in England. But Carteret, supremely confident as always, soon wrought his own downfall. He urged George I to a more belligerent attitude towards Russia than the King was prepared to accept, and placed him in an embarrassing position by intriguing for the marriage of the niece of the Countess von Platen, George's Roman Catholic mistress, to a French nobleman. His agent was Sir Luke Schaub, British ambassador at Paris, an incompetent

[1] I.e. those who had refused to take the oath of allegiance to William and Mary in 1689.

bungler who forced the Regent to confess to the English King that he could not elevate the nobleman to the dukedom that George considered the essential pre-requisite to the marriage. Carteret was under a cloud, and it only required Walpole's mastery of the Commons in the session of 1724 to persuade the King where his best interest lay. Schaub was dismissed in disgrace, to be replaced by Horace Walpole, who had already been sent to Paris as understudy, and Carteret was relegated to the Lord-Lieutenancy of Ireland, there to quell the disturbances over Wood's Halfpence,[1] which he himself had helped to foster. Newcastle became Secretary of State, and Henry Pelham Secretary at War. William Pulteney clearly felt slighted at being passed over in the promotions, but Walpole was not to know that Pulteney would become one of his most inveterate enemies and preside over his downfall eighteen years later. All that mattered was that the remnants of the Sunderland faction had been broken and that Walpole and his colleagues were now *personae gratae* at Court.

It was not until the death of George I in 1727 that Sir Robert had to face a fresh challenge. The new King was more spirited than his father, with stronger prejudices, but rather less confident in his own ability. He had a stiff and formal manner, loved regularity and displayed a meticulous regard for detail. Although possessed of a strong sense of justice and a certain innate shrewdness that showed itself in occasional wry comments, his mind was not big enough to comprehend complicated problems or to think on a grand scale; and too often his essential common sense was perverted by passion and ill-temper. Physically courageous, as is evident from his conduct at Dettingen, he was politically a coward; yet pride and obstinacy made him reluctant to accept any opinions that could not be represented to him as his own, and on political matters on which he felt strongly he could frequently be moved by nothing short of the certainty of defeat in Parliament. Queen Caroline, to whom he was passionately devoted, had long governed him; ministers could do so only if they first won his trust and affection. For although he was incapable of generosity, he could form strong attachments; and, once he had overcome his initial prejudices, he successively developed a warm regard for Walpole, Carteret, Pelham and Newcastle.

George II, as Prince of Wales, had long presided over his own Court at Leicester House, where the leading figures were Sir Spencer Compton (Speaker of the Commons and Paymaster-General) and the Earls of Chesterfield and Scarborough. When in 1720, Walpole had deserted

---

[1]See pp 45–6.

Leicester House for Administration, he had been denounced by the Prince, and George had a long memory. Nor did he have a higher opinion of Sir Robert's chief colleagues. Brother Horace was a 'dirty buffoon', Newcastle an 'impertinent fool', and Townshend a 'choleric blockhead'. The quartet had therefore some reason for feeling apprehensive on the old King's death, and few contemporaries doubted that a change of Ministry was at hand. When Walpole, on conveying the news of George's I death to his son, was instructed to take his orders from Compton, the die seemed cast; yet within ten days Sir Robert and his colleagues were confirmed in power. Compton proved a broken reed; in Lord Hervey's words, he was 'a plodding, heavy fellow, with great application and no talents . . . much better for a clerk to a minister than for a minister to a Prince'. Moreover, Queen Caroline, who had always admired Walpole and appreciated his political abilities, was determined that he should continue at the head of the Ministry. But it was Walpole's own perspicacity that was decisive. He promised the King a more generous income than any of his predecessors had enjoyed—£800,000 per annum and the surplus of all taxes appropriated to the Civil List, together with a jointure of £100,000 for the Queen. The ease with which he carried these proposals through the Commons greatly impressed George II, and when the King compared the addresses which both Walpole and Compton had prepared for the formal dissolution of Parliament, he could no longer ignore the shortcomings of his favourite. To soften the blow, Compton was made Lord Wilmington, Scarborough Master of the Horse and Chesterfield a Lord of the Bedchamber and Ambassador to The Hague; but Walpole and his colleagues continued undisturbed at the head of affairs. Yet the former Leicester House clique was never wholly assimilated into the Administration, and in future was to seize every opportunity to shake the King's confidence in his chief minister. Wilmington in particular never forgave Walpole, and continued spasmodically and ineffectually to intrigue against him until at last in 1742 he succeeded in wresting the Treasury from Walpole's hands—a belated and Pyrrhic victory.

The next stage in Walpole's drive for personal supremacy saw the breach of a political and personal friendship that had endured for thirty years. Walpole and Townshend had travelled a long way together, but from 1725 their association was subjected to ever-increasing strains. Walpole, though anxious for peace and suspicious of the merits of the French alliance, had been content at first to leave foreign affairs, of which he had little experience, in his brother-in-law's hands. But he soon tired of having to defend Townshend's policies in the Commons. He disliked Townshend's Treaty of Hanover in 1725, which was widely ascribed in

England to Hanoverian influences; he deplored the subsidies lavished on Sweden and various German princes; and he was uneasy at both the neglect of Portugal and the alienation of Russia. Inevitably he was forced to assume a greater voice in foreign affairs, and the Treaty of Seville with Spain in 1729 signified his determination to wrest the initiative from Townshend and was the logical prelude to the return to the old Imperial alliance by the second Treaty of Vienna in 1731. Personal factors also exacerbated relations between the two ministers. Townshend's proud aristocratic nature made him resent the signs of Walpole's growing wealth and power—as evident in Norfolk (where Houghton was rapidly overshadowing Raynham) as at Westminster—and he could scarcely remain insensitive of the fact that he was being gradually eased into the position of junior partner. The death in 1726 of Dorothy, Townshend's wife and Walpole's sister, removed the strongest remaining personal link between the two men, and only Townshend's love of power kept him from resigning. Eventually, on 15 May 1730, he reluctantly surrendered the seals, to be replaced by the more malleable Lord Harrington, recently ennobled for his successful negotiation of the Treaty of Seville. With Newcastle and Harrington as Secretaries of State, Walpole could be confident that his views on foreign politics would no longer be frustrated by independent action.

Secure at Court and in the Cabinet, Walpole as yet had little to fear in Parliament. The Tories who comprised the great majority of his opponents were essentially back-benchers, who suffered from the taint of Jacobitism. Carteret, who had been dropped from office in 1730, and Chesterfield, who had hoped to succeed Townshend, were ripe for Opposition but had not yet broken with the Ministry. It was thus left to Pulteney to lead the attacks on Sir Robert, but for years he was unable to make any serious impact on the solid Administration majority in the Commons. Outside Parliament the heart and soul of Opposition had become Bolingbroke, who in 1725 had been pardoned and restored to his estates but not to his seat in the Lords. He never forgave Walpole for insisting on excluding him from formal politics and proceeded to devote his considerable abilities and energy to uniting the heterogeneous opposition and overturning the Ministry. From 1726 he and Pulteney had been attacking Walpole in *The Craftsman*, and in 1730 he published his *Remarks on the History of England*, portraying Sir Robert as the political heir of all the oppressors under whom England had ever suffered. Gradually this virulent propaganda campaign wrought its effect upon the independent element in the Commons. In important debates like that on the payment of arrears on the Civil List in April 1729, or on the failure to prevent

French restoration of the harbour of Dunkirk in February 1730, Walpole had been able to count on a majority of about 120. But when the motions concerned subjects on which independent feeling ran high, this figure began to show signs of a substantial reduction. Thus the continuation of the Hessian troops in English pay was approved by a majority of only seventy-nine and, in 1732 and 1733 attempts to reduce the standing army were defeated by only seventy and sixty-eight votes respectively. But the Opposition badly needed a single clear-cut issue upon which to focus their efforts, and this they eventually found in Walpole's excise scheme of 1733.

There was nothing new about excise duties, which had first been levied by Pym in 1643, but they had always been unpopular in the country, partly because they affected many of the necessities of life, and partly because the activities of the excise officers made evasion of payment very difficult. At the time of the Hanoverian succession the chief items affected were beer, ale, spirits, cider, perry, candles, leather, soap, paper, starch, salt and malt; to these Walpole in 1724 had added tea, coffee and chocolate. Instead of paying duties on landing goods in the country, the merchant stored them in warehouses under the control of excise-officers, and the excise duty was paid only if the goods were taken out for home consumption. If they were re-exported no duty need be paid. This system helped to mitigate many frauds and abuses, simplified rates and modes of collection, increased the revenue, and tended to make London a free port and hence increase its importance as a commercial entrepot. Convinced of the merits of excise and encouraged by the success of the measures of 1724 (which had increased the annual yield by £125,000) Walpole determined to extend the system, hoping to make possible the lowering of the land-tax, and thereby attach both merchant and landed interests ever more firmly to the dynasty and to his own Administration. To this end in 1732 he re-introduced the excise on salt which had been abandoned two years previously, and lowered the land-tax from two shillings to one shilling in the pound. Even these modest proposals, which might have been expected to meet with an enthusiastic reception in a predominantly land-owning assembly, were approved in Committee and on the Report by majorities of only thirty-nine and twenty-nine respectively. Yet Walpole, allowing perhaps for the fact that office-holders were normally allowed a free vote on questions of Ways and Means, remained confident that his policy would soon be universally applauded. By extending the excise to tobacco and wine he felt certain that he would be able to abolish the land-tax completely except in time of war, and the overwhelming evidence of frauds produced by a parliamentary investigating committee of 1732 was a convincing condemnation of the existing customs system and ample justification for the change. But Walpole had reckoned without the Englishman's instinctive hatred of excise and the Opposition's infinite capacity for mischief. Pamphlets poured from the presses, predicting a general excise, the invasion of homes by hordes of excise-men, and the corruption of parliamentary boroughs by the enfranchisement of these minor officials. The country rang with cries of 'No slavery, no excise, no wooden shoes'.

From the counties and larger boroughs instructions flooded in to members exhorting them to vote against excise, and on 14 March 1733—the day on which Walpole was to propose the excise on tobacco—the intense excitement produced a House of 473 members, the highest attendance since Walpole's accession to power. The debate, held in the presence of the Prince of Wales, many foreign ambassadors and a great mass of peers, was furious and lengthy; yet when Walpole divided the House shortly after midnight, he triumphed by sixty-one votes, and faced the Easter recess quietly confident that the measure would pass with relative ease. But in London and Liverpool newspapers supporting excise were publicly burnt, and further instructions to members threatened rejection at the next general election to all who supported Walpole. Equally ominous, a whispering campaign against Sir Robert was launched at Court, and office-holders in both Houses began to waver in their allegiance. Of the former Leicester House clique, Chesterfield, Scarborough and Clinton proclaimed their open opposition; Lord Stair unsuccessfully closeted the Queen; Bolton and Cobham loudly denounced the measure; and the influence of all these peers was exercised over their friends and relatives in the Commons. On the motion for the second reading, on 4 April, Walpole's majority dropped alarmingly to thirty-six, and in a thin House the next day to a mere sixteen. In the face of widespread desertions and abstentions he found himself threatened with possible defeat in both Houses, and reluctantly advised the King that the bill must be dropped. He did indeed offer his resignation but George II refused even to contemplate so drastic a step. Secure in royal confidence, Walpole made one final stand before submitting to the inevitable, but on 10 April the City of London's petition against the bill was rejected in a House of 411 by a mere seventeen votes. To a small gathering of his friends at supper that night he wearily confided: 'This dance, it will no further go'; and on the following day he announced to the Commons that the bill was to be postponed until 12 June. As Parliament would not then be in session, this was a tacit acceptance of defeat. All that night the City abandoned itself to bonfires, fireworks and noisy celebration. But this mob violence caused severe misgivings in the Commons, where even the Opposition leaders joined the next day in condemning the excesses. Walpole skilfully turned the general alarm to his own advantage, and on 22 April, when a petition against excises on tea and coffee was presented, it was rejected by a majority of one hundred. Two days later, in a ballot for a committee to look into frauds in the customs, the Government's nominees were supported by a majority of eighty-five in a huge House of 503 members. The situation in the Commons had been completely retrieved.

With the King firmly behind Walpole, there was little chance of Opposition success at Court, but there were many peers who, jealous of the dominance which Sir Robert had long exercised, were prepared to make an all-out attempt to secure his defeat in the Lords. At least ten office-holding noblemen had openly opposed the Excise Bill, and the subsequent dismissal of Chesterfield and Clinton merely increased aristocratic resentment of Walpole's power at Court. Even the bishops were rumoured to be wavering. Aware of the imminent challenge, Walpole and his fellow-ministers, supported by the King and Queen, made desperate efforts to rally every potential Government supporter. But on 24 May, on an Administration motion relating to an enquiry into the management of the estates of the South Sea directors, the Lords divided seventy-five to seventy-five, and in accordance with the custom of the House the motion was declared lost. This was a new and devastating experience for Walpole, for it had always been assumed that the Upper House was an impregnable ministerial strong-hold with the bishops and Scottish and office-holding peers normally constituting a comfortable majority. Drastic action had become necessary, and the remainder of May was spent closeting every wavering peer, threatening the office-holders who had deserted, and cajoling those whose consciences or ambitions made them vulnerable. These efforts were rewarded on 2 June, when a motion to appoint a joint committee of both Houses to inquire into South Sea Company affairs was defeated by seventy-five votes to seventy. The margin of success was narrow, but it signified the turn of the tide in Walpole's favour. Stern action was taken against the deserters and Stair, Marchmont, Montrose and Bolton were dismissed from office. More than this, Bolton and Cobham were deprived of their regiments, an unprecedented penalty for political apostasy. But it gave striking evidence of George II's devotion to Walpole, for the army was the King's own particular love, jealously guarded against the encroachments of ministerial patronage. Sir Robert was again firmly in the saddle.

The excise crisis had stirred up intense passions, severely shaken

Walpole's pride and self-confidence, and demonstrated to the nation that his position was not as impregnable as it seemed. Yet it would be unwise to regard it as other than a passing storm in an otherwise placid political tea-cup. When the Opposition tried to revive hostility to excise in the general election of 1734, it proved little more than a damp squib, and there is no evidence that it materially affected results in more than a tiny handful of constituencies. Even before the election, Walpole had secured a great personal triumph at the expense of his arch-rival, Bolingbroke. In a debate over the proposed repeal of the Septennial Act, on 13 March 1734, Wyndham had archly suggested: 'Let us suppose a gentleman at the head of the Administration, whose only safety depends upon corrupting the members of this house'; and then proceeded to delight the Commons by a witty exposition of the devious means by which the web of patronage could be spun. Walpole gleefully seized upon the same device of supposition to deliver a blistering attack on the man who, since his return from exile, had been the heart and soul of Opposition. His thundering denunciation concluded:

> Let us farther suppose this anti-minister to have travelled, and at every court where he was, thinking himself the greatest minister, and making it his trade to betray the secrets of every court where he had before been; void of all faith and honour, and betraying every master he ever served. I could carry my suppositions a great deal farther, and I may say I mean no person now in being; but if we can suppose such a one, can there be imagined a greater disgrace to human nature than such a wretch as this?

This was superb, fighting rhetoric, which secured the rejection of repeal by 247 votes to 184, and convinced the Opposition that they could no longer afford the luxury of Bolingbroke's unstable and treacherous genius. At Pulteney's urging he retired to France shortly afterwards, leaving a vacuum that was filled three years later when Frederick, Prince of Wales became the patron of the Opposition. Walpole had thus staged a brilliant recovery, and sober reflection persuaded most members that, whatever the merits and demerits of excise, he gave the country the kind of Government it wanted. What were the bases of his domestic and foreign policies?

The aims of Walpole's economic policy were quite clear-cut. He wished to restore public confidence after the chaos of the South Sea Bubble, to reduce further the national debt and the interest charges upon it, to lower taxation (especially the land-tax), to stimulate production in agriculture and industry, and to expand the volume of English trade. By these means he hoped to rally the support of both landed and merchant classes behind the Hanoverian dynasty and the Ministry, and he was convinced that peace both at home and abroad was essential to the success of his plans. The eclipse of Jacobitism, combined with his own retention of power for twenty-one years, might seem at first sight convincing vindication of his ability as a financier and economist. But there were many reasons other than economic for the endurance both of Walpole and the new dynasty; and when his policy is examined in detail his financial and commercial achievements seem less impressive than has often been claimed.

Sir Robert has been widely and justifiably praised for his restoration of stability after the South Sea crash. But, as Professor Plumb has emphasized, Walpole's success was the result of political courage and determination, not of financial acumen. He did not originally criticize the principle of the South Sea Company's scheme; he bought and sold stock at the wrong times and was saved from considerable personal losses only by the caution of his bankers; the engraftment scheme by which he proposed to restore public credit was not his own idea, but that of Robert Jacombe, and anyway it was never put into practice; and the final settlement of terms for the unfortunate annuitants was an administrative rather than a financial issue. Walpole, far from being hailed by contemporaries as a financial genius, was widely execrated for his protection of those politicians who had been involved in the scandal and for the rigour of the eventual settlement. Yet he at least had the courage to maintain an unpopular but sensible position and allow time for stability to return. His limitations as a financier were far outweighed by his intuitive skill as a politician.

In the opening decades of the eighteenth century there was general alarm at the extent to which the national debt had grown during the wars of William's and Anne's reigns. By 1697 it had reached £14,000,000, by 1717 £40,000,000 and by 1721 £54,000,000. At George I's accession half this debt was held by three great joint-stock companies—the Bank of England, the South Sea Company, and the East India Company—at an interest rate of 6 per cent, and the remainder by private individuals (mostly in the form of annuities) at rates varying from 6 per cent to 9 per cent. The total interest charge was over £3,000,000 per annum, and many feared that the nation would never prosper under so great a burden. This led Walpole, in 1717, to consider the possibility of reducing the debt by the establishment of a Sinking Fund. There was nothing original about this idea, which had been used by the Dutch in 1655, the Papacy in 1685 and the French in 1714. Moreover, it was William Paterson, the founder of the Bank of England, who worked out the details of the scheme, and Stanhope who was to put it into effect after Walpole's resignation in 1717. Nonetheless, Walpole deserves full credit for taking the initiative.

As a result, a conversion of the redeemable debt was carried out which reduced the interest rate from 6 per cent to 5 per cent, and the annual saving of £234,455 became the basis of the Sinking Fund, which was to be used to pay off the capital of the debt. But in practice Walpole achieved much less than he had hoped. The interest rate was admittedly further reduced to 4 per cent in 1727, but this was the result of the South Sea conversion of 1720, which owed nothing to Walpole. The capital had fallen by 1739 (the last year of peace) to £46,000,000 and the annual interest charge to £2,000,000; but if £8,000,000 had been paid off in the course of eighteen years, the income of the Sinking Fund had amounted to over £10,000,000 in the years 1721-8 alone. It is clear that the Fund rapidly came to be diverted to purposes other than the ostensible one of reducing the debt. Thus in 1724 it was raided to make good a loss on gold coin, in 1727 to augment George II's Civil List by £100,000 (thereby helping to secure Walpole's continuance in office), and in 1730 to repeal the salt duties of £500,000 per annum. After 1733 it was regarded merely as a source of revenue that could be tapped for extraordinary expenditure, and in 1737 Walpole openly opposed Sir John Barnard's scheme for a further reduction of the debt. Yet if Sir Robert failed to achieve his original object, this was largely the result of a significant change in the public attitude. Increasing political stability and the beginnings of economic expansion slowly convinced people that the debt, far from being an intolerable burden, was an excellent investment, and Walpole was fully justified in claiming that the public creditors no longer wished to be repaid. A pamphlet of 1735 remarked that 'the Sinking Fund was now grown to a great maturity and produced annually about £1,200,000 and was become almost a terror to all the individual proprietors of the Public Debts'. As with South Sea Company affairs, Walpole approached the problem as a politician rather than as an economist. Nor, although the South Sea Company fiasco had clearly indicated the danger of allowing too great a concentration of financial power, does he seem to have been unduly worried by the fact that almost the whole of the debt had fallen into the hands of the three great companies. It was left to Henry Pelham after 1743 to restore the balance by having greater recourse to private creditors.

Walpole fully appreciated that a low level of taxation was the surest way to political popularity. The window-tax was retained because of the ease of assessment, but the land-tax was reduced in 1721 from three shillings to two shillings in the pound, and even to one shilling in 1732 and 1733. Only during the brief Spanish war was it raised in 1727 to four shillings. Yet the efforts of the Opposition thwarted his attempt to abolish the land-tax, the opposition to his Ministry continued to flourish and, since peace was the essential prerequisite to low taxation, the failure of his foreign policy by 1739 inevitably completed the destruction of his plans.

In the spheres of commerce and industry Walpole is sometimes seen as an innovator—as an early advocate of free trade and the forerunner of the younger Pitt, Peel, Huskisson and Gladstone. This is clearly untrue for Walpole was guided in economics, as in politics, by expediency rather than principle. His basic ideas had been outlined in the Speech from the Throne on 19 October 1721:

> In this situation of affairs, we should be extremely wanting to ourselves, if we neglected to improve the favourable opportunity which this general tranquillity gives us, of extending our commerce, upon which the richness and grandeur of this nation chiefly depend. It is very obvious that nothing would more conduce to the obtaining so public a good, than to make the exportation of our own manufactures, and the importation of the commodities used in the manufacturing of them, as practicable and as easy as may be; by this means the balance of trade may be preserved in our favour, our navigation increased, and greater numbers of our poor employed.

To these ends he abolished duties on the export of agricultural produce and on over one hundred manufactured articles; provided bounties to encourage the export of grain, spirits, silk, sail-cloths and refined sugar; removed import duties on dyes, undressed flax and raw silk in order to stimulate the relevant industries; laid down minimum standards of quality and measurement for bales of broadcloths and serges, linen, sail-cloths, bricks and tiles; protected home industries by export tariffs on rival manufactures; and passed acts in 1721 and 1726 for the regulation of wages by JPs and prohibiting combinations of workmen to secure better pay or conditions of labour. Later in the century, political economists saw Walpole as the inaugurator of a new era of British prosperity, George Chalmers declaring that the year 1722 'must always form an epoch, as memorable for a great operation in commercial policy as the establishment of the sinking fund had been in finance a few years before'. This was a wild exaggeration. Certainly the overall volume of trade expanded appreciably in the course of Sir Robert's long Ministry. Exports (including re-exports) from England and Wales increased from £7,201,000 in 1721 to £10,000,196 in 1738, the last full year of peace; during the remaining three war years of his Ministry they averaged only £8,870,000. Imports between 1721 and 1738 rose from £5,908,000 to £7,439,000, and averaged marginally more than this during the ensuing war years. England's favourable balance of trade thus improved between 1721 and 1738 from £1,293,000 to £2,757,000, and at first sight Walpole's policy would seem to have been a striking success. Yet exports increased more steeply during the twenty years after his fall than they had during his Ministry; and imports had risen appreciably more in the first twenty years of the century. Moreover, if the figures for 1721-38 are broken down the picture becomes rather less rosy. Domestic exports showed little increase at all in the 1720s, and in several years actually decreased; and the favourable balance which England had enjoyed in the early 1720s actually declined between 1725 and 1737. Indeed, if the export of specie is taken into consideration, 1722 was the only year in which Walpole achieved a net favourable balance before 1736. Before then it is dangerous to speak of significant commercial expansion. Even Walpole's attempts to boost particular imports and exports were not uniformly successful. The bounty on refined sugar was accompanied by a rapid rise in its export but that on silk could not prevent a reduction; the abolition of the duty on undressed flax doubtless helped to stimulate a significant increase in its import, but the removal of that on raw silk appears to have had no effect at all. Walpole's tariff policy was by no means the only factor affecting trade in these years, and the statistical information is incomplete and difficult to interpret. But until much more work has been done by economic historians it is as well to be cautious in assessing the merits of Walpole's commercial measures.

As far as colonies were concerned, economic self-sufficiency remained the major aim, and this meant some subordination of colonial interests to those of the mother-country—hence Walpole's Molasses Act of 1733 to protect British West Indian sugar from the competition of the foreign West Indies, and his Hat Act of 1732 to prevent colonial manufacturers from competing with their English counterparts. Yet he made little attempt to enforce these acts, and in 1733 and 1735 he modified the existing regulations by allowing Carolina and Georgia to export rice direct to southern Europe instead of first landing it in England. His refusal even to consider direct taxation of the American colonies bears out the impression that he valued tranquillity in America no less than in England and Europe; and his policy of 'salutary neglect' so much admired by Edmund Burke, left many unsolved problems for his successors, whose attempted solutions provoked revolution and war.

All in all, Walpole presided over a period of reasonable and growing prosperity, especially in the late 1730s, and his strong political rule, by ensuring stability and peace, created excellent conditions for revival after the wars of William and Anne and the financial collapse of 1720. His economic policy sought to stimulate further this prosperity and, up to a point, succeeded. But he seldom pursued his aims to the very end, and their precise effect is difficult to assess. Even the merchant and monied classes, who might have been expected to applaud his policy, were divided in their attitude. The Bank of England and the East India Company (whose charter he renewed in 1733) were solidly behind him, but a host of smaller merchants, especially in the City of London, were his resolute opponents. And in the end it was the violence of the South Sea Company that forced him into a war with Spain that destroyed the peace which, rightly or wrongly, he considered essential to national prosperity.

To speak of Walpole's social policy would be meaningless. He merely followed the prevailing trend of opinion, which for the most part wished only to preserve the *status quo*, but was sometimes unexpectedly and genuinely moved by the first stirrings of a social conscience that was to become more vocal as the century progressed. The fear of rising poor rates provoked the Act of 1723, insisting on the workhouse test as a prerequisite to relief, and allowing local authorities to farm out the care of the poor, a practice that gravely accentuated existing evils. The poor did not lack their occasional champions, of whom one of the more vociferous and influential—William Hay—even persuaded the House of Commons in 1735 to pass resolutions condemning the existing state of affairs and advocating discrimination between treatment of the able-bodied, the idle and disorderly, and the infirm and young; but these resolutions proved sterile in the face of the masterly inactivity of Walpole's ministry.

Sir Robert may have been able to ignore the inhumanity of the primitive system of poor relief, but he was forced to face up to the concurrent evil of excessive gin consumption among the lower classes. Increasing revulsion at this widespread drunkenness produced the act of 1729, which imposed a duty on cheap spirits and introduced a fee of £20 for a retailer's licence. The opposition of wheat-growers to the resulting fall in consumption persuaded Walpole to repeal this act in 1733, but these vested interests could not prevail against the mounting horror that accompanied the fresh orgy of drunkenness. Walpole was compelled to action for the third time, and Sir Joseph Jekyll's Act of 1736 raised the duty to £1 a gallon and the licence fee to £50. But this new severity merely induced widespread evasion, and the problem was bequeathed to Walpole's successors.

The only other social question to achieve prominence in Sir Robert's day was that of the conditions in debtors' prisons, of which the Fleet and Marshalsea were the most notorious. The efforts of James Oglethorpe secured a Parliamentary committee the report of which in February 1729 was the prelude to the dismissal of the sadistic Warden Bambridge of the

Fleet and some of his more brutal subordinates. The appalling revelations in the report also forced the Government to make a few minor improvements in prison conditions, but neither this committee, nor its successor instigated by William Hay in 1735, could provoke Walpole and his fellow-ministers to serious action. It was left to Oglethorpe in his private capacity to raise subscriptions for liquidating the debts of the more deserving, and to persist in the face of Sir Robert's disapproval until he had secured from the King a royal charter conferring on a board of trustees the territory in America that was soon to become Georgia, and was to serve initially as a refuge for those who would otherwise have perished in the disease-ridden squalor of an English debtors' prison. In his attitude to social problems Walpole amply vindicated his proud assertion that he was no saint and no reformer.

Sir Robert was not a devout man and his attitudes to religious problems were dictated largely by their political implications. Since the Tories, traditional champions of the Anglican Church, were rent by the non-juror schism and discredited by the taint of Jacobitism, Walpole and his followers were able to stand forth as the only trustworthy guardians of the establishment. The treatment of Protestant Dissenters was therefore a delicate matter. Sir Robert's natural inclination was to meet their reasonable demands for further relief from penal legislation. They were Whig supporters whose reliability had been proved both in 1685–8 and in 1715, some fourteen thousand of them had the vote in parliamentary elections, and they played an increasingly important part in the economic development of the nation. Yet he was loath to provide the Tories with any excuse for claiming that the Church was threatened, or to alienate the bishops and lesser clergy whose policical activities were invaluable to any eighteenth-century government. In 1723 he provided a mild sedative in the form of the *Regium Donum*, an annual grant of £500 (later raised to £1,000) for the widows of Dissenting ministers; and from 1728 onward he promoted more or less annual Indemnity Acts which gave partial protection to Dissenters who had accepted office without taking the Sacrament. But the Committee of Dissenting Deputies (Presbyterians, Independents and Baptists), formed in 1732, regarded these concessions as inadequate and were exhorted by their rank and file to press for total repeal of the Test and Corporation Acts. Walpole, with the Excise Bill crisis already imminent, was in no mood to risk alienating supporters by becoming involved in religious controversy. He persuaded the Committee that the time was inopportune, and when they resumed their campaign after the election of 1734 he pleaded in excuse the pressure of business in a newly-elected Parliament. When in 1736 and again in 1739 the Deputies proceeded, against Walpole's advice, to move for repeal in the House of Commons they were heavily defeated. Lord Hervey claimed that Walpole had packed the Committee with men who would be guided by him, and that the Dissenters' cause was betrayed by their own leaders. Some credence is given to this claim by the fact that no fewer than thirteen out of the twenty-one members (including Samuel Holden, their Chairman until 1736) had the kind of background that would make them very reluctant to embarrass the Administration, but it seems at least as likely that the Deputies, like Walpole, were political realists who appreciated the difficulty of the situation. At all events Sir Robert adroitly extricated himself from a delicate situation without losing the support of either the episcopate or the Dissenters.

Similar tactics were used in dealing with the Quaker attempts to make obligatory the cheaper methods of prosecution and distraint for non-payment of tithes, permitted by the Act of 1696. From 1729 to 1735 Walpole dealt courteously and sympathetically but evasively with their successive representations, but after he had vindicated his support for the Church by opposing the motion to repeal the Test and Corporation Acts in 1736, he supported their Tithe Bill which, because of the widespread sympathy for their position, passed through its various stages in the Commons without much obstruction. But the Church's vigorous opposition was expressed through the Bishops in the House of Lords, where the bill was easily defeated. The only result was the final breach between Walpole and Bishop Gibson, who was furious at Walpole's support of the measure, and whose control of ecclesiastical patronage[1] was forthwith handed over to the Duke of Newcastle. After 1736 Walpole reverted to fobbing off the Quakers with polite excuses and since, like the other Dissenters, they could hope for nothing from an Opposition in which Tories were numerically predominant, their campaign was similarly doomed to failure.

In foreign affairs the primary aim of British policy continued to be the preservation of peace by co-operation with France. After the end of the Northern War in 1721, the chief threats to peace came from the provocative tactics of Charles VI who, freed from the Turkish menace by the Peace of Passarowitz, proved singularly reluctant to invest Don Carlos with the promised Italian duchies, and offended British and Dutch merchant opinion by the formation in 1722 of the Ostend Company; and from Philip V of Spain, who was irritated by the loss of Gibraltar, resentful of the trading privileges extracted by England at Utrecht, and

---

[1]See pp 153–4.

dominated above all by a determination to force the Emperor's hand over Italy. A dramatic change in the diplomatic tempo occurred at the end of 1724 when Spain decided to quicken the pace by sending Ripperda to treat unilaterally with the Emperor. In the face of Imperial coolness his mission would probably have failed had not France chosen this particular moment to insult Spain by abruptly returning the seven-year-old Infanta (affianced to Louis XV by the Treaty of Madrid) to her parents. Philip and Elizabeth responded by breaking off diplomatic relations with France and ordering Ripperda to settle with the Emperor on any terms he could obtain. The results were embodied in three Treaties of Vienna on 30 April 1725, of which only the first was made public. Charles VI confirmed the Quadruple Alliance, in return for which Philip guaranteed the Pragmatic Sanction, that pathetic and worthless document by which the Emperor hoped to safeguard the succession of his daughter Maria Theresa to his hereditary lands, and which was to prove the Achilles heel of Imperial diplomacy for more than a decade. By the secret articles Charles made vague promises to assist Spain in regaining Gibraltar and Minorca, and Philip granted extended trading privileges to the Emperor and undertook to support the claims of the Ostend Company. This was a very poor bargain for Spain, roused both England and France to feverish activity, and soon divided the Continent into two armed camps. France envisaged the revival of the ancient Hapsburg menace, while in Britain merchant opinion was hostile and the old bogey of foreign aid for the Pretender was resurrected. Until 1725 Britain had generally been content to follow France's lead, but now she seized the diplomatic initiative, and at the same time the first signs of divergence between Townshend and Walpole began to appear. Townshend, sceptical anyway of the value of the traditional alliance with the Emperor and unwilling to risk disruption of the profitable English trade with Spain, favoured vigorous measures against Charles VI. Walpole's conservative temperament made him more reluctant to break with Britain's ancient ally, and with some justification he considered that the navy could be used more effectively against Spain. But Townshend for the moment had his way, aided by George I's ever-present concern for the protection of his Electorate. Thus in the summer of 1725 England and Prussia concluded the Treaty of Hanover. Ostensibly each Power guaranteed the other's possessions, Prussia being won over by a promise of assistance in gaining the succession to Julich and Berg. But England's real objects were to gain support against attacks on Hanover and Gibraltar, strengthen her hand against the Ostend Company, and provide a bulwark against the united potential of the Empire, Spain and Russia. The immediate result was a more precise definition of the alliance between Spain and the Empire by a further Treaty of Vienna of 5 November 1725 in which Charles VI in a panic committed himself whole-heartedly to Spain in the event of war. His fears were premature, for Russia, impatient at France's reluctance to ally with her and anxious at the increasingly strained relations with Britain over Bremen and Verden, Mecklenburg, and Russian intrigues in Sweden, joined the Vienna allies on 26 August; and two months later Frederick William, apprehensive of the threat to his dominions implicit in the Austro-Russian alliance, deserted England and signed the Treaty of Wüsterhausen with the Emperor, guaranteeing the Pragmatic Sanction in return for vague promises about Julich and Berg.

These setbacks galvanized Townshend into further activity. The ever lethargic United Provinces were hustled into joining the Hanover allies in August 1726, while judicious bribery of Swedish senators and the despatch of a British fleet to the Baltic to overawe Russia helped to facilitate Sweden's accession in March 1727. Further subsidy treaties won the support of Denmark and Hesse, although the Emperor's counter-negotiations secured for the Vienna allies the adhesion of various other German states. By the end of 1727 the Vienna Powers could command 387,000 troops, their Hanover rivals only 315,000. But while in the event of war the latter could concentrate their armies within the Empire, Charles had to maintain further detachments in Hungary, on the Turkish border and in Italy; and the naval superiority of the maritime Powers ensured control of the Baltic, the Spanish coast and the West Indies. All in all, Townshend had done a first-class job.

Despite the darkening clouds on the international horizon, only Spain showed much enthusiasm for war. Ripperda's wild threats provoked England into sending Admiral Hosier to Porto Bello in April 1726 to blockade the Spanish treasure fleet and thus make impossible the payment of promised Spanish subsidies to the Emperor. But the dismissal of Ripperda the following month did little to ease Anglo-Spanish tension, especially since the fallen minister promptly revealed all the secret provisions of the Treaties of Vienna to the British Ambassador at Madrid, and Spain retaliated against Hosier's blockade by impounding British ships in Spanish ports. Townshend therefore sent a second fleet under Jennings to cruise off the Spanish coast, and in February 1727 England was forced into a war with Spain which she did not want. Fortunately, neither France nor the Emperor showed any desire to extend the scope of the conflict. The dismissal of Ripperda had made possible without loss of prestige the overthrow of the Duc de Bourbon (who had been responsible for the Franco-Spanish breach) and his replacement by the pacific Fleury, who was convinced that war could benefit only England. Equally, the Emperor had no desire to pander to Spanish ambitions and was beginning to wonder whether the Ostend Company was worth all the trouble it was causing him. This enabled Fleury to promote negotiations between the Emperor and England which culminated in the Preliminaries of 31 May 1727, and to which Spain—deserted by Charles, who was dismayed by the seeming impregnability of Gibraltar, and cut off from the trade with the West Indies that was her life blood—was forced to adhere. From this agreement England gained the suspension for seven years of the Ostend Company and a promise of the settlement of commercial disputes with Spain. For a time indeed Spain, encouraged by Fleury's friendly overtures, was inclined to evade the Preliminaries but, after a series of inconclusive negotiations and an abortive Congress at Soissons, she finally came to terms with England by the Treaty of Seville of 9 November 1729. England's trading privileges were confirmed in return for Anglo-French support in forcing Charles VI's hand over the Italian duchies. But the Emperor's continued procrastination, together with France's reluctance to force his hand (which Fleury believed could be done only by war or by guaranteeing the Pragmatic Sanction) so infuriated Spain that at the end of 1730 she declared the Treaty of Seville null and void.

At this stage Walpole himself finally took command of English foreign policy. For five years he had remained uneasy at Townshend's greater hostility towards the Empire than Spain, convinced that this policy was more in French than British interests, and troubled by the Opposition's claim that it was dictated largely by royal anxiety for the protection of Hanover. Nor did he like Townshend's neglect of Portugal (England's traditional ally against Spain) or his exacerbation of Anglo-Russian relations by expensive subsidies to Sweden, whom Walpole considered a weak and unreliable ally. On Townshend's resignation in May 1730 Walpole therefore determined to return to the Imperial alliance. In the 'Second' Treaty of Vienna of 16 March 1731 England guaranteed the Pragmatic Sanction, while Charles agreed to the total abolition of the Ostend Company and to the admission of Spanish garrisons into the Italian duchies, which they entered peacefully in October. Spain in gratitude renewed the Treaty of Seville and agreed to the appointment of Commissioners to settle reparations for damages to English shipping. Walpole could claim that he had succeeded in removing the last causes of European friction and had reconstituted the Anglo-Imperial alliance without breaking with either France or Spain. His control over all aspects of policy was now complete.

Up to this point English diplomacy had been conspicuously successful.

The French alliance, in which, since 1725, England had clearly been the senior partner, had proved more beneficial to her than to France. While Anglo-Spanish friction remained, France was unable to reap any advantage from her close family connection with Spain, and her commerce was restricted by the destruction of Dunkirk and the cessation of the works at Mardyke. More and more dependent on the English navy, she allowed her own fleet to decline at a time when the whole emphasis of her policy should have been on commercial and colonial development. In North America, India, the West Indies and the Levant her potential was great, but her statesmen lacked the imperial vision of a Chatham and the focus of her interests remained essentially continental. Not that England at this stage showed much greater awareness of her imperial destiny, but her policy was at least directed towards naval supremacy and commercial expansion. Ever sensitive of her position in the Baltic and the Mediterranean, she was equally determined to preserve her trading rights with Spanish America and, if possible, her flourishing commerce with old Spain. From time to time the Opposition accused the Administration of being unduly influenced by Hanoverian considerations but in fact there was little real conflict between British and Electoral interests. Support for Sweden against Russia was dictated as much by British commercial considerations as by Hanoverian fears, and the Treaty of Hanover had sought much more than the mere defence of the Electorate.

Yet after 1731 Walpole did little to consolidate the commanding position he had won. Within a few years the French, Spanish and Imperial alliances had all been appreciably weakened, and the diplomatic initiative had clearly passed to the astute Fleury and his Anglophobe foreign minister Chauvelin. With honeyed words Fleury wooed Horace Walpole and Lord Waldegrave (successive British Ambassadors at Paris) into a sense of false security, while the sources of Anglo-French friction grew apace. Over Canada, the West Indies, Dunkirk and Mardyke, trivial arguments contributed to mounting tension, while the Family Compact of 1733 between France and Spain, and the treaty of neutrality between France and Holland seriously weakened England's position. Although the alliance with France did not formally lapse until 1744 it was, after 1731, little more than an insidious soporific to England. Continuing commercial disputes with Spain equally diminished the utility of the Treaty of Seville and were ultimately to involve Walpole in a war that spelt political ruin. But, in the light of England's declining influence, his greatest mistake was to stand aside from the War of the Polish Succession which broke out in 1733. Though English interests were not directly involved in the Polish issue, French aggression in Germany and Italy could scarcely fail to affect the European balance of power. But Walpole's pacifism eventually prevailed against the conviction of George II and Harrington that the Emperor should be supported. Consequently Charles VI, offered English mediation instead of troops, considered himself betrayed, and Walpole's crude attempts to influence the peace negotiations were neatly foiled by Fleury. By the third Treaty of Vienna in 1738 France gained the reversion to Lorraine, Don Carlos exchanged Parma and Tuscany for the more substantial two Sicilies, and the Emperor won nothing but a worthless French guarantee of the Pragmatic Sanction. Anglo-Imperial friendship was gravely weakened, the Bourbon Powers had consolidated their position, and England, deprived for the first time in twenty years of a voice in European affairs, was left in far from splendid isolation. Walpole was content that peace and prosperity had been preserved, but he lacked the perception to see that France, her succession secured at last by the marriage of the King and birth of an heir, had resumed her aggressive career, and that British interests in Europe and the Empire would not be safe until she was checked. Not for the last time in British history a profound desire for peace at any price was to breed a major war and leave the nation hopelessly unprepared when conflict broke out.

In Ireland, too, Walpole had his difficulties. Dominated by the Protestant ascendancy, the vast bulk of the impoverished Roman Catholic population played no part in the political life of the nation. But the Protestants themselves were far from satisfied with their constitutional and economic subjection to England. In 1722 came the first opportunity for them to stand forth as the patriotic defenders of Irish rights. In response to the chronic shortage of coin in Ireland, the English treasury granted to the Duchess of Kendal a patent for the issue of a new copper coinage, which she promptly sold to one William Wood for £10,000. By this patent Wood was empowered over the following fourteen years to mint Irish halfpence and farthings to the total value of £100,800. But the failure to consult either the Irish Government or Parliament, together with reports that the first instalment was sub-standard and the knowledge that the profits were to be enjoyed by an Englishman, rapidly produced a furore of opposition. Fomented by Lord Chancellor Midleton, exaggerated by the timidity of Lord-Lieutenant Grafton and encouraged by the support of the disgruntled Carteret, the clamour was elevated to a new level by the publication of Dean Swift's *The Drapier's Letters*, which raised the whole question of Anglo-Irish relationships and for the first time united all classes and all religions against English tyranny. Walpole deftly attempted to extricate himself from the crisis by recalling Grafton and demoting Carteret from the Secretaryship of State to the Lord-Lieutenancy, thereby at one and the same time ridding himself of a troublesome rival at Court and providing Ireland with a much-needed strong man. But Carteret could not quell the storm, and in 1725 Walpole was forced to withdraw the patent. Peace was now quickly restored, but the English Government had learnt the need for more effective parliamentary management, which was handed over to the 'undertakers', a group of Anglo-Irish politicians who guaranteed to carry English policy through Parliament in return for the lion's share of the spoils. This new system endured until the 1760s and succeeded in drawing the teeth from Irish 'patriotic' parliamentary opposition.

All in all Walpole had steered a steady if unspectacular course. Peace had been preserved, prosperity was returning, and vested interests had been respected. It has been argued that Sir Robert, by refusing to face thorny problems, merely bequeathed them to his successors, and in respect of foreign, colonial, economic and religious policy there is some strength in this argument. But if parliamentary support were any guide, the country was behind him. He lost sixteen seats at the general election of 1734, but could still in a full Commons count on a majority of almost one hundred; and the purge of malcontents after the excise crisis had strengthened his Administration even though it had augmented the ranks of the Opposition. But the following eight years produced a concatenation of events that eroded his parliamentary support and a change in the climate of opinion that undermined the basis of his political strength and challenged the pacifism in which he so genuinely believed.

Part of the gradual weakening of Walpole's position after 1734 arose from a natural reaction against an Administration that had been long in power. Differences over policy, disappointments over preferment and frustrated ambitions all combined to increase the ranks of his opponents, until after the election of 1741 it became problematic whether he could maintain an adequate working majority in the Commons. Yet it would be a mistake to attribute minor electoral set-backs to alienated public opinion, and it is characteristic that in Scotland and Cornwall, where Walpole lost most heavily in 1741, the political opinions of voters were almost completely irrelevant. The real barometer of politics was the changing balance of forces in the Commons, where, after 1734, Walpole found himself confronted by an ever-increasing array of Opposition talent whose rhetorical outbursts could frequently sway those independent members on whose support Sir Robert in the last resort had to depend. Before the excise crisis his opponents, suffering from the stigma of factiousness implicit in 'formed Opposition' to His Majesty's Government and from the Jacobite taint attaching to the Tories, were rent by divisions, lacking competent leaders and unable to find sufficiently vital issues on which to make a stand. But the Excise Bill fiasco not only gave them their first taste of success, but marked the turning point in their fortunes. The ensuing purge of defecting office-holders greatly strengthened the Opposition benches in the Lords, and, through the influence of individual peers, in the Commons. The dismissal, for example, of Lord Cobham, who was anything but a distinguished politician, might seem of little importance. But by 1741 his relatives in the Lower House included Richard, George and James Grenville, William Pitt and George Lyttelton—all resolute opponents of Walpole, two of them future premiers, and the rest destined for at least junior ministerial office. Similarly Walpole's quarrel with the Duke of Argyll who quitted office in 1740 led the Duke to oppose the Earl of Islay (his brother and Sir Robert's electoral manager in Scotland) in 1741 and for the only time in the century return an Opposition majority from north of the border. In this way Walpole helped to build up one of the most formidable Oppositions of the century. Between the elections of 1734 and 1741 his majority dropped by more than fifty. Jealous of sharing power with able men, he allowed his known preference for mediocrities to drive ambitious newcomers into the arms of Carteret and Pulteney who had now become the real leaders of the Opposition in each House.

In 1737 the Opposition had an even more important windfall. Frederick, Prince of Wales, always on bad terms with his father, gave fresh offence by allowing the Opposition to move in Parliament for the doubling of his annual allowance, deeply wounded George II by his heartless behaviour during the dying agonies of the Queen, and provoked a complete break by carrying off his wife from St James's in the midst of her labour so that his child should not be born within sight of the King. As a result the princely court was declared out-of-bounds to all Government politicians and Frederick became the patron of the parliamentary Opposition. While this made Walpole's opponents personally as well as politically anathema to the King, it bolstered their fortunes in several important ways. Firstly, it gave them an aura of respectability and a focal point for organization; secondly, it meant that the Prince's followers in both Houses would now vote against Walpole instead of for him, and by 1741 there were no fewer than twenty in the Commons alone; thirdly, it enabled the Prince, allied with Lord Falmouth and aided by the expert electoral management of Thomas Pitt, to administer a heavy defeat to the Administration in 1741 in their normally impregnable stronghold of Cornwall. Finally when in January 1742 Frederick refused to be bought off by the addition of £50,000 to his annual allowance as long as Walpole remained in office, Sir Robert was left as the only apparent obstacle to the widely-desired reconciliation between father and son. Thus Frederick's and Walpole's fortunes were inextricably intertwined.

Walpoles advancing years and recurrent ill-health also contributed to his political decline. On the one hand they subjected him to periodic fits of despondency during which he lost his masterly touch; on the other they confirmed the younger generation of politicians in their impression that there was little to be gained by hitching their wagon to Sir Robert's falling star. Nor did the divisions within his Administration breed confidence in his ability to weather the storm. Newcastle and Harrington were increasingly critical of his pacific attitude in foreign affairs, while Wilmington, Dorset and Bubb Dodington were ready to desert him on the slightest excuse. In Scotland Walpole's popularity was undermined by his suppression of the Porteous riots in 1737, and in London the middling merchants, tradesmen and master craftsmen far outnumbered the big monied men whose vested interests in the Bank of England and the great trading companies made them Walpole's natural allies. As early as 1725 Sir Robert had felt it necessary to force through a London Election Act disfranchising some three thousand freemen and legalizing the aldermanic veto over the proceedings of the Common Council. Metropolitan radicalism was encouraged by opposition propaganda in such journals as *The Craftsman*, *The True Briton* and *Common Sense*, and by virulent attacks on ministers from the stage. Tolerant though Walpole was of criticism, the constant jibes and innuendoes of Henry Fielding, John Gay and other Opposition dramatists provoked him in 1737 into passing the Playhouse Act, whereby all new plays had to be submitted to the Lord Chancellor for approval.

Yet although the Opposition's fortunes were rising, it is easy to exaggerate Walpole's decline. If on a 'popular' measure like the Place Bill of 1740 he might escape defeat by only sixteen votes, he maintained on most issues throughout the 1734–41 Parliament a majority of at least fifty, despite the defection of the Prince and his followers in 1737. Moreover, the Opposition could easily over-play its hand, as in February 1741, when its premature move to address the King for Walpole's dismissal was ignominiously defeated by the staggering majority of 184 votes. On domestic issues the Opposition could make little head-way, but the real challenge to Sir Robert's authority came from the gathering war-clouds that had begun to darken Anglo-Spanish relations.

Trade with Spain was an important part of British commerce. Not only did Spain import large quantities of woollen cloth and fish in exchange

Hyde Park Corner Turnpike, with a view of St George's Hospital, 1797

Charles James Fox

for fine wool and the materials for cleansing and dyeing it, but she also purchased many commodities required by her American colonies, and in return Britain gained gold and silver with which to finance other important branches of her trade. Unfortunately, the Spanish penchant for obstructive tactics hampered even this legitimate trade, while the direct commerce with Spanish America provided endless sources of friction. Although the ships of the South Sea Company engaged in a certain amount of illicit trade, this was done tactfully and often with the connivance of the Spaniards themselves. The real irritation from the Spanish point of view was the widespread contraband activity of the British West Indian and mainland colonists. To cope with this the Spanish governors licensed an increasing number of *guarda-costas*, many of whom were little better than pirates. Since they were rewarded by a share of any captured ships, they had every incentive to prey on British shipping, and the right of search they claimed was a constant irritant to British opinion. The resulting depredations were most numerous during the early unsettled years between 1713 and 1731, when 180 British ships were said to have been illegally pillaged, but after England became instrumental in installing Don Carlos in his Italian duchies, Spain became much more accommodating. From 1734 to 1737 only twenty ships were seized, many of them justifiably, and it was ironical that Spanish tolerance, by encouraging colonial smugglers, provoked a fresh crisis that was to culminate in war.

The increase in *guarda-costas* in 1737 resulted in the capture of twelve British vessels. Britain protested, Spain was conciliatory but evasive. West Indian merchants petitioned Parliament, the Opposition clamoured for blood, and claims for depredations in the earlier period were resurrected. Walpole and the Spanish Government did everything in their power to avert a breach, but two developments rendered their efforts useless. In March 1738 news reached England that sailors from four captured British ships had been forced to work their passages to Europe, only to be incarcerated in a Spanish prison. This was in fact normal practice and the Spanish authorities in this particular case had shown more than usual leniency. But Pitt and other Opposition speakers were quick to demand vindication of national honour. It was at this stage that the celebrated Captain Jenkins appeared earless before the Commons, though his ship had been captured as long ago as 1731 and his claim had never been conceded by the commissioners. Even the pacific Walpole was forced to make strong representations to Madrid, send a squadron to the Mediterranean, and increase the number of seamen by ten thousand. The second blow to Sir Robert's policy came from the entanglement of British claims for depredations with the financial affairs of the South Sea Company. Philip V was prepared to pay £95,000 compensation, but wanted the Company to contribute towards it the £68,000 arrears of duties which they admittedly owed him. This was the basis of the Convention of the Pardo which was submitted to Parliament in January 1739, other disputes being referred to plenipotentiaries. But the South Sea directors refused to co-operate and the fury of the Opposition ruined all hopes of accommodation. In the fullest House since the excise crisis the Convention was approved by the Commons by only twenty-eight votes (260–232). Opposition pamphlets inflamed the country, while memorials from the trading ports poured into Parliament. Spain, bolstered by a marriage alliance with France, at last lost all patience, and on 19 October 1739 Walpole was reluctantly forced to accede to the demand for war. In retrospect it is tempting to admire Pitt's vision of expanding trade and the Empire, and deplore Walpole's unimaginative pacifism. Yet like other Opposition leaders, Pitt was intent mainly on encompassing Walpole's defeat in order to force himself into office, and sought to utilize a jingoistic merchant opinion that foolishly believed that the colonial wealth of a supposedly weak Spain was theirs for the taking. Irritating as Spanish provocations might have been, British and colonial merchants and seamen were far from blameless, and in the last resort the genuine and patient attempts of both Governments to preserve the peace and maintain a valuable trade with Old Spain were frustrated by the greed of colonial contraband traders, the irresponsibility of the parliamentary Opposition, and the recalcitrance of the South Sea Company directors.

Walpole's days were now numbered. His heart was not in the war and he proved hopelessly inadequate as a war leader. The early success of Admiral Vernon in capturing Porto Bello was more than offset by its later abandonment and by the failure of the attacks on Cartagena and Cuba. The death of the Emperor Charles VI in October 1740, followed by Frederick the Great's invasion of Silesia in December, entangled Britain in a European conflict in support of Maria Theresa, whose inheritance had been little safeguarded by the Pragmatic Sanction. Spain and Sardinia were eager for aggrandizement in Italy, while the Elector of Bavaria with French support campaigned for the Imperial title against Maria Theresa's husband, Francis, Duke of Tuscany. French armies poured into Germany and George II, desperate for the safety of his Electorate, defied the combined advice of his English ministers, signed a treaty for the neutrality of Hanover, and promised his vote to the Bavarian candidate. Maria Theresa began to despair of English aid, the United Provinces as usual dragged their feet, and Walpole seemed incapable of decisive action.

When the new Parliament met in December 1741 the Opposition mounted an attack that seven times defeated Walpole in the lobbies within the following two months. At last Sir Robert, convinced that the King's business could no longer be carried on while he remained in office, persuaded the reluctant George II to accept his resignation. The Robinocracy was over.

Since the surest way for any minister to lose office is to mismanage a major war, it is less surprising that Walpole should have fallen in February 1742 than that he should have survived for over two years after the outbreak of the conflict. Part of the explanation lies in the strength of the position that he had built up, a position that represents his unique contribution to eighteenth-century constitutional development. By remaining in the Commons he had made himself an essential link between that House and the King, created the new and vital office of 'Minister for the King in the House of Commons', and laid the basis for the eighteenth-century premiership, which rested on the confidence of the King, the leadership of the Commons and the headship of the Treasury. In so doing he created a pattern of politics that conquered the sterile instability of previous decades and enabled King and Parliament to co-operate in the government of the country along mutually acceptable lines. This was Walpole's most enduring legacy.[1]

By acquiescing against his will in war with Spain and by hopelessly mismanaging it, Walpole undermined the position he had built up. The King, it it true, never lost confidence in him despite major disagreements over the conduct of the war. It is often argued that the death of Queen Caroline in 1737 gravely diminished Sir Robert's influence with the King, but this was not so. Essential as had been Caroline's support to Walpole in 1727 and in the ensuing few years when George II was still resentful and suspicious of him, Caroline's mediation had long before 1737 become redundant. Indeed, as Lord Hervey shrewdly saw, the death of Caroline strengthened Walpole's position rather than weakened it, for thenceforth he dealt directly with the King instead of through the Queen. This is borne out by the fact that George remained loyal to him to the very end, and even after his fall was ready on the slightest hint of political crisis to send a messenger to Houghton to seek his advice. But whatever the King might feel, the Commons had lost confidence in Sir Robert, and he could no longer act as an effective link between the twin sources of political power, both of whom wanted the vigorous prosecution of the war. His fall was politically inevitable and constitutionally necessary.

---

[1]For a fuller explanation of these developments see pp 103–5.

But behind the political and constitutional implications of the developing war situation lay a deeper explanation for Walpole's defeat. It was the climate of opinion, not Sir Robert, that had changed. England had needed a breathing space after the exhausting wars of William and Anne, the factious strife of Whig and Tory, and the financial chaos of the South Sea Bubble. This Walpole had provided. But by the late 1730s recuperation was over and a new temper was stirring the country. With the dynasty secured and peace and stability restored, England was ready again to listen to the voice of destiny, exhorting her on the road to commercial and imperial expansion. This strident voice belonged not to the pacific Walpole but to William Pitt, though its message was as yet imperfectly understood. Sir Robert had served his purpose and outlived his usefulness. His way was no longer England's way.

3

CARTERET AND THE PELHAMS 1742–54

THE overthrow of Walpole did not mean the unqualified triumph of his opponents. George II, resentful at having his Closet stormed, wanted ministerial changes reduced to a minimum, and the constitutional conventions of the age required no more than that he should reconstruct his Ministry in such a manner as to enable the resumption of effective Government. Here he was aided both by the relative solidarity of Walpole's following and by the divisions within the ranks of the Opposition. Sir Robert had not created a party in the modern sense, but throughout his long Ministry his basic support had come from a large body of members known as 'the Old Corps of Whigs'. Within its ranks were the leading Government politicians, the more or less permanent office-holders who constituted the Court and Treasury party, and a group of Court independents.[1] Walpole had long since persuaded the King that they were the only reliable basis for any Administration, and their wavering before his fall was quickly checked by their determination to thwart the Opposition, which was anyway in no position to consolidate its victory. Its temporary unanimity had arisen only from a common desire to oust Sir Robert, and the great mass of Tory back-benchers profoundly distrusted the entire Opposition Whig front bench, which was itself bitterly divided. Argyll and his followers rightly suspected that Carteret and Pulteney sought places only for themselves and their few personal supporters, and that they had little sympathy for Argyll's belief in the necessity for a 'broad-bottom' Administration.

Naturally enough, the King chose to treat with the more moderate Carteret and Pulteney. Since Pulteney had many times boasted of his indifference to office, he could be fobbed off with mere membership of the Cabinet, while the ineffectual but unobjectionable Wilmington was at last elevated to his long-desired headship of the Treasury, with Samuel Sandys

---

[1]For a fuller explanation of this classification of members see pp 105–9.

as Chancellor of the Exchequer. Carteret was made Secretary of State in place of Harrington, who moved to the Lord Presidency of the Council. Further 'New Whigs' (as the followers of Carteret and Pulteney came to be called) were insinuated into the Treasury and Admiralty Boards, and reconciliation was at last effected between George II and the Prince of Wales, who gained his extra £50,000 allowance and forthwith instructed his servants to support the new Ministry. Argyll, temporarily persuaded by his supporters to accept office, resigned within a month, convinced that Walpole was still 'minister behind the curtain'. Together with Cobham, Chesterfield, Dodington, Pitt and others he led the Opposition in a triple campaign to court popularity. They dissociated themselves completely from the New Whigs, pressed for the prosecution of Walpole and pushed forward the inevitable 'popular' bills. But the Committee of Enquiry could make no headway against the loyalty of Walpole's former colleagues, successive Place and Pension Bills were rejected by the Lords, and a motion to repeal the Septennial Act did not even pass the Commons. Relations between the Opposition and the New Whigs became ever more embittered, and the alliance of the latter with the Old Corps was cemented by the grant of further places in July, care being taken to mollify any Old Whigs dispossessed of office. Pulteney was forced to retire to the Upper House and political ignominy as Lord Bath, and Henry Pelham became the accepted leader of the Commons. Superficially, the triumph of the King and the Old Corps might seem complete, yet it was another four years before stability returned to the body politic. Pelham might lead the Commons, but it was Carteret, a gifted Classical scholar with a taste for good Burgundy, who came rapidly to engross the confidence of George II as he had much earlier that of George I. Carteret's command of the German language and his readiness to indulge the King's Hanoverian predilections were admittedly great advantages. But he was also a political buccaneer, a minister of the pre-Walpolian era, whose maxim was 'give any man the Crown on his side and he can defy everything'. Had this been true, Walpole would still have been in office, but it was not until 1746 that Carteret was finally persuaded of his error. Meanwhile both the stability of politics and the conduct of the war were disrupted by the failure to find a true successor to Sir Robert.

It is tempting to attribute the improved war situation in 1742 to the advent of Carteret, but in fact the tide had begun to turn before he assumed office. In the previous August, Charles Emmanuel of Sardinia, suspicious of Spanish designs in Italy, had abandoned his temporary flirtation with the Bourbon Powers and had begun negotiations with Maria Theresa. These culminated in the Treaty of Worms in 1743, for which Carteret claimed full credit. British diplomacy had also been able in October to effect a temporary truce between Austria and Prussia, which allowed the Austrian army to check the French and capture Munich on 12 February 1742, the very day on which the Bavarian Elector was crowned Emperor. Finally, Frederick's renewed attack on Moravia in December had proved a failure. Newcastle had first advocated negotiations with Sardinia and had urged an accommodation between Austria and Prussia, which was carried a stage further in the Peace of Breslau in June 1742, whereby Maria Theresa grudgingly ceded Silesia to Frederick. He had also recommended the formation of a composite army for the defence of the Low Countries, which resulted in the embarkation of sixteen thousand British troops in April. Parliament played its part by voting a subsidy of £500,000 of which £300,000 was to go to Maria Theresa and the remainder to Charles Emmanuel. Carteret's sole contribution at this stage was to persuade George II to abandon a more permanent version of the Hanoverian neutrality, but this was more than offset by his encouragement of the King's reluctance to open a campaign in Germany lest Frederick be provoked into an attack on Hanover. Indeed, George II, delighted by the withdrawal of the French army to cope with the Austrian troops released by the Prussian truce, determined to reduce the Hanoverian army; and, in order to avoid the loss to the Allies of sixteen thousand seasoned troops, the Cabinet was compelled to take the Hanoverians into British pay, a move that, however justifiable from a military point of view, was to subject the Administration to severe political criticism.

With one French army bottled up by the Austrians in Prague, and the other hastening to its assistance, Britain had every reason for decisive intervention in support of the Queen of Hungary. But George II was still fearful for the safety of his Electorate and reluctant to expose his Hanoverian troops to a hazardous march so late in the year; the Dutch were quick to use the failure of Hanover to engage in the war as a principal, instead of merely supplying mercenary troops, as an excuse for their own dilatory conduct; and the British commander, Lord Stair, confused the issue by advocating a scatter-brained scheme for a direct attack on Paris. As a result the summer and autumn of 1742 were wasted in futile inactivity in Flanders. Nonetheless the new Administration had agreed tolerably well, and the prospects seemed brighter than at any time since the outbreak of war. The parliamentary session of 1742-3 saw the Opposition roundly criticizing the Cabinet's lack of vigour, but on most issues the Administration found itself able to command a majority of nearly one hundred, and even the controversial employment of the Hanoverian troops was endorsed by sixty-seven votes, despite Pitt's violent and ill-founded charge that England had become 'a province to a despicable Electorate'. But when Carteret set out for Hanover with the King in May 1743 a rift developed within the Ministry that was to hamstring the war effort and provoke a fresh political crisis.

Several examples have already been discussed of the way in which ministers at home distrusted those who accompanied the King abroad, and in Carteret's case there were more than usual grounds for suspicion. He took no pains to conceal his good-natured contempt for his fellow-ministers, treating Newcastle as a fool and Henry Pelham as a petty clerk. Pelham's competent leadership of the Commons in the previous session had won from the King the promise of the reversion to Wilmington's post in the event of the latter's death, but when Wilmington died in July, Bath staked a belated claim to the headship of the Treasury and was supported in Hanover by Carteret. There seems no reason to doubt Carteret's assertion that he was merely honouring an earlier pledge to Bath, and the King was not so foolish as to accept his recommendation, but it is easy to understand the Pelhams' resentment—resentment that was intensified by Carteret's infuriating habit of keeping the ministers at home completely in the dark with regard to the complicated diplomatic manoeuvres in which he was soon engaged. Encouraged by George II's victory over the French at Dettingen, Carteret was tempted to flirt with Prince William of Hesse's ill-conceived scheme for detaching the Emperor from France. Quite apart from the fact that Charles VII demanded in return a substantial subsidy which Parliament was certain to reject, the Austrians and Dutch were likely to be seriously alienated by the secret and unilateral attempt at separate peace negotiations known as the Treaty of Hanau; and the protests of his fellow-ministers eventually succeeded in persuading Carteret to abandon the scheme. But Prince William responded by withdrawing his support from the Allies and even joining France in the following year. Frederick the Great was furious at the rejection of the Emperor's terms and made this an excuse for re-entering the war in 1744. Carteret's secret diplomacy had badly misfired.

Temperamentally incapable of being disheartened by failure, Carteret immediately threw himself into further diplomatic negotiations. The somewhat vague alliance with Sardinia had long required more precise definition, and a note of urgency was added by French approaches to Charles Emmanuel, whom Britain, not without justification, suspected of being willing to sell himself to the highest bidder. Provisional terms had been hammered out before Carteret left England, and on 2 September 1743 was concluded the Treaty of Worms, by which, in return for a slice of Austrian territory in Italy, the Sardinian King undertook to support the Allies until peace was made. But Maria Theresa, already offended by the Hanau negotiations, seized the opportunity to extract from Carteret a 'Separate Declaration' pledging British assistance in gaining adequate compensation for the loss of Silesia and for her cessions in Italy. This new development was greeted unenthusiastically by the ministers at home, but even more objectionable was the further 'Supplementary Convention' upon which Maria Theresa insisted, and which promised the continuation of her subsidy, previously granted on an annual basis, for the duration of the war. Considering that Britain had entered the war largely to preserve the integrity of Maria Theresa's dominions and was contributing substantial military and financial assistance, the Pelhams had no doubt that Parliament would regard the Convention as an unjustified piece of extortion by the Queen of Hungary. Their views were shared by most of their colleagues and when, after Carteret's return, ratification was considered at a full Cabinet meeting, rejection was advised by nine of the thirteen members. Relations with Maria Theresa were thereby further exacerbated, and co-operation between Britain and Austria became ever more half-hearted. Frederick of Prussia took further umbrage because the Treaty failed to recognize the cession of Silesia; and France, fearful that Sardinian support of the Allies would swing the balance of power against her, showed a greater readiness to back Spanish claims in Italy and began to consider entering the war as a principal instead of merely acting as an auxiliary of the Emperor. No doubt the Pelhams underrated the difficulties of Carteret's position, but he had made no attempt to keep his colleagues adequately informed, and had disregarded likely reactions in Parliament. Newcastle had some justification for his angry assertion that 'dexterity with Princes, to seem to promise all and intend nothing, will as little do as with private persons'. Carteret had irritated Britain's allies, strengthened the resolution of her enemies, and embarrassed the Administration of which he was the supposed leader.

Henry Pelham, despite his recent promotion, viewed the future with little confidence. George II was irritated by the frustration of Carteret's schemes, Carteret himself was as arrogant and high-handed as ever, Bath was resentful at his failure to gain the Treasury, and the Old Corps was jealous of Carteret's obvious dominance over the King. Moreover, the rising tide of anti-Hanoverian opinion looked like providing the Opposition with substantial grounds for appealing to the prejudices of independent back-benchers. The widespread resentment at British employment of the Hanoverian troops was heightened by suspicions that Carteret's policy was dictated by Germanic rather than British interests, and by the tactless behaviour of George II, who wore the yellow sash of

Hanover at Dettingen and made little attempt to conceal his partiality for his Electoral troops. The accounts that reached England of his slights to British officers were doubtless exaggerated, but the failure of the Pragmatic army to follow up the victory at Dettingen certainly stemmed from the King's reluctance to endanger his Electorate, and the prolonged inactivity so infuriated Lord Stair that he resigned his command. Anti-Hanoverian pamphlets and articles poured from Opposition pens, and so worried was the majority of the Cabinet that only intervention by Lord Orford (as Walpole had become in 1742) dissuaded them from abandoning the employment of the Electoral troops—a move that would certainly have produced a crisis in the Closet and a grave diminution of allied military strength.

As events turned out, the Administration survived the parliamentary session of 1743-4 without too much difficulty. The morale of the Old Corps was given a minor boost before Christmas when they received preferential treatment in a re-shuffle of offices, and the Opposition was unable to maintain a united front. Pitt, Lyttelton, Chesterfield and their associates supported the idea of a vigorous campaign against France, and were even prepared to ally with the Pelhams in order to frustrate the policy of Carteret; but Cobham, the Grenvilles and others wanted an immediate end to what they considered a futile and expensive war. Thus on most vital issues the Administration found that it could maintain a substantial majority in the Commons (although on at least two occasions its confidence was badly shaken), but its success was due largely to a set of favourable circumstances which might well prove temporary. Firstly, the personal intervention of Orford played a major part in quieting the apprehensions of the Old Corps; secondly, the threat of a French invasion in February 1744, together with France's formal declaration of war against Britain in March, caused a patriotic rallying behind the Ministry and a reaction against the irresponsible philippics of the more extreme leaders of the Opposition; and finally, the moderate, conciliatory leadership of Pelham overcame for the moment the general distrust of Carteret. Even so, Pelham found himself actually defeated over a minor matter of supply, and the crucial vote for the payment of the Hanoverian troops was carried by a majority of only forty-five. The symptoms that had preceded Walpole's fall were re-appearing—wavering among the independents and deliberate abstention among supporters of the Government. It had become clear by the end of the session that, without a marked improvement in the war situation, no Ministry of which Carteret was the presumed leader was likely to survive another session in the Commons.

Unfortunately for the Pelhams the spring and summer of 1744 brought nothing but further failure and frustration. French successes in Flanders were halted only temporarily by an Austrian attack on Alsace; constant bickering between British, Dutch and Austrian generals neutralized all attempts to galvanize the Pragmatic army into activity; Frederick of Prussia re-entered the war, invaded Bohemia, captured Prague and drove the Austrians from the country; Charles Emmanuel, defeated in Italy and threatened with invasion by a Franco-Spanish army, protested bitterly at the lack of help from Maria Theresa and hinted that he might be forced to go over to the Bourbon Powers; and the King of Naples seized the opportunity to abandon his neutrality and ally with Spain. This succession of reverses brought to a head the friction between Carteret, backed by the King, and the Pelhams, supported by the great majority of the Cabinet. All attempts to rouse the Dutch were foiled by the determination of George II and Carteret not to give them any excuse for demanding direct Hanoverian participation in the war. The King was further irritated by Newcastle's insistence that he should at this vital stage remain in England rather than assume the direct command of the army abroad, and by the Ministry's refusal to subsidize the Elector of Saxony to defend Maria Theresa against Frederick, whose re-opening of the Hanau controversy revived old arguments within the Ministry. The Pelhams saw plainly that the Opposition would be enormously strengthened by the developments of the summer and that the doubts of many of the Old Corps would not again be readily allayed. Carteret continued to dictate policy without consulting his colleagues or giving a thought to parliamentary opinion; Henry Pelham was left to defend the Administration as best he could. The whole basis of his parliamentary support was now endangered.

Equally the position of the Pelhams in the Closet had become intolerable. When Parliament was in session George II, realizing that Henry Pelham held the whip hand, grudgingly conceded his requests; but during the summer recess he would listen to no one but Carteret. In desperation the Pelhams made their stand in September. The memorial which Hardwicke was asked to present to the King, and which had the support of no fewer than eleven members of the Cabinet, insisted only on the absolute necessity of securing the immediate and full co-operation of the Dutch; but in the Closet it was made quite clear that the ministers concerned would no longer serve in a cabinet dominated by Earl Granville (as Carteret became on the death of his mother in October). When George II protested to Newcastle that, when ministers disagreed, 'it is hard if I may not determine amongst you', the Duke politely but firmly replied:

> To be sure, Sir, your Majesty ought, must and does; but then, as is the Constitution, your Majesty will have the goodness to excuse those from executing what they think wrong or not for your service.

The King responded by attempting to detach Harrington from his fellow-ministers, and his efforts were backed by a simultaneous approach from the Prince of Wales, for once acting in concert with his father. When neither succeeded George II turned instead to the Opposition, offering a broad-bottom Ministry (exclusive of the Pelhams), if only Granville could be retained. But the Pelhams had already taken the precaution of opening negotiations with their opponents, promising a general dismissal of the New Whigs, ample places for the Opposition leaders, and a more systematic and vigorous war policy. Given the choice between Granville and the Pelhams, there could be no doubt which the Opposition would prefer. In despair George II appealed to Lord Orford, only to be advised to defer to the wishes of the Cabinet majority. With the Old Corps and the Opposition both determined on his downfall, Granville could do nothing but resign, and on 23 November, for the second time in two years, the King had to part with a minister in whom he still reposed the fullest confidence. Superficially, he could this time attribute his defeat to ministerial factiousness, yet the parallel with 1742 was obvious. The only difference was that on this occasion parliamentary defeat was imminent, not actual; but in the last resort favour in the Closet had again to yield to power in the Commons.

The aim of the Pelhams was not merely to enforce Carteret's resignation but so to enlarge the base of the Administration that all shades of political opinion might be brought to support a vigorous and single-minded prosecution of the war. Most of the New Whigs were dismissed to make way for the so-called 'new allies', though the Prince's supporters were carefully excluded from this purge, and both Bath and Granville promised that, even though dismissed, they and their followers would not oppose necessary war measures. Thus Bedford became First Lord of the Admiralty, Chesterfield Lord-Lieutenant of Ireland, Gower Lord Privy Seal and Dodington Treasurer of the Navy. Sandwich and George Grenville were given seats at the Admiralty and Lyttelton at the Treasury Board, but Carteret's vacated Secretaryship of State was reserved for the trustworthy Harrington. By these and other less important changes the Pelhams successfully bought off the leading Opposition spokesmen with the single exception of Pitt, whose violent diatribes against Hanover and reflections on the King's conduct at Dettingen had made George II place an absolute veto on his suggested appointment as Secretary at War.

But Pitt was prepared to wait for the royal anger to fade and expressed himself satisfied with the favours granted to his associates. The prospects for political stability seemed greater than they had been for some years.

Although Henry Pelham in many ways adhered closely to Walpole's principles, he differed from his predecessor and mentor in at least one important respect. Whereas Walpole, impatient of men of ability around him, had driven the most gifted politicians of his time into Opposition and thereby made a rod for his own back, Pelham set out to reverse the process. By depriving his opponents of actual and potential leaders he hoped to strengthen the Government, emasculate the Opposition and make his own position impregnable. This was no lust for power, but arose from a naturally conciliatory disposition and a genuine desire to avoid needless factious rivalry. So determined was Pelham to win universal support that he even attempted the impossible—to reconcile the Tories. Since 1715 there had been a steady succession of defections from the Tory ranks as those for whom the attraction of office became too much forsook their Tory heritage and became Whigs. It was always possible, if one chose the right moment, to wean these men from the Opposition, as had been recently shown by the readiness of Gower and John Pitt to join the broad-bottom Administration. But in 1744 Pelham tried to reach out further and win the support of the irreconcilable hard-core of Tory back-benchers, to whom constant Opposition had become almost second nature. Two of their most prominent spokesmen, John Philipps and Sir John Hinde Cotton, were offered and accepted office, and the great experiment was under way. But both responded by opposing from its own front bench the Administration of which they were members. Within six months Philipps had resigned, within eighteen Cotton was dismissed, and both returned to the Tory back-benches. Nor did the offer of peerages to selected Tories prove more successful, and Pelham had almost despaired when Bolingbroke (by now a friend of Hardwicke's and intent on playing the role of elder statesman) suggested a device that might have the desired effect. While the genuine Tory found it no hardship to forgo office in the central Administration, he deeply resented exclusion from the Commissions of the Peace. The Pelhams were therefore advised by Bolingbroke to support the Tories in their current attempt to win fairer representation in this sphere and, after lengthy negotiations with the Tory leaders, they managed to persuade the King to issue a declaration that thenceforth appointments to Commissions of the Peace would be made 'without distinction of parties'. So gratified were the Tories by this concession that for a few months they actually began to support the Administration and to vote for the war supplies. But the success of the Pelhams' strategem was short-lived. The summer recess gave the Tories time for reflection, and by the beginning of the next parliamentary session all were back in Opposition again. It was to be another decade before they finally tired of opposing all governments, but Henry Pelham first sowed the seeds of doubt in their minds.

Although the Old Corps were inclined to grumble that there were 'so many new faces' in the Administration, and the dismissed New Whigs seized every opportunity to create dissension between the ministers and their new allies, the parliamentary session of 1744-5 was the quietest for many years. Measures relating to the war were frequently passed without a division, and even the Ministry's device of getting rid of the direct employment of the Hanoverian troops by increasing Maria Theresa's annual subsidy so that she could pay them, was accepted with no more than passing jibes from the depleted Opposition benches. In both Houses the debating talent of former Opposition spokesmen and the solid numerical strength of the Old Corps made a formidable combination. The Tories might oscillate and the New Whigs intrigue behind the scenes, but the broad-bottom Administration was successfully launched, and Henry Pelham's ascendancy over the Commons was at last undisputed. To consolidate the position he had won in Parliament he had now to secure the confidence of the King. This was to be no easy task, for George II did not conceal his hostility towards ministers who had forced him to part with Granville and to employ men who for years had obstructed his affairs and many of whom he personally disliked.

So obvious was the King's determination to deny the favour of the Closet to the Pelhams and their new associates that even before the end of 1744 the dismissal of the Ministry was rumoured as imminent. In a special audience in January 1745 Hardwicke endeavoured to convince George II that his ministers sought only to carry on his government efficiently, and that they could not hope to do this without his confidence and support. But he was unable to soften the royal resentment, and during the following months the King criticized every opinion submitted by his ministers, accusing them of deceit, treachery and stupidity. Meanwhile Granville remained the power behind the throne, his advice—especially over foreign affairs—being constantly sought and followed by the King. Thus George II was furious at the Pelhams' recommendation of the Duke of Cumberland as Commander-in-Chief of the British forces in Europe, and at their successful opposition to the Duke's marriage to a Danish Princess; while on the unexpected but convenient death of the Emperor Charles VII it was Granville to whom the King and the Austrian Ambassador turned to discuss possible candidates for the vacant Imperial throne. The Pelham Administration existed in name only, thwarted at every turn by the continuing influence of Granville as 'minister behind the curtain'. Newcastle had every justification for his protest at the end of February that the 'King's servants must be his ministers, exclusive of all others, or they cannot remain his servants'. Yet the Pelhams, still uncomfortable at having forced the King's hand over the dismissal of Granville, were reluctant to bring further pressure to bear, and not until George II set out for Hanover in May did they respectfully indicate that they could not undertake to manage a further session of Parliament without a greater display of royal confidence in them.

Unfortunately, the events of the summer made it still more difficult for the Pelhams to risk a political crisis by taking a stand against the King. Cumberland's defeat at Fontenoy in May was the prelude to a French drive through Flanders that ended only at Ostend and disrupted the lines of communication between Britain and her forces abroad. Nor was the situation any better in Germany, where the belated adhesion of Saxony to the allied cause failed to stem the advances of Frederick, who invaded Saxony and captured Dresden; nor in Italy, where the Genoese had joined the Spaniards and a joint army invaded Lombardy. But the greatest ministerial headache came with the landing of the Young Pretender in Scotland in July. Within a month the Stuart standard had been raised at Glenfinnan and Charles Edward was marching eastwards, gathering support from the clans as he advanced. In retrospect the Forty-Five seems as inevitably doomed to failure as had been the Fifteen, but at the time the threat seemed very real. Britain was in the midst of an unsuccessful war, the country was denuded of troops except for some three or four thousand on garrison duty in Scotland under the ineffectual Sir John Cope, the King was abroad and the Ministry bitterly divided. Even though Granville's direct influence on policy was prevented by the King's absence, his three followers on the Regency Board (Bath, Tweeddale and Stair) did their best to make effective action impossible. Particularly dangerous was the attitude of the two Scots, Tweeddale and Stair, both of whom treated the rebellion as a mere trifle, unworthy of serious consideration. As Tweeddale was Secretary of State for Scotland, his refusal to co-operate gravely impeded ministerial efforts to organize resistance, especially since he was on bad terms with the Duke of Argyll[1] and Duncan Forbes (Lord President of the Court of Session), the two Scots best equipped to maintain the Hanoverian interest north of the border. So rent by futile bickering were the

[1] I.e. the former Earl of Islay, who had succeeded to the title on his brother's death in 1743.

meetings of the Regency that the King was eventually persuaded at the end of August to return to England to assume command of the Government.

Cope allowed himself to be out-manoeuvred by the Pretender, who was able to march first to Perth, where he proclaimed his father King and himself Regent, and then to Edinburgh, where he set up his Court at Holyrood. A brisk victory over Cope at Prestonpans boosted morale and attracted further recruits, until by the end of October he could boast a force of between seven and nine thousand. This was sufficient to command respect in Scotland, but quite inadequate for the invasion of England upon which Charles Edward, against the advice of Lord George Murray and others, forthwith embarked. By this time all but two thousand of the British troops abroad had been recalled, together with six thousand Dutch and Hessians; and Wade and Cumberland had hastily marched north to Newcastle upon Tyne and Lichfield. Outnumbered by more than three to one, Charles Edward avoided contact with the enemy by taking the westward route, capturing Carlisle and marching as far south as Derby by 4 December. But here the projected advance on London ended. Englishmen, apart from a few Roman Catholic families in Lancashire, showed scant enthusiasm for the Jacobite cause, the hoped-for French diversion failed to materialize, and many of the Highlanders lost heart and deserted. The Pretender was prepared to risk all in an attempt to storm the capital, but most of his officers and advisers were against him. There has since been much argument as to what would have happened had he persisted in his original plan. Certainly London was in a panic and, with the forces concentrated in the north and Midlands, could have offered little armed resistance to an attack; equally the Government was divided and the popularity of the monarch at a low ebb. But the appeal of the Roman Catholic Stuarts was even less in 1745 than it had been in 1715, and it seems certain that the substantial armies of Wade and Cumberland would soon have been able to reverse any transient victory by Charles Edward.

At all events the Highlanders retreated and managed to cross the border without running foul of either English army. Here the prospects at first seemed brighter, since Aberdeen and Stirling were in rebel hands, recruits were still pouring in, and Charles Edward enjoyed a few minor victories. But once Cumberland with his well-disciplined force (its supply lines protected by the fleet) reached Scotland, the end could not be long in coming. At Culloden Moor in April 1746 he finally caught up with the retreating, half-starved, quarrelling rebels and roundly defeated them. The Young Pretender was left to make his way back to France as best he could, and Jacobitism was finally discredited. The romantic appeal and personal charm of Charles Edward had proved no substitute for sound judgment and leadership, nor could he hope to prevail against French inactivity, English indifference and superior armed force. It only remained for Cumberland to pursue the fugitives—relentlessly, perhaps, but scarcely with the savagery implied in his nickname of 'the Butcher'—and for the Government to punish the guilty, a process culminating in the spectacular trial of the four rebel peers (Lords Kilmarnoch, Cromartie, Balmerino and Lovat) in 1747. In all about eighty perished on the scaffold, the estates of the leaders were forfeited, the Jacobite clergy were compelled to take the oath of allegiance, and the wearing of the kilt or tartans and the bearing of arms in the Highlands was forbidden. More important in breaking the power of the great clans was the abolition of the hereditary jurisdictions of the chiefs, which they had exercised independently of the King's courts, and of their feudal right to claim military service from their tenants. But firmness was tempered with clemency. Compensation, which amounted eventually to over £150,000, was allowed to chiefs who voluntarily surrendered their jurisdictions, and the proceeds of the forfeited estates were used for improving agriculture and industry, expanding the system of roads begun earlier by Wade, and assisting the civilizing of the Highlands by the provision of new schools. Progress was often slow and uneven, but after 1745 the Highlands at last began to share in some of the undoubted benefits which the Union had earlier brought to the Lowlands.

Before the rebellion was finally crushed, the deteriorating relations between George II and his ministers had reached breaking-point. Even before his reluctant return to England, the King had been further irritated by the Pelhams' insistence that Britain mediate a new truce between Austria and Prussia, so that the allied forces could be concentrated in Flanders and Italy. By the middle of 1745 he was therefore determined to change his Ministry as soon as opportunity offered and, actively encouraged by Granville and his friends, he treated his ministers with the utmost contempt. Henry Pelham despairingly complained that 'we are not permitted either to give our advice or to act in consequence of any advice that is given', and that 'if successors could be found for my brother and myself there would be no hesitation in removing us whether we would or no'; and Newcastle admitted that 'nothing but a rebellion in the heart of the kingdom would or should hinder us from retiring from the most disagreeable and perhaps the most dangerous situation that ever ministers were in'. Most of the 'new allies' were in favour of immediate resignation, but the leaders of the Old Corps, with a generation of support for the

Crown behind them, took their responsibilities more seriously. While the rebellion was at its height they could not bring confusion to the King's affairs by quitting office. For a brief time towards the end of the year, when the foolish optimism of Granville and Tweeddale was discredited by the rapid advances of the rebels, and the summoning of Parliament made vital the co-operation of the Pelhams, George II did indeed moderate his tone. Nevertheless, the ministers' lack of credit in the Closet was soon reflected in the Commons, where many members were uneasy at the resulting inability of the Administration to take decisive action, and where Pitt saw fit to resume his offensive against the ministers by a series of aggressive motions. Acutely aware of their waning power, the Pelhams sought to come to terms with Pitt, but could make no headway against the King's stubborn refusal to consider his appointment as Secretary at War. Indeed, when Pitt's increasing violence was seen to be alienating rather than winning support in the Commons, and the rebels were in full retreat, George II felt strong enough to take the initiative and, on 6 February 1746, he asked Bath, in conjunction with Granville, to form an alternative Ministry.

Events now worked rapidly towards a crisis. Pitt tried to relieve the tension by withdrawing his claims to office, but the issue went much deeper than the preferment of a single troublesome politician. When Bath openly insinuated that a change of Ministry was imminent the Pelhams decided that, with the danger of the rebellion virtually over, they could at last afford to seek relief. On 8 February Hardwicke, Harrington, Newcastle and Pelham took the decision that they had been postponing for nearly twelve months and agreed to resign their offices. So widespread was the sympathy for the ministers and so universal the detestation of Granville and Bath that some forty other office-holders beat a track to the Closet to surrender their posts. Desperately George II tried to launch his new Administration, but few were prepared to join it. In London 'no Pelham, no money' was the cry, as the City promptly withdrew the offer of £300,000 which it had promised to advance to Henry Pelham for the year's supply. George II, when told bluntly that no more than thirty peers and eighty commoners would even consider supporting his new Ministry, locked himself up in his Closet, refused to accept any further resignations, and asked the Pelhams to come back. The great experiment was over, the lessons of 1742 and 1744 underlined, the influence of Granville finally destroyed, and the Pelhams at long last ministers in something more than name alone.

Naturally enough they would not return to office without adequate guarantees. George II had to promise full support for his ministers and agree to the dismissal of the leading New Whigs still in office and to the preferment of Pitt, who was made joint Vice-Treasurer of Ireland in February and Paymaster-General of the Forces in May. These were stiff but not unreasonable terms, yet even at this moment of crushing defeat the King was able to deny the Secretaryship at War to Pitt and to protect from dismissal Edward and William Finch, two Household officials who had been a principal channel of communication between Granville and the Closet. However powerful Henry Pelham's position might now be, he was still reluctant to force the King's hand where his personal sympathies and antipathies were involved. With the preferment of Pitt, the last commoner capable of heading an Opposition was converted to Administration, minor changes of office made the basis of support for the Ministry still broader, and the remainder of the parliamentary session was singularly free of trouble. It remained only for Pelham to consolidate his position by an early dissolution, which he advised in June 1747, twelve months before a general election would normally have been held. There were sound reasons for his decision. Firstly, the Ministry wished to take advantage of the national relief at the successful crushing of the rebellion; secondly, tentative negotiations for a truce in Europe suggested that by 1748 Britain might be either saddled with an unsatisfactory peace or called upon to make fresh financial sacrifices in an increasingly futile conflict; and finally, the Prince of Wales at the beginning of 1747 announced his reversion to Opposition which, even it if represented a return to healthy political normality, argued for a snap election before he had time to organize his campaign.

The general election of 1747 proved a truimph for Henry Pelham. Despite a last-minute alliance with the Tories, the Prince could not repeat his successes of 1741. In Scotland the new Duke of Argyll was one of the staunchest of the Old Corps; in Cornwall Lord Falmouth had returned to alliance with the Ministry, and Thomas Pitt's frantic efforts were mostly doomed to failure, leaving him 'damnably mortified' and almost ashamed to face the Prince. According to Newcastle's calculations the election had provided the Ministry with a handsome majority of 125, more than enough to confirm Henry Pelham's final mastery of the House of Commons, where the Opposition was now confined to the Prince's little knot of third-rate politicians and the general mass of Tory backbenchers. Within Parliament Pelham's supremacy now rivalled that of Walpole at the peak of his power; concurrently, his credit in the Closet began to rise. At first George II had accepted the Pelhams with weary resignation, but once he had finally reconciled himself to the loss of Granville, he found the ease with which Government measures were carried through Parliament a welcome relief from the bitter debates of recent years. Gradually he came to appreciate the quiet competence of Henry Pelham as a parliamentary manager and the manifest if inarticulate devotion of Newcastle to his King and country. The humiliating defeat of the Prince of Wales in the 1747 election completed the Pelhams' admission to royal favour, and Henry was able to add the favour of the Closet to the power of the Commons. Even to Newcastle, the most jealous of men where political power was concerned, brother Henry had become 'the premier'.

Despite the suppression of the rebellion and the return of political stability, there was no corresponding transformation in the position of Britain and her Allies abroad where, amid fluctuating fortunes, the war moved inexorably towards stalemate. In the Low Countries the situation had steadily deteriorated. The withdrawal of British troops in 1745 had been followed by the loss of Brussels, Antwerp and Namur, leaving Marshall Saxe virtual master of the Austrian Netherlands and free to invade Holland, where a belated realization of imminent catastrophe brought about the overthrow of the ineffectual republican Government and its replacement by William of Orange as hereditary stadtholder. Unfortunately William was no military leader, and Dutch morale was soon severely shaken by the fall in September 1747 of their principal border fortress, Bergen-op-Zoom. Meanwhile, the Pragmatic army continued to be hamstrung by the bickerings, recriminations and jealousies of its generals, and Cumberland—no match for the brilliant Saxe—was defeated at Lauffeld in July. In Germany and Italy the Allies fared rather better. The death of Charles VII in 1745 had been followed by the election of Maria Theresa's husband, Francis, as Emperor, and the new Elector of Bavaria proved only too willing to make peace with Austria. Maria Theresa, freed from pressure elsewhere, was able, with the assistance of Saxony, to drive the Prussians from Bohemia, and in December 1745 Frederick agreed by the Peace of Dresden to withdraw again from the war. The death of Philip V in July 1746 also benefited the Allies, for his successor, Ferdinand VI, was eager for peace and friendship with England. Partly because of this and partly because Maria Theresa was able after the Prussian peace to provide greater assistance, Charles Emmanuel was able to resume the offensive in Italy, reversing the French successes of 1745 and clearing the peninsula of enemy troops by the end of 1746. A further ray of hope came from the Anglo-Russian Convention of 1747 by which thirty thousand Russian troops were gained for an annual subsidy of £100,000. These minor successes, however, did not compensate for the disasters in the Low Countries, and it was only at sea that Britain had any cause for jubilation. The capture of Louisburg by British colonial troops in 1745, together with the loss of Madras to the French in the following year, served to remind Englishmen that the war was not confined to Europe. An attack on Quebec was accordingly planned, but a series of unfortunate delays killed the project and the naval forces which had been prepared were employed instead on a futile expedition to L'Orient. Nevertheless, the increasing importance attached by France and Spain to naval and colonial warfare (reflected in the preparation of convoys to protect their commerce with the East and West Indies, and of expeditions to defend Canada and relieve Pondicherry) confirmed English ministers in their growing conviction of the value of British sea-power. Provisions were accordingly made for guarding the main French and Spanish ports, and 1747 saw three notable naval successes—Anson's victory off Finisterre in May, Captain Fox's capture in June of forty-eight ships from a French convoy, and Hawke's triumph over the French off Belleisle in October.

Prussia and Sardinia by now had gained their immediate objectives, the United Provinces were at the mercy of France, and Spain was disillusioned with the conflict. France, though successful in Europe, found her commerce destroyed, her colonies exposed to attack, and her navy threatened with annihilation. Britain, despite her naval successes, was disheartened by repeated failures on the Continent, and by the meagre return for the £1,750,000 she was paying out annually in subsidies. Newcastle and Hardwicke were inclined to favour a last desperate effort in the hope of being able to negotiate from a position of strength; Henry Pelham, who had to find the money, was for peace at any price. Tentative negotiations, begun at Breda as early as October 1746, proved abortive; but by the time the conference reassembled at Aix-la-Chapelle in 1748, no one save Maria Theresa was willing to prolong the conflict, and a futile and unintelligible war was terminated by an equally futile and unintelligible peace. Britain returned Louisburg in exchange for Madras, France evacuated the Low Countries, Spain gained Parma and Piacenza for Don Philip, Prussia was confirmed in her possession of Silesia and Glatz, and Sardinia (as had been promised by the Treaty of Worms) was ceded part of the Milanese by Austria. Spain extended the existing trading privileges to Britain for a further four years, but the much-vexed 'right of search' was not even mentioned. In some ways the war had settled nothing. The issue that had begun to emerge as vital, the commercial and colonial rivalry between France and Britain in North America, the West Indies and India, was left in suspense. In this respect the peace was a mere truce. But in Europe 1748 marked a real turning-point. The cession to Prussia of Silesia, with its flourishing linen industry and vast resources of iron ore, profoundly altered the balance of power within Germany. Austrian hegemony was thereafter no more than a pipe dream, and the way was open for the gradual emergence of Prussia as a great Power. Equally significant for the future, the traditional Anglo-Austrian alliance was dealt a blow from which it never recovered. Maria Theresa, furious at having to cede territory to Prussia and Sardinia and return the barrier fortresses to the Dutch, considered herself basely betrayed by Britain who, for her part, believed that Austria had proved a selfish, unreliable and expensive ally. However Newcastle might strive to maintain the Hapsburg alliance, British and Austrian aims had nothing in common. Britain's enemies were still the Bourbon Powers, her European interests the protection of the Netherlands and Hanover; Austria sought allies only against Prussian aggrandizement.

The end of the war was an immense relief to Henry Pelham who, like Walpole earlier and Lord North later, had little sympathy with foreign and imperial aggrandizement, and deplored the disruption of the national economy which war entailed. Thus peace ushered in six years of stable, unexciting but competent Government under a Prime Minister whose heart was in financial stability, political conciliation and modest domestic reform. Superficially Pelham might seem little more than a pale imitation of Walpole, yet although he lacked the stature of Sir Robert, he also lacked that cynical arrogance and passion for power which had intensified political rivalries and threatened to corrupt public life. At bottom Pelham was more honest, more disinterested and of a more liberal disposition. Despite a touch of peevishness in the face of opposition, he was patently candid and straightforward in his dealings with both colleagues and opponents. If caution and timidity prevented him from achieving complete political dominance, sincerity and integrity made him universally liked and respected. His letters and speeches were models of unaffected common sense—clear, crisp and scrupulously relevant; and of his chosen sphere of finance he was the acknowledged master. With loving care he husbanded the nation's resources, and where Sir Robert had lavishly dispensed government patronage in the pursuit of political and personal ends, Pelham preferred to disarm opposition by sweet reasonableness. In comparing him with Walpole, George II was forced to concede to Newcastle 'that with regard to money matters, your brother does that, understands that, much better'.

Yet even Pelham had his problems. Newcastle's neurotic jealousy of his fellow Secretaries of State forced periodic ministerial changes: Harrington (whom the King had never forgiven for refusing to desert the Pelhams) quit in protest in 1746, his successor, Chesterfield, refused to act any longer as Newcastle's 'commis' in 1748, and Bedford, the next co-Secretary, was stung into resignation by the dismissal of his crony, Sandwich, from the Admiralty in 1751. On this last occasion Anson succeeded Sandwich as First Lord and began his career as one of the great naval administrators of the century. Granville (by then converted to the role of whimsical elder statesman) returned to office as Lord President of the Council, and Newcastle at last found a congenial colleague in the self-effacing Holderness. More unsettling was the renewed political activity of Frederick, Prince of Wales. As the King grew older the 'reversionary interest' became a more powerful magnet to ambitious politicians and the 'shadow court' at Leicester House more substantial. In 1749 George Bubb Dodington, that 'prize political harlot of the eighteenth century', resigned office, once more forsaking the father for the son. Frederick himself, in conjunction with his prospective Prime Minister, Lord Egmont, began to make elaborate preparations for the new reign. The Pelhams and their 'tools' were to be dismissed, a new ministry formed, and virtue was to triumph over all.[1] But suddenly in March 1751 these visions of power were blasted by the unexpected death of the Prince. Thus formal Opposition was left to Bedford and his tiny band of followers, half-heartedly supported by Tory back-benchers who no longer saw any point even in attending parliamentary debates. In the absence of an adult heir to the throne, Bedford and Sandwich gravitated further towards the King's second son, Cumberland, who, although still Commander-in-Chief, had severed his earlier connection with the Pelhams, and whose hatred of Leicester House had led to the circulation of fatuous rumours that he was planning a military *coup d'état*. The Cumberland-Bedford group attempted to embarrass the Ministry over issues such as the Regency Bill of 1751 (when Cumberland was disgruntled to find the Princess of Wales rather than himself named as Regent), the Jew Bill of 1753, and the ridiculous charges of Jacobitism levied in 1752 against members of the Princess's household who were said to be indoctrinating the young Prince George with authoritarian notions of government. Henry Fox, ostensibly a firm adherent of the Ministry, created additional friction by his association with Cumberland, his rivalry with Pitt, and his bitter opposition to Lord Chancellor Hardwicke's Marriage Act of 1753. Even at the highest ministerial level Newcastle and Pelham were constantly bickering, despite their deep and sincere fraternal affection for each other. Pelham was invariably irritated when Newcastle's

---

[1]See pp 110–11.

jealousies forced political changes that disrupted his conciliatory plans, and he had little sympathy with his brother's ambitious diplomatic schemes which threatened to involve the Government in additional expense. Despite the constant mediation of Hardwicke, who had always shown endless patience in his strange but necessary role as political wet-nurse to Newcastle, the two brothers were at one stage reduced to communicating with each other only through the medium of Andrew Stone, Newcastle's private secretary. Yet these were but minor ripples on the placid political surface. Opposition had almost withered away and Horace Walpole could write: 'A bird might build her nest in the Speaker's chair, or in his peruke. There won't be a debate that can disturb her.'

In the sphere of foreign affairs the Ministry's record was at best undistinguished. Few believed that the Treaty of Aix-la-Chappelle had ended the traditional enmity between Britain and France, yet little effort was made to prepare for the next round of hostilities. The French Government irritatingly refused to evacuate St Lucia, St Vincent and Dominica, occupied Tobago, and in 1752 attempted secretly to fortify Dunkirk. In America the British colonies viewed with alarm the chain of French forts that was extending gradually from Canada to Louisiana, and quarrels over the frontiers of Nova Scotia saw the dispatch of a British naval squadron in 1751. On the other side of the globe intermittent rivalry between the English and French East Indian Companies was carried a stage further in 1751 when Robert Clive thwarted the plans of Dupleix by seizing Arcot and re-establishing British control over the Carnatic. But at home Newcastle, whose understanding of international rivalry was limited to the European scene, remained wedded to the anachronistic Austrian alliance, and was encouraged in his conservative myopia by the predilections of the King. George II's hatred of his nephew Frederick the Great (who was quarrelling with him over East Friesland), together with traditional regard for the Empire of which Hanover was an integral part, drew him naturally towards Austria, to whose alliance with Russia Britain acceded in 1750, though she would have nothing to do with the secret engagements for the recovery of Silesia. It was in this context that Newcastle conceived a somewhat eccentric scheme for ensuring European stability in the event of the death of the Holy Roman Emperor, Maria Theresa's husband. Thirty years of successful electioneering in England tempted him to extend his field of patronage, and in 1750 he persuaded his colleagues to sanction a plan for securing the election of the Archduke Joseph as King of the Romans, thereby ensuring his elevation to the Imperial dignity on the death of his father. But the votes of electoral princes proved more expensive than those of English borough constituents even though the subsidies secured the aid of mercenary troops in the event of war, and Austria and the Netherlands were persuaded to share the burden. The support of Cologne, Bavaria and Saxony was purchased in the course of 1750–1, but even before negotiations with the Palatinate in 1752 proved abortive, Pelham and other ministers were in revolt against growing financial burdens in time of peace for an object which at best was of doubtful value. The Bavarian and Saxon subsidies were continued, but that with Cologne was repudiated, and the grandiose scheme was quietly shelved. In 1764, Joseph was elected King of the Romans without any assistance from England, but by then the Anglo-Austrian alliance had long since been torpedoed by Kaunitz and Newcastle's pipe-dreams had yielded to Pitt's ruthless realism.

Meanwhile Pelham set about adjusting the nation's finances to peace-time conditions. By 1750 the army had been reduced from fifty thousand to 18,850, the navy from 51,550 to ten thousand (in 1751, despite the protests of Pitt, he reduced it further to eight thousand, but relented the following year), and the bill for foreign subsidies and the hire of mercenary troops from £1,677,000 to a mere £61,000. In the last year of the war national expenditure had reached nearly £12,000,000; by 1750 it was down to £7,000,000, and in consequence the land-tax dropped from its war-time level of four shillings in the pound to three shillings by 1749 and two shillings by 1752. At the same time Pelham turned his attention to the problem of the national debt, of which during the war the capital had risen from £46,000,000 to £77,000,000, and the annual interest charge from £2,047,000 to £2,981,000. Unlike Walpole, Pelham had been uneasy at too great dependence on the three dominant City companies, which since the 1720s had held most of the debt. In financing the war he had therefore resorted much more to borrowing from the general public, so that by 1748 no less than £25,000,000 of the debt was held by private investors. In his capable hands the credit of the Government had become sufficiently secure for it to be able to borrow from the public on favourable terms, and the individual was able to acquire a stake in the nation on a scale hitherto unknown. Public finance was in the first stage of democratization. Partly in consequence of this process, the debt had become spread among fourteen different stocks, on most of which an interest of 4 per cent was being paid at a time when the prevailing rate had shrunk to 3 per cent. In order to reduce the annual burden of interest Pelham in 1749 introduced a scheme whereby the holders of securities at 4 per cent should be offered 3·5 per cent until 1757 and 3 per cent thereafter, with the option of having their stock redeemed by loans which could be easily floated at 3 per cent. Not unnaturally the scheme encountered considerable opposition from the stock-holders, especially from the proprietors of the three City Companies who between them held over a quarter of the 4 per cents. But Pelham, who was more alive than Walpole to City opinion, played his cards with considerable care. In 1746 he had repealed Walpole's Act of 1725 which had confirmed the aldermanic veto over resolutions of the Common Council; before introducing his scheme he had held private consultations with the directors of the three companies, and enlisted the support of Sir John Barnard, the City's great authority on finance; and in 1750 he exerted a little gentle pressure on recalcitrant stock-holders by passing a second act reducing the interest to 3·5 per cent in 1755 instead of 1757. In the end the holders of all save £3,000,000 of the stock capitulated, and the conversion produced an annual saving in interest payments of £270,000 by 1751, £350,000 by 1755 and £544,000 by 1757. In 1751 Pelham simplified the structure of the debt by reducing the fourteen classes of stock to a mere five, of which the most celebrated were the 3 per cent Consols, which by the end of the century were to become by far the most important element in the national debt.

Although Pelham's most striking achievements were in the field of public finance, his Ministry proved readier to face existing domestic problems, even at the cost of unpopularity, than Walpole's had been. Chesterfield's reform of the calendar, which by adopting the Gregorian system brought English practice into line with that of the Continent, was carried through in 1751 despite the howls of the uninformed mob to 'give us back our eleven days'. A further onslaught was made on the gin trade by denying retail trade to distillers and confining their sales to innkeepers, victuallers and other licensed vendors occupying premises of an annual rental value of at least £10. Hardwicke's Marriage Act of 1753, by insisting on the consent of guardians in the case of minors, the calling of banns and the requirement of residence, ended the abuse of clandestine marriages, often conducted by bogus clergymen and contracted for financial gain by unscrupulous adventurers, prostitutes and other social parasites. Unfortunately, one of Pelham's most enlightened reforms, the Jewish Naturalization Act of 1753[1] was repealed the following year in the face of the violent hostility of vested financial interests in the City, Tory xenophobia, vitriolic and ill-informed propaganda, and the exaggerated fear of unfavourable repercussions in the forthcoming general

[1]This very modest reform merely made it easier for Jews to become naturalized by private Act. It allowed them to omit the words 'on the true faith of a Christian' from the oaths of supremacy and allegiance.

election. A succession of minor measures sought to encourage commerce and industry, and to mitigate the violence and licentiousness of the times. Trade with Africa was facilitated and expanded, insurance rates on shipping between England and India regulated, the import of Irish wool permitted, and support given to the manufacture of silks and Scottish linens, the development of the herring fisheries, and the production in the American colonies of cotton, potash and naval stores. The colonization of Nova Scotia was promoted by the grant of lands and other benefits to disbanded servicemen, and the issue of paper money in the colonies restricted in order to prevent wholesale inflation, though the Government continued blind to the difficulties inherent in colonial shortage of specie. Acts were passed for the prevention of robbery and murder, the regulation of places of public entertainment, the punishment of the keepers of disorderly houses, the remedying of abuses in the collection of turnpike tolls and the more effective employment of the poor. The foundation of the British Museum in 1753 completed a record of modest but enlightened domestic progress.

Peace, stability, conciliation and reform were the keynotes of Henry Pelham's Administration. By 1754 a more perceptive statesman might have noticed the gradual darkening of the international horizon and seen that Britain's destiny was soon to deviate sharply from the paths which Pelham was happy to tread. But fortunately he was spared the fate that had overcome Walpole and was to overcome Lord North—that of a peace-time minister committed to the uncongenial tack of managing a full-scale war. On 6 March 1754 he died of erysipelas, and an ageing King who had grown to appreciate the advantages of political tranquillity sorrowfully predicted 'I shall now have no more peace'. In more ways than George II realized, the death of Henry Pelham was to mark the end of an era.

4

CHALLENGE AND RESPONSE: 1754–60

THE removal of the sober guiding hand of Henry Pelham allowed the fermentation of latent political rivalries and ushered in a period of mounting faction against a background of deteriorating international relations. Only the challenge implicit in the resumption of hostilities with France eventually forced the politicians of the day to come to terms with one another, and even the widespread support for the resulting Pitt-Newcastle coalition could not conceal the fact that the political world of Walpole and Pelham was in the throes of dissolution. This process began on the morrow of Pelham's death. Newcastle, distraught with grief, could not face the ordeal of public business and Hardwicke was left to settle with the King the manner in which the crucial vacancy should be filled. Common sense dictated that the Walpolian-Pelhamite system should be continued by the appointment of a new Minister for the King in the House of Commons; and the most obvious candidates were William Pitt, Henry Fox and William Murray. But Murray, though a proved and able supporter of the Pelhams, was too timid to aspire to the highest office and looked on politics largely as a means of furthering his legal career; and neither Hardwicke nor Newcastle could warm to the prospect of conceding the 'plenitude of power' to such domineering and ambitious men as Fox or Pitt. In retrospect it may seem that Pitt's claims were so obvious that only a corrupt and aristocratic political system could ignore them, yet contemporaries had little enough reason to see things in this light. Universally feared in the early 1740s for his scathing criticism and intermittent bouts of demonic energy, Pitt, since his acquisition of office in 1746, had withdrawn from the centre of the political stage, and in 1754 was in the throes of gout. His earlier factiousness, wild irresponsibility and dramatic *volte-faces* (for which he spent most of his later life apologizing) had alienated not only George II and the leading politicians, but also the great mass of independent opinion in the Commons. Ostentatiously scorning to cultivate a connection of his own, he was related to Lyttelton and the Grenvilles, but preferred for the most part to plough his lonely furrow. The future was to see him emerge dramatically from semi-retirement, but at the beginning of 1754 men had almost forgotten how disruptive a force he could be in politics.

On the surface Fox's prospects seemed much brighter. Despite his Tory origins he had long since become one of the leading political lights among the Old Corps. A friend of both Walpole and Pelham, a good debater and shrewd parliamentary tactician, he had climbed the ladder of preferment in orthodox style and was popular with the King. His promotion would be welcomed by Cumberland and Bedford, and might well remove the last vestiges of Opposition. Yet Fox had his enemies. His ambition and avarice were too obvious not to offend, his association with Cumberland made him *persona non grata* to Leicester House, his sardonic outbursts against Scots and lawyers had irritated two powerful elements in the Commons, and his scathing attacks on Hardwicke had alienated the man in whose hands the reconstruction of the Ministry largely rested. Nor did Fox, who had been overtly understudying Pelham, improve his prospects by making profuse apologies to Hardwicke almost before Pelham's body was cold. Nonetheless George II, appalled at the thought of having Pitt in his Closet, clearly favoured his rival, and Hardwicke was forced to accept a compromise. With singularly bad judgment he persuaded the King that no real successor to Pelham was necessary and that Newcastle as First Lord of the Treasury could manage the Commons from the House of Lords. Legge was to become Chancellor of the Exchequer, Holderness move to the Northern Department and Fox be made Southern Secretary. Fox had no experience of foreign affairs and, in Hardwicke's words 'if the power of the Treasury, the secret service and the House of Commons is once settled in safe hands, the office will carry very little effective power with it'. These proposals were submitted to the Cabinet for approval and were readily endorsed. Fox accepted, but, on being told bluntly by Newcastle that control of the secret service funds and of elections would be denied him, promptly reversed his decision and reverted to the more congenial office of Secretary at War. With some relief Newcastle and Hardwicke chose as Secretary of State Sir Thomas Robinson, competent in diplomatic affairs but dangerously inexperienced in the House of Commons. In order to placate Pitt, who remained as Paymaster of the forces, George Grenville and Lyttelton were promoted, and the Ministry faced the future with a confidence that was little justified.

Thus in 1754 Newcastle was for the first time responsible for the management of a general election. It is too often assumed that his had been the guiding hand throughout the elections of the 1730s and 1740s, but his activities then had been confined to those relatively few constituencies where his personal influence was predominant or which he managed on behalf of the Treasury. At the height of his power he could in his private capacity return no more than nine members, and frequently he had to be content with fewer. Walpole and Pelham had managed their own elections and on Pelham's death Newcastle had to burn a great deal of midnight oil before he was fully apprised of the preparations already made for the coming contest. But this was a field in which he was thoroughly at home, and his endless patience and attention to detail produced a majority for the Administration of over two hundred, the largest of the century. Yet under eighteenth-century conditions even a steam-roller majority required leadership in the Commons, and this had not been provided. Under Carteret in 1742-4 the Administration had constantly to muster its flock and rally those who were tempted to stray; under Newcastle in 1754-6 the flock lacked a shepherd.

Thomas Pelham-Holles, first Duke of Newcastle, was temperamentally ill-equipped to lead the nation at a time of crisis. A constant prey to neurotic fears and jealousies, he was driven to despair by the most trivial criticism and to panic by the slightest signs of political opposition. In his tortured imagination everyone was suspect save Hardwicke, and even he had to weigh every word in conversation or correspondence lest some accidental nuance might offend the hypersensitive Duke. With his constant bustle, excited and disjointed discourse, alternating bouts of elation and misery, and ridiculous fear of damp beds, Newcastle was something of a walking caricature. Yet behind these strange external eccentricities lay many virtues and an ample fund of shrewd common sense; it was not patronage alone that kept him in major office for over forty years. Good natured, generous to a fault, of unimpeachable morals, he was incorruptible in an age when standards of public life were often depressingly low. Far from profiting from his success he spent some £300,000 of his own money in furthering the political interests of the successive administrations of which he was a member. Though he lacked the breadth of vision and single-minded determination of Pitt, his voluminous correspondence shows him to have had a more comprehensive grasp of continental politics than most of his contemporaries. He was also to prove a careful and competent First Lord of the Treasury. Despite appearances Newcastle was no fool, and in an era when principles were too often sacrificed to personal ambition and self-interest he was conspicuous for his complete disinterestedness—a lovable professional in politics who too often became the butt of small-minded and ungenerous amateurs.

While Newcastle spent the summer of 1754 congratulating himself on the size of his electoral victory, disappointed politicians were preparing for revenge. Fox, already regretting his haste in refusing promotion, grew more resentful when his attempts to blackmail his way into power were rebuffed by Newcastle and Hardwicke, and set about restoring his credit through the medium of the King's mistress, Lady Yarmouth. In October he defied the entire Cabinet by authorizing the dispatch of officers to command troops in America whose raising had not even been formally approved. Meanwhile Pitt, furious that Robinson, a political nonentity, had been promoted over his head, and fortified personally and politically by his marriage to Lady Hester Grenville, was preparing a dramatic return to political activity. Frustrated ambition drew Fox and Pitt together, while Henry Bilson Legge, resentful that Newcastle was tactlessly by-passing him at the Treasury Board and fearful of having to stand up to Fox and Pitt in the Commons, was predicting that 'this Parliament would not go on without a minister in it . . . who shall go to the King himself, speak from himself'. The opening of the session on 14 November lent weight to his words. Pitt, aided rather cautiously by Fox, turned his scathing rhetoric on Newcastle, Robinson and Murray in rapid succession. Scarcely veiled threats were directed at Murray's supposed Jacobite associations, Robinson's parliamentary inexperience was derided, and the House was obliquely warned of Newcastle's potential power by suggesting that it might soon 'degenerate into a little assembly, serving no other purpose than to register the arbitrary edicts of one too-powerful subject'. This was too much for the timid Duke. Fox was silenced by the offer of a seat in the Cabinet, offices were found for some of his more important associates (Hartington, Marlborough and Rutland), and the growing power of the Fox-Cumberland connection was further demonstrated when Cumberland was made head of the Council of Regency when the King left for Hanover in the summer. But although these changes secured a relatively placid parliamentary session, they provided no lasting solution. Fox, who had not gained the leadership of the Commons, was still dissatisfied, Leicester House was furious at Cumberland's elevation and was preparing to revert to political Opposition, and Pitt ostentatiously declared his connection with Fox at an end and opened negotiations with the Dowager Princess. Newcastle's worries were scarcely diminished when in May 1755 Admiral Boscawen failed to prevent French reinforcements reaching America and when subsidy treaties had to be concluded with Hesse-Cassel and Russia in order to ensure the assistance of sixty-seven thousand troops in the event of war. These treaties were bound to provoke the usual caustic criticism in the

Commons, where the problem of leadership became ever more urgent. George II, by then in Hanover, was reluctantly persuaded to consider the addition of Pitt to the Cabinet, and in the ensuing weeks Hardwicke and Newcastle held a series of meetings with their formidable colleague. At first he showed a disposition to be reasonable, but when Legge provoked a minor crisis by refusing to sign the Treasury warrants for the Hessian subsidy, Fox threatened to join the Opposition unless he were further satisfied, and news arrived from America of the virtual annihilation of Braddock's force at Fort Duquesne, Pitt realized the increasing strength of his position. He therefore denounced the treaties, protested 'that the business of the House of Commons could not go on without there was a minister . . . who should go directly between the King and them', and insisted on 'an office of *advice* as well as of *execution*'. It was clear that either Pitt or Fox must be gratified, and although Hardwicke still favoured the former, the King on his return from Hanover was in no mood to listen to Pitt's peremptory demands. As a result Fox was elevated in September to the offices of Secretary of State and leader of the Commons, and five of his followers were promised promotion.

From the time of his appointment until the assembly of Parliament on 13 November Fox was occupied chiefly with canvassing support for the subsidy treaties. On paper the Administration's majority in the Commons was still over two hundred but, as Walpole and Carteret had found to their cost, an unpopular foreign policy was the quickest solvent of political allegiances. Pitt, Legge and the Grenvilles were known to be violently opposed to the subsidies, while Leicester House were furious with Fox's further promotion and their new leader, Lord Bute, was attempting to stir up opposition in the City. When the testing-time came with the debate on the Address-in-Reply the Administration enjoyed an apparently sweeping victory by a majority of 206. But Pitt derided the junction of Newcastle and Fox in his celebrated Rhône-Saône speech and the most spirited attacks on the Government came from its own front bench. With war imminent and the country ill-prepared, this insubordination could not be tolerated. Pitt, Legge, George Grenville and Charles Townshend were dismissed and James Grenville resigned in order to avoid a similar fate. The alignment of political forces was at last clear-cut, and the subsidy treaties were eventually carried by substantial majorities. But the events of early 1756 were soon to pose new problems.

The Convention of St Petersburg, by which the subsidy agreement with Russia had been concluded, triggered off a series of events that was to culminate in the dramatic reversal of alliances known as the Diplomatic Revolution. Ever since 1749 the Austrian Government under the influence

William Pitt (Elder)

Robert Walpole

of Kaunitz had been toying with the idea of forming alliances with Russia and France in order to isolate Frederick the Great and regain Silesia. At first the French court was unimpressed by Kaunitz's advances but, as the divergence between Austrian and British interests became evident and the naval and colonial conflict between France and Britain was resumed, the diplomatic climate became more favourable to radical change. The crucial stimulus to the realignment of forces came from Frederick who, already alarmed by the anti-Prussian trend of Russian policy, was thrown into a panic by the Convention of St Petersburg. Unwilling to be dragged by his ally France into a war in which colonial interests were likely to predominate, and determined at all costs to avoid a combined attack from Britain, Austria and Russia, Frederick turned a ready ear to overtures from a British Government intent on securing the safety of Hanover. The result, in January 1756, was the Convention of Westminster, by which Britain and Prussia agreed to the neutrality of Germany in the event of war. Logically France should have been delighted at this opportunity to concentrate on the colonial conflict with Britain, but Louis XV was deeply offended by Frederick's show of independence and fell a willing victim to renewed approaches from Kaunitz. In May the defensive first Treaty of Versailles was signed, by which Austrian neutrality in the Franco-British struggle was ensured in return for Louis's promise to respect Austrian possessions. Each nation also undertook to aid the other if attacked. The Tsarina Elizabeth was equally furious to find that the Anglo-Russian alliance was not to be directed against Prussia, and by April Russia and Austria were discussing plans for the dismemberment of Frederick's territories. Within a few months a radical reversal of alliances had been effected. Newcastle, who had no wish to disrupt the old system, had sought only to provide additional guarantees for the security of Hanover, and neither France nor Britain was eager for a resumption of European conflict. But the increasing coolness between Britain and Austria, together with the fears, jealousies and ambitions of the rulers of France, Russia and Prussia, had converted a minor diplomatic gambit into a major realignment of the Powers. War was no more inevitable than before, but if it should come Britain had gained a much more valuable ally than she had lost, and France was well on the way towards involving herself in European entanglements on behalf of Austria that could only divert her from the all-important maritime and colonial conflict with Britain.

These developments and their practical corollaries dominated the latter part of the parliamentary session of 1755–6. The agreement with Prussia was inevitably denounced by Pitt and his associates as a Hanoverian measure. With Hanoverian neutrality secured, it was widely feared that the full force of French arms would be directed against Britain, and Belleisle's collection of sixty thousand men on the French channel coast threw the country and the Ministry into a panic. Steps were taken to augment the armed forces and as an interim precaution six thousand Hessians and eight thousand Hanoverians were brought over to England in May. Pitt rose dramatically from his sick-bed to fulminate against the use of foreign troops but, as in the 1740s, the Commons were more intent on being protected than on enquiring into the identity of their protectors. Yet dwindling majorities showed a clear waning of confidence in the Ministry, and when a financial resolution was passed by only nine votes the writing was on the wall. Although the Administration otherwise managed to survive the session with reasonable comfort, it was evident that only a vigorous and successful policy could avert a political crisis in the immediate future.

As luck would have it the summer and autumn of 1756 were disastrous for Newcastle and his fellow-ministers. The fleet had been concentrated in home waters to repel the threatened French invasion, but by March it had become obvious that the initial enemy attack was likely to be launched against the important naval base of Minorca. After some confusion and delay Admiral Byng's inadequately equipped and under-manned fleet was despatched to the Mediterranean, and on 15 May war was duly declared against France. Byng's ill-fated expedition was refused additional troops by the Governor of Gibraltar, who informed him that the French had already landed on Minorca. On 20 May he engaged the enemy fleet, similar in strength to his own but the condition and morale of which were considerably better. Psychologically on the defensive and hampered by antiquated and restrictive fighting instructions, Byng could do no more than fight an indecisive action; and, fortified by the resolution of a council of war that was convinced of the impracticability of relieving Minorca and afraid of endangering Gibraltar by their failure, he decided to retire to the Rock and keep his fleet intact. The inevitable result was the fall of Minorca on 28 June. When the news reached London there was universal dismay. The unfortunate Byng, against whom the initial hostility was directed, was made a scapegoat by a terrified Ministry, but his supersession and imprisonment to await court-martial converted him to the role of national hero and idol of the parliamentary Opposition. In Canada the postponed attack on Fort Niagara was a failure, and Montcalm, the new French commander, captured Fort Oswego. Thus the opening of the maritime and colonial struggle brought nothing but disaster for Britain and, at the end of August, she was faced with a full-scale continental struggle when Frederick of Prussia, in full knowledge of Austro-Russian military preparations, seized the initiative by invading Saxony and formally opening the Seven Years' War.

This rapid deterioration in the international situation provided the first impetus to the fall of Newcastle and the rise of Pitt, but political developments at home determined the precise timing of the crisis. Leadership in the Commons became ever more vital, but in May William Murray became Lord Chief Justice Mansfield, and Newcastle lost his only reliable lieutenant in the Lower House. He was now completely at the mercy of Fox, and worse was to come. When Prince George reached the age of eighteen in May, the King gave him an annual allowance of £40,000 and a special suite of apartments, in order to remove the political influence which his mother was falsely believed to be exerting upon him. The Prince readily accepted the allowance, but asked both to be allowed to remain with his mother and to have Lord Bute as his Groom of the Stole and effective head of his household. This infuriated George II who knew that Bute was friendly with Pitt and was foolish enough to believe that he was also the lover of the Dowager Princess. But when it quickly became obvious that Leicester House was prepared to revert to political Opposition to achieve its ends, even the King could appreciate the likely impact on the coming parliamentary session, and in October he at last conceded both the Prince's demands. Unfortunately, Newcastle was relieved of one crisis only to be confronted by another. Fox's conduct had for many months been at best enigmatic. In the Commons he had supported Pitt's Militia Bill in defiance of his fellow-ministers, and shortly afterwards he had intrigued with foreign diplomats behind his colleagues' backs in a foolish attempt to win Spanish support by ceding Gibraltar. The King quickly realized Fox's incompetence as Secretary of State and hoped for the return of the more congenial Robinson who, whatever his parliamentary shortcomings, understood diplomacy and could converse with George II in his own tongue. When Fox, from the outset of the quarrel with Leicester House, urged submission on the King, his influence in the Closet further declined, and the war disasters of 1756 (especially the loss of Minorca) reduced him to complete panic. With Murray out of the Commons he would bear the brunt of the parliamentary attack, and on 15 October 'he thought it prudent to avoid the storm' by announcing his intention to resign. Newcastle was now left with the ineffectual Lyttelton (who had at last broken completely with Pitt and been made Chancellor of the Exchequer) as his only supporter of consequence in the Lower House. Considering the ominous war situation, political survival seemed well-nigh impossible.

It was clear that Pitt must be won over, as even the King, livid with rage at Fox's desertion, was forced to concede. But Pitt was shrewd enough to realize that his bargaining power was greater than ever before. He still sat for Newcastle's pocket borough, and a mere twelve months earlier had freely acknowledged that the friendship of Newcastle and Hardwicke 'constituted the only honour of his public life'. But all this was conveniently forgotten,and when he was offered the Secretaryship of State he was in his most imperious and uncompromising mood, refusing point blank to serve in any Ministry with Newcastle. The old Duke willingly consented to resign in order to ease matters, and on 27 October the King in desperation commissioned Fox to form a Ministry with Pitt. But Pitt rejected Fox's overtures as contemptuously as those of Hardwicke, and is said to have remarked to the Duke of Devonshire that 'I am sure I can save the country and nobody else can'. His conduct to date gave little enough cause for this overweening confidence, but so widely was he feared that no one could be found to serve without him. The King was helpless, and on 29 October Devonshire was given the task of forming a Ministry, exclusive of Newcastle and Fox, in which Pitt was to be Secretary of State and the effective leader. The Closet had been successfully stormed.

The new Administration was weak and unstable, and Pitt suffered from the great disadvantage of having forced himself upon the King. But unlike Newcastle, he ignored his colleagues rather than allowing himself to be brow-beaten by them. His advocacy of a Country war policy[1] had won him much support in the City and among the Tories, and he enjoyed the favour of the Prince of Wales and his circle. Dr Johnson's celebrated remark that Walpole was a minister given by the King to the people, and Pitt a minister given by the people to the King, is at best a half-truth. In 1756 Pitt climbed to power on the shoulders of Leicester House rather than the people. Nor in the ensuing five months did he do much to broaden the basis of his strength. Periodic attacks of gout prevented him from appearing more than fifteen times in the House of Commons and six times in the royal Closet, where he proved so obsequious that Horace Walpole could acidly assert that 'you could see the tip of his hooked nose between his legs'. His own political following was also too limited to allow major changes of personnel. Lord Temple (who was particularly odious to the King) became First Lord of the Admiralty, George Grenville Treasurer of the Navy, James Grenville a Junior Lord

---

[1]I.e. concentration upon naval and colonial warfare, with only limited military involvement in Europe.

of the Treasury, and Henry Bilson Legge Chancellor of the Exchequer; Newcastle, Hardwicke, Fox and Anson were ousted. But for the rest Pitt had to take over the existing Ministry. Granville continued as Lord President of the Council, Holderness as Secretary for the Northern Department, and Barrington as Secretary at War. To cap it all the titular head of the Ministry, as First Lord of the Treasury, was the Duke of Devonshire, one of the most attractive and disinterested of mid-eighteenth-century politicians, but also the intimate friend of Henry Fox, Pitt's chief political rival. The widespread lack of confidence in the new Administration was reflected in Newcastle's continued popularity. Lyttelton remarked that 'the Duke of Newcastle has been more visited and had greater professions of attachment to him than when at the head of the Treasury'. Indeed, it was widely believed that if Newcastle should choose to oppose the new Administration—and especially if Fox should join him—it would not last a day; but the leaders of the Old Corps had been denouncing formed Opposition for so long that they could not readily embark upon it. As for Pitt, his conduct in office contrasted strangely with the attitude he had adopted whilst in Opposition. He had earlier demanded a parliamentary enquiry into the conduct of the previous ministers, especially with regard to the loss of Minorca. Since he had no wish to unite Fox and Newcastle, this idea was now abandoned, and it was left to Fox to move for an enquiry in order to vindicate himself and his colleagues. The Militia Act which Pitt had long been demanding was introduced by George Townshend at the beginning of the parliamentary session but got no further before the Ministry came to an end. Admiral Byng, whose cause Pitt had so passionately espoused, was left to his unhappy fate after a half-hearted attempt to get him reprieved. But most startling of all were Pitt's dramatic *volte-faces* in war policy. For long he had thundered against Hanover, yet his first appearance as chief minister in the House of Commons was to ask for a vote of supply 'for the just and necessary defence and preservation of the Electoral dominions'. Of Newcastle's alliance with Prussia he had earlier declared that he would not have signed it for all the Cabinet offices put together; yet it was now embraced and extended. In the King's speech Frederick the Great became 'my good ally the King of Prussia', and he received a letter from Pitt in which he was gratified to find himself described as 'a Prince who stands the unshaken bulwark of Europe'. Little wonder that there were raised eye-brows and cynical smiles in the House of Commons.

To be fair to Pitt he showed, even during the brief five months of his first Administration, a broader grasp than Newcastle of the over-all war situation, a clearer appreciation of the importance of colonial and naval strategy, and a greater willingness to rally the support of the nation. 'The succour and preservation of America' was made a principal object of policy, and an immediate decision was taken to send an army and a fleet across the Atlantic. In his letters to the colonial governors Pitt strove, though with little enough success, to arouse the Americans into making common cause with the mother-country. Steps were taken to augment the navy in home waters and in India, where Pitt again showed himself more alive to the French threat than his predecessors had been. At home he courted popularity by providing for the early removal of the Hanoverians and Hessians who had been brought over to defend the nation in the event of a French invasion, and by raising new British regiments to replace them. He even introduced the controversial but successful experiment of including among the new regiments two drawn from the Highland clans which had rebelled against the dynasty a mere eleven years earlier.

Whatever new energy Pitt breathed into the war effort, his strengths were heavily outweighed by his weaknesses and the new Administration inspired little confidence. The absence of any immediate success in America, the failure to keep the French fleets blockaded in home waters and thereby deprive Canada of reinforcements and supplies, the continuing rise in corn prices, and Pitt's equivocal attitude over Byng all contributed to his waning popularity. But in the end it was the antagonism of the King, Fox and the Duke of Cumberland that proved decisive. Pitt's association with Leicester House may have been a useful insurance in the event of the death of George II, but it scarcely improved his credit at St James's or with the Fox-Cumberland set. By refusing to take up the command of the army of observation in Germany while Pitt was chief minister, Cumberland provided his father with the excuse he needed; and on 6 April 1757 George II bluntly ordered Pitt to return the seals of his office. For the next three months the nation was left virtually without an Administration in the midst of a major war.

The detailed negotiations of these months are highly complex and of little general interest. Legge and the Grenvilles followed Pitt out of office, but Devonshire soldiered on in theoretical command of a Ministry that lacked any effective leadership. George II, at first determined not to go cap in hand to Pitt as he had been forced to go to the Pelhams in February 1746, tried every conceivable combination, using first Fox and later the second Earl Waldegrave as his intermediaries. But Pitt after his dismissal enjoyed a popularity that had eluded him as chief minister. The circumstances of his fall, coupled with the general panic at the ensuing political chaos, induced a wave of popular feeling in his favour. London was merely the first of a host of cities that voted him their freedom, though the fact that the mediocre Legge was similarly honoured might be thought to diminish the value of these gestures. At all events it became increasingly obvious that a junction between Newcastle and Pitt was the only way out of the political deadlock, and on 29 June Hardwicke eventually succeeded in effecting the necessary coalition. The final outcome has been seen as confirming the corrupt nature of eighteenth-century politics, in that Pitt—the great genius of the age and the idol of the public—could not maintain himself in power without the aid of Newcastle's parliamentary myrmidons. But it is equally true that Newcastle, the greatest parliamentary manager and borough-monger of his time, could not maintain his Ministry without the aid of Pitt, whose personal following in the House of Commons was negligible. Men were too frightened of Pitt to serve without him in a Ministry that had to inherit a difficult and initially unsuccessful war. Thus only he could provide the necessary leadership in the Commons and link with Leicester House, as even Newcastle was forced to admit. When the King castigated him for pressing Pitt's claims, the old Duke could only respond tremulously: 'I can't come in without bringing in my enemy, Mr Pitt. He turned me out. But I can't serve without my enemy'; and again, 'No one will have a majority at present, against Mr Pitt. No man, Sir, will in the present conjecture, set his face against Mr Pitt in the House of Commons.' Thus the Pitt-Newcastle coalition was born, with Pitt taking over primary responsibility for the conduct of the war, and Newcastle left with the problem of finding the necessary money and at the same time supervising government patronage. The strongest Ministry of the century was at last on its feet.

The new Administration embraced almost every conceivable shade of political opinion. Pitt returned to his former post as Secretary of State for the Southern Department, and as Holderness continued as his co-Secretary he was assured of the dominant voice in foreign affairs. Of his followers, Legge resumed office as Chancellor of the Exchequer, with James Grenville as a Junior Lord of the Treausry to offset the influence there of Newcastle's friends. George Grenville returned to the Treasurership of the Navy, Charles Pratt (the future Lord Camden) became Attorney-General and Temple was pacified by being made Lord Privy Seal. Fox was happy enough to accept the highly lucrative office of Paymaster of the Forces, from which he was to derive a considerable fortune; and of his friends Devonshire became Lord Chamberlain, and Bedford Lord-Lieutenant of Ireland. Finally, the interests of the Old Corps were protected by Newcastle's return as First Lord of the Treasury, Hardwicke's inclusion in the Cabinet (though he declined to resume the Lord Chancellorship), Charles Yorke's appointment as Solicitor-General, Lord Barrington's continuation as Secretary at War, and the reinstatement of Anson as First Lord of the Admiralty and Halifax as First Lord of Trade and Plantations. Lord Granville remained as Lord President of the Council. Since Pitt continued to enjoy considerable Tory support, Opposition virtually ceased to exist, but one point of importance for the future should be made. The Old Corps, deprived of a leader in the Commons since the death of Henry Pelham, had already tended to lose its sense of corporate solidarity. Only to a very limited extent was this regained after 1757, for the Pitt-Newcastle coalition was so broadly based, and Tory support of Government so much of a novelty, that the Old Corps was submerged in a welter of new faces. The pattern of early eighteenth-century politics was in the process of disintegration.

The war situation which greeted the new Ministry was anything but encouraging. In Europe, Frederick had failed to dislodge the Austrians from Prague and in June was badly defeated by Marshal Daun at Kolin. The 'army of observation', established earlier by Pitt in western Germany, and consisting of thirty-six thousand Hanoverians and twenty-four thousand Prussians and Hessians soon showed that it was fit for little but observation! Cumberland's ineffectual leadership resulted in July in its defeat at Hastenbeck by the French who proceeded to occupy Hesse-Cassel and most of Hanover. A panic-stricken George II, without consulting his British ministers, authorized Cumberland to negotiate for the neutrality of Hanover but he was thunder-struck by the resulting Convention of Closterseven in September, which represented a complete capitulation, left Hanover to its fate, and exposed Frederick to attack from the west. On 7 October an angry Cabinet refused further financial support for the army in Germany while the Convention remained in force. The same day Pitt's expensive, ill-planned and weakly-led expedition against the French at Rochefort returned to England without having achieved anything of significance, and nine days later the Russians occupied Berlin. The dismal European scene was scarcely relieved by the knowledge that the French had garrisoned Ostend and Nieuport in the Austrian Netherlands, whence they were free to prey on British merchantmen or prepare to launch an attack on England. Nor were these misfortunes offset by success in the colonial theatres of war. Although in Canada the cautious Loudon had been reinforced and a fleet sent out under Holbourne, the French forces had been similarly augmented and Loudon could not bring himself to risk at attack on Louisburg from which the French still commanded the St Lawrence. Concurrently Montcalm's capture of

Fort William Henry in August increased the French threat to the middle colonies. From India the bleak news of the Black Hole of Calcutta finally reached England, where the implementation of Pitt's much-vaunted Militia Act brought not rejoicing but riots and disturbances—both from those who deplored the expense and those who feared with some justification that they would be illegally forced into service abroad. By the end of October 1757 Frederick the Great was gloomily contemplating suicide, the British Cabinet was considering ceding Gibraltar in an attempt to win Spanish support, Newcastle was pathetically wooing Madame de Pompadour with presents of pineapples and a telescope, and even Pitt was 'sunk into little less than despair of the public'.

Fortunately within a few weeks this almost universal gloom was to be dispersed. Frederick, although heavily outnumbered, defeated the Franco-Imperial army at Rossbach and the Austrians at Leuthen. Amidst general rejoicing at these successes the British Cabinet repudiated the Convention of Closterseven and resumed financial responsibility for the army of observation. This was placed under the command of the able Prince Ferdinand of Brunswick, who proceeded to seize Verden, drive the French back across the Rhine and roundly defeat them at Crefeld. Encouraged by this sudden turn of the tide Pitt, despite the mutterings of Leicester House and the Tories, committed himself increasingly to support of the continental war. By the second Treaty of Westminster in April 1758 both Prussia and Britain pledged themselves not to make separate peace, and Frederick was voted an annual subsidy of £670,000. The army of observation was augmented by nine thousand British troops under Marlborough and Lord George Sackville, and the Hanoverians were taken into British pay. Though France counter-attacked, Ferdinand yielded little. Frederick, with his flank secured, was able to defeat the Russians at Zorndorf in August and, despite a minor defeat by the Austrians at Hochkirk, managed to retain control of Saxony and Silesia.

The three campaigns in America also met with general if limited success. Pitt, perhaps unwisely, replaced Loudon by Abercromby who was instructed to advance from New York via Lake George and Lake Champlain, take Crown Point and Ticonderoga, and eventually strike at either Montreal or Quebec. But at Ticonderoga he failed to make any impression on Montcalm's entrenched position and had to retreat. On the other hand Amherst, who was entrusted with the attack on Louisburg successfully stormed that fortress on 26 July; and the third expedition under Colonel Forbes followed up Bradstreet's capture of Fort Frontenac by occupying Fort Duquesne in November, leaving the British in control of Lake Ontario and commanding the Ohio valley. Meanwhile, bad harvests kept the French Canadians short of supplies, British naval strength minimized the hopes of aid from France and, with the waning of French prestige and the dwindling of the customary presents, the Indians showed less inclination to support their former allies.

On the African coast French power was similarly checked when a small force of ships and marines seized Fort Louis at the mouth of the Senegal in April 1758, and when a second expedition captured Goree at the end of the year. These proved useful bases for procuring gold dust, ivory and gum arabic from the interior, and for diverting the supply of slaves from the French West Indies to the British colonies. From India came the news that Clive had routed Surajah Dowlah at Plassey in June of the previous year, replaced him as Nawab of Bengal by the puppet Mir Jafar, and made it possible for the East India Company to assume virtual control of Bengal, Bihar and Orissa. Compared to this major success Lally's capture of Fort St David and siege of Madras seemed relatively minor setbacks. At sea the British gained minor victories off Cartagena and in the Basque roads, and only Pitt's raids on the French coast (at St Malo in January, Cherbourg in August and St Malo again in September) proved more or less abortive. On balance 1758 was a year of solid if unspectacular progress.

By 1759 no fewer than ninety-one thousand British soldiers (excluding the militia) and sixty thousand seamen were serving in the various theatres of war, and nearly £13,000,000 was voted for the coming year without a word of protest. The ensuing victories proved commensurate with the effort. In America Amherst took Fort Niagara in June, and Ticonderoga and Crown Point within the following two months, and in September Wolfe and Saunders dealt a shattering blow to French power in Canada by capturing Quebec. In the West Indies a projected attack on Martinique came to naught, but the valuable sugar island of Guadeloupe was taken in May. The invasion of England planned by Choiseul, who had assumed control of the French war effort in November 1758, was thwarted by the bombardment of Le Havre in July, by Boscawen's destruction of the Toulon fleet off Lagos on 18 August, and by Hawke's decisive victory over the Brest fleet in November. In India the arrival of Admiral Pocock's squadron compelled Lally to raise the siege of Madras, while further north the British captured Masulipatam, a centre of French influence on the east coast. To supporters of a Country war policy 1759 was indeed the *annus mirabilis*. Only in Europe was there no occasion for jubilation. Even Ferdinand's important victory over the French at Minden in August was marred by the court-martial and temporary disgrace of Lord George Sackville for alleged cowardice in the face of the enemy. Elsewhere the Russians invaded Brandenburg, captured Frankfurt, and in August joined the Austrians in shattering Frederick's army at Kunersdorf. For the remainder of the year Frederick could do no more than play for time.

If 1759 saw British power and Pitt's popularity at their zenith it also offered warnings to the more acute observers. A record £15,500,000 was voted for the following year, but the ever-increasing burden of taxation brought in its wake a rising demand for peace, encouraged by the knowledge that recent British successes made it possible to negotiate from a position of strength. Danes, Swedes, Dutch and Spanish all showed increasing resentment at British insistence on searching neutral shipping for goods destined for France; and the accession in August of the Anglophobe Charles III to the throne of Spain made the continuation of Spanish neutrality at best problematical. At first indeed he offered to mediate between Britain and France, but Pitt refused to consider peace and by 1760 Charles had resumed his earlier hostility. At home the Militia Act continued to provoke periodic disturbances and it became obvious that only in times of dire emergency was it likely to be effective. On balance Pitt was probably justified in his belief that British gains had not yet been sufficiently consolidated, that further victories in Europe were necessary to ensure the retention of colonial acquisitions, and that a premature peace would be too reminiscent of Utrecht to enhance Britain's value as an ally in any future war. Yet Horace Walpole was later to write with perception as well as the gift of hindsight that by the end of 1759 'Europe began to take umbrage at our success'. The continuation of the war had become a calculated risk.

During 1760 Britain continued to prosper in the colonial conflict. With the surrender of Montreal in September Canada was lost to France, and in India Lally was decisively defeated by Eyre Coote in January, leaving little but Pondicherry in French hands. But in Europe, despite the doubling in the number of British troops and the subsidization of more German ones, decisive victories were not forthcoming. In the west, successes at Emsdorf and Warburg were cancelled out by defeats at Corbach and Campen, and Ferdinand could do no more than prevent the French from joining their Austrian and Russian allies in a massive attack on Frederick who, after initial reverses in Saxony and the temporary loss of Berlin, managed to retrieve the situation by victories over the Austrians at Liegnitz and Torgau. Pitt was now more than ever committed to a European war that seemed likely to result in a stalemate, and the movement for peace was bound to thrive on this change of emphasis. Yet the prevailing attitude was still one of ebullient confidence when the political situation was transformed by the sudden death of George II in the early morning of 25 October. At home and abroad the future suddenly became uncertain.

The credit for Britain's resounding victories in the late 1750s has gone almost exclusively to Pitt. A modern scholarly appraisal of his war administration has yet to be written, but it seems likely that the traditional picture stands in need of modification. Pitt was undoubtedly an able war minister, whose breadth of vision, grasp of detail, tireless energy, capacity to inspire and supreme conviction in the rightness of his own judgment enabled him to tower above his colleagues. He was also a singularly unpleasant man—ungenerous, ruthless, inconsistent, irresponsible, theatrical and arrogant. He could command fear and respect, but seldom love, loyalty or even mild affection. If he was something of an egocentric genius, his alternating bouts of wild exhilaration and acute misery—especially in his later life—suggest that he was also a manic-depressive. Certainly he was an impossible colleague, who gave scant credit to Newcastle for providing the vast sums of money that were constantly demanded of the Treasury; to Henry Pelham, whose financial reorganization had placed the national economy on a much sounder basis and had paved the way for closer co-operation between Government and the City; or to Anson for his invaluable work at the head of the Admiralty. Compared to the ministers who had muddled their way through the War of the Austrian Succession, Pitt also had the considerable advantage of a better ally in the King of Prussia, and Scotland was no longer a potential Jacobite spring-board for the invasion of England. Any war leader needs a lot of luck; there is a suspicion that Pitt had more than his fair share. His overall strategy in America was shrewd and consistent, but elsewhere he was rather less impressive. Only gradually did he appreciate the need for the whole-hearted support of Frederick the Great, and the victories in India owed little to his efforts. His intermittent abortive raids on the French coast may have been useful in temporarily diverting the enemy's attention from elsewhere in Europe, but they showed scant return for the substantial expense they involved and were bitterly criticized by his colleagues. His naval appointments were for the most part strikingly successful (though here again Anson's role deserves closer examination), but his military ones, in which admittedly he had sometimes to bow to the King's prejudices, were less so. For a man who could think and plan on a grand scale he could be extraordinarily small-minded and mean. His personal hatred of Lord Mansfield led him to create a minor crisis in 1757–8 over Mansfield's interpretation of the right to a writ of *habeas corpus*. He was even prepared to withdraw his opposition to Hessian subsidies to get his own way over this legal issue, and on failing he petulantly opposed a projected increase in judges' salaries. When his brother-in-law Lord Temple was very reasonably refused the Garter by the King in 1759 he darkly threatened resignation in order to force George II's hand, and he deliberately provoked a bitter altercation within the Cabinet by encouraging Holderness to take offence at a private correspondence between Newcastle and Hardwicke's son Joseph Yorke, Ambassador at The Hague. His peevish irresponsibility, which had hampered his early career because it had been manifested over major issues, was now concentrated on trivia, but it stemmed from the same scarcely-veiled contempt for his colleagues and for the conventions of the time. An outsider in politics who scorned to play the game according to the accepted rules, Pitt would never have achieved fame without the aid of a national crisis. The urgency of the times forced his contemporaries to overcome their instinctive distrust of him, and his successes temporarily established him in a position of political dominance that perhaps only Winston Churchill has since equalled. His secret was his capacity to instil fear in his generals, his admirals and his fellow-ministers, and any criticism of the policy or the man was stifled at source. But if nothing succeeds like success, nothing fails like failure. By 1760 doubts concerning the wisdom of continuing the war were beginning to appear, and the Ministry was so lacking in cohesion—for in the last analysis Pitt was an autocrat, not a leader—that even a minor change in circumstances could cause its rapid disintegration. A change of King, and especially the accession of a monarch who hated both Pitt and the war, was rather more than a minor change of circumstance.

5

THE PATTERN OF POLITICS

THE system of government inherited by George I defied precise definition, and the experience of his two predecessors might seem to suggest that it could breed only chronic political instability and bitter factional strife. The authors of the so-called revolutionary settlement (based above all on the Bill of Rights of 1689, the Toleration Act of 1690, the Triennial Act of 1694 and the Act of Settlement of 1701) had in fact settled remarkably little—largely because the alteration in the hereditary succession had seemed to remove the necessity for major constitutional change. Had James II been permitted to retain the throne, the need for adequate safeguards might well have confined subsequent political life in Britain to the inflexibility inherent in a written constitution. As it was, the execution of one king and the dethronement of another left a legacy from the seventeenth century that might reasonably be expected to deter subsequent monarchs from attempting to rule in a manner repugnant to the interests and prejudices of the parliamentary classes. True, one or two loose ends were conveniently tied up. The royal suspending power was declared illegal, and the dispensing power was brought under parliamentary control; the maintenance of a standing army without the approval of Parliament was forbidden, and was in practice authorized by an annual Mutiny Act; judges were freed from undue royal pressure by being granted tenure during good behaviour instead of at the pleasure of the King; the habit of voting supply annually did more to prevent a return to non-parliamentary rule than the re-iterated provision that not more than three years should elapse without the summoning of a Parliament and indeed, re-inforced by the need for a Mutiny Act, ensured annual sessions; and the accompanying requirement that Parliament should not last longer than three years removed the possibility of a monarch retaining indefinitely a House of Commons politically emasculated by the use of royal patronage—though only at the cost of encouraging factiousness and an almost permanent electioneering atmosphere.

Thus royal government, in the sense that it had existed under the

Tudors and early Stuarts became even more impracticable than it had been under Charles II and James II; yet the conventions of modern parliamentary government still lay far in the future. The King retained a considerable reservoir of power and was very much in the forefront of the political stage. He was the chief executive officer of the realm, the fountain of honour and justice, and the maker of peace and war. If many of his former prerogatives had been whittled away in the course of the seventeenth century, it was still generally recognized that he retained the last and most vital of those prerogatives, the right to appoint and dismiss ministers—though it rapidly became obvious that those ministers must be able to command the confidence of Parliament, and especially of the House of Commons, if the King's business was effectively to be carried on. This brings us to the central paradox of the system of mixed government which developed out of the revolutionary settlement—the co-existence of a royal executive with increasing parliamentary struggles for office which, if successful, could deprive the monarch of his freedom in the choice of ministers. The key to the eventual and permanent loss of that freedom was of course the emergence of a well-organized, well-disciplined party which could command the support of a working majority in both houses of Parliament and use its power to designate ministers to the King. But in the first half of the eighteenth century this was never the case, and even after 1760 it was to be so only rarely, fleetingly and under quite exceptional circumstances. Meanwhile the first two Georges intermittently did battle with successive generations of politicians who, while paying lip-service to the royal right to choose ministers, did their best to circumvent that right. Men continued to talk in seventeenth-century terms, but increasingly behaved in a manner more consistent with the conventions of the nineteenth century. Nonetheless, despite outward appearances and a long subsequent tradition that monarchical power underwent a marked decline between 1714 and 1760, it is possible to argue that the early Hanoverians held their own remarkably well. At the same time a system of government was evolved and a pattern of politics emerged that ensured a greater degree of political stability than William and Anne had ever known. In 1714 it had appeared that royal power had been curbed only at the cost of accepting political anarchy; by 1760 British government was the envy of contemporary Europe.

It is not difficult to understand why the first two Georges were for long believed to have been ineffectual nonentities. Devoid of personal charm, ill-tempered, stubborn and opinionated, they neither commanded the affection of their subjects nor were they able to gain the approval of historians. Both kings lamented the idiosyncracies of the British constitution, which denied them the untrammelled power that they enjoyed in their beloved Hanover, and both found foreign affairs more to their taste than the intricacies of domestic politics. But even George I's ignorance of the English language[1] did not persuade him to leave the direction of internal affairs exclusively to his ministers, and his son took great pains to instruct himself in detail on every aspect of policy. Their partiality for Hanover, which brought them perhaps more unpopularity than their intermittent sacrifice of British to Electoral interests deserved, provided such politicians as the elder Pitt with an opportunity to rouse public hostility towards them, but the political difficulties which they encountered were merely exacerbated by their Germanic origin and their unattractive personalities. At bottom, those difficulties arose partly from the fact that since 1688 Parliament had become a permanent feature of political life, and kings had therefore to learn to secure its co-operation in the government of the realm; partly from the limitations which both Georges voluntarily imposed upon their freedom of action, and which more intelligent monarchs might have avoided. This brings us to the heart of the dilemma in which they found themselves, to the basic problem left unsolved by the makers of the revolutionary settlement; it also invites, before attempting a final assessment of the fortunes of the early Hanoverian monarchy, an examination of the structure and organization of the House of Commons.

Though the events of 1688-9 had underlined the lesson that in a head-on collision between King and parliamentary classes the former would have to yield, the authors of the subsequent settlement paid curiously little attention to the equally fundamental though less dramatic issue of maintaining harmony in day-to-day government between the executive and the legislature—between the King and his ministers on the one hand, and Parliament on the other. The ultimate solution was of course to be found in the gradual withdrawal of the monarch from active politics and the emergence of a system of Cabinet Government whereby the members of the executive were chosen from the ranks of the party which enjoyed, at least temporarily, the confidence of a working majority in Parliament. But at the beginning of the eighteenth century neither of these developments could be foreseen, and neither would anyway have been considered desirable. Indeed, in the Act of Settlement an attempt

---

[1]French was spoken at Court under George I, while George II spoke English fluently, though with a strong guttural accent.

was made to exclude all office-holders from the House of Commons, which, if it had become law, would not only have frustrated the emergence of Cabinet Government, but would have invited perennial political deadlock by creating a complete divorce between executive and legislature. Happily the advantage of having ministers in the Commons, where they could readily be called to account, quickly became obvious; and the Regency Act of 1705 repealed the offending clause before it could ever come into effect. Instead, holders of all offices created after 1705 were excluded, but any member of the Commons on appointment to an office already in existence before that date had merely to vacate his seat and was immediately eligible for re-election. Thus the way was at least left open for creating harmony between the two main centres of power that prevailed throughout the period of mixed government—the Closet and the Commons.

The royal Closet—the small room in which successive Kings granted audience to their ministers, usually individually but sometimes (especially if they wished to play upon personal rivalries) in pairs—was for most of the eighteenth century on a higher political level than the Cabinet. Under the later Stuarts the so-called Cabinet Council had tended to replace the Privy Council, because the latter had become too large and unwieldy to cope effectively with the increasing amount of government business. Not unnaturally the smaller body was resented by suspicious members of Parliament, just as the Privy Council had been when it had replaced the larger amorphous *consilium regis* in the sixteenth century; and an attempt was made in the Act of Settlement to restore the Privy Council to full executive power. But prejudice could not prevail against pragmatic necessity, and when in 1713 Lord Cholmondeley tried to invoke a debate in the Privy Council on the terms of the peace treaties, he was told bluntly that they had been approved by the Cabinet Council and all that was required was formal ratification. In time the Cabinet Council, which included not only the heads of the chief administrative departments but also the Archbishop of Canterbury and a collection of household officers such as the Groom of the Stole, the Lord Steward and the Master of the Horse, also became too large for convenient consultation, and from its ranks a smaller 'efficient' Cabinet emerged, which was confined to effective heads of departments and was to prove the direct ancestor of the modern Cabinet. Though many attempts have been made to identify the date of its birth, none has succeeded. It is clear that by 1760 it was unusual for the 'nominal' Cabinet to meet except to hear a draft of the King's Speech before the opening of each parliamentary session and to consider appeals for royal clemency in criminal cases. Romney Sedgwick long ago suggested[1] that the efficient Cabinet existed as early as 1739-41, when the King while in Hanover frequently sent despatches to England with instructions that they were to be submitted only to those lords who were normally consulted on affairs of a secret nature. But this seems to refer, so to speak, to the Closet without the King—to those ministers who would be consulted individually by the King when he was in England, but who temporarily assumed a kind of corporate identity, distinct from the larger Council of Regency, when he was abroad. At this stage there is no convincing proof of the separate existence of efficient and nominal Cabinets. When there were no issues of real political importance to be discussed, it was natural enough that many 'honorific' members of the Cabinet should prefer to remain in the country or concentrate on the duties of their offices, and that most meetings should be confined to key ministers such as the First Lord of the Treasury, the Lord Chancellor, the two (or three) Secretaries of State, and the Lord President of the Council. But when excitement ran high, as it did for example during the French invasion scare of early 1744 and the Jacobite rebellion of the following year, all members were anxious to attend in order to keep abreast of affairs and the leading ministers were only too ready to encourage their attendance so that they could spread responsibility as widely as possible. Thus during 1742 and 1743 Cabinet meetings were rarely attended by more than five to ten members, and were held only at irregular intervals, but the temporary crises of 1744 and 1745 brought an increase in attendance to as many as twenty and more, and meetings were summoned daily, and even on occasions twice a day. As was so often the case with the development of constitutional conventions in England, pragmatic considerations were decisive.

The powers of early eighteenth-century Cabinets were nowhere defined by law; indeed their existence was not even formally recognized. They considered matters submitted to them by the King, but invited royal displeasure if they discussed issues without his prior permission. Though previous monarchs had presided over Cabinet meetings, George I decided to break with past tradition, partly no doubt because of his inability to speak English and partly perhaps because he was unwilling to accord a similar privilege to his despised son, who acted as Regent when he himself was spending his summers in Hanover. It would be a mistake to assume that the absence of the King (George II continued his father's practice) meant a significant decline in royal authority, or automatically opened the way for the development of the prime ministership and other

---

[1]See *English Historical Review*, 1919, p. 290.

aspects of modern Cabinet Government. Although the minister who assumed the chairmanship obviously enjoyed an enhanced status, the origins of the premiership—as we shall see—were more broadly based; and despite the attempts of Walpole to impose a degree of discipline upon his Cabinet colleagues (for instance, his dismissal of Townshend and his purge after the Excise Bill) the notion of Cabinet solidarity was still unformulated. Ministerial responsibility in the eighteenth century was individual rather than collective. Ministers were responsible not so much to Parliament, but politically to the King and legally to the law. Thus for Parliament to force a monarch to dismiss a minister or ministers merely because of disagreement over policy was regarded as 'storming the Closet', an activity that was at best irresponsible, at worst treasonable. Impeachment therefore remained the only respectable method of getting rid of an unacceptable minister, though in practice it was too cumbersome, archaic and inefficient a procedure to survive, and Oxford and Bolingbroke were the last to be impeached for purely political reasons. But after the Commons in 1742 administered its first major rebuff to George II by withdrawing its confidence from Walpole and forcing him to resign, members felt it necessary to appoint a secret committee to search for evidence of high crimes and misdemeanours in order to salve their consciences. Furthermore, although they had ousted Walpole for his part in mismanaging the war, they did not dream of dictating to the King whom he should employ in his place. The royal power of appointment was as yet unchallenged. Even when, in 1756 and again in 1757, George II found himself compelled to accept the elder Pitt, it was not the House of Commons that ensured his elevation, but the reluctance of any other prominent politician to serve without him, and Pitt's determination that he would have none but the first place. A megalomaniac like Pitt might temporarily succeed, where Walpole had failed, in imposing his will upon his Cabinet colleagues, but most Cabinets of the early Hanoverian period, especially during 1739-44 and 1754-6 were rent by bitter disputes, and individual members had no hesitation in making their differences public. In such circumstances the position of the Cabinet *vis-à-vis* the King was seldom particularly strong, though on the occasions when harmony prevailed it could become a useful vehicle for discussing a common plan of attack when ministers attempted individually to drive home their points in the Closet. It was still in the latter that policy was hammered out, and it is easy to believe that the King was there able to exercise a more decisive influence than he would have done at Cabinet meetings.

This makes it obvious that the Cabinet was scarcely an effective link between Closet and Commons, nor until the development of true party discipline could it hope to be so. The necessary link could meanwhile be partially supplied by the eighteenth-century equivalent of party discipline on the Government side of the House—royal patronage, or Influence as it came to be called. It is no accident that modern party whips hold office at the Treasury, where in the age of Walpole and Pelham it was said that 'numberless sturdy beggars apply, who cannot all be satisfied, nor all with safety be refused'. The use of Influence had been denounced by Country members ever since the days of Charles II when Danby had first applied himself to the mammoth task of building up a substantial Court party in the Commons; and the exclusion of specific classes of office-holders and pensioners by the Place and Pension Acts of 1700, 1701, 1716 and 1742, together with the 'place clause' of the Act of Settlement and a host of other abortive measures, testified to the continuing Country suspicion that the independence of Parliament was being undermined. But notwithstanding constant charges of 'corruption' and 'dependence', the need for some such form of constitutional lubricant was generally recognized by impartial observers such as David Hume, who wrote of Influence in 1741 that 'some degree and some kind of it are inseparable from the very nature of the constitution, and necessary to the preservation of our mixed government'. It is too easy from the comfortable democratic vantage-point of the twentieth century thoughtlessly to condemn a political system that was based in part upon an elaborate network of patronage confined to a narrow section of the community, and easier still to misinterpret the way in which that system operated. Admittedly, large numbers of electors openly sold their votes to the highest bidder, and there were few members of either House of Parliament who did not look upon their membership as an opportunity to seek royal favour, whether for themselves, their relatives or their constituents. But the modern elector is similarly seduced by party promises, and many members still seek and are granted recompense for faithful service. At all events, very serious reservations must be made about the too-often assumed corollary that eighteenth-century Ministries could maintain themselves in power through the bought support of a venal majority in the Commons. Without Influence, the nucleus of supporters it could provide and the electoral resources to keep them in Parliament, few ministers would have found it easy to survive; but even such masters of the patronage system as Walpole and Newcastle had to bow to defeat, and the elder Pitt, who scorned to cultivate even a small connection of his own, twice managed to thrust himself into power by sheer force of personality. Influence was certainly essential to the establishment of political stability, but it could never save a Ministry that had insufficient debating strength and administrative talent to command the confidence of a House of Commons which was in fact far more independent than its twentieth-century descendant.

This becomes obvious when one looks at the nature and extent of Influence. Firstly, the attitude of the electors deserves attention. Except in the counties, the two universities and a handful of the more open boroughs, and then only on the rare occasions when national issues arose, they paid little or no heed to the way in which their members were likely to vote in the Commons. They regarded their franchises, as indeed did the Courts, as a kind of personal property on which they expected to make a profit at least once every seven years. They were keenly interested in the amount of money a candidate might be prepared to pay them, the support which he enjoyed from local magnates, or the concessions which he might be able to extract from Parliament for the constituency. But they did not normally regard it as their function to make and break Ministries, or to assist in the determination of national policy. In 1757, for example, there was a revolution in the Cornish borough of Grampound. The fifty or so voters, dissatisfied with their existing patrons, Lord Edgcumbe, Christopher Hawkins and Robert Andrews, transferred their allegiance to Edward Eliot and William Trevanion. But at the ensuing election of 1761 they returned the sitting members, both of whom, like all five patrons, were supporters of the Government. Thus the local revolt had no effect at all at Westminster. As far as the English constituencies were concerned, Government or private patronage prevailed only in the boroughs. No English county seat was under the control of a single individual, and the prohibitive cost of fighting an election (that of Oxfordshire in 1754 cost the Tories alone over £20,000) discouraged contests. It was therefore quite common for the leading magnate of the county to nominate one member and for the country gentlemen to determine the other; but if the magnate was ill-advised enough to attempt to capture both seats he invariably lost the one on which he could otherwise count. In many, indeed most, of the 203 English boroughs with their complex array of franchises, it was quite otherwise. All male inhabitants had the vote in a dozen of them; in thirty-six the ancient 'scot and lot' franchise was scarcely less wide; there were six where all freeholders voted; in the ninety-four where all freemen were enfranchised the way was open for the mayor and corporation to create new freemen on the very eve of an election; in twenty-six the franchise was confined to members of the corporation, who frequently turned their privilege to good advantage; and in the final twenty-nine (the notorious burgage boroughs) it was attached to particular plots of land, the purchase of a majority of which guaranteed control. The size of the electorate varied from the seven to eight thousand of London or Westminster to the three or four of Old Sarum. But venality was not in inverse proportion to size. Some of the smallest boroughs, like Bath and Devizes, showed a sturdy independence; large ones, such as Bedford and Gloucester, could prove the most avaricious. The English boroughs produced 405 members of the House of Commons of whom, at various times between 1714 and 1760, some 220 to 245 were returned by private patrons or by Government departments such as the Treasury, Admiralty or Post Office, which exercised influence in certain constituencies where their minor local officials could dominate the electorate. Depending upon the efficiency with which they could muster their electoral troops, the Government was thus able to control between twenty and twenty-five seats and, in co-operation with a local patron (such as Lord Edgcumbe or Lord Falmouth in Cornwall), might manage to influence a further twenty to thirty-five. But even at its most efficacious it could not hope to return as many as a sixth of the borough members, and usually it had to rest content with significantly fewer. The remaining borough seats were under the control of private patrons, who might of course be supporters of the Opposition no less than of the Government. Those patrons who were commoners normally returned themselves and constituted the most independent element in the House. Others returned their relatives, regardless of their political complexion, for kinship almost invariably rose above politics at election time. Thus only any marketable surplus would be made available to Government or Opposition leaders who knew of supporters still seeking seats. If we take the election of 1741 as an example, only ninety-nine out of the two hundred members returned by private borough patrons owed their return exclusively to their political views; sixty-nine were supporters of the Government, thirty of the Opposition. The Government advantage was therefore a mere thirty-nine, and of these many subsequently voted against ministers on occasions that in modern times would see the issue of a three-line whip. If we add the forty-one members returned for Government boroughs, the ministerial advantage rises to seventy-one, of whom no fewer than thirty-five subsequently crossed the floor of the House at times when their support was desperately needed. Clearly the effect of borough patronage was not to provide the ministerial benches with a massive docile majority. Its purpose, from the Government's point of view, was to make available a small group of seats for those men of business and other office-holders whose presence in Parliament was deemed essential, and who could not afford the £1-2,000 that a contested borough was likely to cost. The private patron's aim was to provide himself (if a commoner) and his family with avenues to the Commons, and to sell any surplus on the open market to those who might share his political views. Since such purchasers normally paid the market price, their continued political allegiance during the following seven years was at best dubious.

Nor was Influence in the House of Commons, in the form of places and pensions, as uniformly and widely beneficial to the Government as its detractors claimed. Admittedly, the number of office-holders in the Commons was substantial—usually some 150–160, or about 28 per cent of the total membership of the House; and during the Seven Years' War as many as 220, or almost 40 per cent. If one adds the army and naval officers who held nothing but their commissions (and it is not clear that one should do so) the proportion was about one-third, except during 1756-60, when it rose to perhaps 45 per cent. Under normal circumstances the placemen were far from constituting a working majority, nor indeed were they all reliable supporters of the Government. If one looks at the 157 place-holders in the Commons in 1741, no fewer than thirty-three prove to be active members of the Opposition, nineteen of them holding their offices of the Prince of Wales and the others enjoying sinecures for life (and therefore thoroughly independent) or judicial office. Even of the remaining 124, at least nineteen voted against the Government on crucial occasions during the life of the 1741-7 Parliament. As in the constituencies, it is easy to exaggerate the effects of Influence. It is easy, too, to overlook the fact that eighteenth-century members were paid no salaries, and therefore expected some recompense for their substantial financial outlay in getting themselves elected and maintaining houses in London during the parliamentary sessions. If they could command no royal favour they were likely to be looked upon as men of little consequence, though the true Country member would confine his requests to a seat on his local commission of the peace or a minor concession for a friend, relative or constituent. Occasionally, of course, troublesome opponents in the Commons were bought off by preferment. But for the most part offices were rewards for the faithful rather than enticements to political subservience, and charity rather than corruption frequently characterized their distribution. For every satisfied recipient there was also apt to be a host of disappointed suppliants. Patronage could breed opponents as well as confirm allies and win converts, and the obligations which it engendered were often complex and conflicting.

Influence was nonetheless one significant link between King and Commons; Sir Robert Walpole first provided the other. Previously, commoners, on elevation to high ministerial office, had sought and obtained elevation to the House of Lords. But Walpole was shrewd enough to see that only the Commons could rival the Closet as a source of political power, and throughout his long years as First Lord of the Treasury he declined to quit the lower House. He was thereby able to create a new office—that of Minister for the King in the House of Commons or (as it was alternatively called) Minister for the House of Commons in the Closet. As such he could act as mediator between King and Commons, convey the wishes and prejudices of each to the other, and suggest a compromise when conflict threatened. Lord Hervey, an unusually perceptive political observer, was the first to see that Walpole's fall in 1742 left a power vacuum. To Hervey the 'favour of the Closet' meant the confidence of the King, the 'power of the Closet' the ability to bring pressure on the King arising from leadership of the Commons. As early as July 1742 he was urging George II to appoint a true successor to Walpole, pointing out that 'at present, the favour is all bestowed on Lord Carteret, and all the power exercised by Mr Pulteney. This cannot last; favour and power must go on together, or neither can go on long.' But it was not until 1744 that Henry Pelham managed to gain the undisputed leadership of the Commons, and it took him a further two years to win the confidence of the King. Only then did real stability return to the body politic, and it did not survive Pelham's death in 1754. Of course prominent peers in the Ministry found it irksome to have to accord primacy to a commoner, and Newcastle had early and petulantly protested at brother Henry's assumption of Walpole's 'old method of being the first person upon all occasions', though he conceded that his brother's 'superior interest in the Closet and situation in the House of Commons' were indeed great advantages. When Pelham died, Hardwicke was obtuse enough to advise George II that no successor need be appointed, and that Newcastle could manage the Commons from the remote reaches of the House of Lords. But by 1757 he was forced to admit that the earlier precedents of a peer as effective first minister 'had been overruled by the long habit of seeing Sir Robert Walpole and Mr Pelham in the House of Commons'. Indeed, the ministries presided over by peers lasted few more months than those presided over by commoners did years, as the contrast between those of Walpole and Pelham on the one hand, and of Carteret and Newcastle on the other, amply illustrate.

The new office held by Walpole and Pelham did more than provide an essential link between King and Commons; it laid the basis for the emergence of the eighteenth-century prime ministership. This was quite different from its twentieth-century counterpart, for the prime minister was not the leader of a united party, was never invited by the King to form an administration of his own choosing, had grave difficulty in imposing any degree of solidarity upon his Cabinet colleagues, and did not expect them to quit office with him when he resigned or was dismissed. In theory every minister was responsible to the King only for the affairs of his own department, and the very idea of a 'first' or 'sole' minister was regarded as savouring of royal favouritism, apeing undesirable French practice, and generally alien to the spirit of the developing constitution. But there were never more than two commoners in the Cabinet, and usually only one of any real political importance. This minister became the front line of defence in the Commons, not merely for the business of his department, but for all aspects of the Government's policy. He was therefore able to gain an accretion of power that enabled him, in a very real sense, to rise above his aristocratic colleagues and become a 'prime' minister. The so-called 'plenitude of power' normally rested upon a three-fold basis—the confidence of the King, the leadership of the Commons, and the headship of the Treasury. The last of these depended not so much upon the management of the public finances, important though this was, as upon the distribution of patronage. It was a less essential ingredient of primacy than the other two, and so formidable a commoner as the elder Pitt, between 1757 and 1761, could leave the First Lordship of the Treasury to Newcastle without unduly diminishing his power. But Walpole and Pelham possessed all three elements, and it was Pelham in the forties who was first widely described in contemporary correspondence as the 'premier'.

The early eighteenth-century House of Commons did not readily lend itself to domination by even the most assiduous and conciliatory of prime ministers. It had no party organization in any coherent sense, partly because the great issues around which parties tend to crystallize were absent, partly because the bitter, factious conflicts of Anne's reign had discredited the very idea of party, and partly because the great majority of the House had cogent reasons for not wishing to become associated with incipient party leaders. Nonetheless the desire of politicians to increase their bargaining power—and hence their chance of retaining or gaining office—led them to attempt to build up personal followings, though it was not till the 1760s that these assumed any great political importance in the political life of the nation. Meanwhile the Commons at any one time could be divided broadly into the supporters and opponents of Administration or, as they were sometimes called, Court and Country. Yet this obvious division concealed a more fundamental one into three different types of member, which can be most conveniently explained by reference to the following diagram:

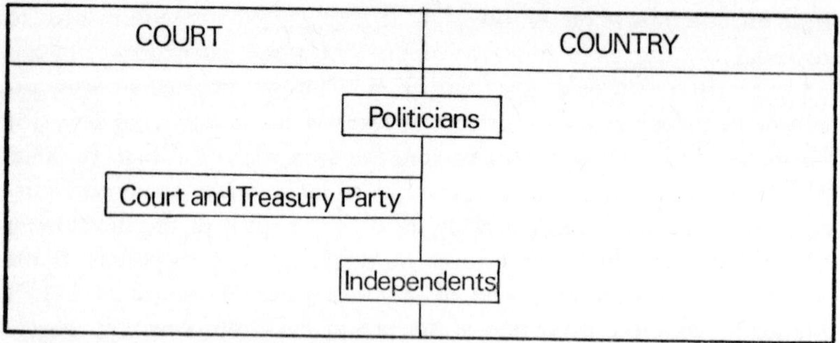

Firstly there were the politicians, who included in their ranks members of the most prominent political families of the times, occupied the two front benches, dominated the debates, and frequently created the erroneous impression of a two-party system at work. They played the political game with unremitting enthusiasm, members of the Administration hoping quickly to scale the ladder of preferment, opponents seeking to force themselves into office. On the Government front bench were inevitably Walpole, Pelham, Henry Fox, William Murray, Thomas Winnington and a host of others who never rose above the second rank; among the Opposition at one time or another could be found men such as William Pulteney, William Pitt, George Lyttelton, George Bubb Dodington and the Grenville brothers, all of whom managed eventually to sail into ministerial harbour. In round figures the politicians usually numbered around a hundred but, because of their incessant activity, they have tended to monopolize the attention of historians.

Next came, for want of a better term, the Court and Treasury Party—placemen like their ministerial betters, but with few ambitions other than security of tenure. Because this was their primary aim, they were reluctant to commit themselves too closely to particular politicians, even though many of them had originally been granted office at the behest of those politicians. They preferred instead to acknowledge their allegiance direct to the King, and were prepared for the most part to give faithful support to any ministers whom he chose to appoint. When Ministries changed there was a reshuffling of politicians, but the vast majority of the Court and Treasury Party were left undisturbed, whether they be Court officials, sinecurists, forerunners of the modern civil servants, or holders of military governorships. Their common bond was dependence upon the Crown for their salaries, and often for their parliamentary seats as well. They had achieved a modest competence through their membership of the Commons, and desired no more. Thus young Horace Walpole was able for no fewer than fifty-nine years to enjoy his triple sinecures as Clerk of the Estreats, Usher of the Exchequer and Comptroller of the Pipe, Thomas Hervey peacefully to draw his salary for his scarcely arduous duties as Superintendent of the King's Gardens and Waterworks, and General Charles Churchill (the illegitimate nephew of the great Duke of Marlborough) to occupy for more than two decades the offices of Groom of the Bedchamber, Governor of Plymouth and Deputy Ranger of St James's Park—as well as to marry his illegitimate son (also an MP and sinecurist) to the illegitimate daughter of Sir Robert Walpole. The total number of the Court and Treasury Party in early Hanoverian times was usually about one hundred to one hundred and twenty, and perhaps twenty more if one includes *all* military and naval personnel, not merely those who held office.

The remaining 300–350 members have been called 'independents', though perhaps a more appropriate title might be 'non-dependents'. They differed from the politicians in that they were essentially back benchers, and from the Court and Treasury Party in that they relied upon the Crown neither for their incomes nor their parliamentary seats. This did not preclude them from seeking favours for others, but there is no evidence that this significantly affected their voting behaviour. The basic inclination of the Court independent was to support ministers because they constituted the King's Government, and therefore merited support as long as they governed in accordance with established traditions. The attitude, on the other hand, of the characteristic Country independent was one of barely disguised hostility to all Government, and a deep-seated suspicion of executive power and of politicians of every shade. But independent opinion could prove very fluid on many issues, and was apt to be swayed in the course of debate if sensitive nerves were struck. It could turn swiftly and with devastating results against either a maladroit Administration or an unscrupulous Opposition.

The terms 'Court 'and 'Country', have thus far been used in their most general sense—the former to include the 'in' politicians for the time being, the more or less permanent 'ins' of the Court and Treasury Party, and a group of Court independents; the latter to embrace the Opposition front bench as well as the Country back benchers. But just as the Court and Treasury Party was the true core of the Court, so the true Country member was found only on the Opposition back benches. Country attitudes, which were in evidence from the early seventeenth century, persisted far longer into the eighteenth than has often been recognized. They derived from an instinctive distrust of the central Government and its ever-spreading tentacles, and their upholders saw themselves as inheriting the former role of the Commons as a whole, before it had begun to succumb to the pernicious influence of the Court. To curb that influence they eagerly supported all attempts to reduce the numbers of placemen and pensioners in Parliament, and argued for measures to mitigate corruption in the boroughs. They were also passionately devoted to frugal administration and low taxation, hostile to the maintenance of even a token standing army in time of peace and, if war should come, favoured naval and colonial combat in preference to expensive military entanglements on the Continent. Thus we find them opposing the Septennial Act and constantly moving for its repeal, resisting the payment of debts on the King's Civil List (which they saw as an engine of corruption), denouncing the employment of Hanoverian and Hessian mercenaries, and rising against Walpole's Excise Bill, which seemed calculated to threaten the privacy of their homes and flood the constituencies with hordes of excise officers who could upset the local balances of political power. But suspicious though they might be of ministerial motives, they were equally determined not to be made stepping-stones to power by ambitious Opposition politicians intent only upon storming the Closet. Thus in February 1741, at a time when Walpole's majority was normally only about forty, the premature attempt of Pulteney to secure the dismissal of the prime minister caused a massive revolt among Country members, and gave Walpole victory by 184 votes—the highest majority of his political career.

It is only fair to add that the three basic types of member identified in the diagram are sometimes difficult to distinguish, and that in the course of their parliamentary lives some members moved from one category to another. Especially towards the end of a long Administration the lines between the ministerial politicians and the Court and Treasury Party became blurred, so long had they acted in unison. Even the particular office which a man held did not necessarily determine his type. As Secretary at War, Henry Fox, like Walpole and Pelham before him, was obviously a politician on the way up; but Lord Barrington was subsequently to hold the same office for twenty years without ever changing his Court and Treasury mentality. On the other hand, many who might originally have harboured political ambitions quickly realized their limitations, settled for permanent office at a modest level, and quietly shed their connections with their former associates. As for the independents, domestic extravagance and electoral fever could in time erode their position, and not a few were eventually forced to abandon their principles and seek financial salvation through the largesse of the Crown. But at any one time most members fitted at least temporarily into one of the three main categories which, despite their merging penumbrae, serve better than any other classification to depict the varieties of political motivation.

The nature of the parliamentary conflict in early Hanoverian England thus becomes clear. It was essentially between two opposing sets of politicians, of whom the ministerial set had the very substantial advantage of general support from the King and from the Court and Treasury Party. To the latter the Opposition leaders had no counterpart unless the Prince of Wales was acting as their patron, when the officers of his court could provide them with a little parcel of perhaps twenty placemen. Yet the Government advantage was never sufficient to ensure them a working majority, for which they needed in addition the support of at least a few score of independents. It was therefore for the souls of these independents that the politicians did battle.

The task facing Opposition leaders was indeed formidable. As long as the King was the effective leader of the Government the notion of 'His Majesty's Opposition' was a contradiction in terms. It was generally accepted (as even Elizabeth I had long before acknowledged) that any member was free to vote according to his conscience on a particular issue. But for members to band together in a 'formed Opposition' for the purpose of continually opposing and harassing ministers in order to force their removal was widely regarded as irresponsible, factious and even treasonable. Hardwicke's comment in 1757 was typical: 'For my own part I am determined not to go into a *form'd general Opposition*. I have seen so much of them that I am convinc'd that they are the most wicked combinations that men can enter into;—worse and more corrupt than any Administration.' But since there were never enough offices to satisfy all those who sought them, and since genuine differences over policy intermittently arose, Oppositions inevitably developed and sometimes, as in 1742 and 1756, even succeeded in storming the Closet. Nevertheless their leaders felt psychologically at a disadvantage and constantly tried to forestall charges of unconstitutional behaviour. At the practical level they sought and frequently secured the patronage of the Prince of Wales. There was no such thing as a shadow Cabinet, but from 1717 to 1720, from 1737 to 1742, from 1747 to 1751, and from 1755 to 1757 there was a shadow Court at Leicester House. It was clearly preposterous to accuse ministerial opponents of disloyalty to the dynasty—a charge that might seem to gain credence from the fact that the great majority of them were Tories suspected of Jacobite sympathies—if they were gathering under the aegis of the Hanoverian heir to the throne. At the theoretical level they claimed that they were opposing not the King's Government, but a group of 'evil counsellors' who had forced themselves upon the monarch.

Their aim was therefore to rescue the King from the clutches of an oligarchical cabal. This polite fiction, which had obvious seventeenth-century origins, became the stock-in-trade of Leicester House, and was to assume new significance in the reign of George III.

The role of Leicester House deserves special attention. To quote Romney Sedgwick:[1]

> At all times and in all countries, heirs to the throne have tended to quarrel with reigning monarchs, but only in England between the Revolution of 1688 and the First Reform Act of 1832 have they been provided with a safe agreeable means of expressing their resentment and securing redress of their grievances by placing themselves at the head of the Opposition and embarrassing the Government.

George II and George III as Princes of Wales, and Frederick until his death in 1751, intermittently courted the Opposition—not only to annoy the reigning monarchs, but also to gain concessions for themselves. Thus the future George II in 1720 secured the removal of the tiresome social sanctions which his father had imposed upon him, Frederick in 1742 achieved the doubling of his personal allowance, and the future George III in 1756 finally won royal approval of the appointment of Lord Bute to the headship of his Household. But the heirs apparent also sought to prepare for their own reigns, when the existing rascally ministers would be ejected and replaced by Leicester House minions. Everyone thus expected Walpole to be dismissed when George II succeeded to the throne in 1727, and he was saved only by the support of Queen Caroline and the manifest incompetence of Sir Spencer Compton. Frederick was above all determined to avoid similar failure when the great day came, and from 1749 to 1751 made extraordinarily detailed plans for the first fifteen days after his father's death. All ministerial changes were outlined; Pelham was to be kicked up to the House of Lords, Fox and Pitt bought off with some profitable employments inconsistent with a seat in the Commons, William Murray elevated to the Chief Justiceship of the Common Pleas, and so it went on. Not only was Frederick's speech to the Commons prepared, but even the Address by which a dutiful House would respond 'upon this sad occasion'. The Tories would be wooed, and special care taken to prevent despair among the 'underlings of Office'—the Court and Treasury Party—who would of course continue undisturbed by ministerial changes. Finally, a list of members for every constituency was prepared, with notes on whether they could be allowed to continue in a new Parliament, and suggestions for effecting the defeat of those who were unacceptable.

---

[1] *Letters from George III to Lord Bute, 1756–66*, p. xii.

Frederick and his future chief minister, Lord Egmont, had taken every care to ensure that the death of George II would see a new dawn of salvation for the country, but unfortunately—as in all of Frederick's activities—the outcome was more appropriate to comic opera than high drama. Intent on venturing out in bleak weather to see how his father looked (George II had been ill and his son's hopes had correspondingly risen), Frederick caught a chill and two weeks later was himself dead. Leicester House was in sorry disarray. Thomas Pitt, who had spent a fortune electioneering on behalf of the Prince, added an unbalanced mind to his already unbalanced accounts, and George Bubb Dodington who, with his infallibly bad sense of timing, had once again deserted the King for the Prince, recorded touchingly in his diary: 'Lord of Mercy, thy hand that wounds alone can heal!' In due course all members of the Prince's faction made their peace with the King—except Egmont, who could not bring himself to play second fiddle. Eventually he was to serve the new Prince of Wales, and even find employment under the Crown when young George succeeded to the throne in 1760.

The various elements among the Opposition had other reasons for allying with successive heirs apparent besides the aura of political respectability which they thereby gained. Leicester House provided them with a social centre and a focal point for their embryonic organization. Chesterfield put his finger on a fundamental weakness of Opposition when he confided to Dodington in 1741:

> I entirely agree with you, that we ought to have meetings to concert measures before the meeting of the Parliament, but that I likewise know will not happen. I have been these seven years endeavouring to bring it about, and have not been able. Fox-hunting, gardening, planting or indifference have kept our people in the country, till the very day before the meeting of Parliament.

The really able politicians among the Opposition merely used successive Princes for as long as this served their purpose; if thereby they sufficiently enhanced their nuisance value to be able to force themselves into office with the King, they had no hesitation in dropping the Prince who, not unnaturally, denounced them in no uncertain terms. Thus Walpole was to George II a rogue and a rascal who had sold him out, Frederick considered his former followers to have behaved 'very dishonourably', 'disgracefully' and 'offensively', and Pitt to the future George III was 'the blackest of hearts' who should be made 'to smart for his ingratitude' in the new reign. But the less ambitious—the counterpart of the Court and Treasury Party—were content to settle for modest office under the Prince and do his bidding; and among the Country independents many showed a passing interest in Leicester House because successive heirs tended to adopt a Country policy in order to cultivate independent support. Thus in 1747 the Tories agreed to co-ordinate efforts with Frederick in the general election of that year, because he promised that when he came to the throne he would promote such measures as a Place Bill, non-discrimination in the appointment of justices of the peace and a reduced Civil List. But when the reigning monarch was old and ill the pull of Leicester House was at its greatest. Then the so-called 'reversionary interest' came into its own. Frederick made a scarcely-veiled reference to the future when, in attempting in 1744 to bully Lord Harrington into deserting the Pelhams, he remarked: 'My Lord, remember the King is 61, and I am 37.' By 1750 many ambitious men were coming to the conclusion that 'selling spot to buy futures' might not be a bad gamble. As Lord Hervey had remarked long before: 'anybody who could get no ready money would rather have a bad promissory note than nothing.' But Frederick's death halted the movement towards Leicester House, and the striking success of the Ministry during the Seven Years' War prevented the young Prince George from taking advantage of the reversionary interest between 1757 and the death of his grandfather. Nonetheless, Hardwicke put his finger on a fundamental requirement of political stability when in April 1757 he advised Newcastle: 'no solid plan of administration can be made . . . but such a one as may, if possible, unite the whole Royal Family and bring *the succession* to support and give quiet to *the possession*. Everything else will be perpetual conflict.'

In surveying the composition of the Commons and the nature of the parliamentary conflict little use has been made of the terms 'Whig' and 'Tory', yet it is scarcely enough merely to agree with Namier that 'they explain little but themselves require much explaining'. Every single member of the Commons between 1714 and 1760 adopted one or other of these labels, and we must assume that they had some reason for doing so. But this does not mean that the basic political conflict was, as it had been under Anne, between Whig and Tory; in so far as it transcended that between Court and Country, it was between Whig and Whig. At least so it was at Westminster. In the constituencies the old Whig-Tory rivalry survived much longer, even if it often did no more than confer a specious aura of principle upon traditional struggles between prominent local families. But in the central political arena 1715 had marked a fundamental turning-point. Before then Tory politicians were as common as Whig ones; the Court and Treasury Party had embraced men of either party, or indeed of both at the same time; and the ranks of the independents were similarly mixed, though Country Whigs were becoming increasingly difficult to find. But the involvement of a handful of the Tory leaders in the Jacobite Rebellion of 1715, confirming as it did the suspicion of George I that the Whigs alone could be trusted to preserve the new dynasty, meant that thereafter, with exceptions that could literally be counted upon the fingers of one hand, no Tory again held office. Hence the so-called Whig supremacy. With remarkable speed the Tories became confined to a collection of one hundred to one hundred and fifty Country back benchers, who appeared in every House of Commons of the early Hanoverian period, and who profoundly distrusted a succession of Opposition Whig front benchers whose leadership they fretfully followed. The principles with which, at one time or another, the Tories had been associated—support of the royal prerogative against the attempted encroachments of Parliament, of the Anglican Church against Protestant nonconformity, of the landed against the monied interest, of Stuart against Hanoverian dynasty, and of naval and colonial warfare against expensive military commitments in Europe—had all been overtaken by events. The royal prerogative, which was now rarely discussed, was supported by those who for the time being were beneficiaries under it, and criticized (if at all) by those out of favour; and the complete reversal of the earlier Tory attitude was best illustrated by their partial justification of their electoral alliance with the Prince of Wales on the ground that 'he offers such terms in future for securing the Liberty of the Subject, and for setting bounds to the Prerogative, as never were proposed by anyone related to the Crown'. After 1714 religion ceased to be a central issue of political debate, and even the repeal of the Occasional Conformity and Schism Acts and the developing practice of granting annual indemnity Acts to those who ignored the requirement for religious tests did not arouse the old Tory battle-cry of 'the Church in danger'. Similarly, the conflict between landed and monied interests subsided to such an extent that when Walpole, surely the epitome of Whiggery, introduced the Excise Bill which, among other things, proposed to extract more money from the supposedly Whig merchants in order to lower the land-tax on the supposedly Tory landed gentry, every Tory in the House of Commons opposed him. Differences of opinion over the conduct of war still continued, but the 'blue-water school' had long since become 'Country' rather than 'Tory'. Only loyalty to the Hanoverian dynasty continued to be argued by some as a badge of differentiation, and in the official *History of Parliament* Romney Sedgwick, as recently as 1970, committed himself to the view that the Tories 'were a predominantly Jacobite party, engaged in attempts to restore the Stuarts by a rising with foreign assistance'. It is difficult to accept this claim. After 1715 those Tories who still sought preferment avoided disqualification for office by quietly dropping their Tory identity and gradually infiltrating the amorphous body of Whigs. This was the route taken by the Finches, Foxes, Leveson-Gowers and scores of others, as the old Tory party lost its Court wing, and was thereby reduced to a host of Country back benchers. These retained their Tory identity as a gesture of defiance, to show that they cared not a fig for Hanoverian kings or Whig ministers; and they liked nothing better than to gather over dinner, toast the Pretender and thump on the table as they shouted *redeat*. But when the Pretender actually came over in 1745, no more than a handful of Tories in the then House of Commons showed any enthusiasm for his cause, and the reaction of the overwhelming majority is best indicated by the words in which Lord Egmont in 1750 described Thomas Rowney, member for Oxford:

> It is remarkable of this man, who is a rough clownish country gentleman, always reputed a rank Jacobite, and has drunk the Pretender's health 500 times, that when the Pretender's son came into England, he was frightened out of his wits, and ordered his chaplain to pray for King George, which he had never suffered him to do in his life before.

In essence then, the Tories of early Hanoverian England were those who had Tory ancestors and who continued to behave as Country members, opposed in general to the measures of the Court; in terms of policy they were indistinguishable from genuine Country Whigs. Although generations of politically active men continued to describe themselves as 'good Whigs', they could be virulent opponents of Government as well as staunch supporters, and it is difficult to find any common bond between them other than the fact that they rejected the title of 'Tory'. In so far as any body apart from the Tories was conscious of a corporate sense of identity it was the Old Corps of Whigs—that large amalgam of prominent Whig political families, Court and Treasury Party and Court Independents who across the generations gave a general support to the Ministries of Walpole and Pelham. Their continued presence contributed as much to the stability of Administration as that of the Tories did to the ranks of the Opposition, but after the death of Pelham in 1754 they began to disintegrate, with results that were to be important in the new reign. The Tories, too, in the 1750s began to lose their sense of separate identity. The game of opposing every Administration was beginning to wear a little thin, especially to a rising generation to whom the conflicts of bygone days meant little, and the supposedly 'Country' war policy of the elder Pitt brought many of them round to support of the Ministry. The old order was clearly changing before George III came to the throne.

It is now possible to see in rather clearer perspective the political conflicts of the times, and the role in those conflicts of both King and Commons. The King appointed his ministers, who in turn sought to achieve a permanent working majority in the Commons. So strong was royal influence in the Upper House that ministers had few worries there, and only once—during the Excise Bill crisis—did a Government have to bow momentarily to defeat. In the Commons, too, patronage provided a substantial nucleus of support, and sufficient independent backing was normally available to ensure survival. For lasting political stability a 'Minister for the King in the House of Commons' was necessary and, as an added guarantee, it was advisable for St James's to come to terms with Leicester House. When a Ministry was overturned in the Commons rather than dismissed by the King, this was achieved in the following manner. The Opposition leaders, who had always to espouse a Country policy to command any significant support, found an issue that so stirred independent opinion that a massive swing away from the Government occurred at that level. It might be the Excise Bill of 1733, but the best issue was a mismanaged war—as in 1739-42. When, as a result of independent defections, the Administration's majority dropped to about twenty, a new force came into play. Although the great majority of the Court and Treasury Party stood firm, and a few even took their courage in both hands and tried to anticipate their royal master by linking forces with the Opposition, a significant number sought safety in abstaining. They invented any excuse to absent themselves from the Commons until the issue was decided. Thus at the time of the Excise Bill Lord Hervey could lament to the Queen that

> a great many in the King's service . . . have taken the quiet part of lying by till things are ripe for a revolution in the ministry, at which juncture it is expected they will break forth and show themselves not less inveterate enemies to Sir Robert Walpole than the others, though they have had a little more caution in appearing so.

In 1742 Lord Hartington similarly deplored the 'parcel of such shabby fellows who will not attend'. These abstentions, if left unchecked, could finally deprive the Ministry of its majority. In 1733 Walpole avoided defeat by dropping the offensive measure; in 1742 only his resignation could reverse the tide.

These were the conditions under which the first two Georges endeavoured to remain effective heads of the executive, and maintain their freedom of choice with regard to the appointment and dismissal of ministers. In view of the striking contrast that is generally portrayed between their activities and that of George III, it is necessary to emphasize the degree of success they enjoyed and to place their undoubted failures in clear perspective. George I admittedly remains a somewhat elusive figure, but the absence of any significant correspondence from him or his son (in contrast to George III) should not delude us into believing that they were mere constitutional figureheads; and for George II there is much alternative evidence of the very active role which he played. The approval of both monarchs was required in all questions of patronage, and the army was a particularly sensitive area. Old Horace Walpole remarked that his brother, Sir Robert, was constantly told by the King that he knew nothing of military matters, and that he was frequently blamed by disappointed aspirants for promotion when he was powerless to advance their interests; and Pelham similarly admitted that he and Newcastle 'did not meddle in the army', which was strictly the province of the King and the Duke of Cumberland. George II was equally adamant about the granting of peerages, and even so brilliant a lawyer and devoted a supporter of Government as William Murray had the greatest difficulty in gaining a peerage on his elevation in 1756 to the Chief Justiceship of the King's Bench. The right to appoint to the Order of the Garter was also jealously preserved by the King, and despite the strenuous support of both Newcastle and Pitt, Lord Temple had almost to prostrate himself before George II in order to gain the coveted ribbon in 1759. In ecclesiastical affairs, too, the King frequently rejected the advice of Newcastle who, after 1737, liked to think of himself as the 'ecclesiastical minister'; and when a general election came around every last detail was submitted to the monarch for consideration and comment. Daily audiences in the Closet were thus far from mere formalities and, when political rivalries ran high, individual ministers were subjected to severe royal abuse. When Pelham and Newcastle were fighting against Granville for political survival in 1744–6, every day produced 'some new disagreeable incident in the Closet', and Newcastle sorrowfully reported the King's language as '*incapacity* to my brother, spectator of other people's policy and measures, and yesterday pitiful fellows'. Of course, however much the King might bluster, he was sometimes forced by political circumstances to yield. Then all he could do was protest that 'Ministers are the Kings in this country', that 'he did not look upon himself as King whilst he was in the hands of these scoundrels', and that he was weary of being teased about 'that d—d House of Commons'. Yet did he really fare so badly?

There was one area in which the influence of both Georges was normally decisive, and that was the fundamental one of foreign affairs. Here the interests of Hanover usually prevailed, even if they were by no means as irreconcilable with those of Britain as successive Opposition leaders claimed. George I and his Hanoverian advisers largely decided foreign policy during the last years of the Northern War, and his son during the War of the Austrian Succession repeatedly flouted the advice of most of his ministers. He frustrated Walpole's attempt in 1740 to detach Frederick of Prussia from France, in the following year unilaterally signed a treaty for the neutrality of Hanover, and in 1742 and 1743 refused to allow British troops to assume the offensive in Germany because he feared that Frederick the Great would respond by carrying out his threat to invade the Electorate. He further hamstrung the allied war effort by refusing to bring pressure to bear upon the Dutch in case in return they should demand that Hanover engage in the war as a principal instead of merely supplying mercenaries. Little wonder that the annual vote of supply in the Commons for the upkeep of the Hanoverian troops threw ministers into a panic, especially since George II in the field showed blatant partiality towards his German officers and openly snubbed their British counterparts. Even as late as the opening months of the Seven Years' War George II was still intriguing behind the backs of his ministers in order to extricate Hanover from the conflict, though military events soon forced him to change his attitude.

Over policy no less than patronage the first two Georges therefore kept tight control; over the appointment and dismissal of ministers their record was—at least *prima facie*—less impressive. Here the performance of George II in particular is often said to have indicated a serious decline in royal power. He failed to save Walpole in 1742 and Granville in 1744; he suffered severe defeat when in February 1746 he endeavoured to replace the Pelhams by a Ministry based upon Granville and Bath; and in 1756 and again in 1757 he had the elder Pitt forced upon him. This indeed appears to give some credence to the notion of 'a King in toils' so assiduously cultivated by Leicester House and widely accepted by historians. Yet, as we shall see, between 1760 and 1784 George III fared little better during years that are generally assumed to have seen an increase of monarchical power. The reasons for the failures of George II are clear and, for the most part, central to the nature of the eighteenth-century constitution. If political harmony and stability were to be preserved, a chief minister in the Commons was essential and Leicester House had to be weaned from Opposition. Walpole's loss of the confidence of the Commons was primarily responsible for his fall in 1742; the absence of a leader there who had the King's confidence led to the ousting of Granville in 1744 and to the success of Pitt in 1756 and 1757. Leicester House also played a crucial role both in the defeat of Walpole and the elevation of

Pitt. George III was later to be no more able than his predecessors to ignore the basic facts of political life. The fiasco of 1746 is more complicated, though again George II's refusal to give his confidence to Pelham, who by then had won undisputed control over the Commons, provided the setting for the debacle. Granville, since his enforced dismissal at the end of 1744, had remained 'minister behind the curtain', and it was universally known that his advice was followed in preference to that of the combined Cabinet—whether it be over war policy or the need for effective measures to put down the Jacobite rebellion. Ministers were thus being held responsible in Parliament for a policy in the formulation of which they had virtually no part, and only the emergency of the rebellion deterred them from resignation. In the end it was not their collective action that provoked the crisis, but a clear invitation from the King to Granville and Bath to form an alternative Ministry. Only then did Pelham, Newcastle, Hardwicke and Harrington hand in their joint resignations, though so intolerable had the situation become that a host of other office-holders hastened to follow suit. No adequate support could be found for the King's new ministers, and within days he had to return cap-in-hand to the Pelhams, who not unnaturally insisted upon the exclusion of Granville and Bath from royal confidence as the price of their return. George II never had the faintest chance of success. The fall of Walpole had made abundantly clear that an unacceptable minister could not be maintained by the King alone. By 1746 Granville and Bath had become the two most notoriously unpopular politicians of the century—*personae non gratae* to the Old Corps because they had been instrumental in ousting Walpole, and equally so to the Opposition because they had immediately sneaked into power and deserted their former colleagues. The greatest political genius in the world could not have formed a stable Ministry around these two men—and George II was no political genius. Had he sought merely to oust Pelham, Newcastle and a few others, he might well have succeeded. But it was his own fatal error of judgment rather than the strength of the politicians that ensured his defeat. The day of royal favourites was long since over.

If George II's failures are for the most part attributable to the nature of the contemporary constitution, it must be admitted that both he and George I voluntarily limited their own freedom of action. Both came to feel that in the last analysis any Ministry must rest upon the solid basis of the Old Corps of Whigs; both were unwilling to negotiate with the Tories, though since these soon ceased to be ministerial material, this did not restrict their choice as much as might at first sight appear; and both were singularly reluctant to treat with anyone who had been associated with the despised heirs apparent. This did not leave much room for manoeuvre, and of course greatly strengthened the hands of successive leaders of the Old Corps. Yet the correspondence of those leaders leaves no doubt that the monarch exercised real power. Hardwicke remarked in 1740 that the King 'was a kind of centre of unity; at least his final opinion concluded everybody else'; and in 1754 he told Pitt 'that there are certain things which ministers cannot do directly; and that, in political arrangements, prudence often dictates to submit to the *minus malum* and to leave it to time and incidents, and perhaps to ill-judging opposers, to help forward the rest'. But the last word must be left to the most politically adroit of George II's ministers. In 1743 Walpole wrote thus to his friend and political pupil, Henry Pelham:

> The King must, with tenderness and management, be shewn what he may with reason depend upon, and what he will be deceived and lost if he places any confidence and reliance in . . . This leads me to the most delicate part of the whole; I mean your behaviour, and your manner of treating this subject with him. It is a great misfortune that you have not time; for time and address have often carried things, that met at first onset, with great reluctance . . . Address and Management are the weapons you must fight and defend with; plain truths will not be relished at first, in opposition to prejudices, conceived and infused in favour of his own partialities; and you must dress up all you offer, with the appearance of no other view or tendency, but to promote his service in his own way, to the utmost of your power.

This is scarcely the picture of 'a King in toils'.

If the pattern of politics in early Hanoverian England emerges with reasonable clarity, it must not be forgotten that in the life of the ordinary citizen the central government played relatively little part; and that except at election times—and then only in a limited sense—the stuff of national politics was little discussed in the constituencies. Here of course there is a striking contrast with previous reigns when the political battle had raged as bitterly in almost every corner of England as it had at Westminster. But in the years after 1714 political passions quickly subsided; septennial Parliaments encouraged the spread of patronage, reduced the number of elections and helped to deprive them of political significance; and the electorate as a whole became narrower and less volatile. As Professor Plumb so brilliantly demonstrated in his Ford Lectures,[1] the growth of political stability in England owed as much to the changing climate of opinion in the constituencies and to the entrenchment of oligarchic interests in them as it did to the growing influence of the

---

[1] *The Growth of Political Stability in England 1675–1725* (1967).

executive over the legislature; and both reflected the increasing sense of identity among the governing classes. But not everyone would agree with Professor Plumb's conclusion that the rage of party was thereby merely replaced by the pursuit of place, or that patronage created 'an almost impregnable citadel, impervious to defeat, indifferent to social change'. Genuine differences of opinion still continued to exist, and the 'honest and disinterested' part of the House of Commons, to which David Hume paid tribute, was still a real force in politics. Yet much of the tension admittedly went out of political life at both national and local levels, and it became ever more obvious that the function of the central Government was confined to maintaining law and order, conducting foreign policy (and, if need be, war), and implementing the minimum of economic control consistent with the maintenance of national prosperity. As little government as possible was not an index of oligarchic ignorance or indifference, but in accord with the most articulate 'Country' opinion of the time; it represented the ideals not only of Walpole and what has misleadingly been called his 'single party' Government, but also those of his most vigorous Tory opponents. It is therefore not surprising that it was only at the local level that the ordinary individual was likely to be subject to much real authority.

The chief organs of local government had largely freed themselves from central control in the course of the previous century, and were therefore theoretically able to respond in many different ways to the new challenges of social and economic change. But the men who held power in the localities tended to become self-perpetuating oligarchies, and their social homogeneity ensured a certain similarity of approach to problems that by 1800 were to become too vast for them to handle effectively. Before 1760, however, most local government officials showed some capacity for adapting to the new situation caused by agricultural change and increasing industrialization, even though shifts in population frequently placed the burden on areas that were least equipped to cope with them. The basic unit remained the ecclesiastical parish, where the chief duties continued to devolve upon the churchwarden, the overseer of the poor, the surveyor of the highways and the petty constable. Under the supervision of the local justices, who appointed all of them but the churchwarden, these unpaid officials and their subordinates were responsible for regulating the life of the village in accordance with established law and custom.

Within each county the dominant figure was the Lord-Lieutenant, who was appointed by the King and was normally a local magnate. But except in so far as he commanded the county militia, and therefore assumed significance in time of war or rebellion, his chief duty was to appoint the justices of the peace, who still formed the real cornerstone of local government. In quarter sessions the justices tried a wide variety of criminal cases, and gave the lie to Montesquieu's 'separation of the powers' by wielding substantial executive authority in supervising roads, bridges, gaols, houses of correction, and—to a diminishing extent—wages and prices. In petty sessions lesser offenders were tried and similar administrative duties carried out; and even a single justice could exercise significant judicial and executive authority. Despite the notoriety attaching to the 'trading justices' of Middlesex, most JPs behaved fairly and conscientiously, showing a keen appreciation of the need for more complex machinery and making increasing use of contracting, salaried experts and special committees to examine new problems.

Outside the jurisdiction of the county officials lay some two hundred municipal boroughs, whose chief officers were *ex officio* justices, and who by royal charter or prescriptive right had acquired control of their own affairs. The normal form of government was by mayor, aldermen and common councilmen, usually but not invariably chosen by the freemen of the borough. In practice the boroughs showed the same tendency towards oligarchy that prevailed in the counties, though again the general outlook was often innovative and progressive. Only London perhaps could really boast a governmental structure that was in any sense democratic, though between 1725 and 1746 effective power rested in the Court of Aldermen, and the Court of Common Council was subject to its veto. But in 1746 Pelham removed the aldermanic veto, and thereafter the aldermen tended to concentrate on their judicial duties and the Common Council increasingly to exercise the real executive power. Since the aldermen represented the great monied interest in the City, and the common councilmen the 'middling and lesser' citizens, their political conflict was reflected at the national level. The monied interest was closely connected to the Government, while the smaller merchants tended to adopt a Tory, and later radical, point of view. Both Pelham and Pitt took great pains to woo the City, and during the 1760s it was to achieve a prominence in national politics that had eluded it in the earlier half of the century.

At the local level, then, the individual came face to face with the law and was forced to accept a share of the responsibility for maintaining tolerable standards in community life. The almost universal and deep-seated distrust of the central Government meant an increasing burden of duties for local authorities, especially with growing urbanization and a rapidly developing transport system. Turnpike trusts were created in ever greater numbers, and *ad hoc* commissions were established by Parliament to provide services such as paving and lighting. If at the national level a system of Government that had threatened anarchy under William and Anne was successfully modified to produce a surprising degree of political stability, it was no less an achievement that the antiquated structure of local government managed with remarkable resilience to adapt itself to changes that might well have induced chronic disorder and widespread misery. Oligarchy bred neither indifference nor stagnation.

6

ECONOMIC AND SOCIAL DEVELOPMENT

UNTIL comparatively recently, the social and economic developments of the first half of the eighteenth century attracted relatively little attention, largely because they seemed dwarfed in importance after 1760 by what have been traditionally, and perhaps misleadingly, called the Agricultural and Industrial Revolutions. But scholars of the past two decades—economists no less than historians—have increasingly stressed the continuity of social and economic change and, in their search for the underlying causes of the twin 'revolutions', have both set them in clearer perspective and shed much additional light on early Hanoverian England. Yet if our knowledge has thereby been enlarged, recent research has raised as many problems as it has solved. A bewildering array of statistical information—much of it incomplete, inaccurate and capable of yielding contradictory conclusions—has facilitated the questioning of old assumptions rather than the postulation of new ones. Furthermore, the increasing obsession with English industrialization as a 'case study' (which might be made to yield a magic formula for economic growth in the contemporary underdeveloped world) can be as present-minded and selective in its choice of evidence as was Whig preoccupation with parliamentary government in the field of politics. Any attempt, in the light of present knowledge, to assess the changes in social and economic life under the first two Georges must of necessity be tentative; one must also beware the wisdom of hindsight.

In so far as over-all economic growth in the period can be measured, it seems likely that the first thirty years saw no more than 0·3 per cent per annum expansion in total output, but that after 1745 there was a sharp acceleration to an annual growth rate of about 1 per cent—not high, perhaps, but respectable enough for a pre-industrial society. This growth owed much to developments during the half century before 1714, when England solved most of her remaining political and constitutional problems, emerged as a major European power, and devoted her attention increasingly to economic advancement and colonial expansion. By the time of the accession of the Hanoverians she had long since outstripped the Dutch, and in the process borrowed much from her former rivals in the realms of commerce, technology, finance and agriculture. Shipping and trade had expanded under the dual umbrella of protective legislation and naval power, increased production of food had largely overcome the recurrent scarcity of Tudor and early Stuart times, scientific curiosity was provoking interest in manufactures and technology, and the facilities for both public and private credit were more sophisticated. England was fast becoming an entrepôt and, although London was still dominant, the western ports were beginning to emerge, feeding on a growing colonial trade that was reflected in increased imports, home consumption and re-exports, but had scarcely as yet begun to challenge the export trade in woollen cloth that for over two centuries had been the crucial index of England's economic prosperity. All this provided a sound basis on which the abundant intelligence and enterprise of eighteenth-century Englishmen could and did build; and the creation in 1754 of the Society for the Encouragement of Arts, Manufactures and Commerce recognized the accomplishments of the first two generations and looked forward to a still brighter future.

The economic achievements of the early eighteenth century were indeed a triumph of private enterprise rather than of conscious government policy, though such mercantilist regulation as existed (notwithstanding the strictures of subsequent advocates of free trade and *laissez-faire*) probably aided development rather than hindered it. The landed interest enjoyed the protection of the Corn Laws against imports unless the price of corn was unduly high, and the encouragement of export bounties when it was low; the Acts of Trade and Navigation stimulated commerce, manufacturing and shipping; and an increasingly aggressive foreign policy showed growing awareness of the importance of new markets and new sources of raw materials. A reasonably equitable and, for the age, well administered system of taxation hampered neither trade nor industry, and although in time of war it could bear heavily on the poorer classes and (through the land-tax) on the lesser gentry, was not really socially divisive. Economic regulation no longer aimed primarily at the preservation of a hierarchical social order but at the encouragement of productivity, and such matters as manufacturing standards and wage rates were increasingly left to the free play of market forces. The Government attempted not so much to direct the economy as to create the conditions under which individual enterprise might flourish, untrammelled by the guild restrictions, internal tolls and legal barriers between classes that thwarted the economic progress of so many contemporary European nations. Only the Netherlands could boast as favourable a climate for expansion, and they were already past their zenith.

Among the most stable elements in the early Hanoverian economy were population, prices and wages. Though all statistics of population before the first census in 1801 represent varying degrees of intelligent guess-work, and some recent scholars have suggested that they may seriously underestimate numbers at the beginning of the eighteenth century, the balance of opinion still inclines towards a figure of some six million for England and Wales in 1715, remaining virtually static or even declining for the next three decades and then rising by perhaps half a million between 1745 and 1760. Most of this modest increase appears to have been concentrated in the counties in which there was growing industrial activity (Lancashire, Warwickshire, Staffordshire and the West Riding of Yorkshire), and to have been due to a rising birth-rate, coupled possibly with a declining death-rate after about 1740. In the south and east there was little change, largely because of a continuing high death-rate, with infant mortality possibly as high as 50 per cent in London. These decades saw the height of the gin mania, but there must have been some improvement with the tightening of the licensing laws in 1751, and over the country as a whole cheaper and more plentiful food gradually exercised a beneficial effect. In general, population was being drawn, mostly by local migration, to the western ports and the inland towns which supplied them with manufactured goods. In 1715 London had perhaps 500,000 inhabitants, Edinburgh 35,000, and only Bristol and Norwich more than 20,000; by 1763 Bristol had risen to 100,000, Liverpool (already the chief slaving port), Sheffield, Manchester and Birmingham had between 30,000 and 50,000, and Whitehaven and Glasgow were growing fast. Urbanization was well under way.

Although the best available cost-of-living index is severely limited by its being based on contract prices and confined to London and southern England, the picture it presents is in keeping with contemporary comment. Apart from a brief rise in the late 1720s, counterbalanced by a fall in the early 1730s, these prices remained remarkably constant and below the 1700 level until the mid-fifties, when they rose sharply. It is impossible to tell whether a similar pattern prevailed in the north, or whether—as in the cases of population and wages—the pattern was different. Certainly northern wage-earners fared better than their southern counterparts, the index for both money wages and real wages in Lancashire rising sharply in the early 1720s and early 1730s, and then remaining steady till the mid-fifties when, because of rising prices, there was a marked decline in real wages. London wages showed less variation, failing to advance significantly in the early decades, though stabilizing after 1735 at a slightly higher rate than in 1714, until the same sharp fall was experienced in the mid-1750s. Wage-earners in the north from 1730 to 1755 appear to have been about 30 per cent better off than they had been in 1714, those in London only some 10 per cent. The relevant indices apply largely to agriculture and the building trade, but it seems reasonable to assume that at least similar gains were made by those engaged in industry. Certainly low prices (especially for bread) and steady or rising wages, brought a higher standard of living to the labouring classes, at least until about 1755.

Any or all of the chief sectors of the economy could be temporarily shaken by short-term fluctuations. The bad harvests of 1727, 1728, 1740, 1751 and 1756 hit the farming community and (through high corn prices) the poorer sections of society, while the prolonged cattle plague of the late forties and early fifties severely affected the fortunes of the graziers and produced a serious shortage of animal foods, especially since sheep were at the same time decimated by three successive bitter winters. Apart from weather and disease, passing crises (whether political as in the cases of the two Jacobite rebellions or financial as with the bursting of the South Sea Bubble) could briefly damage confidence and put a damper on economic enterprise. But by far the most significant short-term fluctuations were caused by war. Whether the over-all effects of war upon the economy were beneficial or retrogade has long been debated. On the credit side lay the acquisition of new markets and new sources of raw materials, the boost in naval construction, the high level of employment arising from increased government expenditure, the encouragement of the metallurgical and clothing industries (at least for those who benefited from government contracts), the removal of foreign competition for other industries such as silk and linen, and even a limited stimulus to invention in relevant fields, of which Wilkinson's device for boring cannon is the most commonly quoted example. But against these had to be balanced the general distortion of the peace-time economy (especially the decline in housing and transport improvements), the interference with foreign trade, the depreciation of the currency and the strain on the balance of payments. While there may be no safe generalization, it seems evident that the brief conflicts with Spain in 1718-20 and 1726-28 damaged trade more than they benefited any other sector; that the prolonged war of 1739-48 was at least initially prejudicial; but that the Seven Years' War, with Pitt's increased emphasis on commercial and colonial considerations, was both less disruptive and more rewarding. Though the settlement of 1763, by conceding Guadeloupe and fishing rights off Newfoundland, created some doubts about the economic profitability of the war, the balance of opinion still inclined towards the view that British prosperity had to be won at the expense of France, whose potential seemed inherently greater, and whose advance in America and India must be permanently halted. The cost of withstanding France could already be measured by the staggering increase of the national debt, which the wars of William's and Anne's reigns had already raised to £36,000,000 by 1714, and which increased to £76,000,000 by 1748 and to £132,000,000 by 1763. Rather more than 70 per cent of the cost of each major war was met by borrowing and the remainder chiefly by increases in the land-tax and the excise. Land and assessed taxes supplied some 25–30 per cent of war-time taxation, customs 20–25 per cent, and the excise as much as 40–45 per cent. It is difficult to assess the impact of rising indebtedness and taxation upon the national economy. Until direct borrowing from the public became common from the 1740s onwards, the chief beneficiaries were the three great corporations,[1] and thereafter there was some strength in the argument that the poorer classes were bearing an undue burden of taxation in order to pay interest to an increasing number of fund-holders. As investment in the funds became increasingly popular, it seems likely that capital was diverted from trade and industry, and the high land-tax certainly impeded agricultural development. The impression remained, however, that England's bellicose search for 'profit and power' may have been more of a stimulus to economic growth than the pacifism that Sir Robert Walpole so strongly believed to be an essential pillar of English prosperity. It can scarcely be mere coincidence that total output increased most markedly in the last fifteen years of George II's reign, half of which were spent in major conflict with France.

In 1760 as in 1714 English society was still overwhelmingly rural, some 75 per cent of the population being involved primarily in agriculture, although at the upper levels many had additional interests in commerce and manufacturing, and at the lower an increasing number augmented their meagre incomes by participation in domestic industry. Socially, the natural division was into peerage, gentry, freeholders, tenant farmers, and cottagers and labourers; economically it makes more sense to divide the first three groups into landlords (who comprised the peerage and most of the gentry) and owner-occupiers (freeholders and lesser gentry), at the same time distinguishing between the greater landlords with incomes of £3,000 or more a year, and the lesser who comprised the main body of the gentry. But many owner-occupiers rented some land, some of the lesser

---

[1] See p 34.

gentry had fallen behind the wealthier freeholders, and the more prosperous tenant farmers had overtaken the smaller freeholders.

At first sight it would appear that all these groups—except perhaps the labourers—declined in prosperity during the early Hanoverian period. Corn prices remained lower than they had been in the decade before 1714 and, except during the late twenties and late fifties, significantly so. Meat prices fared marginally better, but the overall picture is one of agricultural depression, reaching its nadir between 1730 and 1750. Landlords were faced with falling rents and accumulating arrears, owner-occupiers and tenants with declining incomes. Bankruptcies were common, and many of the smaller men were forced to sell their holdings before conditions began to improve in the 1750s. Those primarily concerned with dairy produce fared better than those dependent on arable farming, but even here cattle disease, severe winters and war taxation took their toll. Yet the period 1714–60 saw surprisingly little agricultural stagnation, change and improvement were evident in many areas, total output increased by about 10 per cent, the export of corn more than doubled, and there appears to have been a net increase in agricultural investment. During these years all the features of the so-called Agricultural Revolution were in evidence, though the stimulus came not from rising demand and higher profits, but from a determination to survive in the face of adversity. This meant greater diversification, more specialization, improved husbandry and better organization, as well as a decided move towards larger estates and a further extension of the landlord-tenant system at the expense of the small freeholder. The impact of science and technology was negligible until the nineteenth century.

Local variations were of prime importance, depending partly on the topography and nature of the soil, partly on the proximity of developing urban centres. The highland zone, traditionally the rearing country for cattle and sheep, saw little change, but it was quite otherwise in the lowlands. Here the ill-drained clay vales and heavy loams, characteristic of much of the Midlands, alternated with the free-draining soils of the chalk and limestone uplands (for example, the Cotswolds and the Wessex uplands), the lighter loams, and the more fertile sands, especially in East Anglia. The heavy lands had long been the chief granaries of the nation, but despite various experiments with drainage and the spread of floating water-meadows, most of them proved unsuitable for the introduction of new crops (especially roots) and were increasingly converted to pasture. Their inhabitants looked to dairying and fattening to improve their fortunes, and were able to benefit from the ever greater expansion of domestic industry such as hosiery, lace and leather work, and nail-making.

But it was the lighter soils that were the real centre of agricultural advance. Traditionally, because of their relative infertility, they had been devoted to pastoral farming, but from the late seventeenth century onwards the introduction of convertible husbandry (most often the Norfolk system of crop rotation, involving turnips, barley or oats, clover or rye, and wheat) made them ideally suited to mixed farming. The alternate use of fodder and corn crops removed the necessity for fallowing, the sowing of legumes such as clover, sainfoin or lucerne added to soil fertility through nitrogen fixing, and better fodder enabled the land to carry additional stock, thereby enriching the soil with more manure, and raising the total crop yield. Agricultural prosperity was therefore moving from the heavier lands to the lighter ones of the south and east, while industry was becoming more important in the Midlands and the north. As communications improved, the north and south were tending to become complementary markets.

Long before 1714 there had been a degree of specialization in agriculture, with the environs of London—and to a lesser extent Norwich and Bristol—providing a variety of food for the urban population and fodder for their animals. The growth of urbanization merely increased this tendency. Subsistence farming had almost ceased, and even a modest holding of a dozen acres was likely to produce a surplus for marketing. Gloucestershire and Wiltshire were plentiful sources of cheese and bacon, East Anglia of turkeys and geese; Kent and Worcestershire had their hop fields and orchards, the West Country its cider. All this helped to cushion the impact of falling prices, but improved husbandry, and to a lesser extent better organization, provided the most potent weapons in the struggle for survival. Here the traditionally great figures have lost something of their former lustre. Jethro Tull's fanatical enthusiasm for tillage may have been infectious, but his much-lauded invention of the seed-drill drew upon earlier experience and had little practical effect before the nineteenth century. 'Turnip' Townshend, with his passion for manures, mortgages and long leases, merely popularized methods in use in both Holland and England in the previous century, and on balance his earlier political career may have established a better claim to fame than his later agricultural one. Even Robert Bakewell, whose celebrated experiments in breeding were far from unique, met with only limited success. He deserves credit for his part in developing the modern shire horse, but neither his New Leicesters nor his New Longhorns were prolific breeders, both ran too easily to fat, and the fleeces of the former and milk of the latter were far from perfect. Perhaps the main contribution of these three enthusiasts was their great capacity for popularizing trends which had long been apparent. They epitomized the bustle, energy and enterprise of early eighteenth-century agriculture.

Of organizational changes the most obvious was the sharp increase in enclosures, although the most dramatic acceleration did not to come till the closing decades of the century. An average of only some thirteen hundred acres a year was enclosed by Act under George I; under his son more than nine thousand. How much more was enclosed by private agreement, often enrolled in Chancery, may never be known, but it seems likely that it substantially exceeded the amount approved by parliamentary authority. Most of it was concentrated in the Midlands and in the central southern counties, where perhaps half the arable land was still in the form of open fields. If the latter were not always as resistant to change as has sometimes been claimed, their increasing disappearance certainly saw a marked improvement in efficiency and productivity. Farms became more compact, a better balance was achieved between arable and pasture, exhausted land was revived, areas of common and waste were brought under cultivation, better care of animals was ensured, and a certain amount of ley-farming was introduced on the better drained soils. The mere fact that a doubling of the rental value was the normal corollary of enclosure testified to its economic desirability, but inevitably it sometimes squeezed the smaller farmer out of business and deprived the cottager of at least some of his former rights. Yet it is easy to exaggerate. Some small freeholders consolidated and even extended their holdings, some could meet the costs (which varied greatly but averaged about twenty-eight shillings an acre) by selling a little land or mortgaging their whole properties, some were anyway absentee owners who seized the favourable opportunity to sell. While enclosure accelerated the existing tendency towards larger farming units, this was often achieved merely by increasing the area under cultivation, and there is little evidence that small farmers were generally opposed to enclosure, even it if meant a change to tenant status. The cottager fared rather worse, though the rights to common and waste which he had hitherto enjoyed were frequently of little practical value, and in many cases he retained a tiny plot of land even if his rights had been customary rather than legally secured. Since enclosure, with its consequent need for reclamation, fencing and hedging, required more rather than less labour, it did not generally induce poverty among agricultural labourers until the population began to rise at a greater rate than could be absorbed.

In general, then, the trend was towards larger farms and the spread of tenant farming. It is easy to sentimentalize about the decline of the small freeholder, but his lot had become increasingly hard, and in an era of low prices may well have improved if he sold his land and used the proceeds to stock a new holding as tenant and adopt improved methods. Ownership could be a positive burden, and many tenants were significantly better off than freeholders or even small squires. A long lease was obviously an advantage, though the demand for efficient tenants normally ensured a high degree of security for good farmers, even those dependent on annual agreements. Long leases were anyway mostly confined to larger farms, and since most of them did not prescribe specific modes of farming, it may be doubted whether they were as much the instruments of improvement as was once believed. By and large the landlords assumed a tolerably benevolent role, if only because of self-interest. In times of hardship they frequently reduced rents, allowed arrears temporarily to accumulate, paid for new buildings, financed improvements, and assumed responsibility for the land-tax which in more prosperous days was handed on to their tenants. On the whole, the spread of the landlord-tenant relationship helped to increase output and buttressed agriculture against the worst effects of a long period of low prices.

Aided by low interest rates and the development of the long-term mortgage, agriculture thus faced up to its problems and, by the mid-fifties, emerged from two decades of relative depression with a sounder structure and significantly improved techniques. Virtually all facets of change had their origins in the previous century, but adversity had much hastened the pace of improvement. Rising real incomes led to capital accumulation by many of the larger landlords, some of whom developed mineral resources on their lands, while others invested in transport and urban housing; and to increased demand, not only for food, but also for a limited range of manufactured goods, among the lower orders of agricultural society. In a period when the European market for English manufactures was sluggish, grain exports helped to maintain a favourable balance of payments. All in all, agriculture provided a useful underpinning for an economy which, until at least the middle forties, needed all the stimulus it could get.

As with agriculture, advances in overseas trade during the early Hanoverian period owed much to the developments of the previous half-century, which had seen the passage of the basic mercantilist legislation, improved ship design and construction, the extension of naval power and the establishment of superiority over the Dutch. While the export trade to Europe was still dominated by woollen and worsted goods, the British possessions in the New World had begun to emerge as a small but significant market for other manufactures, and re-exports of produce from there and from India had already assumed an important role. New export industries such as silk and linen were still in their infancy, as were new techniques in textiles and metals. The Treaty of Utrecht had provided an entry to Spanish American commerce and extended the activities of the slave-traders. The breach in the privileges of the great chartered companies (the Eastland and Royal African Companies had lost their monopolies before 1714, and in 1708 the old East India Company had been forced to amalgamate with the new) indicated a move towards the freer trade which had always prevailed between Britain and her American possessions. More so even than in agriculture the way was open to the enterprising.

Naturally enough, the expansion of commerce between 1714 and 1760 reflected and developed these earlier trends. Shipping, though not maintaining the spectacular acceleration of the seventeenth century, probably increased in tonnage by about 30 per cent; domestic exports rose by more than 80 per cent (£4·8 to £8·9 million), re-exports by almost 50 per cent (£2·4 to £3·6 million), and imports by 40 per cent (£6·2 to £8·8 million). But this general picture of a 60 per cent increase in the total value of overseas trade concealed many variations in the fortunes of each branch. During the first two decades imports and re-exports expanded most rapidly, with little significant rise in exports before the mid-thirties. In the early forties imports, after a few stagnant years, slumped badly, but the upward movement was resumed and intensified after 1745. Exports, apart from brief dips during the War of the Austrian Succession and in the early fifties, moved strongly ahead, and generally speaking the years after 1745 saw rapid advances in all but re-exports. Throughout the period overseas commerce showed an increasingly favourable balance, except for a lean period in the twenties, and the over-all volume of trade a steady increase of about 15 per cent per decade except for a brief recession during the opening years of the Austrian war. Finally, re-exports fared better than the export of British manufactures until about 1745, after which their fortunes were reversed. Every branch of trade thus had its sluggish period, but the over-all growth, in spite of the interruptions of two major and two minor wars, testified to an essentially healthy and flexible economy.

Perhaps even more significant than the general increase were the changes in the character and geographical distribution of British exports. Woollen and worsted yarn and manufactures continued to dominate, and in the last decade their value was 50 per cent higher than it had been in the first. But their proportion of total domestic exports dropped from about 75 per cent to 60 per cent, and other infant industries showed a much greater potential. Iron and steel exports increased four-fold and non-ferrous metals and manufactures doubled. Equally impressive were the new textiles, silk yarn and manufactures more than doubling, cotton increasing six-fold, and linen exports leaping to thirteen times their earlier value. As yet, of course, none of these could in absolute terms begin to compete with wool, of which the annual export value in the fifties was nearly £5·5 million. The combined metal industries during the same decade contributed less than £900,000, linen just over £300,000, silk nearly £200,000 and cotton only £100,000. Nonetheless the changes were striking evidence of diversification and innovation in British industry, and of the capacity of changing markets to absorb new products.

Naturally enough, Europe continued as Britain's leading market for both domestic exports and re-exports, but her intake increased by only 25 per cent (from £5·6 to £7·5 million) between the first and last decades of the period, while her share of the total export market dropped from 77 per cent to 60 per cent. Infant competitors showed a much greater propensity for increase. Exports to Africa nearly doubled, those to Asia rose almost nine-fold, and those to British North America and the West Indies increased by almost 250 per cent. It was the American market, especially the thirteen colonies, which had the most significant record, its share of the total market doubling from 10 per cent (or £730,000) to 20 per cent (or £2·5 million), and the growing colonial societies showing an increasing eagerness for a diversity of small manufactured goods, such as axes, nails, firearms, buckets, saddles, handkerchiefs. By 1760 British overseas possessions and dependencies in America, Africa and India were probably absorbing 40 per cent of English domestic exports.

Similar trends were evident in the import field. In 1715–24 Europe had provided £3·39 million worth (or 53 per cent) of British imports; in the 1750s £3·87 million worth (or 43 per cent). While the value of imports from Europe had thus risen by only 12 per cent, those from British colonies in the New World had increased by 75 per cent—from £1·49 to £2·6 million, or from 24 per cent to 30 per cent of the total. By 1760 even Asia was providing goods to the value of more than a quarter of the intake from Europe, where Holland, which had been the single most important source of British imports in 1700, had declined to tenth position. These changes reflected above all a growing demand, in Europe no less than in England, for tea, coffee, sugar and tobacco, which together constituted a high proportion of colonial imports, although rice, pitch, tar and timber were rapidly assuming significant proportions. Considering the ever more vital role of the colonies in expanding British commerce, it is not surprising that the Government of the mother-country increasingly turned its attention to the enforcement of the protective laws on which that commerce depended, and the Seven Years' War merely intensified the problem. Finally, a further element in the 'colonial' trade should not be forgotten. The annual value of commerce with Ireland more than doubled in the early Hanoverian period, imports in the 1750s reaching more than £700,000 a year, exports more than £600,000 and re-exports almost £450,000.

The most obvious impact of these developments upon the English domestic scene was the stimulus provided to nascent industries, but equally important was the ending of London's overwhelming dominance and the development of the western ports (Bristol and Liverpool) and the inland towns which supplied them. The seventy-three ships which had entered Bristol from the New World in 1687 had doubled by 1760, while the twenty-one ships entering Liverpool had increased to almost two hundred. A significant part of their rising prosperity was based upon the inhuman traffic in slaves, the expansion of which may be illustrated by the fact that the two to three thousand tons of shipping leaving England for Africa in 1714 had risen to more than fifteen thousand tons by the early sixties. England's economic fortunes were increasingly bound up with her growing maritime and colonial strength, as was testified by the belligerence of her merchants in forcing war with Spain in 1739, and by the elder Pitt's emphasis on commercial and colonial aggression and his tendency to turn his back on Europe.

The available statistics for overseas trade, whatever their many limitations, support the broad trends of which contemporaries wrote and spoke, and enable a reasonably comprehensive picture to emerge. In the case of industrial output it is very different. Although the excise series give some indication of variations in the production of beer, spirits, soap, leather, tallow candles and starch, they obviously underestimate output—in some cases substantially—because of the widespread evasion of duty. With the more important textile and metal industries, imports of raw materials and exports of the finished products offer virtually the only guide, though occasionally local production figures are available. When the evidence is so meagre and fragmentary, generalization is both difficult and dangerous. It has been estimated that the output of the so-called home industries (essentially those of the excise series) increased by only 14 per cent between 1700 and 1760, while that of the export industries (primarily textiles and metals) more than doubled. Were this true, it would be necessary to accord the export boom, more particularly from the mid-forties onwards, a predominant role in stimulating subsequent industrial expansion; but to do this would involve uncritical acceptance of the implications of artificially selective and incomplete statistics. The problems may best be appreciated by looking quickly at the individual industries.

The export figures have already given striking proof of the further expansion of the textile industries. For woollens and worsteds, the admittedly unreliable production figures for the West Riding (which for broad cloths begin in 1727 and for narrow cloths only in 1739) suggest a much greater increase in output than the 50 per cent rise in exports would indicate, and it is tempting to see home demand as an even more significant stimulus. But Yorkshire enjoyed quite unprecedented prosperity in the early eighteenth century, benefiting from its ample supply of water, coal, wool and cheap labour, and enjoying the increasing popularity of its worsteds. This advance was gained at the expense of other areas that had hitherto occupied an important place in the woollen industry. The new draperies of Essex and the serges of Devon and Somerset suffered a sharp decline, and only Norwich with its 'stuffs' could even pretend to compete with the West Riding. Trends in total output must therefore remain ill-defined, though the substantial rise in the number of sheep, together with significant imports of Spanish and Irish wool, confirm the picture of steady growth. The only production figures for linen are for Scotland, where output perhaps increased six times, an acceleration that was matched by exports from Northern Ireland. According to contemporary estimates, English production (centred in Lancashire) may have been about five times that of Scotland in 1730, but little more than double by 1760. In all cases the thirteen-fold increase in linen exports from England and Wales clearly gives a misleading impression, though the rapid expansion of the industry is not in dispute. If the imports of raw and thrown silk are any indication of the progress of the silk industry of the Midlands it was steady until the thirties, when John Lombe's factory at Derby failed, and the ensuing slump lasted until a rapid up-swing began in the fifties. The industry is chiefly interesting as one of the earliest examples of mechanized, power-driven factory production, which provided valuable lessons for Lombe's successors in Derby and Stockport. Finally among the textiles comes cotton, where the retained imports of raw material suggest an increase of about 70 per cent between 1714 and 1760, and which appears to have enjoyed a steady rise in output except for a mild recession in the twenties and early thirties. It was of course concentrated around Manchester and Glasgow, in both of which it was beginning by 1760 to outstrip linen. Advantageously placed for the importation of West Indian cotton, both areas also enjoyed ample supplies of local coal and rapidly built up a body of reasonably cheap skilled labour. As yet there was little mechanization, and the great age of cotton was still some way ahead.

Textiles certainly showed impressive increases in output, especially from the mid-forties, and the centres of prosperity had moved to the north and, to a lesser extent, the Midlands; yet in 1760 there was little hint of anything that could genuinely be called factory production. The conversion of raw wool into woollen cloth, for example, involved a wide variety of processes—sorting, cleaning, dyeing, combing or carding, spinning, weaving, fulling, washing, stretching, bleaching, dressing and shearing. Most of these were still carried out in the home, whether by men or by women and children. But fulling and dressing took place in mills, and dyeing required vats and other large equipment. Some processes were thus likely to be the part-time occupations of those primarily engaged in agriculture, but in the areas of principal concentration full-time operatives increasingly appeared in small workshops and water-driven mills. Nonetheless, Lombe's silk factory was not yet used as a pattern, either in silk or other textiles, and large-scale mechanization and production had still to come. Spinning remained the great bottle-neck, and would have been more so if John Kay's flying-shuttle of 1733 (which greatly speeded up weaving) had been put into general use before the second half of the century. While a few wealthy men were beginning to emerge in the worsted industry, investment was generally still on a relatively small scale, though increasing numbers of workers were coming to depend upon the limited capital of merchants, clothiers and linen-drapers.

Progress in coal production is particularly difficult to assess. While exports doubled between 1714 and 1760, coastal traffic both out of Newcastle and into London rose by little more than 20–30 per cent. The discrepancy may be partly explained by the increasing local use of coal in industry, especially perhaps in the Midlands, where coal and metal production advanced together. As yet coal was used for heating rather than power, for Abraham Darby's discovery in 1709 of a method for smelting iron ore with coke was for long concealed within his Quaker circle, and even large furnaces still continued to smelt with charcoal. But heating, in the textile no less than in the metallurgical industries, consumed considerable quantities of coal, and the export figures are therefore likely to be a more reliable guide to the rise in production than those of the coastal traffic. Nonetheless, the progress of coal-mining, considering the substantial natural resources, was relatively slow, partly because of the lack of mechanical devices, partly because of the technical problems involved in the presence in the mines of gas and water. The problem of drainage was only gradually overcome by the increased use of Thomas Newcomen's pumping engine, invented as early as 1708, but initially more widely used in the tin mines of Cornwall than in the coal mines of the Midlands and the north. Since fuel was basic to most processes of production, the relatively meagre supply of coal hampered industrial development in other spheres. Nevertheless, as the coal-fields of the Midlands quickly overtook those of Durham and Northumberland, so Birmingham, Wolverhampton and Sheffield became the centres of the metal industries.

For the production of iron there are not even unreliable statistics, and the increase of only 50 per cent in the import of bar iron between 1714 and 1760 gives little impression of significant growth. But the fact that iron and steel exports quadrupled, together with ample contemporary evidence of the spread of blast furnaces, forges, blade mills and slitting mills, suggests at least a steady increase in output, which must have owed something to the stimulus of recurrent wars. As long as charcoal was still used for smelting, ironworks tended to be located near woodlands, but as Darby's process gradually spread, furnaces and foundries began to spring up around the chief Midlands coalfields, and the universal use of coal in the manufacture (as distinct from the production) of iron encouraged similar geographical concentration. Cast iron was used chiefly for pots, pans and various forms of ordnance; wrought iron for nails, tools, chains, locks and bolts, horseshoes, bits, stirrups and agricultural implements; steel for cutlery, swords, razors, clocks and watches. For the most part, both production and manufacture were conducted on a relatively small scale in a multitude of furnaces, forges, mills, shops and sheds, where an increasing army of gunsmiths, swordsmiths, tool makers, cutlers, chain makers and locksmiths plied their trades. But equipment, fuel and raw materials were costly, and the need for significant capital outlay saw the rise of a few large manufacturers such as John Taylor and Ambrose Crowley, the standardization of machinery, and even a move towards a primitive form of factory production. Similar advances were made in copper and tin, where Cornish production figures suggest at least a doubling in the first half of the century, though in both cases the real increase in output came after the mid-forties. Growing colonial demand was clearly important in the expansion of the metal industries, though home consumption must also have been significant.

On the basis of the excise series the 'home' industries maintained fairly steady production throughout the period, though the output of starch, paper and candles all showed a significant rise from the late forties or early fifties. Spirits were rather a special case, output more than doubling at the height of the gin mania in the 1730s and 1740s, but dropping sharply after the Act of 1751. The paper industry undoubtedly benefited from the protective duties against foreign imports and, notwithstanding the rapid increase in newspapers, books and pamphlets, was supplying most of Britain's needs by 1760. The rise in starch output naturally reflected that of the textiles, and increasing urbanization may well have increased the demand for candles. Beer withstood the challenge of coffee and gin, but suffered from the rapidly rising imports of tea, although the introduction of cheap 'porter' in 1722 soon created a mass market, and Whitbread, Barclay and Truman were all well-established long before 1760. While the greatest concentration of brewers was in London, the barley lands of the Trent valley were already supplying growing competition in Newark, Burton, Nottingham and Derby. Finally, the development of porcelain and pottery deserves a few words, though before 1750 only a limited amount of imitation 'Delft' ware was produced in London and Bristol. Thereafter Chelsea and Bow porcelain rapidly achieved popularity, and similar enterprises began to take root in the Midlands, especially in Staffordshire, where ample clay, coal and lead for glazing were ready at hand. But Josiah Wedgwood began work at Burslem only in 1759, and the great days of the potteries still lay ahead.

An observer of the English industrial scene in 1760 would have needed to be clairvoyant to guess that within a few decades economic and social transformation would be effected on a scale that could be called 'revolutionary', but he would have seen much to ponder and (unless he were a humanitarian) to applaud. The availability and mobility of capital may still have been limited, most roads were little better than mud tracks, river transport was slow and expensive, and most individual industries had bottle-necks which the primitive technology of the age had not yet succeeded in clearing. Despite the growth of towns, few industries other than brewing, soap-boiling and sugar-refining were essentially urban in character, and most were still conducted on a domestic or semi-domestic basis, with all the interruptions and inconveniences inherent in a system of ill-supervised, part-time workers, many of whom were likely to lay down their tools during harvest and, within the limits imposed by the necessity for survival, whenever else the urge seized them. Yet all this paled into insignificance beside the vitality and spirit of enterprise that almost everywhere prevailed. Although industry was still widely dispersed (not least because falling water was still almost the sole source of power), and investment still mostly on a modest scale, a few major entrepreneurs had already emerged, and factories on a limited scale had begun to appear. But what must have impressed most were the increased specialization and diversification, and the spread throughout a growing section of the population of a wide variety of industrial activities and skills. The progress of the previous forty-five years may have been erratic in most sectors, the immediate post-war boom giving way to stagnation and even decline from the mid-twenties to the mid-forties. But from then onwards expansion was almost universal and even the advent of the Seven Years' War failed to halt it. It is tempting to see the export trade, especially to the colonies, as the chief industrial stimulus, but despite the paucity of information it is likely that home demand in an era of rising real wages had a considerable effect, especially in periods when exports were temporarily sluggish.

It is clear, then, that in all principal sectors of the economy—agriculture, commerce and industry—the years 1714 to 1760 saw significant expansion. If estimates of total output are to be believed, that expansion was of the order of 40 per cent. Admittedly each sector had its years of relative stagnation, but when overseas demand diminished that at home frequently appeared to take up any slack in the economy. What is less clear is whether any decisive turning-point can be discerned. It has been suggested that after the fairly modest expansion of 1714-45—little more than 15 per cent—the mid-forties saw the beginning of an acceleration comparable to that of the 1780s. Certainly most indicators showed a pronounced upswing after 1745, and overall growth never again declined to the pace of the first three decades after 1714. But the acceleration had slackened somewhat by the mid-fifties, and even the ending of the Seven Years' War did not produce a return to the boom years of 1745-55. In a century of so many wars, with their erratic and conflicting effects upon the economy, it is difficult to identify major turning points. The most one can safely say is that many enterprising men had built successfully upon the foundations laid during the half century before 1714, and that the progress made by 1760 gave every reason for confidence in the future. A national economy, as distinct from a collection of local economies, was beginning to emerge, but only just; and the forces of innovation and growth, powerful and pervasive as they were, had still to contend with those of conservatism and inertia.

The social structure of early Hanoverian England does not readily lend itself to even tentative quantitative analysis, or indeed to any very precise qualitative treatment. One can of course distinguish broadly between the landed classes (peerage, gentry, freeholders and tenant farmers), the commercial and manufacturing classes (including artisans, handicraftsmen and shopkeepers), the professional classes (mostly army and naval officers, clergy and lawyers), the labourers and the poor. Yet, except at the lowest levels, there was much intermingling of activities and much mobility between these classes and within the sub-divisions of each. Since land above all conferred social status, as well as establishing a qualification for membership of Parliament, an increasing number of small properties became the country residences of successful merchants and professional men, while many of the leading industrialists of the period (including rather more than half of the forty-three who sat in the Commons between 1715 and 1754) continued to regard themselves as country gentlemen who had merely developed the mineral resources on their properties. It was by no means uncommon for a small farmer or craftsman to become a tolerably wealthy manufacturer, and for him or his son to slide comfortably into the ranks of the gentry. But the movement was by no means always upwards. Many small freeholders joined the ranks of the agricultural labourers, many of the gentry over-committed themselves (not least by reckless involvement in electioneering) even to the extent of financial ruin, and many merchants ended in bankruptcy. The speculation mania, of which the South Sea Bubble was merely the prime example, was not the only road to disaster; and, although the growth of large estates and the emergence of rich merchants and even a few great manufacturers was a feature of the period, wealth did not invariably beget more wealth, nor did those of relatively humble background necessarily become poorer. The enterprising went on to ever greater fame and fortune; the sluggish, the careless and the unlucky—of whatever rank or class—frequently plummeted to obscurity and insolvency. Prosperity went above all to particular groups of people who happened to be engaged in activities where there was substantial growth—to the big monied men of the metropolis, to the squires and tenant farmers of East Anglia, to the gentlemen graziers of the Midlands, to the merchants of Bristol and Liverpool, and to the manufacturers of textiles in Yorkshire and Lancashire.

At the top of the social pyramid the peerage remained a relatively closed caste, neither George I nor George II showing any enthusiasm for significantly increasing its ranks. Had the ambitions of members of the House of Commons not ensured the rejection of the Peerage Bill in 1719, it would have become even more closed. When additions were made, the existing phalanx of Whig magnates, who engrossed so many offices in the Government and at Court, and who normally exercised considerable political influence in their respective counties, was merely joined by other men of substantial estates who in some way (whether by political services, hard cash or, as in the cases of Hugh Boscawen and Richard Edgcumbe, electoral interest) had established their claim to recognition. But the law was also a major pathway to a title, as was amply demonstrated by the careers of Philip Yorke, Charles Talbot, Robert Raymond, Peter King, Robert Henley and others. Military success might bring a peerage to William Cadogan and James Stanhope, though the latter had equal claims as a diplomat or as a statesman; and a distinguished career in the navy (aided, admittedly, by a circumnavigation of the globe and marriage to the daughter of the Earl of Hardwicke) ensured a baronetcy for George Anson. If a remarkable ministerial career won an earldom for Robert Walpole, William Pulteney was similarly rewarded for twenty years of contumacious Opposition, although his vast wealth could more than support the title, and the chief object was to get him out of the House of Commons. Those in commerce and industry still had to be content for the most part with knighthoods or baronetcies. Sir Jacob Bouverie, a prominent Turkey merchant, managed to acquire a viscountcy, but only—it was said—at the cost of a contribution of £12,000 to the King's mistress, Lady Yarmouth; and it was with great difficulty and in the face of much hostile comment that Sir Henry Liddell, one of the cartel who dominated the northern coal industry, gained his baronetcy.

It is, however, artificial to isolate the peerage even for purposes of social analysis. Within the ranks of the landed classes many of the wealthier gentry had higher incomes than the poorer peers, a handful might rival the prosperity of all but the greatest magnates, and constant intermarriage further blurred the social and economic divisions. There were probably about four hundred great landlords with incomes of at least £3,000 a year, of whom little more than half comprised the peerage. The remainder of the gentry—baronets, knights, esquires or merely gentlemen—may have numbered fifteen to twenty thousand, and their incomes varied from perhaps £200 to £3,000. In addition there were probably 100–150,000 freeholders, most of whose incomes would be less than £100, but a minority of whom could boast of double that amount; and perhaps an even larger, and certainly growing, number of tenant farmers in a similar financial situation. Despite the overlapping of incomes between these categories, and despite the movement towards larger estates, it was almost as difficult to enter the ranks of the great landlords as it was to gain a peerage. Since a property worth £1,000 a year—sufficient to establish one among the middling gentry—could involve a capital outlay of about £30,000, very few were likely in a single generation to reach the higher levels of landed society. Even if tolerable fortunes were made from trade, from the law or (as with Robert Walpole and Henry Fox) from office, suitable properties were not always available. Strict family settlements (which acted as restraints upon spendthrift heirs) and the readier availability of long-term mortgages at reasonably low interest rates combined to preserve the large estates and even make them larger. But perhaps still more important was the seemingly infinite capacity of the existing landed aristocracy for attracting heiresses and absorbing other people's fortunes. The Duke of Bedford may have been an improving landlord, but the growing prosperity of the family was built upon the earlier marriage, in 1695, of Wriothesley Russell to the grand-daughter of the great East Indian merchant, Sir Josiah Child; the Duke of Newcastle would have had to curb his passion for electioneering had his father not been sufficiently far-sighted to marry the heiress to the Holles fortune; and when, in 1756, the second Earl of Ashburnham took as his wife the grand-daughter of the ironmaster Ambrose Crowley, he was merely following a well-established family tradition. To reach the top, therefore, required time as well as enterprise, and the establishment of a great landed family was usually the work of several generations, although the plight of many lesser gentry and freeholders made available smaller properties which served as a useful basis on which to build.

Within the ranks of the landed classes there was clearly a great difference between the life-styles of the greatest landowners and those of the humblest freeholders and tenant farmers, yet the transformation across the social spectrum was very gradual and there were no clear dividing lines. Great landlords did not noticeably prosper during the early eighteenth century, though their fortunes changed markedly for the better after the 1750s. Most lived extravagantly, spending lavishly on building, parks, gardens, education, entertaining, sport, electioneering and charity. Although a few, such as Townshend, Bedford, Ducie, Egremont and Halifax, experimented with the new methods of agriculture, their activities were mainly confined to consolidating their estates, bringing waste into cultivation, and improving the administration of their lands with the aid of efficient stewards. They created a favourable environment for progressive farming, hoping thereby to benefit from higher rents; but before the 1750s they were fortunate if their efforts enabled them to maintain their existing incomes. Quite apart from the agricultural depression, political considerations sometimes dictated low rents, and the dispersion of many of the large estates hampered efficiency. Some great lords, such as Rutland, Portland and Kingston, benefited from substantial resources of coal on their properties, and others (Scarborough, Burlington and Devonshire, for example) boosted their revenues by investing in urban property—especially in London, as the names of many of its streets and squares testify. But declining rents were a common complaint, and it is easy to understand the growing attractions of office (even though it meant maintaining an establishment in London), the popularity of investment in the Funds and the passion for profitable marriages. The lesser landowners, except for the really small men, mostly managed to hold their own or even advance a little. Many of the gentry and freeholders (and indeed tenant farmers) adopted improved methods of agriculture, and although extravagance could also take its toll with them, their pretensions were relatively modest. They were of course less well-placed than their wealthy neighbours to withstand the burden of war-time taxation and were more likely to be hard hit by the effects of bad harvests and animal disease—especially if they had already mortgaged their estates. Many therefore found it difficult to maintain their social positions and administrative responsibilities, and the gentry families who survived frequently did so by entering the ranks of the professional classes, merchants, tradesmen and manufacturers—just as the freeholders eked out their incomes by engaging in transport, mining, glove-making, hosiery and similar pursuits. Though towards the bottom of the social scale shared inheritance was more widespread than primogeniture, many younger sons sought security by becoming attorneys, doctors, surveyors or government officials of one kind and another. The most impecunious or least enterprising of the small holders could not cope with the difficult conditions and declined to the status of labourers in agriculture or industry.

Except in London and a few large towns, the landed classes dominated the political life of the nation. The great landlords virtually monopolized the House of Lords and provided some of the wealthiest members of the Commons, where anyway their sons, brothers and other relatives readily found seats; and as Lords-Lieutenants and Deputy Lieutenants they exercised considerable control in their respective counties. The richer gentry, and some not so rich, also sought membership of Parliament as a matter of prestige and occasionally as a path to office. But for most of the landed majority in the Commons their centre of gravity remained firmly in the localities, and they were frequently more concerned with legislation of local significance, such as that relating to turnpikes, enclosures and other improvements, than with matters of national politics—though in the latter they were likely to maintain a traditional Country attitude. There is little evidence to suggest that members of the landed classes abused their political power, or that Parliament was any less sensitive to the national interest than it is today—and in most cases political attitudes, like electoral behaviour, were dependent on personal relationships rather than issues or principles. The lesser gentry confined themselves to participation in local government, where they augmented the ranks of the JPs. Again self-interest was normally subordinated to considerations of justice, though the excessive eighteenth-century respect for property and the continued prevalence of barbaric forms of punishment ensured ruthless treatment of poachers and other petty thieves. Finally, at the base of the political structure came the freeholders, who constituted the main body of electors in the counties and who fulfilled their local obligations by serving as churchwardens, overseers of the poor, surveyors and constables. In such well-populated counties as Yorkshire and Middlesex their collective political importance could be considerable, and in others such as Kent and Sussex their economic strength provided a sturdy political independence. If the landed interest as a whole seemed almost to monopolize political power, it was after all overwhelmingly the principal interest of the nation, and constant movement between all sectors of the landed classes and those engaged in trade, industry and the professions helped to preserve a tolerably balanced attitude towards life. By comparison with most contemporary European nations, narrow vested interests seldom prevailed within the English political system.

Much of the homogeneity of outlook of the ruling classes in eighteenth-century England sprang from a common system of education and from acceptance of common cultural values. The public schools and the two universities, whatever the limitations of their predominantly but by no means exclusively classical education, were not solely the preserves of great wealth. Sons of peers rubbed shoulders with those of gentry, freeholders, tenant farmers, lawyers, clergy, merchants and craftsmen, though the general standard of behaviour was such that private tuition at home was frequently preferred for the eldest sons of those who could afford it. The grammar schools and local boarding schools (including some for girls) catered mostly for the children of the gentry and farmers, while the elementary charity schools provided rudimentary instruction in the three Rs for the children of agricultural labourers. The landlord class could therefore boast a general familiarity with the classics, philosophy and literature, and the wealthier had the additional advantage of a year or two at the Inns of Court. For a few the crowning experience was the Grand Tour, or at least a brief spell abroad, to familiarize them with foreign languages, improve their manners and generally broaden their outlook—even if it usually resulted in confirming their instinctive conviction of the superiority of the English way of life. Most landlords, then, were reasonably civilized and liberal-minded human beings, and their country houses were local centres of social activity and constant hospitality. Though travel was still expensive, the wealthy could afford to take the waters regularly at fashionable spas like Bath and Tunbridge Wells, while others occasionally visited the smaller resorts. The London season, with its interminable round of balls, receptions and theatres represented the peak of social activity, but was beyond the reach of all but the most affluent.

Frederick, Lord North, Earl of Guildford

Henry Pelham

Whatever the attractions of the metropolis, landlords were most at ease in their country houses—from the splendour of Blenheim and Chatsworth to the modest dwellings of the lesser gentry. It was here that they felt a sense of achievement and permanence, and here they were likely to indulge themselves in ostentatious building and landscape gardening, and in collecting pictures, statuary, *objets d'art*, fabrics, carpets and tapestries from Europe and beyond. A substantial body of domestic servants, most of whom lived in and led a tolerably comfortable existence, coped with the strenuous demands of a hospitality that was traditional among landed families. A light breakfast of tea or coffee, with bread and butter, was taken between 9 and 10 am, and an equally light supper of assorted cold meats towards midnight. But it was dinner, normally served in the mid-afternoon, that provided the main social occasion and the opportunity for gross over-indulgence. A vast spread of roast meats, game, poultry, pies, tarts, fruit and nuts kept the company occupied for a couple of hours, to be followed, after the ladies had withdrawn, by a similar period of steady drinking. Though society had become more genteel than it had been in the previous century, and excessive drunkenness was frowned upon in polite circles, table manners were still a little on the crude side. Spitting and scratching at table were still practised with relish, and chamber-pots on the sideboards were readily accessible for those whose taste for wine exceeded their capacity. Though the well-to-do ate rather more than heartily, their diet was less well-balanced than that of their poorer neighbours, and deficiency in iron and vitamins frequently induced anaemia and 'land scurvy', which were scarcely cured by the combination of bleeding, purging and blistering that was the common remedy for anything not requiring surgery.

The daily lives of the freeholders and tenant farmers were much more dreary than those of the landlord class, though their standard of living was a great deal better than that of most of their European counterparts. Their houses—and, except during the thirties and forties, the re-building and improvement of the previous century was continued—might have only five to ten main rooms, compared to the twenty to forty of the richer gentry; and kitchen, bakehouse, dairy and buttery could take up much of the available space. But foreigners were greatly impressed by their neatness and cleanliness; and the furniture and furnishings, if predominantly utilitarian, were tasteful and well-kept. The larger houses—usually timber-framed but sometimes of stone—could accommodate a few of the more important farm servants, though as prosperous times returned it became common for separate quarters to be provided. Food was wholesome rather than varied, with meat, bacon, bread, cheese, milk, beer, vegetables and fruit providing the staple. For the most part they had to supply their own entertainment, and they could not normally afford to engage in the aristocratic pastimes of hunting and shooting. But there were race-meetings, boxing, cock-fighting and cricket matches to provide amusement, local fairs were highly popular, and periodic visits to the local market towns helped to relieve the monotony. During the years of agricultural depression, the average farmer might have difficulty in making ends meet, but his way of life was neither devoid of dignity nor lacking in variety. Not infrequently he had more reasons to count his blessings than many of the poorer gentry, committed to habits and obligations that they could ill afford.

Of those who may broadly, if anachronistically, be called the middle classes—clergy, lawyers, merchants, manufacturers, shopkeepers, tradesmen and artisans—it is difficult to generalize. The higher clergy, with emoluments ranging from £400 to £7,000, could rival the nobility and gentry in wealth and leisure and, with the increasing laicization of religion, led not dissimilar lives. The twenty-six spiritual peers usually formed a reliable body of support for the government in the House of Lords, and many of their lesser colleagues were active in local politics. Since the ladder of clerical preferment was difficult to scale without influential support, the clergy were among the most anxious to tap the springs of patronage. But the higher clergy were as far removed from the village parsons as were the landed magnates from the freeholders. The more fortunate rectors and vicars might enjoy relative comfort on £200 to £400 a year, but most country benefices or curacies were worth little more than £50 to £100, and some even less. Moreover, the curacies conferred no security of tenure, and indeed a great many who entered Holy Orders had to look outside the Church to survive. But for those who managed, whether through influence or ability, to acquire a reasonable benefice, life was not without its compensations. Behind the squire stood the parson, and although there might be intermittent disputes over tithes, the Church was too highly regarded as a pillar of rural society for its servants not to be received as respected members of the village community.

The legal profession, like the Church, offered handsome prizes and even a title to those who really prospered, and a comfortable income—similar to that of a good clerical benefice—to the main body of its members. But here too the supply always exceeded the demand. As Joseph Addison had lamented when he surveyed the two professions: 'They are each of them overburdened with practitioners, and filled with multitudes of ingenious gentlemen that starve one another.'

The really successful merchants and manufacturers chose to buy their way into landed society, some on a grand scale, but most simply by purchasing small properties in the environs of London and other commercial and industrial centres. Despite a certain undercurrent of resentment at their intrusion, they could scarcely be rejected by neighbours who were only too eager to tap their wealth through intermarriage or investment. Some indeed were merely returning to the land, from which also their ranks were being continuously augmented. The directors of the great monied companies and a host of the more substantial men in London and the provinces found their way into the House of Commons (where they constituted about 10 per cent of the total membership), and a few used their influence to gain government contracts and further increase their fortunes. They also tended to dominate the local politics of the metropolis, chief ports and inland towns, though in difficult times they could be challenged by the middling and smaller men in the same way as, in the countryside, the gentry could, if hard pressed or tactlessly treated, resist aristocratic control. If men like Sir Gilbert Heathcote (Governor of the Bank and one of the greatest exporters of his time) and Sir James Bateman (a director of both the Bank and the South Sea Company) could amass fortunes larger than those of all but a handful of the landed magnates, buy up huge estates and ensure aristocratic marriages and even peerages for their descendants, lesser figures were often content to plough back their profits, concentrate on building up their businesses, and lead a comfortable but unpretentious life. Especially was this the case with the growing number of Protestant Dissenters, who played so important a role in the commercial and industrial life of the period. Shopkeepers, tradesmen and artisans grew in number with the expansion of commerce and industry, absorbing the overflow from the lower reaches of the landed classes, and achieving a similar, or rather better, standard of living.

Thus far we have surveyed the upper half of the population—those who in Gregory King's somewhat prejudiced eyes 'increased the wealth of the country'. Failures could of course be found in every one of their varied walks of life, and amongst the less well-to-do failure could mean descent into the ranks of the anonymous masses. But the great majority survived and not a few prospered and rose in the social scale. Below them lay a vast ill-differentiated mass of actual or potential workers—agricultural and industrial labourers, cottagers, domestic servants, common seamen and soldiers, squatters on the outskirts of villages, paupers in the towns and vagrants; those in fact whom King saw as 'diminishing the wealth of the country'. Their fortunes could vary as widely as those of the classes above them, and it is perhaps impossible to reconstruct satisctfaorily 'the short and simple annals of the poor', especially since much contemporary comment suffers from a built-in hostility towards their apparent fecklessness and perversity. The lives of many of them were indeed 'poor, nasty, brutish and short', and they would doubtless have been astonished to find that historians intent on condemning the human effects of the later Industrial Revolution would see them as beneficiaries of a golden, pre-industrial age. The conditions in which they lived, particularly in London and the infant manufacturing towns, were often primitive and insanitary; in both agriculture and industry underemployment was the norm, much of the work was seasonal, and economic fluctuations could violently interrupt the little security they enjoyed at other times; wages (especially in the armed forces and in industry) were often paid irregularly and well in arrears, and since a large part of them might be in kind rather than cash, they offered little opportunity for varied spending. Though living-in domestic and farm servants enjoyed reasonable security and comfort, the great mass of the working classes were at the mercy of their employers and, although rather ineffectual combinations of workers were beginning to appear, rioting and other forms of violence were virtually their only weapons when their position became intolerable rather than merely precarious. When clothiers like William Temple could passionately assert that the only sensible way to deal with workers was 'to lay them under the necessity of labouring all the time they can spare from rest and sleep, in order to produce the common necessaries of life', it is understandable that, in perverse fashion, they frequently chose to work as little as possible—often no more than a four-day week—or that they downed tools whenever a fair, wake, race-meeting, cock-fight or public execution happened to attract their attention. Those living perpetually on the margin of subsistence felt little incentive to improve their position, nor did their meagre and erratic wages often enable them to do so. If employed full-time, agricultural labourers earned between seven and eight shillings a week, those in industry from seven to fifteen shillings, and in London skilled labourers fourteen shillings and craftsmen half as much again. But a system based primarily on temporary hiring or piece-work afforded little security or confidence in the future. In times of dearth many workers faced starvation, and could depend only on charity or poor relief; in times of relative plenty they preferred to take life easy and squander any petty surplus on beer or gin.

Yet the picture was by no means one of unrelieved gloom. The long years of rising real wages offered many an opportunity to stabilize and even improve their position; standards of diet, clothing and housing tended to rise; an expanding and more diversified economy provided a wider variety of jobs; family incomes were boosted by the increasing employment of women and children; and charity schools brought a degree of literacy and stimulated imagination and ambition. As early as 1728 Defoe could claim that the working classes 'lye warm, live in plenty, work hard, and know no want'—certainly an exaggeration, especially in the less progressive areas, but an indication of steadily improving conditions. The more prosperous labourers appear even to have developed a taste for cheap manufactured articles, and experience of a fuller life encouraged the growth of less haphazard working habits. Skilled workers in agriculture and industry were increasingly hired for a year at a time, and if some cottagers and squatters were hit by enclosures and consolidation of farms, they and their families often found employment in industry. As always, there were the unemployables who lacked either the will or the inclination to work—beggars, vagrants, thieves, highwaymen and prostitutes. But apart from the growing body of fully-employed workers (many of whom themselves hired apprentices, journeymen and women to work alongside them) a host of others managed to eke out some kind of living in rural cottages or urban garrets. Even in industry relationships between employers and employed had not yet become wholly impersonal, and by no means all entrepreneurs were as callous as William Temple. The early phase of industry absorbed something of the casual, leisurely flavour of agricultural life, though the combination of home and miniature factory often created appalling living conditions and constituted a serious hazard to health. Indeed, towards mid-century it began to be argued that the incentive of higher wages might be more conducive to national prosperity as well as to human happiness than the maintenance of a surplus pool of labour at or near the subsistence level, and that the provision of gainful employment for the lower orders should be a prime object of public policy.

Thus, though by modern standards the condition of the working classes might seem deplorable, there is some reason to believe that many of them were sharing in the rising prosperity. Except in so far as a few were entitled to vote in a handful of urban constituencies, they were, of course, denied any formal role in the political life of the nation, remaining in the eyes of the propertied classes 'the illiterate rabble, who have neither the capacity for judging any matters of government, nor property to be concerned for'. Yet at least in the towns they were by no means all illiterate, many took an interest in political issues that were important or touched their lives, and by temporarily assuming their designated role of 'rabble' they could—as on the occasion of the Excise Bill of 1733 or the Jewish Naturalization Act of 1753—swell the voices of protest and help to secure a change of government policy. It was perhaps a combination of genuine concern for their unenviable lot, fear for the potential threat that their numbers posed for a society that had no adequate machinery for dealing with disturbances, and a conviction that they might become a source of wealth rather than a drain upon it that engendered a growing debate about the problem of the 'labouring poor', and raised the issue whether poverty and labour need necessarily be synonymous. The problem of the poor was of course an old one, and since the Elizabethan codification of the Poor Laws had formally been the responsibility of the parishes. The increasing absence of supervision by the central Government was further reflected in the Settlement Act of 1662, which authorized parishes to oust immigrant paupers and which, despite the undoubted hardship it brought to individuals, was probably necessary if the more conscientious parishes were not to be inundated with hopeful outsiders. But although by 1753 the estimated cost of the poor rate had reached £1,000,000 a year, this represented but part of the attempt to alleviate poverty. Individual charities continued to provide food, clothing, almshouses and other forms of temporary relief, and an increasing body of benefactors (especially the merchants in London and the chief towns) turned to the endowment of apprenticeships and the establishment of charity schools which eventually provided some sort of education for about sixty thousand children in England. Although doubts were voiced about the wisdom of imparting knowledge to those who were meant to be hewers of wood and drawers of water, and an element of self-interest was intermingled with genuine philanthropy in the apprenticeship schemes, it would be cynical in the extreme to ignore the real spirit of compassion behind the work of men like Thomas Coram, James Oglethorpe, William Hay and Jonas Hanway. Yet most large-scale attempts to solve the problem of the poor foundered in the face of conflicting opinions, administrative inadequacy and personal dishonesty. The workhouse was the most commonly proposed remedy, and its subsequent pejorative connotations should not blind us to the fact that in origin it was often meant to serve a genuinely constructive purpose. Bristol and other towns took the lead in establishing these institutions, and their maintenance by combinations of parishes was authorized by a succession of Acts in the twenties and thirties. But although their inmates were usefully enough employed in spinning, knitting and other similar pursuits, the supervision was inadequate and haphazard, and Defoe was merely the first of many to see them—quite wrongly—as representing unfair competition with private industry and lowering the quality and prestige of British manufactured goods. Most notorious of the various swindles connected with the poor was the Charitable Corporation, founded as far back as 1707 to lend small sums of money to poor people to keep them out of the clutches of usurers. By the early thirties it had a capital of more than £300,000, but several of its directors appear to have followed the advice of one of their number, Denis Bond, who was said to have remarked 'Damn the poor; let us go into the City where we may make money'. When the coffers of the corporation were found to be empty the chief embezzlers were expelled from the House of Commons and their estates forfeited, but their notorious activities must have dimmed the enthusiasm of many who had advocated such schemes. By mid-century the workhouse system was largely abandoned, though the early private factories took over some of their constructive aspects (including schools and dormitories for children) and proved both more durable and more profitable.

Early Hanoverian England provided an almost ideal setting for the nobility and the gentry, and for any who could reasonably aspire to join their ranks. It also held out promise to those who, whether from native ability, sheer industry or expertise in finding a benevolent patron, were willing and able to seize the opportunity for self-betterment. But against the elegant living and self-assurance of the men of property must be set the squalor and poverty of the many for whom the morrow nearly always seemed insecure. The world of Gainsborough and Reynolds was very different from the world of Hogarth. Yet the ruling classes were more enlightened and benevolent in England than almost anywhere in Europe, the opportunities for enterprise more widespread, and the lot of even the humblest labourer less devoid of hope. If it was still in many ways a violent age—nowhere more so than in the barbarity of its penal system—it was not totally without social conscience. If many of the rich eventually grew richer, it was not necessarily at the expense of their fellow-men; nor, on the whole did the poor grow poorer. Such economic progress as was made brought benefits, if unevenly, to all sections of society; and when in some areas local conditions temporarily frustrated advancement, it was not the poor alone who suffered. Most Englishmen by 1760 had more reason for confidence than they had had at the turn of the century; most foreign visitors were impressed and not a little envious.

7

RELIGIOUS, INTELLECTUAL AND CULTURAL LIFE

By comparison with previous generations, the Englishmen of the early eighteenth century displayed little religious fervour, and by the mid-twenties is must have been difficult to believe that as recently as the reign of Anne religion had still been a major divisive force in national life. A thorough-going Erastianism had quickly pervaded the Anglican Church, the Roman Catholics—except during brief periods of Jacobite activity—were only too happy to remain inconspicuous, and the non-conformist sects appeared more interested in commercial and industrial enterprise than in taking a stand upon religious principles. This mood of apathy is not difficult to explain. The prominence of religious conflict during the previous two centuries had been due largely to the fact that the religious and political aspects of life were intimately intertwined. When Henry VIII had added the headship of the Church to that of the State, religious dissent came increasingly to be equated with political opposition, and heresy with treason. It seemed to contemporaries inconceivable that men of differing religious faiths could live in peace within a single political community, or that religious toleration could be granted without endangering the safety of the State. The first stage in the secularization of politics had come with the Restoration settlement, when the attempt to maintain a single Established Church was finally abandoned, the existence of Protestant Dissent legally recognized, and freedom of worship within certain limits formally permitted, even if Dissenters were at the same time condemned to second-class citizenship. But in the minds of most Englishmen, Roman Catholics were still too firmly associated with authoritarian government to be given similar privileges, and the activities of James II and the subsequent Jacobite movement ensured that the laws against Papists were retained and even strengthened. Thus Protestant Dissenters, who had refused to be seduced by the promises of James II or to flirt with the idea of a Stuart restoration, had become politically respectable and were duly rewarded by the Toleration Act of 1689, the Act for Quieting Corporations of 1718, the repeal of the Occasional Conformity and Schism Acts in 1719, and by a degree of *de facto* relief from the provisions of the Test and Corporation Acts through the annual granting of indemnity. But as long as the Jacobite threat remained, Roman Catholics would be politically suspect and subject to renewed persecution in times of crisis. Nonetheless, most of them were in normal circumstances permitted to worship in peace by their Anglican neighbours, who had no wish to disturb local tranquillity and who shared the comfortable and tolerant rationalism of the age. All these developments were symptomatic of a growing maturity and an unwillingness any longer to allow religious animosities to embitter national life, yet most historians have been as unsympathetic in their treatment both of the Established Church and of the dissenting groups under the early Hanoverians as they have been in their assessment of the political conventions of the period. Only the non-jurors, Methodists and Evangelicals have been the subject of favourable comment.

It is easy to understand why the Anglican Church of the early eighteenth century should have had a bad press, and why even its attempted rehabilitation by the late Norman Sykes[1] won only partial acceptance. Once Toryism had been discredited in 1715, the Whigs were left as the only champions of the Established Church, and the way was open for a latitudinarian approach in religion no less than in politics. The nonjuring schism had already deprived the Church of many of its most conservative members, and the views of the predominantly Tory lower clergy had scant opportunity for expression after the suspension of a bitterly-divided convocation in 1717 and again in 1741. High Anglican clerics had as little impact on the religious life of the nation as Tory back-benchers had upon its political life. Meanwhile a generation of Whig bishops became intimately associated with the leaders of the Old Corps of Whigs, as was evident from the close relation between Bishop Gibson and Robert Walpole until the breach between them in 1736, and by Newcastle's obsession with questions of ecclesiastical patronage thereafter. In the House of Lords the bishops proved one of the most solid blocks of support for successive administrations, and in the constituencies they and a host of lesser clergy became deeply involved in politics. Bishop Hare of Chichester was one of Newcastle's most trusted lieutenants in Sussex during the election of 1734, and Archbishop Herring of York was even prepared to take up arms against the Jacobite rebels in 1745.

[1]See especially his *Church and State in Eighteenth Century England* (1934).

Political service had become the most obvious way to preferment, as could be seen from Benjamin Hoadly's rapid progress through the sees of Bangor, Hereford, Salisbury and Winchester. Tory sympathies on the other hand condemned Thomas Secker for sixteen years to the relatively penurious bishoprics of Bristol and Oxford, and Thomas Newton's friendship with William Pulteney delayed his elevation to episcopal status until after the accession of George III. A royal chaplaincy, and especially attendance upon the King in Hanover, was another orthodox route to preferment, as to a lesser extent was a tutorship to a scion of a prominent political family; and, as might be expected in this highly aristocratic age, many younger sons of the nobility, such as James Yorke, Henry Egerton and Frederick Cornwallis, enjoyed accelerated promotion. It was therefore not surprising that the more successful among the Anglican clergy should be accused of servility, time-serving and neglect of their pastoral duties, or that much attention should be focused upon the poverty of the humbler clerics in contrast to the wealth of those who enjoyed the fruits of pluralism and non-residence.

Yet the growth of religious stability in England was no less beneficial than the growth of political stability, and neither was based upon privilege and patronage alone; nor should realism be confused with lack of principle or moral fibre. The non-jurors scarcely deserved Macaulay's caustic rebuke that they sacrificed 'both liberty and order to a superstition as stupid and degrading as the Egyptian worship of cats and onions', and their sincerity and piety have never been called in question. But they were living in the religious and political past, committed to a doctrine of divine indefeasible hereditary right which had no place in post-revolutionary Britain. Their protest was indeed political rather than religious, and in their own way they were as Erastian as those whom they felt compelled to criticize. Little wonder that the main body of the Church sought security by turning to that Whiggery of which the distinguishing characteristic constituted, in the words of Bishop Gibson, 'the settled principle of maintaining the Protestant Succession, the Church Establishment and the Toleration'. Nor did the conventions of the eighteenth-century Church break with the past as dramatically as has sometimes been suggested. Pluralism and non-residence had not disappeared with the Reformation, and the holding of benefices *in commendam* would last as long as the wide disparity between clerical emoluments persisted. Clerical participation in political life was perhaps more intense in the seventeenth century than in the eighteenth; it is far from clear that the principles upon which either Laudians or Puritans acted were in any way morally superior to those which motivated the clergy of Georgian

England, and they were certainly much more disruptive of national unity. Of course any system based to a considerable extent upon patronage is bound to have its full quota of sycophants, and Bishop Hoadly was the obvious counterpart of politicians like George Bubb Dodington. Yet as long as there are patrons talent will never be at a discount. George Grenville distinguished between bishoprics 'for men of ability and learning' and those for 'men of family and fashion'. Occupants of the latter have received much more attention than those of the former, but the Georgian bench of bishops was not obviously inferior in either ability or piety to those of previous ages. Potter, Secker, Gibson, Hurd, Warburton, Hume, Herring and many others were men of real learning and deep religious conviction. Equally, James Woodforde's attractive *Diary of a Country Parson* is but the best-known of a series of contemporary clerical diaries that serve to remind us that the calumnies heaped upon the Hanoverian clergy are not always based upon fact. When the political conventions of the age are seen in clear perspective, it becomes less easy to condemn a Church that turned with relief from the sterile conflicts of the past to uphold a settlement that was firmly based upon the consensus of the politically active nation.

Not the least achievements of the early Hanoverian Church were its spirited defence of Christianity against the onslaughts of Deism and its philosophical vindication of its own position. The reaction against the sectarian conflicts of the previous century, the growing interest in science, and the new preoccupation with the harmony and order of the universe all helped to create an atmosphere favourable to natural religion, which postulated a single rational, reliable, beneficent Deity and looked to the general religious consciousness of mankind to provide a basis for unity. Though Deism was not new, the climate of opinion was peculiarly favourable to its reception, and Bolingbroke was only the most prominent of many who at least temporarily embraced its principles. These were most cogently expressed in John Toland's *Christianity not Mysterious* and Matthew Tyndal's *Christianity as Old as the Creation*, and their basic appeal was perhaps best summarized in Pope's couplet,

> For modes of faith let graceless zealots fight;
> He can't be wrong whose life is in the right.

But even in the early eighteenth century the Church was not sufficiently Latitudinarian to abandon the cause of revealed religion. Of the many refutations of Deism the best known are William Law's *Serious Call to a Devout and Holy Life*, which was to charm such severe critics as Dr Johnson and Edward Gibbon, and which provided an early example of that personal and devotional religion that was to become characteristic of both Methodists and Evangelicals; and Joseph Butler's *Analogy of Religion*, the sweet reasonableness and sincerity of which quickly established it as one of the great classic defences of Christianity.

Inevitably, it was the precise nature of the relationship between Church and State that provoked the most heated controversy of the period. The refusal of the non-jurors to take the oath of allegiance to William III, their denial of the legitimacy of their subsequent deprivations, their assertion of the Church as an independent *societas perfecta*, and their accusations of Erastianism against the established clergy could scarcely be allowed to pass unchallenged. But the form of Bishop Hoadly's repudiation raised more problems for the Church than it solved. In so far as he asserted the legality of the deprivations and justified the non-jurors' successors in ecclesiastical office, he was merely voicing opinions that commanded general acceptance. But when, in his celebrated sermon of 31 March 1717, preached from the text 'My Kingdom is not of this world', he ridiculed the authority of the visible Church and argued the right of unfettered private judgment as the essence of Christianity, he inaugurated an orgy of controversy. It was difficult to escape the logic of William Law's riposte that Hoadly had dissolved the whole fabric of organized religion, or to deny that his extreme Erastianism was potentially more disruptive of society than the doctrines of non-jurors and Deists. The Bangorian controversy also brought Hoadly the unsolicited notoriety of being the ostensible cause of the suspension of Convocation, though it could scarcely be foreseen that it would not effectively resume its sessions until the middle of the following century. Hoadly's views were clearly anathema to most of the Tory High Churchmen in the lower house, and the Government's anxiety to avoid any heightening of the religious temperature was perfectly natural. But so tumultuous had been the recent sessions of Convocation that it had largely wrought its own downfall, and the imminent resumption of conflict between the two houses was merely a convenient excuse for prorogation. Indeed, since Convocation in 1664 had surrendered its right of voting clerical subsidies, the chief reason for its periodic summons had disappeared and it had scarcely met between then and 1700. In suspending its activities in 1717 the Whig Government was merely reverting to normal practice and hardly deserves the condemnation it has received. In theory the absence of regular assemblies isolated the clergy and prevented common action and contemplation of reform, but in practice the immediate recrudescence of conflict when it was briefly summoned in 1741 underlined the futility of its proceedings and the harmful effect that they were likely to have upon the Church.

Expediency dictated not only the suspension of Convocation, but also the increasingly tolerant attitude towards Protestant nonconformity, and it was left to William Warburton in *The Alliance between Church and State* (published in 1736) to justify the attitudes of the early Hanoverian Church and its Whig champions in terms that could command general respect. Taking as his starting-point the social contract which all good Whigs recognized as the origin of the State, Warburton postulated a similar basis for the Church, which he saw as a separate society concerned not with the temporal happiness of man, but with his eternal salvation. Between these two originally sovereign and independent societies a compact was arranged for their mutual support and benefit. The State gained from the religious sanctions which its institutions thereby acquired, its chief executive became also the head of the Church, and its authority was necessary before the officers of the Church could exercise their spiritual authority. But in return the Church received the protection of the State, public provision for its clergy, a share in the legislature of the realm, and the enactment of religious tests to prevent members of other religious societies from sharing its privileges. Notwithstanding these tests, full freedom was granted to every man to worship according to his conscience. Thus the basis of Whiggism as defined by Bishop Gibson was convincingly vindicated in terms of utility, and the social purpose of religion fully recognized. Though Warburton did not realize it, his adoption of the theory of the two societies opened the way for the complete secularization of politics, but this was not to be achieved until the 1820s, and not until the days of the Oxford Movement was the search for ecclesiastical independence resumed.

The same lack of vigour and proselytizing zeal that characterized the Established Church was found among the ranks of dissenters. Content enough with the limited toleration that they enjoyed, most Protestant nonconformists showed little desire to revive the conflicts of the past, and many members of the younger generation even found it socially and politically expedient to drift back into the Anglican fold. Others, encouraged perhaps by the spirit of free enquiry that was an essential part of education in the dissenting academies, flirted with Arian, Socinian and unitarian doctrines, but they produced no thinkers who could compare with the leading Anglican divines. For the most part they wore their religion more easily than their rigid seventeenth-century ancestors and welcomed both material success and the relative absence of religious controversy. Not unnaturally, considering the savage penal laws that still remained on the statute books and their intermittent involvement with Jacobitism, the Roman Catholics preferred to remain even more unobtrusive, and their religion probably reached its lowest ebb in England since the Reformation. In general, the great masses of the British people were little touched by religious experience, neither Anglicans nor dissenters showing much concern for their material welfare, still less for their immortal souls.

But it would be unpardonable to leave the early eighteenth-century religious scene without at least passing reference to the birth of Methodism, even if its major impact did not come until after 1760. In 1729 Charles Wesley formed the Holy Club at Oxford and was soon joined by his more celebrated brother, John, and by George Whitefield. These three and their few associates reacted strongly against the prevailing religious trends, and at first devoted themselves to disciplined lives of scripture reading, prayer and good works. But after they had experienced personal 'conversion' they developed a burning desire to arouse their fellow men to the need for salvation, rejected the current cult of reasonableness, and embraced 'enthusiasm' in religion at a time when, despite the individual efforts of a few evangelists such as Griffith Jones, it was still highly unfashionable. It was Whitefield, whose first impassioned sermon was said to have driven fifteen people mad, who set the tone for the movement with his open-air address in February 1739 to the Kingswood colliers at Bristol. John Wesley, who had initially been dubious about the propriety of open-air preaching, soon joined Whitefield in Bristol, and only a few months later was proclaiming the world as his parish. During the remaining fifty-two years of his life he was to travel some 250,000 miles, preach over forty thousand sermons, and dominate a movement that brought deep emotional religious experience to countless thousands among the neglected masses of the emerging industrial society. Though in time Methodism achieved respectability and, because of its emphasis upon hard work and discipline, came to be regarded as socially useful, it was at first greeted with widespread hostility. The appeal to emotion, the use of lay-preachers and of huge open-air meetings that often culminated in riots, and the implicit criticism of the ways of organized religion were all seen as disruptive in an age that placed a premium upon order and reason. Although the Wesleys had no wish to break with the Established Church, and although many of its members such as William Grimshaw, John Berridge, John Fletcher and William Romaine sympathized with Wesley's aims and were themselves evangelical in outlook, the bishops and most parish priests were suspicious and resentful. The Methodists were therefore forced gradually to move away from the Church, form their own organization and rely eventually upon non-episcopal ordination. This merely confirmed suspicions of their radical nature, and Selina, Countess of Huntingdon, who became Whitefield's patron, was one of the very few from the upper ranks of society to embrace Methodist views. At first Whitefield, because of his remarkable gift for preaching, tended to command most attention, but his rigid Calvinism conflicted with the Arminianism of the Wesleys, the breach which developed between them in 1740 was never completely healed, and John Wesley's genius for organization soon made him the undisputed leader of the movement. By 1760 much of the initial hostility had disappeared and he was already recognized as a major force in the religious life of the nation.

The general intellectual climate was characterized by the same passion for order, reasonableness and moderation that made the ruling classes distrustful of Methodism and lent an air of urbanity, if not complacency, to much of the literary and artistic endeavour of the age. The tone had been set by the earlier writings of Sir Isaac Newton and John Locke. Newton had at least implicitly resolved the old conflict between reason and revelation by postulating an orderly universe governed by natural laws, the handiwork of an essentially reasonable Creator. Locke had seen the origins of civil government in a social contract by which reasonable men conditionally surrendered to the State their individual rights to enforce the laws of nature in order that those rights to life, liberty and property might be more effectively preserved; and at a practical level he had vindicated the right of revolution if the conditions of the contract were broken, the separation of the powers, majority rule, and the divorce of Church and State. The thought of Locke was supremely rational and secular, too much so indeed for many of his contemporaries; and it pointed the way to the utilitarianism of David Hume and Jeremy Bentham. In so far as it seemed to provide a philosophical justification for the Glorious Revolution (though the *Two Treatises of Government* were in fact written before 1688), it commanded general approval. But it is at least possible that Locke's writings were more closely studied and his ideas more widely followed in America and in France than they were in England.

Since reason had triumphed with the establishment of limited monarchy and the emergence of a stable form of mixed government, the era of the first two Georges was not one of profound political speculation. Indeed only two writers merit comment—Bolingbroke and Hume. Bolingbroke, a man of great natural abilities and pathetically bad judgment, was one of those splendid failures in which the eighteenth century abounds, and his rather superficial writings (Lord Morley called him 'a solemn trifler') were allowed to rest in decent obscurity until the current fashion for intellectual history resurrected them. Now, unhappily, there are almost as many bad books on Bolingbroke as there are on Pitt. Apart from his somewhat ineffectual excursions into Deism, Bolingbroke is chiefly interesting for his scintillating portraits of political life in the age of Walpole and for his succinct statement of the Country position. But this is little more than political journalism of a high order, and when it ceased to serve his purpose (for Bolingbroke was interested in power, not in principled Opposition), the one-time high priest of Toryism roundly condemned his former associates and turned in succession to the ideal of a non-party broad-bottomed Administration and to the need for restoring the ancient constitution through the agency of a patriot king. His writings were essentially tracts for the times and apologia for the twists in his own chequered political career. There seems little reason to quarrel with Harold Laski's verdict that they were 'no more than a mask for ambition born of hate'.

David Hume on the other hand was a thinker of great power and originality. Although his work was more destructive than constructive (he gave as short shrift to the social contract as he did to divine right), and although it lacked the over-all coherence and depth of that of Hobbes and Locke, it was remarkable for its many brilliant shafts of insight, and for the ease with which its author embraced politics, moral philosophy, psychology, metaphysics and economics. His uniformly empirical approach was in bold contrast to the idealism of George Berkeley, who alone among his contemporaries could rival, and even surpass, him in philosophical speculation, and his attitude to all political problems was essentially utilitarian. His liberal economic views, which clearly foreshadow those of Adam Smith, were similarly based upon secure psychological foundations, and his dislike of the divisive effects of organized religion led him wholly to subordinate the Church to the State. Despite this, and despite also his acute analysis of the contemporary political system, his distrust of all innovation and his contempt for the contract theory make him appear peculiarly un-Whiggish. Perhaps no one better illustrates the irrelevance of party labels, expresses more clearly the essence of eighteenth-century politics, or so epitomizes the sturdy common sense that was a vital element in the successful solution of most problems of the age.

The mainstream of British political writing was undoubtedly highly conservative, and even those—such as Bolingbroke—who criticized the existing order of things, looked back to a hypothetical golden age rather than forward to a brave new world. Yet there was also a continuing radical literary tradition, represented by Robert Molesworth, John

Trenchard, Edmund Law, John Toland, Thomas Pownall and other lesser figures. All thought of themselves as the inheritors of the republican thought of Milton, Harrington and Sidney, and all advocated reform that went beyond the limited aspirations of 'Country' critics of Government. These Real Whigs or Commonwealthmen, as they were frequently called, came mainly from the middle classes of society, and were often Deists, Protestant nonconformists, Scots or Irishmen. Although far from revolutionary in doctrine, they resisted the oligarchical tendencies of the age, lamented the increasing influence of the executive over the legislature, demanded a redistribution of the franchise, believed passionately in the natural rights of all men in all countries, sought to extend education and improve the condition of the masses, and advocated complete religious toleration. As might be expected in an era when most foreign visitors as well as most Englishmen were convinced of the beauty of the English constitution, their influence on political life was negligible. But they merit mention because they kept alive political ideas that were to have a significant bearing on the attitudes of the American colonists at the time of the revolution; and because they formed a link between the radicalism of the mid-seventeenth century and that of the late eighteenth, when the torch was handed on to men such as Richard Price, Joseph Priestley, James Burgh and John Cartwright.

In science no one could hope to rival the great Newton, who died in 1727, but whose influence inspired a host of lesser men to modest advances in mathematics, astronomy, chemistry, botany and medicine. Characteristically, many of their achievements were concerned with practical problems, and their activities were frequently many-sided. Among the more prominent mathematicians were Colin MacLaurin, James Stirling and Brook Taylor; the Astronomer-Royal Edmund Halley, who gave his name to the comet the return of which in 1758 he accurately forecast, also spent a year on St Helena and provided mariners with many useful navigational aids for the southern hemisphere; his successor, James Bradley, won international and lasting recognition for his theoretical work in astronomy; and at a more practical level James Dolland perfected the first refractory telescope. In chemistry the experiments of Joseph Black virtually destroyed the old 'phlogiston' theory,[1] identified carbon dioxide in all but name, illuminated the whole process of combustion, and established the concept of latent heat; and in botany the outstanding figure was

---

[1]Phlogiston was a hypothetical substance, formerly believed to exist in all combustible bodies, and to be released in the process of combustion.

Stephen Hales, whose many achievements included the discovery of the phenomenon of arterial pressure. Among the most beneficial advances were those in medicine and surgery, where men of the calibre of William and John Hunter led the way. During the first half of the century anatomy came to be taught in all four English and Scottish universities, and at Edinburgh a chair of clinical medicine was established. With the dissolution in 1745 of the Company of Barbers and Surgeons, surgery began to achieve respectability; although quacks still abounded, an increasing number of doctors came to enjoy high social position and membership of the Royal Society; and the heightened activity in the field of medicine was amply illustrated by the increase between 1700 and 1760 of the number of hospitals in Britain—from two to eleven in London alone.

Developments in art, music and architecture reflected the spirit of the times. Reynolds and Gainsborough had not yet fully established their reputations, and the English passion for portrait-painting had elevated the German Godfrey Kneller to a position of dominance which some felt he little deserved. But Sir James Thornhill produced some notable portraits, and decorative work of real quality on the dome of St Paul's, at Greenwich, and at Blenheim Palace. His son-in-law, William Hogarth, whose satirical genius equalled that of Pope, left us many savage and vivid portrayals of the hypocrisy, violence, crime and misery of the age. In sculpture no Englishman of great talent emerged, but Peter Scheemakers, John Michael Rysbrack and Louis François Roubillac made their homes in England and maintained a standard of work that in time influenced and encouraged less gifted local sculptors. In music the dominant figure was of course George Frederick Handel who, except when he alienated George II for six years by composing a wedding anthem for Frederick, Prince of Wales, enjoyed royal patronage until his death in 1759. In return he composed the *Water Music* for a river-fête organized in 1717 by George I, *Zadok the Priest* for the coronation of George II, the *Te Deum* on the occasion of the King's victory at Dettingen, and the *Firework Music* to celebrate the Peace of Aix-la-Chapelle. English reaction against the artificiality of grand opera helped to divert Handel to the oratorio, with which he achieved almost unqualified success, culminating in the first professional performance of the *Messiah* at Dublin in 1742. Among native Englishmen only Thomas Arne, who composed *Rule Britannia* and whose arrangement of *God Save the King* was first sung at Covent Garden and Drury Lane on the occasion of the Jacobite victory at Prestonpans, deserves special mention—not least for some of his Shakespearean settings. But the widespread love of music was evidenced by aristocratic no less than royal patronage, and the more popular songs were heard in cottages no less than stately homes.

In architecture the influence of Sir Christopher Wren, who died at the age of ninety in 1723, was reflected in the work of Sir John Vanbrugh, who turned with effortless ease from the writing of plays to the design of Blenheim Palace, Castle Howard and Seaton Delaval; and in that of Nicholas Hawksmoor, whose most notable achievements included the Clarendon Building at Oxford, the Codrington Library at All Souls' College, the library of The Queen's College and the western end of Westminster Abbey. With Vanbrugh the classical element in Wren was dwarfed by the baroque, and a reaction soon set in against an ostentatious splendour that ran counter to the growing belief in the harmony between man and nature. Hawksmoor's buildings, though maintaining the same pure symmetry and fine proportions, were less over-powering than those of Vanbrugh; and with James Gibbs, whose Senate House at Cambridge is one of the most elegant examples of the architecture of the period, the Palladian style which became so popular with the Earl of Burlington and William Kent is much in evidence. The love of harmony and order was seen not only in public buildings, stately homes and many humbler dwellings, but also in the streets, crescents and squares of London and Bath, in the natural landscape gardening of Kent and 'Capability' Brown, and in the supremely elegant furniture of Thomas Chippendale.

In the world of literature change was even more apparent. The great survivors from the Augustan age were Alexander Pope, lionized by the parliamentary opposition to Walpole, and Jonathan Swift, condemned for his Tory political writings to the obscurity of an Irish deanery. Pope's urbanity, elegance and command of language—illustrated above all in *The Rape of the Lock*, *An Essay on Criticism* and *An Essay on Man*—can make us forgive the occasional artificiality of his sentiments, and his satires alone establish him among the great figures of eighteenth-century literature. Yet Swift, who wielded the bludgeon rather than the rapier, had the greater intellect, and nothing that Pope wrote can compare with the savage vigour of *Gulliver's Travels* or *The Tale of a Tub*. Pope's hatreds were of individuals and were often spiteful and petty; Swift could warm to individuals but despised the human race.

More typical of future trends were the poetry of James Thomson, William Collins and Thomas Gray, and the novels of Samuel Richardson, Henry Fielding and Tobias Smollett. Although all were bound to some extent by the artificial conventions of the past, their writings were also marked by simplicity and sentiment. The poets showed a love of nature that was to reach maturity with their greater successors of the romantic movement, and the novelists—despite Richardson's tiresome penchant for moralizing—displayed a more subtle understanding of human character and motivation than the Augustans had seen fit to express. Thomson in his *The Seasons*, Collins in his odes *To Evening* and *To Simplicity*, and Gray in *The Bard* and in his word-perfect *Elegy Written in a Country Churchyard* brought a new dimension to English poetry. Richardson's *Pamela* and *Clarissa*, Fielding's *Joseph Andrews* and *Tom Jones*, and Smollett's *Roderick Random* captured something of the vitality, self-confidence and infinite variety of the age. Nor should one forget John Gay, whose *The Beggar's Opera* relentlessly and savagely lampooned the politics of the Walpoleian era in language that all could understand, and which was so successful that its successor, *Polly*, was barred from the stage. Over all presided the towering figure of Samuel Johnson, who had published most of his more important work by 1760, but was still only on the threshold of recognition and awaited Boswell. It is impossible not to warm to his uncompromising Toryism, his resounding eloquence, his boisterous good humour and his many and passionately-held prejudices. But he was born fifty years too late, and should really have been at his prime in the reign of Anne. The man is more engaging than his work and, had it not been for Boswell, he could scarcely have enjoyed so great or so enduring a reputation. Yet it is a testament to his impact upon contemporary society that his ponderous prose and bigoted outlook, which ran counter to every trend of the age, could win greater acclaim than the simple lucid style and liberal empirical attitude of his great protagonist, David Hume.

More important perhaps than the stature of the leading literary figures was the widespread interest in their writings and the rapid growth of the reading public. Newspapers mushroomed in London and the provinces, magazines and reviews (of which the most important were the *Gentleman's Magazine* and the *London Magazine*) enjoyed a great popularity, and the circulating library was launched. Writers of real ability no longer had to rely upon finding a wealthy patron, but could expect ample financial reward for their work. The passion for literary expression was also to enable posterity to enjoy some of the most articulate and informative letters, diaries, journals and memoirs in the English language. By 1760 Horace Walpole had already provided many potential volumes of malicious gossip in his correspondence with that prince of mediocrity, Sir Horace Mann; Lady Mary Wortley Montagu had perceptively and elegantly recorded her travels abroad; the wit and cynicism of Lord Chesterfield had captured the fashionable society of his time in his urbane letters to his illegitimate son. More important for the historian were the diaries kept by the Earls of Marchmont and by Lord Egmont, and the endearing journal of George Bubb Dodington, who summed up his whole political philosophy in the couplet:

> Strive thy little bark to steer
> With the tide, but near the shore.

But the most valuable of all are the memoirs of Lord Hervey and of Horace Walpole, who between them covered the first and last decades of the reign of George II. Both sets of memoirs are shot through with malice, and both have been allowed to colour too much our view of the leading political figures of the age. Hervey could find no merit in anyone but Queen Caroline and Sir Robert Walpole; and Horace Walpole, irritated by the refusal of the Pelhams to let him get his hand yet further into the till, began his memoirs with the express purpose of blackening their characters. When Archdeacon William Coxe sought permission in 1823 to use the family papers of the fourth Duke of Newcastle for his biography of Henry Pelham, the Duke had some grounds for deploring the abuse heaped upon his 'two good uncles, Newcastle and Pelham', and for welcoming what he trusted would be 'an effective antidote to the vilifying and scurrilous invective with which their administration has been so unjustly covered'. Nor was he unduly vindictive in describing Horace Walpole as 'venomous from constitution, rendered more acid by personal hate and frustrated ambition'. Yet Walpole's memoirs, unlike his letters, are remarkable for the accuracy of their political content, and his caustic wit makes them marvellously entertaining. Nevertheless, they can scarcely compare, either for venom or for elegance, with the measured, vitriolic prose of Lord Hervey, who brilliantly depicted life at the Court of George II and, with malice towards all, portrayed the men and women of his day. Even of so harmless a figure as the first Lord Lyttelton he could write:

> His face was so ugly, his person so ill-made, and his carriage so awkward, that every feature was a blemish, every limb an encumbrance, and every motion a disgrace. But, as disagreeable as his figure was, his voice was still more so, and his address more disagreeable than either. He had a great flow of words that were always uttered in a lulling monotony, and the little meaning they had to boast of was generally borrowed from the commonplace maxims and sentiments of moralists, philosophers, patriots and poets, crudely imbibed, half digested, ill put together and confusedly refunded.

But even Hervey eventually met his match, and the last word must go to Pope, whose hermaphrodite insinuations and contempt for Hervey's servility to Sir Robert Walpole and Queen Caroline were etched in pure acid:

Let Sporus tremble—What, that thing of silk,
Sporus, that mere white curd of ass's milk?
Satire or sense, alas! can Sporus feel?
Who breaks a butterfly upon a wheel?
Yet let me flap this bug with gilded wings—
This painted child of dirt, that stinks and stings;
Whose buzz the witty and the fair annoys,
Yet wit ne'er tastes, and beauty ne'er enjoys;
So well-bred spaniels civilly delight
In mumbling of the game they dare not bite.
Eternal smiles his emptiness betray,
As shallow streams run dimpling all the way.
Whether in florid impotence he speaks,
And, as the prompter breathes, the puppet squeaks;
Or at the ear of Eve, familiar toad,
Half froth, half venom, spits himself abroad,
In puns, or politics, or tales, or lies,
Or spite, or smut, or rhymes, or blasphemies.
His wit all see-saw between that and this,
And he himself one vile antithesis.
Amphibious thing, that acting either part,
The trifling head, or the corrupted heart.
Fop at the toilet, flatterer at the board,
Now trips a lady, and now struts a lord.
Eve's tempter thus the rabbins have expressed,
A cherub's face, a reptile all the rest;
Beauty that shocks you, parts that none will trust,
Wit that can creep, and pride that licks the dust.

PART TWO
1760–1815

8

GEORGE III IN SEARCH OF A MINISTRY: 1760–70

THE accession of George III inaugurated a decade of political instability that was halted only by the appointment of Lord North to the headship of the Treasury in 1770. To some extent the roots of this instability went back to the death of Henry Pelham in 1754, and the situation was soon to be aggravated by the post-war depression, the emergence of new radical forces, and the growing dispute between Britain and her American colonies.[1] For the moment we may merely note that the character and upbringing of the new King was a significant element in the political equation. He had been taught at Leicester House to believe that his grandfather had been reduced to a cypher by the politicians of his reign, he regarded Newcastle and his immediate associates as the chief architects of a corrupt system of politics, he loathed Pitt for deserting him in 1757, he detested Hanover and deplored the continuation of the war, and he was determined to inaugurate a new reign of virtue by ousting the old ministers as soon as possible and elevating his dearest friend, Lord Bute, to the highest political office. In many ways George III's most revealing act was the issue, six days after his succession, of a proclamation 'for the encouragement of piety and virtue, and for the prevention of vice, profaneness and immorality'. A naïve young man of twenty-three was about to clean out the Augean stables. But naïvety was only one of the new King's handicaps. He was unfortunate enough to combine a deep sense of responsibility with an enormous inferiority complex. Psychologically incapable of acting the tyrant, even had he wished to do so, he sought above all a strong man on whom he could lean; and he was at first foolish enough to cast the ineffectual Bute in this role. Not surprisingly the result was disastrous.

---

[1]For a more detailed analysis of the changing pattern of politics see pp 277–94.

Yet at first there seemed little enough cause for alarm, for the middle of a war was no time for major ministerial changes. Bute was elevated to the office of Groom of the Stole, an attempt to insinuate a reference in the King's Speech to the 'bloody and expensive' war was modified at Pitt's insistence to acknowledge the conflict as expensive but 'just and necessary', the King surrendered his hereditary revenue in return for a fixed annual Civil List of £800,000, and a supply of nearly £20,000,000 was voted for the coming year without too much difficulty. The general election of 1761 was notable only for the King's refusal to contribute any secret service money towards the expenses, but though Newcastle grumbled he was happy enough to be left in general charge of the election, and the resulting Parliament differed in no essential from its predecessors. In deference to Bute's acknowledged influence in the royal counsels, ministers agreed that he should hold an office of real responsibility, and in March 1761 he was given an English earldom and Holderness's place as Secretary of State, with Charles Jenkinson as his Under-Secretary. Sir Francis Dashwood, one of Bute's protégés, was made Treasurer of the Chamber, Barrington replaced Legge as Chancellor of the Exchequer, and Halifax became Lord-Lieutenant of Ireland—all relatively minor changes but symptomatic of an almost imperceptible swing away from the *status quo*.

Meanwhile, the end of the war seemed to be in sight. The publication in 1760 of Israel Mauduit's *Considerations on the Present German War* had bolstered the conviction of Bute and the King that an early peace was essential; and the English capture of Belleisle, Dominica and Pondicherry had persuaded the French to put out peace-feelers which Frederick the Great, hard pressed by both Austria and Prussia, was inclined to favour. Negotiations were therefore opened in both Paris and London, but Pitt caused a temporary breakdown by insisting that France be absolutely excluded from the Newfoundland fisheries. This encouraged the growing *rapprochement* between France and Spain, and Choiseul responded to Pitt's rigidity by requesting a concurrent settlement of Spanish grievances and by implying that Spain would join the conflict if not satisfied. On 15 August 1761 Pitt declared that all hope of peace was at an end. Shortly afterwards he changed his mind, but the damage had been done. The Family Compact was concluded between France and Spain, with the latter promising to enter the war if peace had not been concluded by May 1762. This threat nettled the English ministers and Newcastle alone opposed Pitt's subsequent official termination of the negotiations. But Pitt was not content to let matters rest there; he insisted upon an immediate declaration of war against Spain so that her treasure fleet could be seized and her colonies attacked. This was too much for ministers such as Bedford who wanted peace at any price, or even Newcastle who was prepared to give further support to Prussia but had no wish to extend the scope of the war. When the Cabinet debated the issue on 2 October 1761, only Temple supported Pitt, who was at his most arrogant:

> In his station and situation [he declared] he was responsible and would not continue without having the direction. That being his case nobody could be surprised that he could go on no longer, and he would repeat it again, that he would be responsible for nothing but what he directed.

Three days later he resigned, with a peerage for his wife and an annual pension of £3,000, at the same time disclaiming all intention of going into Opposition. He was followed by Temple on 9 October.

In retrospect it is tempting to see all this as part of a deep-laid plot, with the King and Bute playing on the other ministers' jealousy of Pitt, and using them to force him out as the essential but unsuspected prerequisite to their own later dismissal. But although George III was undoubtedly delighted, Pitt's fall was the outcome of a growing desire for peace that was increasingly evident in both Parliament and the nation. Pitt preferred to ignore the vast cost and rising unpopularity of the war; he forced the conclusion of the Family Compact when he had every reason to believe that France was genuinely ready for peace; and he was unreasonably arrogant towards the French monarch who, having already been humbled, was peculiarly sensitive to insult. Moreover, other European nations were as little likely to welcome an over-mighty Britain as an over-mighty France. An equitable peace made good political sense.

Pitt had fallen, but fear of his power in the Commons remained. George Grenville (who had broken with both Pitt and Temple) was therefore given Cabinet rank and made Leader of the Lower House; and Henry Fox, mollified by a peerage for his wife, agreed to act under Bute's instructions. Egremont, a staunch friend of both Bute and the King, was elevated to Pitt's Secretaryship. Thereafter Bute, Egremont and Grenville settled everything between them, and poor Newcastle was soon complaining that, although he was ostensible head of the Ministry, he was kept completely in the dark. He knew nothing of the decision to send six thousand men to Portugal, though it was he who had to find the money to support them; negotiations with France were conducted entirely through Bute's brother, James Stuart Mackenzie. Finally, when war was declared against Spain in January 1762 it was against Newcastle's advice. It was ironical that Bute should consent to the extension of the war when he and his fellow-ministers had forced Pitt's resignation over this very issue. But he was uneasy at the continuing enthusiasm of the City for Pitt, and his immediate reaction was to court merchant popularity by rivalling his predecessor in belligerency. The ensuing capture of Martinique, St Lucia, Grenada and St Vincent, together with the dispatch of troops to Portugal and of an expedition to take Havana, seemed to augur well for the future. But oddly enough these successes made Bute panic. He saw himself committed to an expanding war, and sought refuge in trying to disentangle Britain from Europe by breaking with Prussia. His subsequent actions have been the subject of much controversy, but on balance it seems that he acted injudiciously rather than perfidiously. He negotiated secretly with Austria and gave the Russian ambassador in London reason to believe that he was prepared to double-cross Frederick over Silesia. Frederick for his part was being singularly difficult. Assisted at a very crucial stage in his fortunes by the death of his bitter enemy the Tsarina Elizabeth (whereby Russia was converted from a dreaded and powerful foe into an enthusiastic ally, and, even after the rapid murder of the new Tsar, remained, under Catherine the Great, benevolently neutral) Frederick demanded greater British activity, despite the new situation created by the entry of Spain into the war. He even tried to stir up opposition to Bute in England, but Pitt would not play his game. Not unnaturally Bute was irritated and he determined to withhold the annual subsidy already promised to Prussia. This was the issue which was to bring about the final rupture with the most prominent of the old ministers, for Newcastle, Hardwicke and Devonshire, already annoyed at not being consulted, disliked the idea of dishonouring the promise to Prussia. At the Cabinet meeting of 31 April 1762 they opposed Bute's proposal but were overruled. A month later Newcastle surrendered the seals after more than forty years of almost continuous office. Devonshire, though retaining office as Lord Chamberlain, ceased to attend Cabinet meetings, and Hardwicke was no longer summoned. Few other changes were made. Bute at last moved up to the long-coveted Treasury, Grenville to the Secretaryship of State, and Dashwood to the Chancellorship of the Exchequer; and on Anson's death later in the year Halifax took over the Admiralty.

If the changes of personnel were few, 1762 marked in a real sense the end of an era dominated except for Pitt by the politicians of the Old Corps. For the first time in fifty years families like the Pelhams, Yorkes, Walpoles and Cavendishes were on the outside looking in, and the future seemed cold and bleak. Yet, at least superficially, Bute and the King had little to fear. Men who had for two generations been denouncing all formed Opposition as wicked and factious were unlikely to embark on it themselves, while those still in the service of the Crown (especially

Hardwicke's ambitious sons) were not anxious to offend the King. Pitt, an essential element in any Opposition, was obliged to Bute for his pension and his wife's peerage and preferred to play a waiting game in the hope that he might yet be restored to his former power. He was also hated by the Duke of Cumberland, who had broken with Fox when the latter joined forces with Bute, and towards whom Newcastle and his friends were tending to gravitate. The chances of a concerted Opposition therefore seemed slight, yet dissatisfaction was in the air, important people had been offended and any ill-considered action by Bute or the King could easily provoke a crisis.

Meanwhile the war continued to go smoothly. Havana and Manilla were captured from Spain, Frederick drove the Austrians from Silesia, French troops suffered further defeat in Europe, and Portugal, aided by British troops, drove the invading Spaniards from their country. Bute became terror-stricken at the receding prospects of peace and even wrote to Choiseul deploring the French defeats. Lacking any confidence in his ability as a war leader, and fearing the belligerent tendencies of some of his new colleagues, he sent Lyttelton to sound Newcastle and Hardwicke about a possible return to office. Not unnaturally they declined to rally to his aid. When in August 1762 Bute despatched Bedford to Paris to discuss peace terms, his Administration seemed on the point of collapse. Dashwood had proved a broken reed, while Grenville was refusing to accept responsibility for the Commons unless he were given control of patronage, which could only make Bute, as head of the Treasury, appear ridiculous. The King appealed again to Newcastle and Hardwicke—and even to Pitt—to come in and bolster up Bute's Ministry, but all were adamant. George III was beginning to learn—as his grandfather had learnt in 1746—that an Administration could not be built on foundations of sand. Fearful that the projected peace terms would be rejected by a Commons bereft of responsible leadership, Bute turned in desperation to Henry Fox who, in return for the promise of a peerage, agreed to manage the lower House. Grenville for his recalcitrance was relegated to the Admiralty, and Halifax took his place as Secretary of State.

With confidence re-born, the King struck out in blind rage at those who had refused to do his bidding. Early in October Devonshire had refused to attend a Cabinet meeting to discuss the peace terms, and his association with Newcastle convinced the King that both were caballing against Bute. George therefore determined to dismiss him, refused him an audience, and was furious to find that Devonshire, resenting the insult, had deposited the symbol of his office in Lord Egremont's lap. Taking umbrage at the King's treatment of his brother, Lord George Cavendish resigned as Comptroller of the Household, to be followed by the Marquis of Rockingham, until then a Lord of the Bedchamber. The King, more furious than ever, struck Devonshire's name from the list of Privy Councillors, for which the only precedents were Lord Bath (for persistent and contumacious opposition) and Lord George Sackville (for his alleged cowardice at Minden). Nothing was more calculated to arouse the resentment of the leading Old Whig peers than insult and injustice to one of their leaders. Kinoull and Albemarle promptly resigned, and opposition to the peace preliminaries became inevitable. Not that Bute was in any danger. The preliminaries passed the Upper House without a division, and in the two divisions on them in the Commons only ninety-seven members voted against the Government. Nonetheless, George III determined to punish the rump of the Old Corps. Newcastle, Rockingham and Grafton were removed from their Lord-Lieutenancies, and Devonshire forestalled the King by resigning his. Finally came the 'slaughter of the Pelhamite innocents' whereby in the constituencies every trivial friend, relative and dependent of Newcastle's was ruthlessly purged, while the Duke lamented with tears in his eyes the fate of 'the poor unhappy county of Sussex'.

Peace was duly signed on 10 February 1763 and rather surprisingly accepted with little enthusiasm by a nation that only recently had seemed very war-weary. British gains, if less than Pitt had wished, were real and substantial—the whole of Canada, Louisiana east of the Mississippi, Cape Breton and the islands of the St Lawrence, Tobago, Dominica, St Vincent, the Grenadines, Senegal and (from the Spanish) Florida. True, France retained fishing rights in the St Lawrence together with the islands of St Pierre and Miquelon as a base, and recovered Guadeloupe, Martinique, St Lucia, Mariegalante, Desirade and Gorée. But she had also to return Minorca in exchange for Belleisle and agree to demilitarize Dunkirk; and although she regained her factories in India it was only in return for her effective acknowledgment of the supremacy of the British East India Company and of their puppet princes in the Carnatic and the Deccan. Critics could argue that Guadeloupe would have been of much greater immediate value than Canada (though the British West Indian sugar lobby did not welcome the prospect of competition), that the removal of the French menace from the British American mainland colonies would only encourage them to take a more independent line, and that Bute's hasty conclusion of peace had alienated Prussia and left Britain without an ally in Europe in the event of further conflict. Yet Parliament's overwhelming endorsement of the peace terms was more indicative of public opinion than the reactions, for example, of London, Yorkshire and Surrey which refused to send in addresses of thanks.

Nonetheless, there was a vague but widespread suspicion of the new look which George III had imparted to the political scene, and the ensuing abuse was heaped upon the head of Bute, who increased his unpopularity by the introduction of a cider tax in March 1763. As an extension of the excise this was bound to arouse memories of 1733, and was received with rage and rioting in London and the cider counties. The Press—and especially the *North Briton*—violently denounced Bute, playing on the pathological English distrust of all Scotsmen. Within the Cabinet few of his colleagues showed any enthusiasm for his leadership and even the King had come to deplore his 'deficiency in political firmness'. Depressed and unnerved, Bute resigned on 8 April 1763 and the reign of virtue which the King had envisaged in 1760 was over. Since neither Pitt nor Fox was prepared to succeed Bute, and since George III could not bring himself again to approach the leaders of the Old Corps, the headship of the Treasury eventually went to George Grenville. With the two Secretaries, Egremont and Halifax, he formed the so-called Triumvirate which took over the trembling reins of Government from the deflated Scottish favourite. Dashwood was retired with a peerage, while Fox continued as Paymaster and became Lord Holland.

Bute and the King apparently hoped that Grenville, despite earlier evidence of stubbornness, might become a quiet, efficient, co-operative minister, duly respectful towards royal prejudices and susceptibilities. Never were men more mistaken. Up to this time Grenville had had a relatively undistinguished career, being far outshone by the erratic genius of his brother-in-law, Pitt, and by the hot-headed violence of his elder brother, Temple. But at heart he shared the abiding belief of all his family, that in their creation the Almighty had at last achieved perfection. Elevated by a whimsical turn of fate to the headship of the Treasury, he rapidly developed a liking for the first place, and the King soon found that he had to deal not with a pliant nonentity, but with a hard-headed and hard-hearted politician who was not afraid to take a strong line and defend it to the last ditch. Grenville was not an attractive man; indeed he was a crashing bore, with a mind like a cash-register. But he commanded a great deal of respect. His ideal of a carefully-balanced budget, rigid economy at home and abroad and avoidance of continental entanglements, endeared him to the mass of country gentlemen, who were long since weary of heavy wartime taxation. His determination to bring the recalcitrant American colonists to heel, and his conservative hatred of all radical agitation at home likewise reflected the prejudices of most members of Parliament, while his obvious administrative efficiency won the support of many Government servants who had seats in the Lower House. He also had the inestimable advantage of being physically present in the Commons and had he not quickly become *persona non grata* to the King he could probably have maintained his Ministry until his death in 1770.

But it was not to be. Grenville's humourless dogmatism soon became anathema to George III, as did his almost pathological suspicion of Bute and his friends, and his determination to make himself the sole channel to royal favour. Thus even before the Wilkes affair reached its height the King had already twice tried to extricate himself from Grenville's dominance be seeking the assistance of both Pitt and the leaders of the Old Corps. But they were by then more distrustful than ever of the King and insisted on terms that he was unwilling to accept. George III therefore had to go back cap in hand to Grenville whose confidence and determination were merely strengthened by the King's failure. On the death of Egremont, Sandwich became Secretary of State, while Hillsborough took over the Board of Trade from Shelburne (who resigned because Pitt had not been won over) and Bedford entered the Administration as Lord President. Thus the Ministry became more conservative-minded than ever, as it quickly showed in its handling of both Wilkes and America.

John Wilkes, MP for Aylesbury since 1757 and a political associate of Temple, was ambitious, reckless, unprincipled, brazen, ugly, charming and witty. He was also a polemicist and demagogue of near genius. No one could better express in scurrilous form the uneasiness that was felt, especially in the metropolitan area, about the influence of the unpopular Bute, the peace terms and the cider tax. In No. 45 of the *North Briton* he insulted the King and denounced the praise of the peace in the King's Speech as 'the most abandoned instance of ministerial effrontery'. Ministers, perhaps because they felt less secure, were more sensitive than their predecessors had been in the days of Walpole and Pelham; and they feared Wilkes's capacity for arousing the general public. A general warrant, under the authority of Lord Halifax as Secretary of State, was issued for the arrest of the authors, printers and publishers of No. 45. Thus unwittingly Wilkes was launched on a career as the friend of liberty that was to last for a decade. On his arrest and imprisonment in the Tower he was portrayed as the victim of ministerial tyranny, and there was general rejoicing when Chief Justice Pratt (a liberal-minded friend of Pitt) released him on the grounds that his privilege as a member of Parliament exonerated him from imprisonment except for treason, felony or breach of the peace. With splendid effrontery Wilkes pressed home his advantage by re-publishing his libels, suing Halifax and his under-Secretary, Robert Wood, and recovering £1,000 damages. The ministers, humiliated by Wilkes and taunted by vociferous London radicals, could scarcely let the matter rest there. In the Commons on 15 November 1763, they carried by 237 votes to 111 a motion declaring No. 45 to be a 'false, scandalous and seditious libel', likely to excite 'traitorous insurrections against his majesty's Government'. Clearly many of the Commons shared the ministers' fear of Wilkes's potentiality as a demagogue, especially during the period of bad harvests, high prices and increasing unemployment that accompanied the ending of the war. With the aid of Sandwich, who ironically enough had been a former associate of Wilkes in the revels of the Hell-Fire Club, the Administration was able to procure a copy of *The Essay on Woman*, which Wilkes had privately printed and which was held to be obscene and pornographic. Since it contained notes attributed satirically to the Bishop of Gloucester, it was also denounced as a libel in the House of Lords. Wilkes had now been condemned by both Houses and faced warrants for his arrest on charges of seditious libel and obscenity. Already wounded in a duel, he decided that discretion was the better part of valour and withdrew to France, where news soon reached him of his expulsion from the Commons in January 1764 and his outlawry a month later for failure to appear in court to answer the charges against him.

But if the denunciation of No. 45 and the expulsion of Wilkes indicated that independent opinion in the Commons disapproved of both scurrility and obscenity, there was widespread uneasiness about the high-handed methods adopted by the Administration. Since the lapsing of the Licensing Act in 1696 the use of general warrants had been regarded as at best of dubious legality, and the chief political aftermath of this first phase of the Wilkes affair was a motion in the Commons on 15 February 1764 that they were in fact illegal. The Ministry managed to stave off defeat, but only by fourteen votes in a House of 458 members. Nor was the prestige of the Administration much improved when Colonel Barré and General Conway were dismissed from office for opposing their fellow-ministers over Wilkes, and when Charles and John Yorke resigned in protest; while opinion in London was perhaps best indicated by the fact that when the public hangman attempted to burn No. 45, he was interrupted by the mob, and a pair of jack-boots and a petticoat (symbolizing Bute and the Dowager Princess) were burnt instead.

If Grenville's handling of Wilkes had given the parliamentary Opposition an issue on which to make a stand, his conduct of American affairs was to stir up even greater agitation on the other side of the Atlantic. The growing spirit of independence among the mainland colonists had long been a source of concern to successive British Governments. For much of the seventeenth century Britain had been too pre-occupied with her own domestic affairs to exercise effective control over her colonies, while the long wars of William and Anne and the 'salutary neglect' of Walpole had confirmed the colonists' belief in their right to self-government. Colonial governors found it difficult if not impossible to implement imperial policy when they were dependent for their stipends on local assemblies which were only too conscious of their 'power of the purse', but which showed themselves irresponsible in their attitude towards Indian relations and towards the problem of their own defence. During the Seven Years' War the colonists had not only declined to defend themselves (until Pitt had promised to reimburse them) but had encouraged the sale of arms to the enemy. After 1763 British ministers and country gentlemen who had long been suffering a maximum land-tax for a war that was fought at least partially in defence of America felt, not unnaturally, that the time had come to reassert the authority of the mother-country. Under Bute the decision had been taken to station ten thousand troops in the colonies in case of a renewed threat from France; and under Grenville had been issued the Proclamation of 7 October 1763 establishing the Alleghanies as a temporary boundary line beyond which the present colonies should not be allowed to expand. These were the first steps towards the solution of the acutely difficult 'western problem' in which Indian relations, defence and the fur-trade were all intimately interwoven, and the urgency of which was emphasized shortly afterwards by the rising of the Indian chief, Pontiac. But Grenville did not stop there. On the expiry of Walpole's Molasses Act of 1733 he reduced the duty on foreign sugar imported into the colonies from sixpence to threepence, but openly stated in the preamble to his new revenue act that it was necessary to raise money for 'defending, protecting and securing' America; and by enlarging the navy and the customs service he made it clear that the revenue henceforth would be collected, which had certainly not been the case in the past. This of course would not raise all the money that was needed, and he proposed to provide for the remainder by extending the Mutiny Act to America and considering the possibility of a Stamp Act. The ideas of the colonists were sought on the latter and when no alternative sources of supply were suggested the Stamp Act was duly passed on 22 March 1765, without much more than token opposition from the friends of Pitt and Newcastle. For the first time an internal as distinct from an external tax was levied on the Americans, but no one in England foresaw the storm that this innovation would arouse.

Meanwhile Grenville had pursued a policy of rigid economy at home, aided of course by the ending of the war. Annual expenditure was cut from £13,000,000 to £8,000,000, the army reduced from 120,000 to thirty thousand and the navy neglected to the point of danger. All this appealed to the country gentlemen in Parliament, who were also delighted to see Grenville extract £100,000 from the Bank of England as a prerequisite to the renewal of their charter. But if Grenville's credit with the Commons stood high he had not endeared himself to the King. A temporary illness early in 1765 persuaded George III that he should appoint a Council of Regency in case of future incapacity. Grenville successfully dissuaded the King from including his mother, the Dowager Princess, in the Council on the grounds that the Commons would certainly insist on the deletion of her name. But during the debate the Princess's name was actually added without significant opposition. George III was furious at having unnecessarily been made to appear an undutiful son, and Grenville had to bear the brunt of his wrath. Indeed, by the spring of 1765 George III had become thoroughly irritated by Grenville's parsimony, long-windedness, jealousy over questions of patronage and endless complaints about Bute, which culminated in his insistence on the dismissal of Bute's brother-in-law, Stuart MacKenzie. Already the King had approached his uncle, the Duke of Cumberland, to act as intermediary in the formation of a new Ministry, based on the friends of Pitt and Newcastle. But Pitt at first proved too uncompromising in his demands and later refused to come in because Temple would not accept the Treasury. This left Newcastle's friends as the only feasible alternative and, although many of them were reluctant to serve without Pitt, a meeting of some of their leaders at the end of June 1765 decided by twelve votes to five that the invitation should be accepted—provided that the King would agree to dismiss at least some of Bute's friends who were still in office. With this backward glimpse at the purge of 1762 the so-called first Rockingham ministry was formed on 13 July.

The Rockingham Whigs occupy a special place in the historiography of eighteenth-century politics, and deserve careful analysis.[1] But it is here necessary only to emphasize that they consisted chiefly of an older, conservative group of prominent political families from the previous reign—the rump of the Old Corps—and a younger, more ambitious group, of whom the most notable included Edmund Burke, William Dowdeswell and Sir William Meredith. The somewhat uneasy alliance between senior and junior wings had managed to survive the political stresses of 1762–5, and was tending increasingly to turn for leadership from Newcastle to Rockingham, himself a younger man, but linked through Newcastle and the Cavendishes with the Old Corps. Rockingham

[1] See pp 282–8.

also had his own little band of personal followers, drawn largely from his territorial stronghold of Yorkshire. It is not easy to explain the influence which he came eventually to exert over his party. A shockingly poor speaker, an inept politician, dedicated more to the race-track than the Cabinet board, he originally had no clear ideas of importance on any political issue. Yet he came to command intense loyalty, even during sixteen long years in the political wilderness between 1766 and 1782. It is easy to sneer at Rockingham for his amateurism and incapacity, but in an age when personal relationships were all-important in politics, and when (Pitt notwithstanding) men mattered more than measures, one should not underestimate Rockingham's sincerity and capacity for friendship. He was an agreeable companion and a genial host; he enjoyed tremendous popularity in Yorkshire; he had enough money to be disinterested and could, if necessary, afford the luxury of almost permanent Opposition; and he had a propagandist of genius in Edmund Burke, whose ineptitude as a 'man of business' was at first concealed by the activities of Dowdeswell. Rockingham was to become a real force in politics, but in 1765 he was still an unknown quantity.

In July 1765 the essential weakness of the new Ministry was well illustrated by the composition of the efficient Cabinet. The effective chief minister was in fact not Rockingham but Cumberland, formerly Commander-in-Chief but by then holding no office. Until his death in October he presided over every important Cabinet meeting and was consulted on all matters. For three months it was Cumberland's rather than Rockingham's Administration. Rockingham was first Lord of the Treasury, but Conway and Grafton as the two Secretaries of State did most of the real work; Northington (Lord Chancellor) and Egmont (First Lord of the Admiralty) were included as King's Friends or royal observers; Newcastle (Lord Privy Seal) and Winchelsea (Lord President) were political ghosts, shuffling about on a barely familiar political stage. As for the other offices there was a much greater turnover than at any other change of Ministry between 1714 and 1782, when the second Rockingham Ministry was formed. Between thirty and forty offices changed hands. The front benches in both Houses had a decidedly new look, and places were found for most of the more prominent who had been faithful since 1762. Yet in the Commons there were probably no more than about fifty upon whom ministers could rely absolutely. They would inevitably have to depend for survival upon the support of the King's Friends[1] (an amalgam of Court and Treasury Party, Court independents and Bute's

---

[1]See p 279.

Scottish associates) and independents with whom they had no definite connection. If the Administration was more homogeneous than any other of the 1760s it was anything but firmly based, and indeed few contemporaries believed that it would endure. Chesterfield described it as 'a mere jumble of youth and caducity, which cannot be efficient', and Charles Townshend remarked that it was 'a mere lute-string Administration, pretty summer wear, but it will never survive the winter'. Ministerial lack of confidence was shown in frantic attempts to mollify Pitt by providing offices for some of his relatives and by giving Pratt a peerage. Nor did the new Ministry have any clear ideas on policy apart from a vague inclination on the part of its younger members to harness some of the extra-parliamentary forces that had recently appeared. In particular they wished to cultivate the large and influential middling interest in the City, which for the first time had been brought to support Administration under Pitt. In the first half of the century the middling men had been consistently anti-ministerial and had been particularly active at the time of the Excise Bill and the agitation for war with Spain in 1739. More recently they had gained confidence by Pitt's recognition of their importance, become more vocal under the influence of the post-war depression, and been strengthened—at least temporarily—by the tendency towards co-operation of the American and West Indian elements within their ranks. This connection with the merchants (with Barlow Trecothick and the two Fullers providing the liaison) had been gradually forged between 1762 and 1765, and was to colour the whole life and activities of the Ministry. On the other hand, the Rockinghams could be certain of the combined opposition of the highly conservative Bedford and Grenville groups (each numbering perhaps twenty or more), and much would depend on two imponderables. How would Pitt and his tiny band of followers act? And how would the King's Friends react?

To a large extent the story of the first Rockingham Ministry can be written in terms of its American policy. Recognizing the intrinsic weakness of their position, the older members became increasingly reconciled to the eagerness of the younger men to seek merchant support. But they were also as indignant as they were surprised by the strength of American resistance to the Stamp Act, and denounced Patrick Henry's Virginia Resolves as 'an absolute disavowal of the right of the Parliament of Great Britain to impose taxes on the colonies, and a daring attack on the constitution of this country'—words of which Grenville himself might have been proud. Indeed orders were sent to Colonial Governors to take steps to quell the riots, and if necessary to call on the Commander-in-Chief for military aid. Had it not been for the moderating influence of the merchants, both British and colonial, the American Revolution might have broken out under the first Rockingham Ministry, and generations of Whig historians would have been gravely embarrassed. But fortunately wiser counsels prevailed. American non-importation and non-consumption agreements were increasingly striking at the pockets of British merchants, already smarting under the impact of post-war depression. Trade was held up, debts could not be collected, and foreign markets were not yet sufficiently developed to absorb the goods that were piling up in the warehouses. Fearing bankruptcy, the merchants wasted no time in futile theorizing about the rights of Parliament. A committee of London merchants under Trecothick was chosen to organize agitation on a national scale, and many of the Rockinghams supported the circular letter which was sent to thirty of the chief manufacturing and trading towns. Yet the older conservative wing (except for Newcastle) could not readily contemplate anything so 'un-Whiggish' as repealing the Stamp Act and appearing to surrender parliamentary sovereignty over the colonies. When Parliament assemble briefly before Christmas the Ministry failed to take any positive line, and only Grenville's premature and provocative attempts to force a crisis saved them from embarrassment. During the Christmas recess the leaders of the Rockinghams met to discuss the American problem, but so divided were they that they could not even agree to modification of the Stamp Act, let alone its repeal. Indeed, the conservative Charles Yorke not only opposed any concession, but for the first time advocated a Declaratory Act which would emphasize the sovereignty of the British Parliament. In desperation the Rockinghams twice approached Pitt, but his terms were too high to be acceptable either to them or to the King, who spent most of his time trying to instil confidence into his ministers. 'If you continue firm' he wrote, 'I don't doubt of success, but if you in the least seem to hesitate, the inferiors will fly off.' This was sound advice, but it was not followed.

When Parliament reassembled on 14 January the Ministry's uncertainty was demonstrated by the delightful vagueness of the King's speech, which merely commended the American problem to the wisdom of Parliament. This enabled Pitt to take the initiative. He roundly condemned all Grenville's previous American policy, but refused to give his confidence to the Rockinghams. He drew a clear if unrealistic distinction between taxation and legislation, claiming that Parliament had complete power in the latter field, but could not tax the colonists. Consequently he advocated repeal of the Stamp Act, accompanied by a Declaratory Act asserting the power of legislation. Conway openly agreed with Pitt and seemed to imply that his fellow-ministers felt similarly. Further ministerial inactivity was impossible, yet characteristically the immediate reaction was yet another attempt to gain Pitt. This repeated insistence that Pitt in effect should be the successor to Cumberland was too much for the King, who took it as an indication that the Ministry could not carry on, and in the middle of January considered the possibility of forming an alternative Administration, exclusive of the Rockinghams, Grenvilles or Pitt. The King's Friends even met to discuss the situation, but were forced to confess their basic weakness—they lacked a reputable front bench, which could be supplied only from the ranks of the leading politicians. The sole outcome was a further abortive approach to Pitt, followed by the acknowledgment by both the King and the Rockinghams that there was no obvious alternative to a continuation of the present Ministry, however weak it might be.

Meanwhile, merchant activity was rapidly bearing fruit. Local bodies of merchants had been formed in Liverpool, Bristol, Manchester and Glasgow, and twenty-three petitions were received by the Commons between 17 and 29 January. All stressed the disastrous effect of the crisis upon trade and the widespread unemployment in manufacturing and commercial districts. In their delicate position the Rockinghams welcomed this support for decisive action, and uneasily but inexorably moved towards their final position. A parliamentary enquiry into merchant grievances was appointed and witnesses of every type were called. National bankruptcy and widespread social unrest were mournfully predicted and, although there is reason to believe that the Stamp Act crisis had merely aggravated a recession that was already beginning to ease, this general clamour served to overcome the last vestige of the older wing's reluctance to bow to American resistance. Their support for repeal was to be bought by the simultaneous passage of a Declaratory Act which, in the light of the law officers' justifiable suspicion of the validity of Pitt's distinction between taxation and legislation, was to assert the power of Parliament over the colonies 'in all cases whatsoever'. Burke was subsequently to assert: 'The question with me is, not whether you have a right to render your people miserable, but whether it is not in your interest to make them happy.' The Rockinghams, by taking their stand in 1766 on expediency rather than on constitutional propriety, sought their own happiness through continued unity rather than that of the colonists, for their American policy was the outcome of divisions within their own ranks. Only old Newcastle lamented the compromise as illogical, protesting that authority and relief should not go hand in hand.

The Declaratory Act passed without difficulty, only Pitt and a few others protesting in the Commons, and five peers opposing it in the Lords.

Parliament and indeed the vast majority of the politically conscious nation was solidly behind Britain's *right* to tax the colonies. But the repeal of the Stamp Act posed a more difficult problem. Pitt's support could be expected, as could the determined opposition of the conservative Bedfords and Grenvilles. But what of the King, Bute and their friends? The Rockinghams of course had every reason to expect reasonably substantial support from at least the Court and Treasury element of the King's Friends, though the previous decades had seen many abstentions and even desertions within their ranks in times of political crisis.

In the event repeal was carried with surprising ease. When the Opposition tried belatedly to win the support of the King's Friends by substituting 'explain and amend' for 'repeal', they were only partially successful, the decision in favour of repeal being carried by 275 to 167. Nonetheless sixty-one office-holders and twenty-seven Scots (reflecting Bute's influence) voted against the Ministry, which was saved by massive support from the ranks of the independents. There can be little doubt that the latter were putting what they considered to be the national interest above their natural impatience of colonial disaffection, and their attitude merely served to convince the Rockinghams of the iniquity of those King's Friends (approximately a third of the total number) who had opposed repeal.[1]

The Rockinghams had successfully harnessed merchant support, but for a brief time it began to look as though they had made a rod for their own backs. The merchants wrested the initiative from the Ministry, demanding the restraint of Vice-Admiralty Courts in America, the lowering of the duty on molasses and even the removal of restraints on trade. But fortunately for the Rockinghams, once the centre of activity passed to the merchant bodies the earlier rift between North American and West Indian interests reappeared, with the former demanding that Dominica be made a free port through which foreign produce could be imported without restriction. In the end the Ministry managed to maintain its merchant alliance by reducing the duty on foreign molasses from threepence to a penny (which was reluctantly accepted by the West Indians) and by compromising over the free port issue. The North Americans were given Dominica, through which they could import foreign raw cotton for export to Manchester, and probably smuggle foreign sugar, while the West Indians were given a *quid pro quo* in the shape of Jamaica as a free port through which they would be able to smuggle Spanish bullion.

In other fields too the Ministry was active. The Spitalfields weavers

---

[1]For a discussion of the role of the King and his Friends in this crisis see pp 284–6.

were pacified by an Act restraining the importation of foreign silks; the Cider Tax was repealed without a division; resolutions were passed declaring general warrants illegal and condemning the seizure of papers in cases of libel; a treaty of commerce was concluded with Russia; and, despite Pitt's denunciation, Lord George Sackville's name was restored to the list of Privy Councillors. It is easy to see how Burke, in his *Short Account of a Late Administration*, could portray the Rockingham Ministry as pursuing an enlightened and liberal policy. But there was about their measures a hint of weakness, an urge to grant concessions to all who demanded them, a desire to do anything for the sake of an easy life. Their record was one of well-meaning timidity. They had indeed reason to be timid, for they had never managed wholly to control the difficult situation they had inherited. From the time of Cumberland's death the Cabinet was divided and there was little real leadership. Rockingham was perpetually in a panic; Grafton and Conway were constantly urging the need to gain Pitt; Northington and Egmont were increasingly distrusted as royal observers. In Parliament they had to face the combined opposition of Pitt, Grenville, Bedford, Temple and many of Bute's and the King's friends. A strong line might have commanded support, but the one thing the Rockinghams could not do was inspire confidence. Again and again they pathetically courted Pitt, only to meet with contemptuous rejection and a clear statement that he would not serve unless personally summoned by the King. Rockingham and most of his followers never forgave Pitt for his persistent refusal to assist a Ministry with ideas on policy so similar to his own. They had found a new hate symbol; first Bute, then Grenville, and now Pitt. Prejudice prevented them from negotiating with Bute, who alone could have given them the additional support they needed without drastically affecting their policy. They could not stand alone; they could not, or would not, take in others. Grafton resigned because of the failure to gain Pitt, and was replaced by the idiosyncratic Duke of Richmond. For other vacant offices no man of status could be found, so widespread was the belief that the Ministry could not survive. Rockingham even momentarily contemplated alliance with the Bedfords and Grenvilles, which would have made nonsense of everything the Ministry pretended to represent. George III not unreasonably decided that he had to find an alternative Ministry and on 7 July reluctantly approached Pitt, who had made known his determination to break all parties and take his stand on 'not men but measures'. So the King turned to the 'blackest of hearts' to rescue him from those very factions which his own inexperienced and naïve politics had produced. He was still looking for his strong man.

In an audience on 12 July Pitt agreed to accept office, at the same time expressing a willingness to reinstate Bute's friends as places became available. The Rockingham Ministry was at an end, and the most ludicrous of George III's ministerial experiments had begun. It is difficult to imagine anyone less equipped than Pitt to act the conciliatory and healing role necessary to remove the intense political jealousies that the King's well-meaning but ineffectual machinations had produced. The changes of men were in fact relatively few. Of the old Cabinet, Rockingham, Newcastle, Richmond and Winchelsea were dismissed. Egmont resigned, not because he was a Rockingham, but because he disapproved of Pitt's policy. Outside the Cabinet only the three Yorkes, Dartmouth, Dowdeswell and Lord John Cavendish resigned, though several other lesser men were dismissed. Pitt could not afford to dispense with the services of many whom Rockingham had brought in, and Rockingham for his part wanted to retain sufficient followers in office to control the Ministry from within—a futile hope. Of the new office-holders only five including Shelburne, could in any sense be called personal followers of Pitt; Conway and Grafton (who was made First Lord of the Treasury) were half Rockingham, half Pittite; Northington, who was switched to the Lord Presidency, remained a King's Friend; and others of the same allegiance, who had followed Bute and Grenville into Opposition, were re-admitted to office, the best-known being Lord North (Joint Paymaster) and Hillsborough (First Lord of Trade and Plantations). Thus the new Ministry was initially part Pittite, part Rockingham and part King's Friends. Burke's later jibes about the heterogeneous character of the new Ministry were not unjust, but they could equally have been applied to most Ministries of the 1760s, with the possible and partial exception of the Rockingham Administration.

Pitt's advantages lay in the lack of a united Opposition, his past reputation, his continuing extra-parliamentary popularity (especially in the City), and his readiness to co-operate with Bute and to heal the breach within the ranks of the King's Friends. Yet all he was to achieve was to pave the way for the eventual re-emergence of political stability under Lord North. Nor is this surprising. If his Ministry was really to be based upon measures rather than men, the opposition of the Bedfords and Grenvilles, both of whom took a highly conservative line over domestic and colonial affairs, could be expected; and alliance between Pitt and the liberal-minded Rockinghams was the logical conclusion. But most of the Rockinghams distrusted and hated Pitt, and great tact would be required to prevent those who remained in the new Administration from having to choose between two loyalties. No one had ever accused Pitt of being tactful, and by the end of the year his barely veiled contempt for the Rockinghams, and his repeated disregard of them over questions of patronage, had brought about further resignations and launched them upon a career of opposition that was to last sixteen years. By declaring war on party, Pitt merely hardened party lines, and his complete inability to work with his colleagues further confused and embittered the political scene. At the same time his incomprehensible decision to accept a peerage as Lord Chatham diminished his popularity in the country and left a void in the Commons that was not to be filled until the emergence of Lord North. Meanwhile Conway was too sensitive a soul to be an effective leader of the lower House, and Charles Townshend—the only other possibility—was a brilliant, unstable epileptic. Yet the Commons was going to need leadership, for even a reunited Court party needed some degree of independent support, and the country gentlemen no longer regarded Chatham with the same enthusiasm as at the height of the Seven Years' War. They were looking for economical and efficient Government, freedom from continental entanglements, and (notwithstanding their support of repeal of the Stamp Act) a firm line with the American colonies. Grenville, not Chatham, was now their ideal.

Even before he faced his first parliamentary session Chatham was beginning to founder. Townshend was irritated at being denied a peerage for his wife, Conway at being refused promotion in the army, his first and truest love. Having offended the Rockinghams by forcing Lord Edgecumbe to give up his Treasurership of the Chamber in order that it might be given to Newcastle's apostate nephew, John Shelley, Chatham surprisingly looked to the Bedfords for an accession of strength; but he was unprepared to make available sufficient offices to win over a faction that rated men above measures. Nor was he more successful in foreign affairs. Hoping to turn to advantage Frederick the Great's admiration for him, he sought alliance with Prussia as a counter-weight against the Family Compact. But Frederick had not forgiven Britain for her supposed desertion of him in 1762, and with his new ally, Russia, was turning his eyes away from France and the west towards Poland. The projected alliance therefore came to naught. But it was in Parliament that Chatham was to face his real test, and in the session of 1766–7 he found himself in very deep water indeed. Though the Rockinghams, Bedfords and Grenvilles were far from pulling easily together, they found in the land-tax an issue on which they could command substantial independent support; and when Townshend moved on 27 February 1767 to maintain the current rate of four shillings in the pound, the Opposition carried a reduction to three shillings by 206 votes to 188. This was a serious embarrassment to the Administration, but of much greater significance for the future were developments over America and India.

Both Chathamites and Rockinghams had shown themselves sympathetic towards the claims of the colonists, but only on condition that the latter behaved reasonably. Repeal of the Stamp Act had been regarded as a major concession and the Americans were expected to be duly grateful. By the beginning of 1767 it was becoming obvious that this was not the case. Many sufferers from the Stamp Act riots were still awaiting the compensation which Parliament had ordered; several colonies were believed to have refused to accept the extension of the Mutiny Act to America, which Grenville had ordered and even Chatham had approved; and the New York Assembly had had the effrontery to petition Parliament for the major revision of the Acts of Trade and Navigation. No one of any shade of political opinion in England denied that Parliament was wholly competent to legislate for the colonies and to regulate their trade. Relatively few accepted the validity of Chatham's and the colonists' subtle distinction between internal and external taxation, but ironically enough it was left to Townshend, Chatham's own Chancellor of the Exchequer, to denounce it publicly as nonsensical and illusory. This he did on 26 January 1767, when Grenville unsuccessfully moved that the expense of the troops in America should be borne by the colonists themselves. Without ever consulting his colleagues Townshend announced that he had found a way of taxing the colonists that would cause no offence, and pledged himself to do something that very session to ease the financial burden of American defence. Not a voice was raised in protest, and even Chatham, irritated by American recalcitrance over the Mutiny Act, preferred to ignore Townshend's remarks. By the time that the Cabinet came to consider American affairs, events had moved a stage further. The New York Assembly had formally refused to enforce the Mutiny Act, and Massachusetts had actually granted indemnity for all offences committed during the Stamp Act disturbances. The Mutiny Act, the Declaratory Act and the Acts of Trade and Navigation had all now been challenged, and the colonial attitude was denounced by even Chatham, Shelburne, Grafton and Camden. Only Conway still pleaded for conciliation, but the Cabinet determined to introduce an act prohibiting the New York Assembly from passing any legislation until it had accepted the Mutiny Act, and with some apprehension bowed to Townshend's threat that he would resign if he were not allowed to tax American imports.

The ensuing parliamentary debates on America were more than a little complicated, with each of the different factions trying to score off the others. But the general climate of opinion was highly authoritarian and hostile to the colonists. On 13 May Townshend made it clear that since the Americans had expressed a preference for external taxation, that was what he would give them; and he proceeded to introduce his duties on paper, paint, glass, lead and tea, which finally passed as part of the annual supply on 2 June. But although Townshend duties preserved the form of external taxation the preamble made it clear that their primary purpose was not to regulate trade but to raise money for defence *and* for establishing a civil list within the colonies which would make the Governors more independent of the colonial assemblies. The ensuing storm in America might readily have been foreseen, but not even a Rockingham voice appears to have been raised against the new proposals. Expediency is a flexible maxim; and what had been inexpedient under Grenville could be expedient under Townshend, who had after all been brought into office by Rockingham. At all events the debates on the duties went unreported and no contemporary seems to have regarded them as sufficiently important to warrant comment.

Unfortunately for Chatham, the affairs of the East India Company also reached a critical stage during his Administration. Before the 1760s relations between the Company and successive Governments had been generally cordial. As one of the major creditors of the State, the Company fulfilled an important role in public finance and, provided it managed its affairs with tolerable competence, had little to fear from Government intervention. The most that was demanded of it, as in 1730 and 1744, was a financial *quid pro quo* in return for the periodical renewal of its charter. But after 1760 the situation became much more complex. Firstly, the Company acquired substantial new commitments in India as a result of the successes of the Seven Years' War and of Clive's assumption of the Diwani[1] of Bengal in 1765. An enormous increase in wealth was confidently if erroneously predicted, and the resulting speculation played havoc with the Company's stock. Secondly, the 1760s saw growing personal and political rivalry within the ranks of the Company no less than on the parliamentary stage, and political instability was added to economic uncertainty. Changing Administrations and factious Oppositions within Parliament allied with similar groups within the government of the Company, where Clive and Laurence Sulivan were in bitter conflict—Clive fighting to preserve his *jaghir*[2] and Sulivan initially for dominance and ultimately to avoid financial ruin. Indian potentates and dissatisfied

[1]I.e. the right of collecting the revenues.
[2]I.e. the annuity of £25,000 granted to him by the Nawab of Bengal.

Company servants had no hesitation in going over the head of the Company and protesting to prominent ministers and Opposition leaders many of whom had personal and political motives for intervention. Thirdly, there appeared the first glimmerings of a genuine interest in the welfare of native peoples, an interest that was soon to provide a backcloth for the impeachment of Warren Hastings, the agitation for the abolition of the slave-trade, and the growth of an embryonic doctrine of trusteeship in colonial policy. Finally, the Administrations of the day were faced with a greatly increased national debt and widespread opposition to the high level of taxation. Financial considerations therefore directed their attention not only towards the American colonies, but also towards the seemingly vast riches of India, and paved the way for the parliamentary enquiry of 1767, North's Regulating Act of 1773, Fox's India Bill of 1783 and Pitt's India Act of 1784. The traditional independence of the Company was drawing to an end.

If the immediate reason for governmental intervention in 1767 was financial, factiousness and speculation within the Company provided both the opportunity and a plausible excuse. A majority of the Court of Proprietors embarked on an intensive stock-splitting and propaganda campaign directed towards forcing the more responsible but divided Court of Directors to accept a rise in dividend which the speculators considered essential to the maintenance of a bull market. The result was an increase from 6 per cent to 10 per cent in September 1766, and to 12·5 per cent in May 1767. A united and competent Administration might have intervened with every chance of substantial support from a Parliament which disliked stock-jobbers, hated and feared returning wealthy Company servants (the so-called 'nabobs') whom they believed were corrupting political life, and could be expected to welcome a discreet raid on the Company's coffers. But, as over America, the Chatham Ministry proved weak and divided. Chatham himself pursued a typically legalistic line in seeking to assert the right of the Crown to the revenues arising from the newly-acquired territorial rights in Bengal, Bihar and Orissa; though once that right and the concomitant financial benefits were conceded, he was prepared to make concessions to the Company in respect of its administrative responsibilities in the provinces, which he had no wish to see the British Government assume. This unrealistic approach was based on a misconception of the Company's power in India, where it had no territorial possessions as such, but merely held the revenues in quasi-feudal fashion in return for administering the provinces as Diwan of the Mogul Emperor—a feasible proposition for a trading company, but scarcely for the British Crown. Since the primary aim of the Administration was to mulct the Company, the preference of Conway, Townshend and Shelburne for negotiating a settlement with the directors was much more sensible. Chatham's plan for a parliamentary enquiry therefore achieved little save to unite Rockingham and Grenville in defence of the sacred rights of chartered companies. Meanwhile, negotiations with the directors proceeded in defiance of Chatham's instructions, and a compromise was eventually hammered out and embodied in four Acts of Parliament. The Company was confirmed in its territorial rights for a further two years (thus surrendering Chatham's position) in return for an annual payment to the Crown of £400,000; it was granted concessions with regard to the duty and draw-back on tea; proprietors were required to hold stock for six months before they were entitled to vote; and the dividend was pegged at 10 per cent until the beginning of the following parliamentary session. At best this was a temporary solution, and the chief political results were the further undermining of Chatham's authority and the discrediting of Townshend, who had been outmanoeuvred in the later stages of the negotiations by Shelburne, and who was to die in comparative ignominy four months later.

By the end of May 1767 Grafton, who had been left in *de facto* control of the Administration by Chatham, was at his wits' end. Conway and Townshend had defied him over America and India; Shelburne was refusing to attend Cabinet meetings; Rockingham, Bedford and Grenville were even showing a limited ability to pull together in Opposition. Defeat over the land-tax in the Commons had sapped Grafton's confidence, and in the Lords he found it necessary to summon invalid supporters to divisions and even call on the votes of the King's brothers to avoid ignominious defeat. Chatham was able to dissuade him from resignation but he was now convinced that an accession of strength was necessary, and that he must take in either the Bedfords or the Rockinghams, since the King would not consider the return of Grenville. In accordance with Chatham's wishes (which showed how little Chatham really believed in measures rather than men) Grafton first approached Bedford, but the latter's insistence that Temple share the chief authority was unacceptable to the King. This left Grafton free to negotiate with the Rockinghams, whom he much preferred, and for three weeks in July 1767 every possibility was explored. In the end Rockingham failed to gain office because he insisted on his own pre-eminence. He was offered the Headship of the Treasury and provision for all his friends. But he inexplicably refused to come in without the support of the Bedfords (despite their disagreement over both domestic and colonial policy), and as the Bedfords would not desert the Grenvilles, Rockingham had to insist on their inclusion as well, though only in subordinate office. Furthermore, both Bedfords and Grenvilles had to acknowledge Rockingham's supremacy over them, just as the King had to recognize him as pre-eminent over Grafton. Many of his followers deplored his inflexibility, but Rockingham stood firm. The negotiations therefore failed, but the seeming unity among the Opposition did not survive the year. In November Rockingham suddenly announced his determination never to sit in the same Cabinet with Grenville, who for his part denounced the whole colonial policy of the Rockinghams, whom the Bedfords declined to defend. Rockingham was now convinced that Bedford could be as little trusted as Grenville, and his visionary notion of a comprehensive Administration was shattered forever.

Grafton's next move was obvious. He still needed an accession of strength, the Rockinghams had refused to come in alone, and Grenville was still anathema to the King. Only the Bedfords were left, and now that they were convinced of the impossibility of a united Opposition they were prepared to be more reasonable. Thus, in the opening days of December, Weymouth replaced Conway as Secretary of State and North assumed the Leadership of the Commons. Hillsborough became Secretary of State for the Colonies, Gower Lord President, Sandwich Postmaster-General, and Richard Rigby joint Vice-Treasurer of Ireland. The admission of the Bedfords was important for three reasons. Firstly, it signalled the final collapse of Chatham's attempt to break party; far from annihilating faction his Administration had been forced to come to terms with it. Secondly it marked the last chance for more than a decade for the Rockinghams to re-enter the service of the Crown. Finally, and most important for the future, the Cabinet moved right in its colonial policy. Conway had been superseded, Grafton and Camden were to become ever more ineffectual, and Chatham had long since ceased to count for anything. The new recruits—Gower, Weymouth and Hillsborough—were all advocates of coercion. Rockingham had put his own desire for pre-eminence above his concern for America, and the advent of the Bedfords made renewed conflict with the colonies inevitable. But in 1767 nobody spared a thought for America, and questions of policy had never entered significantly into any of the negotiations.

On 1 March Parliament was dissolved and the ensuing general election, in which political issues played virtually no part, and which was characterized by Grafton's ineffectual management, brought only a slight diminution in Government strength. The only excitement was caused by the return of John Wilkes at the top of the poll for Middlesex, to the accompaniment of tremendous mob activity. Since his expulsion from Parliament in 1764, Wilkes had spent most of his time in France, returning only occasionally in abortive attempts to blackmail his way back to favour. In December 1767 he took the offensive by publishing a scathing attack on Chatham. Two months later he returned permanently to England, and for the next few years was to be constantly in the forefront of politics, posing as the self-appointed champion of incipient metropolitan radicalism. In the early 1760s the middling class of lesser merchants, tradesmen and mastercraftsmen in the City, had shown signs of developing attitudes of their own, independent of the parliamentary Opposition. They had already made common cause with Wilkes over the peace terms, the cider tax, and general warrants; and the continuing undercurrent of economic malaise and social unrest after 1764 provided Wilkes with an ideal background to resume his provocative career. Bad harvests, severe winters, post-war depression and unemployment caused partially by the influx of Irish labourers into England all excited mob discontent on which Wilkes could capitalize. When the new Parliament assembled in May 1768 there was widespread rioting, identified with the cause of 'Wilkes and Liberty'. Troops were called out and some people were killed in St George's Fields. For three weeks London was in chaos, and order was restored only with extreme difficulty. In June Wilkes's outlawry was reversed on technical grounds, and he was sentenced to twenty-two months' imprisonment and fined £1,000 for his previous offences. But imprisonment only endowed him with a martyr's crown, and in prison he proved a greater focus for unrest than he had when free.

The dying days of Chatham's Administration were bedevilled by problems abroad no less than at home. British prestige suffered a further blow when the annexation of Corsica by France became imminent, and the reaction in America to the Townshend duties brought a fresh crisis in colonial affairs. In October 1767 Boston had entered into a non-importation agreement, and in January 1768 Massachusetts petitioned King and Parliament against taxation without representation and sent a circular letter to the other colonies urging common action against the aggression of the mother country. When the colonists based their opposition on constitutional grounds rather than commercial expediency they invariably hardened resistance in England. The Massachusetts Assembly was dissolved, two regiments were sent to New England, and a resident governor was appointed in Virginia. Grafton openly acknowledged his dislike of this Bedford policy of coercion, but like Camden lacked the moral courage to resign. Both believing in Chatham's policy, they were too weak to enforce it and could only join in ousting Shelburne, the only other minister who really shared their views. In so doing they lost Chatham as well, though it may be doubted whether his resignation in October

1768 was really a loss. Bristol became Lord Privy Seal, Rochford Secretary of State, and the Cabinet was further weighted in the direction of coercion.

Grafton was now formally head of an Administration that was as divided in its opinions as the Opposition, which however managed two minor victories in the parliamentary session of 1768–9 by unseating Sir James Lowther on petition and passing the *Nullum Tempus* bill against the wishes of the Ministry. But the two crucial issues remained the colonies and Wilkes. In America the resistance of Boston had spread rapidly, and strong remonstrances were presented by Virginia and Pennsylvania. But there was little sympathy in England for this opposition. No one except Chatham and Camden favoured the repeal of the Declaratory Act, no one except the Rockinghams the repeal of the Townshend duties. The sole immediate result was Hillsborough's petition to the King to revive an obsolete statute enabling colonists suspected of treason to be shipped to England for trial. But rising merchant discontent with the decline in American trade that followed the non-importation agreements persuaded Grafton to have second thoughts, and on 1 May 1769 a Cabinet meeting was held to decide whether or not the Townshend duties should be repealed. By a majority of one vote it was decided to retain the duty on tea for the sake of principle, and the way was unconsciously paved for the Boston Tea Party and the final rupture between Britain and America. There can be no doubt that, if the Rockinghams had condescended to join the Ministry in 1768, the vote would have gone the other way.

For the moment Wilkes posed a more immediate problem. To enliven his days in prison he published in the *St James's Chronicle* Weymouth's letter to the Surrey magistrates of the previous 10 May, which had exorted them to call out the army in the event of riots and had resulted in the deaths in St George's Fields. In a provocative introduction Wilkes represented this as a deep-laid ministerial plot against the people. The Lords promptly voted this introduction a seditious libel, and the Commons followed suit on 1 February 1769, despite Burke's warning at making Wilkes any more of a martyr, and Grenville's doubts on the propriety of the Commons taking cognizance of a libel upon a peer. Wilkes's expulsion from the Commons was effected two days later, though Grenville emphasized the weakness of the Commons' case and foretold with remarkable prescience the developments that would inexorably follow. Three times Wilkes was re-elected for Middlesex, and three times his expulsion was re-enacted. On the final occasion his defeated opponent, Colonel Luttrell, was declared elected on the grounds that Wilkes was incapable of sitting in the Commons and that votes cast for him were therefore invalid. While no one could doubt the right of the Commons to expel a member, and while there were even precedents for declaring incapacity, the virtual disfranchisement of the great majority of the freeholders of Middlesex was a very different matter. The vote was regarded as a species of property of which the owner could be deprived only by an act of the whole legislature, and if the Commons were to extend their recent action they would be able to eliminate all opposition. At last the opponents of the Ministry had found an issue on which they could make common cause.

The result was the so-called 'united Opposition' of 1769 to 1771 and an appeal to the country against the Commons. On 21 February 1769 came the formation of the 'Supporters of the Bill of Rights', and instructions were organized from many constituencies to their parliamentary representatives. In this growing agitation the initiative was taken by the metropolitan radicals, led in the absence of Wilkes by the Lord Mayor, William Beckford, with whom Chatham was closely linked. On 24 June a most violent petition was carried at the Guildhall by the Livery of London, and in July the electors of Westminster even petitioned the King to dissolve Parliament. But the radical attempt to extend their agitation to the nation met with only partial success. They wished to use the Middlesex issue as a peg on which to hang various demands for political reform—triennial (if not annual) Parliaments, place and pension bills, and a more adequate representation of the people. In the end eighteen English counties and some dozen of the larger towns were persuaded to send in petitions, but except for those from London and Middlesex these petitions confined themselves to the single issue of Middlesex and the associated rights of freeholders. The electorate as a whole had no wish to become the dupes of metropolitan radicals, and in some constituencies, such as Norfolk and Essex, the Administration was able to prevent any petitions at all. Country gentlemen were basically conservative in their politics, and the freeholders were mostly ignorant or apathetic. The country was not yet ripe for reform. Nor were either Rockingham or Grenville over-anxious to espouse a movement that offended their conservative instincts and was calculated to advance Chatham's political ambitions rather than their own. They supported the more limited petitions, but looked askance at the City. Rockingham indeed had special grounds for caution, for although he was prepared to co-operate with Grenville over the Middlesex issue, he had been alarmed at the reconciliation between Grenville and Temple in November 1768, and was even more disturbed when in the following July Chatham emerged from his retirement and announced his opposition to Grafton's Ministry. When Chatham and Grenville subsequently visited each other and speculation envisaged a Chatham-Temple-Grenville *rapprochement*, Rockingham began to suffer from George III's recurrent nightmare that all might have to submit to 'the family'. But the uneasy alliance between Grenville and Rockingham survived these fears, and for once Chatham went out of his way to be cordial towards Rockingham. A tentative and vague union was thus formed between the three wings of the Opposition, based upon the rights of the freeholders of Middlesex.

By the time that Parliament re-assembled on 9 January 1770 a political crisis was imminent. Camden and Granby were intriguing with Chatham against Grafton, and openly showing their support for Wilkes and their dislike of their ministerial colleagues. The Opposition, on the other hand, was showing ever greater signs of life and unity. In the debate on the Address-in-Reply Camden, Granby and Dunning all voted against their fellow-ministers, and all expressed their intention of resigning. Increasingly unhappy at presiding over a Ministry that was rent from within, Grafton teetered on the brink; and when, on 25 January, the Administration staved off defeat over Middlesex by only forty-four votes (the minority of 180 including many habitual Administration supporters) he insisted at last on resignation. The changes were few, but as Grafton's successor George III chose one of the most likeable and ill-fated of all British premiers, Lord North.

9

SUCCESS AND FAILURE: 1770–82

BEFORE he became First Lord of the Treasury in 1770 Lord North's career had been relatively undistinguished. As an orthodox Old Corps Whig he had entered Parliament for his family borough of Banbury in 1754, and was to continue to represent it until he succeeded his long-lived father as Earl of Guilford in 1790. He had been made a junior Lord of the Treasury by Newcastle in 1759, but after 1760 he gravitated towards the Court and was therefore excluded from the first Rockingham Ministry. The Chatham Administration saw him back in office as joint Paymaster of the Forces, and on Townshend's timely death in 1767 he became Chancellor of the Exchequer. Far from being associated with a faction, he had scarcely a member of the lower House whom he could call his own, and there were at the time of his promotion no other significant new appointments. Few could have guessed that the chronic political instability of the previous decade would be ended within eighteen months of North's accession to power; fewer still that he would preside over the only major war that Britain has ever lost. Physically he was almost as repulsive as John Wilkes, being variously described as ugly, awkward, undignified, gross, unwieldy, of swollen and inflated countenance, and with great bolting eyes and a harsh unmusical voice. But his merits lay elsewhere and were not inconsiderable. He was a skilful debater, able, tactful and sweet-tempered; he had a sparkling wit which he could use to good effect against his more brilliant opponents; and his penchant for simulating sleep on the Treasury front bench was to prove peculiarly disconcerting to those who sat opposite. Above all, he was in the House of Commons, the first chief minister since Grenville to enjoy this inestimable advantage; and his genuine desire for efficient economical Government was quickly to commend him to independent country gentlemen, who were becoming increasingly weary of sterile party manoeuvres. North was sometimes a figure of fun; he was anything but a fool.

On the other hand the Opposition, its appetite whetted by the resignation of Grafton, was in full cry. Rockingham, Chatham and Grenville were still pulling together, however uneasily, and there was much greater talent and debating power on the Opposition front benches than North could hope to muster. When, on 31 January, Dowdeswell returned to the Middlesex issue by moving that incapacitation could be only by Act of Parliament, North was able to kill the motion by only forty votes. But this was the closest that he came to defeat. On 12 February Dowdeswell tested new ground by seeking leave to bring in a bill to disenfranchise the lower revenue officers. This was a 'popular' measure, which was to cause North acute embarrassment in 1780, but as yet there was no widespread demand for economical reform and North was victorious by a majority of seventy-five. The Opposition strength had remained virtually constant, while that of the Administration had increased by almost forty. The waverers, who had abstained in the dying days of Grafton's Ministry, were returning to the fold. Concurrently, Opposition attacks on the Lords over the Middlesex issue were easily defeated, and between mid-February and the Easter recess North was able to consolidate a position that was already beginning to look comfortingly strong.

On 14 March the metropolitan radicals attempted to seize the initiative when William Beckford presented a strong remonstrance from the City to the King, deploring the Administration's conduct over the Middlesex election and seeking both the dismissal of the Ministry and the dissolution of Parliament. As might be expected, George III contemptuously rejected it, and the Administration counter-attacked by moving that copies of the remonstrance and the King's answer to it should be laid before the Commons. Conservative suspicion of City radicalism gave North the enormous majority of 163, and ministers pushed home their advantage by successfully moving that claims to deny the validity of the present Parliament were disruptive of the public peace. Yet in the midst of these ministerial triumphs the Commons produced a characteristic vindication of its independence. On 30 March Grenville introduced his bill for transferring the trial of election petitions from the whole House (where decisions frequently tended to be blatantly partisan) to a small select committee which could examine witnesses on oath. This was opposed by the Ministry, but the Country gentlemen were enthusiastically behind it, and North's attempt to adjourn the question was defeated by a majority of fifty-two. He then wisely withdrew his opposition and in due course the bill was passed for a trial period of seven years. But this was an extraordinary measure and did not indicate any permanent waning in

North's fortunes. The Opposition's motion for an address to the King for retrenchment in the Civil List was defeated by 133 votes, and an attempt to secure a copy of the Pension List by sixty-two. Then came the Easter recess.

In general the Opposition was thoroughly disheartened by its failure to unsettle North. But Chatham refused to give up hope and went out of his way to court Rockingham. 'I have a firm reliance on his zeal for liberty, and will not separate from him', he wrote to Calcraft on 30 March. During the recess, with Rockingham's half-hearted co-operation, he framed a bill for reversing the proceedings of the Commons over the Middlesex election; but this was overwhelmingly rejected in the Lords when Parliament re-assembled. Three days later, on 4 May, Chatham waxed even more violent, condemning the King's answer to the City's remonstrance as violating the subject's right of petition. When this attack was also roundly defeated, Chatham determined to move for the dissolution of Parliament and even managed to persuade the startled Rockinghams that in so doing he was influenced not by popular pressure but by personal conviction. But his motion was so obviously contrary to the opinion of the Lords that it was negatived without even a division. On 19 May the parliamentary session came to an end and North seemed firmly in the saddle.

Despite successive and substantial defeats the united Opposition did not immediately disintegrate. But although colonial issues had been carefully avoided, significant differences of opinion were beginning to appear. Chatham might welcome the attempts of Beckford and the City radicals to force their programme of Parliamentary and economical reform on the leaders of the Opposition, but the Rockinghams were far too conservative to warm to radical measures, and were anyway disinclined to take any steps that might further Chatham's interest in the City. Burke denounced the Bill of Rights people as 'a rotten sub-division of a faction among ourselves', and in late 1770 Rockingham, Sir George Savile and Lord John Cavendish actually dissuaded the Yorkshire freeholders from producing a second petition in favour of the rights of the electors of Middlesex. It was clear that Rockingham's attitude was more typical of Parliament and the electorate than was Chatham's. There was little sympathy for the City's second remonstrance to the King, which Beckford presented on 23 May, adding some violent words of his own in the process. The City might applaud his action and erect a statue in the Guildhall to commemorate the occasion, but the country looked askance at this effrontery, and with the death of Beckford in June, Wilkes, recently released from prison, began to reassume control of the City machine and bend it to his own personal purposes. Thereafter, Chatham's direct contact with, and influence in, the City began to decline.

The divergence of outlook between Chatham and the Rockinghams was amply illustrated in Burke's *Thoughts on the Causes of the Present Discontents*, which appeared in April 1770. Apart from the scorn it poured upon Chatham's previous Administration, it denounced the radical remedies of triennial Parliaments, place bills, and a more equal representation of the people, with which Chatham was known to sympathize; and it postulated a thesis that was to become the basis of all subsequent Whig historiography but which Chatham rightly regarded as fantasy. Not that Burke himself had always believed the nonsense which he wrote in 1770. Five years earlier, on the formation of the Rockingham Administration, he had commented: 'It is certain, that if they act wisely, they cannot fail to make up a lasting Administration. I call taking in Lord Bute, or at least not quarrelling with him . . . acting wisely.' At that stage Burke, unlike the rump of the Old Corps, could see nothing sinister about Bute, yet within twelve months he was ludicrously claiming that the King's Scottish favourite had been largely responsible for Rockingham's fall and was the real power behind the Chatham Administration. By 1770 he had convinced himself that 'the power of the Crown, almost dead and rotten as Prerogative, has grown up anew, with much more strength, and far less odium, under the name of Influence'. The King, he asserted, had assumed to himself the complete control of patronage and had built up a Court party of 'King's Friends' who monopolized all subordinate administrative offices and wielded the real power in the State. Apart from the Rockingham ministry, all Administrations of the 1760s were mere façades, covering arbitrary government by Court favourites. Meanwhile Britain was treated with contempt abroad and had alienated the colonies by extending arbitrary measures to American shores. As a remedy Burke could only propose the development of 'Party', the very solution which Chatham had repeatedly denounced and had tried in practice to smash. It would not have been surprising if the publication of Burke's treatise had provoked Chatham into breaking with the Rockinghams, yet so determined was he at this stage to maintain the united Opposition that he merely referred to a recent pamphlet which, though no doubt well-intentioned, had not in his opinion done much good to the common cause. Mild stuff indeed from one of Chatham's volcanic temperament, but he had not yet given up all hope of overturning North.

The summer of 1770 was notable chiefly for the dispute between Britain and Spain over the Falkland Islands, which looked for some months as if it might lead to war and see Chatham called upon to resume the conflict with the Bourbon Powers. But Spain would not make a stand without the certainty of French support, and in the last analysis France was no more prepared than Britain to fight over a few rocky islands. Totally misjudging the attitude of Parliament and the country, Chatham encouraged the Opposition to behave in a thoroughly irresponsible manner, demanding vindication of the national honour and even denouncing North's eventual settlement as cowardly surrender. All he achieved was the further consolidation of North's position and confirmation of his own increasing isolation. Nonetheless, as long as the Falkland Islands dispute remained in the foreground of politics, Chatham had continued to court Rockingham. In November 1770 he wrote of the Marquis: 'His whole language was, as I expected, honourable, just and sensible. My esteem and confidence in his Lordship's upright intentions grow from every conversation with him.' There was indeed more need than ever for co-operation between Chatham and Rockingham, since the third wing of the Opposition was destroyed by the death of George Grenville on the very day that Parliament met, and by the subsequent conversion to Administration of most of his ablest followers. Thus Suffolk became Lord Privy Seal, Wedderburne Solicitor-General, Thomas Whatley (Grenville's erstwhile man-of-business) a Lord of Trade, and Lord Augustus Hervey a Lord of Admiralty. Yet in the spring of 1771 Chatham suddenly and deliberately torpedoed the alliance with Rockingham, and by the end of the session relations between the two were as frigid as they had been before the united Opposition had been born in the autumn of 1769. The issue over which they formally split was the attempt to reform the law of libel.

In recent trials for seditious libel Lord Mansfield had emphasized that the jury was confined to determining the facts of printing and publication, and that it was the exclusive right of the judge to determine whether or not the material in question was libellous. This interpretation of the law, notwithstanding a few precedents to the contrary, was commonly held by eighteenth-century judges, but their political conservatism could be thought to impose unnecessary restrictions upon the freedom of the Press. Both Chatham and Rockingham adopted a liberal attitude, but Chatham from the outset linked his campaign for the extension of jurors' rights with a demand for an enquiry into the administration of the law, and made it plain that his chief target was Mansfield. The Rockinghams did not share this desire to personalize the issue, and Dowdeswell instead prepared a bill which would simply change the existing law. At first Chatham, furious at the Rockinghams' refusal to follow his lead and indignant at Burke's remark that juries could be just as corrupt as judges, was determined to oppose Dowdeswell's measure. But eventually a meeting was arranged between him and Rockingham, and he agreed to support the bill, though with the intention of changing it in committee from an 'enacting' to a 'declaratory' measure, which would establish that the law had always been otherwise than Mansfield had interpreted it. But when the bill was submitted to the Commons on 7 March the Opposition was rent asunder. Chathamites and Rockinghams openly denounced one another, while ministers delightedly welcomed not only the abandonment of any attempt to reform the law of libel, but the virtual extinction of effective Opposition. Not until 1779 was North again to face a serious threat to his Administration.

The blame for the collapse of the united Opposition rested squarely on Chatham's shoulders, and thereafter he treated Rockingham as contemptuously as he had done before 1769. Why should Chatham have reverted to type at this particular moment? As far as the law of libel was concerned, it is clear that he was much more interested in persecuting his old enemy, Mansfield, than he was in achieving reform. But there was more to it than that. During the first Rockingham Ministry Pitt had despised its leader because of his manifest weakness, and had refused many times to come in and assist him. Yet his own Administration in 1766–8 had proved equally ineffective. Once he had recovered his health, the memory of his failure for a time reduced him to life size. He could see plainly that his only hope of ever regaining power lay through the medium of a united Opposition; and to achieve this he was prepared to become reconciled to Grenville and even to be nice to Rockingham. But to swallow his pride must have been galling indeed to a man of Chatham's temperament, and only the prospect of political success could restrain his megalomania. By early 1771 that prospect had disappeared. North was firmly established in power and the fiasco over the Falkland Islands made even Chatham realize that his belligerent talents were no longer in demand. He therefore chose the first available issue on which to sever his connection with the despised Rockinghams. As so often in the past Chatham's and Rockingham's ideas on policy differed only in detail, and co-operation on broad principles should have been easy. But then most of Chatham's career is a denial of his oft-repeated faith in the importance of 'not men, but measures'.

The Opposition was so disorganized that it could not even take advantage of the Ministry's singularly inept handling of a dispute with some City printers in early 1771. The printing of parliamentary debates had always in theory been a breach of privilege, though in practice various devices were used to get round this difficulty. But since notes could not openly be taken, the quality of the reporting was very poor, and many members who deplored having their opinions misrepresented were inclined to sympathize with the increased public demand for freedom of reporting. In February Colonel George Onslow, irritated at seeing himself described as 'little cocking George' moved successfully for several printers of London papers and journals to be summoned to the House to answer charges of breach of privilege. Some attended and were duly reprimanded by the Speaker. But three of them—Wheble, Thompson and Miller—refused to appear. The Commons, showing again that arbitrary temper which it had manifested several times in the previous few years, asked the King to issue a proclamation for their apprehension—a ridiculous and irregular proceeding. As a result, Wheble was taken collusively by another printer and brought before Alderman John Wilkes, who discharged him on the grounds that no legal charge had been levied against him, and that he had been apprehended in defiance of his own rights and the charter of the City. Characteristically, Wilkes communicated these proceedings in an insolent letter to Lord Halifax, Secretary of State. Thompson was similarly apprehended and discharged by Alderman Oliver. Meanwhile, Wilkes and Almon appear to have concocted a plan for bringing the Commons and the City into even more serious conflict. The third printer, Miller was to allow himself to be taken by a messenger of the Commons, but was to have a City constable in readiness to arrest the messenger for infringing the jurisdiction of the City. This plan worked to perfection, and both Miller and the messenger were duly brought before Lord Mayor Brass Crosby, Wilkes and Oliver. Miller was discharged, and the messenger was bound over on a charge of committing a breach of the peace! The Commons, understandably irritated by this provocative action, reacted in the most authoritarian fashion. All suits arising out of the prosecution of the printers were banned, the offending entries were torn out of the Mansion House minute book, and the Lord Mayor and two aldermen were summoned to the House to answer charges of breach of privilege. Wilkes, with his usual studied insolence, declined to attend save in his proper capacity as legal member for Middlesex; and the Ministry was so chary of tangling with him again that it even adjourned Parliament for ten days so that the order for his appearance might lapse. Crosby and Oliver were duly brought before the House on 25 March and confined to the Tower. Many of the Opposition walked out of the House in disgust at these arbitrary proceedings, but the Commons was legally within its rights and the judges held that they could take no cognizance of the actions, still less release the imprisoned men on writs of *habeas corpus*. The usual rioting took place, Crosby and Oliver were visited while in prison by most of the leading Opposition peers and commoners, and when they were released at the end of the session the City abandoned itself to wild celebration. Thereafter the Commons made no serious attempt to interfere with the printing of parliamentary debates, though it still exercised the right to clear the gallery of strangers.

Throughout these proceedings Chatham had been in something of a quandary. He still wished to maintain his popularity in the City, where the death of Beckford had tended to diminish his direct influence. Indeed, during this session he had repeated his support for a redistribution of parliamentary seats, and even announced his conversion to the idea of triennial Parliaments in an attempt to court the metropolitan radicals. But the conflict with the printers posed a difficult problem. While he had no wish to oppose the City magistrates in the legal exercise of their powers, neither did he want to irritate the Commons by denying their undoubted right to punish for breach of privilege. For weeks he equivocated, persuading his friends among the City members to dissociate themselves from the whole proceedings. But in the end he came out roundly in favour of the City, perhaps because by the end of the session he realized that his support in the Commons had anyway become negligible.

Thus by the spring of 1771 effective Opposition was at an end and for the following two years ministers enjoyed a degree of peace unknown since the death of Henry Pelham. If North resembled Walpole in his lack of long-term plans and his inclination to avoid major issues, he was more akin to Pelham in the loose rein he held over his Cabinet colleagues, his skill in matters financial, and his capacity to build a broadly-based Ministry by attaching moderate men to his Government. Most of Bute's followers had made their peace with Administration in 1766, the Bedfords had come over in 1768, and the Grenvilles in early 1771. But the Ministry was further strengthened by the appointment as Solicitor-General of Edward Thurlow, who in debate could wield the bludgeon as effectively as Attorney-General Wedderburne could use the rapier. Sir Fletcher Norton proved a much more cool-headed and dependable Speaker than Sir John Cust had been at the height of the Middlesex disturbances, and Sandwich—after a brief period as Secretary of State—became a more efficient First Lord of the Admiralty than his political opponents were prepared to concede. The somewhat reactionary influence of the Bedfords was offset to a considerable extent by the return of Grafton to the Ministry as Lord Privy Seal in 1771, and even more by the appointment of North's half-brother, Lord Dartmouth (previously associated with the Rockinghams) as Secretary of State for the Colonies in 1772. Conciliation, moderation and quietly efficient and economical administration increasingly attracted independent support in Parliament, and the return of stable Government was welcomed by civil servants such as John Robinson, Charles Jenkinson and Jeremiah Dyson.

Free from the pressure of significant Opposition North could concentrate on his principle aim of restoring financial stability. Not since Grenville had any first Lord of the Treasury shown such a capacity for the lucid exposition of financial matters, or for the careful management of the nation's finances. Except during the war-scare of 1771 the land-tax was kept at three shillings in the pound until 1774, and North was also determined to budget for at least small annual surpluses with a view to reducing both the capital of, and interest charges on, the national debt. To achieve this he had to introduce new taxes on luxuries, and to persuade holders of existing stock to accept redemption at under par in return for participation in a lottery. Indeed the revenue lottery, as distinct from one associated with the raising of a loan, was but one aspect of North's innovation in financial matters. He also experimented with an inhabited house duty, the scope of which was much wider than that of the land-tax, began the simplification and modernization of the financial system, and—even at the height of the American war—established a non-political commission of experts to recommend permanent reforms. Though the war ruined any chance of his policy being brought to fruition, he laid the basis on which the younger Pitt was to build; and by the time of the outbreak of the war in 1776 he had paid off some £3,500,000 of the national debt.

Like Walpole and Pelham before him, Lord North had shown his capacity as a peace-time minister and parliamentary manager. Yet the problems of Empire, which had temporarily thrust themselves into the forefront, of politics in the 1760s, soon reappeared in accentuated form and involved North in a crisis which he was incapable of fully understanding, still less controlling; and it was the affairs of the East India Company rather than developments in the American colonies that were to provide the initial spark. For several years East Indian affairs had been deceptively quiet, but unfortunately the Company had not taken advantage of the lull to put its house in order. Hostility to its rumoured misrule, aggravated by the horrors of the 1769–70 famine in Bengal and by the ever-growing hatred of the returning 'nabobs', was vigorously and pungently expressed by writers like William Bolts and Alexander Dow, and predisposed Parliament to wax highly critical when the general European credit crisis of 1772 precipitated financial chaos in the company's affairs. Territorial revenue had dropped in India because of trade depression and famine, military expenditure rose with the threat of revived French aggression and increasing instability among native states, and the Company was ill able to afford its annual contribution of £400,000 to the Exchequer. Over-burdened with bonded debt in India and embarrassed by its irresponsible raising of the dividend to 12.5 per cent in March 1772 in order to maintain confidence, it found itself compelled to ask the Government for permission to postpone its customs payments and for a loan to tide it over its difficulties. The response of Parliament was to set up a small select committee of secrecy under Charles Jenkinson to examine the Company's books and report back. Since the Company had invited investigation by seeking financial assistance, the Parliamentary Opposition could scarcely protest—as it had done in the 1760s—that chartered rights were being wantonly flouted by a greedy Government. A renewal in 1773 of the request for a loan and a demand for concession regarding the export of tea led North to insist on concurrent reforms, and the resulting package deal was eventually presented in three acts of Parliament. The Loan Act granted the Company £1,400,000, pegged the annual dividend at 6 per cent until this loan was re-paid, and restricted it to 7 per cent until the bonded debt in India was reduced to £1,000,000. The previous annual payment to the Exchequer was waived, but the Company was forbidden to issue bills of exchange for more than £300,000 per year, thereby restricting an important means by which returning Company servants transferred their fortunes back to England. The Tea Act which, considering its celebrated aftermath, aroused singularly little attention in Parliament, permitted the drawback of duties on all tea above 10 million pounds held in the Company's warehouses, and allowed its export directly to America. The result, it was hoped, would be greatly increased profits for the Company through its ability to under-cut the Dutch, and cheap tea for the delighted colonists. Instead the way was paved for the conversion of the Americans into a nation of coffee-drinkers.

But the most important piece of legislation as far as the future of the Company was concerned was the so-called Regulating Act. An attempt was made to restrain factiousness and instability within the Company by raising the voting qualification from £500 to £1,000 and by insisting that the stock be held for a year before voting. The Court of Directors was also to be elected every four years, with one quarter of its members retiring each year and remaining out of office for at least twelve months. To drive home the advantage which the Administration thus hoped to gain, its supporters were exhorted to take out voting qualifications, and by the end of the year the frantic opposition in the Court of Proprietors had been overcome and East Indian affairs thenceforth became an integral part of Treasury business. The intermittent governmental interference of previous decades had become permanent and formalized. The Act also of course applied itself to the problem of Company rule in India. Bengal was placed under the control of a Governor-General (Warren Hastings) and four councillors (General John Clavering, Richard Barwell, Colonel George Monson and Philip Francis). The subordinate presidencies of Bombay and Madras were to act under the instructions of the Governor and Council of Bengal save when imminent danger made effective consultation impossible or when they had received direct orders from the Company at home. A Supreme Court of Justice was established in Bengal under Sir Elijah Impey as Chief Justice, liberal salaries were provided for the chief administration and judicial officers, Company servants were forbidden to engage in trade, and the acceptance of presents was made illegal.

It is easy in retrospect to criticize the provisions of the Act. The stock-splitting regulations achieved little, and although the potentiality of the major holders for mischief was halved, the many disqualified £500 holders were mostly people who had caused little trouble. Equally, the regulation of the election of directors, though it facilitated governmental management and did something to lessen faction, soon produced a stereotyped situation in which thirty directors held office, with six retiring for one year out of every four. In India the results were even more unfortunate. Hastings was hamstrung by a hostile majority on the Council, led by the able but vindictive and doctrinaire Francis; the Supreme Court and Council were involved in bitter disputes over areas of jurisdiction that had been left ill-defined; and traditional rivalry, poor communications and chronic unrest in southern India all conspired to breed ill-feeling between Bengal and the subordinate presidencies. Yet the Act represented an honest enough attempt to deal with a series of problems, the intricacies of which were as yet little understood by either Government or Opposition; and those few who had the necessary knowledge and experience of Indian affairs were too often intent on pursuing their own selfish interests to offer constructive advice.

At the beginning of North's Ministry, American affairs were as deceptively quiet as those of the East India Company. The repeal of the Stamp Act and of all the Townshend duties save that on tea had temporarily taken the sting out of colonial agitation, and North's appointment of the moderate Dartmouth as Secretary of State for the colonies seemed to augur well for the future. Yet below the surface a whole series of delicate problems remained unsolved. None of these was alone enough to provoke a revolutionary situation, but together they sufficed to maintain a spirit of discontent among various elements of colonial society. All that was needed was a focal point around which the various strands of opposition could unite and a political philosophy which could provide that united opposition with a cause for which it was prepared to fight. The 1770s were to provide both.

This is not the place for a detailed analysis of colonial grievances, real or imagined; nor would such an analysis necessarily shed much light upon the reasons for the breach between Britain and her American colonies. As had already become evident in the course of the 1760s, restrictions upon commerce, manufacturing and currency were irksome when rigidly enforced, but not sufficiently so to provoke rebellion; attempts to regulate westward expansion and to develop a more responsible attitude towards the associated problems of defence and Indian relations aroused dissatisfaction among some elements of colonial society, but commanded a degree of support among others; and if taxation, whether for defence or for the establishment of a civil list, had provoked the most bitter opposition, the repeal of the Stamp Act and partial repeal of the Townshend duties had quelled the clamour, and both the Sugar Act and the tea duty maintained the principle of the British right to tax. When the colonists had appealed on grounds of commercial expediency and adopted measures to hamper British trade, successive Governments had been prepared to listen and even to yield. But when their actions were challenged on the basis of constitutional impropriety the resistance in Britain had been firm and widespread. Unfortunately the debate was increasingly to be conducted in constitutional terms.

Yet to North in 1770 the American situation must have seemed peaceful enough. John Wilkes and Edmund Burke, each in his own way, had done their best to maintain American disaffection and to persuade the colonists that they were fighting the same battle for freedom as were the radicals or Rockingham Whigs. But just as in England the Rockinghams and the radicals deeply suspected each other, so too did the moderate and extremist elements of the colonial opposition to British power. In the late 1760s conservative merchants and planters had joined with radical townspeople and frontiersmen in the battle against taxation, but they were becoming increasingly aware of the danger of flirting with forces which they might be unable to control, and had no wish to see British power replaced by a colonial democracy. This was emphasized after the Boston 'massacre' of 5 March 1770, when British soldiers fired on a mob attacking the customs-house and five Bostonians were killed. Sam Adams and his fellow-radicals did their utmost to exaggerate the unfortunate incident but the conservative merchant aristocracy showed little enthusiasm for mob activity and propaganda. In New York too, after bitter internal conflict, the conservatives regained the upper hand, while in the Carolinas the revolt of the frontier 'Regulators' reminded the authorities of the dangerous game they had been playing. By mid-1770 the solidarity of American resistance to Britain had been broken, and the non-importation agreements had become a dead letter even before the news of North's repeal of all the duties save that on tea reached the colonies. When North, intent evidently on mixing clemency with firmness, made it clear that the new Governor of New York should have his salary paid from local revenues, persuaded the Privy Council to annul an act of the South Carolinas assembly providing for a gift of £1,500 to the Supporters of the Bill of Rights in London, and (in view of the dissaffected disposition of Massachusetts) moved the rendezvous of the Royal Navy in America to Boston and increased the troops there, little excitement resulted. The American merchants appeared to have decided that too much politics was bad for business, and the radicals found their propaganda falling on apathetic ears.

Yet 1772 forcibly placed American no less than Indian affairs on North's agenda, and it was the zealous enforcement of the Acts of Trade that provoked a new crisis. On the morning of 10 June a small band of Rhode Islanders boarded the revenue cutter *Gaspée*, wounded the captain and burned the vessel. Especially as it was known that the radicals were chancing their arms, North could ill afford to ignore this act of violence and defiance. But the Commission of Enquiry which he established ran up against the universal amnesia of the population of Rhode Island, and had to confess itself powerless. The delighted radicals were encouraged to fresh bursts of activity, representing the Commission as an attack on colonial liberty and advocating that Committees of Correspondence be established by the colonial assemblies in order to resist British aggression. Nor was the situation improved when, later in the year, the Government declared its intention to establish a Civil List in Massachusetts where, with the suppression of smuggling, the customs revenue was becoming substantial. Sam Adams was able to use this threat to develop further the creation of Committees of Correspondence, and a powerful revolutionary machine was forged. The publication of Governor Hutchinson's and Lieutenant-Governor Oliver's private letters to England, made available to the Boston radicals by Benjamin Franklin, added further fuel to the flames—especially since they expressed the view that 'there must be a diminution of what are called English liberties' in Massachusetts if the disintegration of the Empire were to be prevented. It was against this background of radical excitement and fears that North introduced his ill-fated Tea Act.

When the East India Company despatched some twelve hundred chests of tea to the American colonies in 1773 it had no more reason than the Government to believe that it was setting in motion a chain of events that was to culminate in revolution; yet the reaction in the colonies was immediate and widespread. Most ports either refused entry to the tea or stored it up unsold, and the tea consignees, condemned as widely as the stamp-masters had been in 1765, mostly resigned. The radicals were aghast at the prospect of a substantial revenue being raised, and even relatively conservative merchants saw their position as middle-men being eroded, and the tea monopoly as the harbinger of further similar invasions of their business. The result was the most celebrated of the many demonstrations—the Boston Tea-Party of 16 December 1773, when 340 chests of tea were dumped in Boston harbour.

The resistance at Boston was much more than symbolic. Its instigators had openly flouted the authority of Parliament, the radicals were committed to physical opposition, and moderate merchant opinion had at least temporarily succumbed to extremist demands. In Britain condemnation was almost unanimous, even Rockingham and Chatham denouncing the conduct of the Bostonians, while Burke confessed that 'the popular current both within doors and without at present sets sharply against America'. Within the Cabinet, moderates like North and Dartmouth were forced to yield to the more conservative elements, and a series of coercive measures was quickly rushed through Parliament. Although at the outset of North's Ministry the Opposition had been able to command as many as 180 votes on important issues, it never divided above sixty-four during all the debates on the coercive measures, and on many occasions it could not muster more than forty votes. Both Chatham and Rockingham were more interested in justifying their own past actions than in offering constructive criticism, and the one serious attempt to pacify the colonists was Rose Fuller's motion of 19 April 1774 to repeal the duty on tea. It was defeated by 182 votes to forty-nine, and the occasion was memorable only for Burke's celebrated speech on American taxation. This was magnificent rhetoric, but merely covered old and familiar ground. Burke ridiculed the earlier Chatham Administration and eulogized that of Rockingham; praised the wisdom of expediency and carefully sidestepped the question of right; argued that taxation alone was at the root of American resistance, yet conceded the necessity for it; and urged the wholly impracticable method of requisitioning troops.

The first of the coercive measures—the Boston Port Act—closed

Boston to shipping until compensation had been paid to the East India Company and to the revenue officers who had been man-handled by the mob. The second—the Massachusetts Government Act—deprived that colony of the right to elect councillors, gave the Governor power to appoint and dismiss all civil officers except judges of the supreme court, substituted nominated jurors for elected ones, and placed severe restrictions upon town-meetings. The Administration of Justice Act provided that, where fair trials could not be expected in Massachusetts, the defendants might be transferred for trial to Britain or to another colony; and the Quartering Act directed local authorities to provide quarters nearby for troops and authorized the Governor to commandeer houses and barns in default of the necessary co-operation.

By these four Acts Parliament hoped to bring Massachusetts to heel and indeed isolate it from the other colonies. Any slender hope of success was shattered by the concurrent passage of the Quebec Act, which was not part of the policy of coercion, but a genuine attempt by Dartmouth to solve at one and the same time the western problem and that of Canadian government. Its Canadian provisions were liberal and humane, but it created greater misgivings in the American colonies than all the other Acts together. Because Quebec was not yet considered ready for an elected legislative assembly, the appointed Governor and Council were continued with full executive and legislative power; French civil law (which knew no jury) was retained and blended in a sensible fashion with the English criminal law; toleration was granted to Roman Catholics, who were given full legal rights, including jury service; and tithes were allowed for the Roman Catholic Church. Finally, the boundaries of Quebec were extended south to the Ohio and west to the Mississippi. In Parliament there was some resistance to religious toleration, and to the denial of the usual civil and political liberties to the small English minority in Quebec; but no one appeared to realize the impact the Act would have on the American colonies. It was indeed ironical that, of all the legislation of the pre-revolutionary decade, the most provocative were acts which sought merely to extricate the East India Company from its difficulties and to provide an equitable government for French Canadians.

The initial reaction in America to the Port Act was somewhat mixed. Many conservatives in Boston were prepared to pay compensation and beg for mercy, but the radicals were determined to fight and quickly spread the word through the Committees of Correspondence. Paul Revere was sent to New York and Philadelphia for aid, and Boston was portrayed as the first line of defence for American liberty. At first the plight of the Bostonians commanded widespread sympathy and there were demonstrations and gestures of defiance in most colonies. Sam Adams was encouraged to draw up the Solemn League and Covenant, demanding non-importation and non-consumption agreements until the Port Act was repealed. He doubtless hoped to win British concessions by applying economic sanctions, as had successfully been done in 1765 and in 1767. But the initiative this time was being taken, not by conservative merchants, but by radicals. The internal conflict that had already been apparent in the 1760s and was to characterize American politics long after the break with Britain had been effected, again burst forth. The middle colonies in particular were unenthusiastic about adopting any measures without prior consultation. John Dickinson and the Quaker oligarchy in Pennsylvania were quick to urge caution, and the New York conservatives demanded the summoning of a Continental Congress where it was hoped their opinions would prevail. Nonetheless supplies of food were sent to aid Boston in withstanding North's blockade and Virginia came out strongly in favour of the radicals.

In this uncertain situation the further coercive measures and the Quebec Act proved decisive. The 'mandamus' councillors were widely condemned and the so-called 'Murder Act' was portrayed as an open invitation to the British troops to murder innocent Americans. The absence of an elected assembly in Canada, together with the lack of *habeas corpus* and of trial by jury in civil cases were depicted as evidence of what the Americans might expect in the near future, and the extension of the boundaries of Quebec was seen as a determination to strangle westward expansion. Most bizarre of all, the toleration of Roman Catholicism was portrayed as the first stage in the introduction of a popish despotism into North America—an idea encouraged, to their discredit, by Chatham, Camden, Fox and Shelburne. No longer was the British Parliament merely chastising the recalcitrant Massachusetts; it was threatening the religion, property and civil liberties of all Americans. So at least was the tenor of radical propaganda.

The first Continental Congress duly assembled in Philadelphia, a notoriously conservative town, but the radicals did not make the mistake of alienating support by proceeding too rashly. The New Englanders remained discreetly in the background, allowing their cause to be taken up by representatives from Virginia and the Carolinas. Even then, the demand was only for the repeal of all repressive legislation enacted since 1763, no challenge was issued to Parliament's right to regulate trade, the King was petitioned for protection against oppressive ministers, and a Declaration of Rights and Grievances was concocted for presentation to the English people. But the turning-point came when the conservative

Joseph Galloway presented his Plan of Union in September 1774. It envisaged a Grand Council of representatives from all the colonies, with jurisdiction over matters of general importance, and its assent would be necessary to validate parliamentary legislation affecting the colonies as a whole. Executive authority would be exercised by a Resident-General representing the Crown and possessing the power of veto over all acts of the Council. It was a statesmanlike attempt at compromise, but it was too radical for the conservatives and too conservative for the radicals. Its defeat by the slender margin of one vote opened the way for the main radical challenge, and Congress was presented with the Suffolk Resolves, nurtured by a ludicrous rumour of large-scale butchery by British troops in Massachusetts. The Resolves demanded defiance of the coercive acts and the withholding of taxes until all privileges had been restored to Massachusetts; they also advocated defensive military preparations and reprisals in the event of the arrest of any patriot leaders. Though this was perilously close to support of a defensive war against Britain, the Resolves were worded in such a way as to make their rejection appear a desertion of Massachusetts. They were therefore adopted somewhat nervously, and moderation was urged towards Gage and his army.

The stand against Britain was reinforced by the formation of the Continental Association, committed to non-importation, non-consumption and non-exportation. Southern agricultural interests were very unenthusiastic about non-exportation, and the northern colonies were dissatisfied when, for the sake of unity, rice had to be conceded as an exception. Nor was the Association made any more popular by the vigorous activities of the inspecting committees which were established to enforce the boycotts. Apart from their ruthless treatment of violators, they sought to encourage frugality and discountenance all forms of dissipation. Many conservatives and even some radicals deplored this latter-day Puritanism, and began to wonder whether American tyranny was preferable to that supposedly exercised by Britain. But there was widespread hope that British bankruptcy would be ensured by the boycotts, and few people seemed to realize that war was imminent. They ignored the highly inflammatory situation that had developed in Massachusetts, where British troops and the New Englanders stood at daggers drawn. Gage was faced with widespread passive resistance, was denied supplies and shelter, and had to listen while a whole series of robberies, rapes and murders was fictitiously attributed to his ill-fed and miserable troops. Meanwhile the radicals were clearly preparing to force a defensive war on Congress by forming companies and assembling military stores. Thus the winter passed in uneasy quiet, with Gage convinced that the New

Englanders could be crushed, but without sufficient men to risk an engagement. Further south the conservatives grew increasingly suspicious of radical intentions, and the refusal of the New York assembly to adopt the Association was a clear indication of continuing colonial divisions. There was even a radical suggestion that the New England militia might be more profitably used against New York than against the British.

In the face of an enemy still at least partially divided, the British Parliament considered the last attempts at conciliation. The general election of 1774 had wrought little change in the composition of the House of Commons, North's estimated following of 321 being almost identical to a calculation that John Robinson had made in 1772. Despite the crisis in colonial relations, political issues were seldom raised in the vast majority of constituencies. Candidates in a few radical strongholds such as Middlesex, Westminster and London were urged to seek conciliation with the colonies, and Bristol was still sufficiently sympathetic towards America to return Edmund Burke. Otherwise all was apathy. The King and his ministers were not unnaturally indignant at the reception accorded the Coercive Acts in the colonies, and horrified at Gage's suggestion that the Acts should be suspended until British forces had been built up. Indeed, North's desire for economy, the continued foolish convictions that Massachusetts could be isolated and that colonial troops were a mere rabble, and the fear of France all combined to restrict British reinforcements to Gage to a mere three ships and some six hundred marines. In so far as strategy was argued within ministerial ranks, Barrington (Secretary at War) wanted naval rather than land forces diverted to the colonies, while Sandwich (First Lord of the Admiralty) advocated the reverse. Barrington indeed favoured the withdrawal of all British troops from Massachusetts, and concentration on a naval blockade of the coast-line. But withdrawal would seriously damage British prestige in America, and Britain at that stage could ill afford ships for the blockade. Sandwich had with difficulty managed to prevent North from reducing the navy, but there had been no increase and many ships were far from sea-worthy—despite the fact that France was said to be fitting out a fleet in Toulon. Moreover North, with almost incredible short-sightedness, chose this moment to reduce the number of seamen by four thousand, merely because the East Indian fleet had been recalled. In these circumstances further attempts at conciliation were understandable.

Within Parliament both Government and Opposition approaches to conciliation were somewhat oblique. North and Dartmouth toyed with the idea of a royal commission to discuss the situation with the colonists, but neither their fellow-ministers nor the King could stomach such weakness. Meanwhile the Rockinghams tried to repeat their past successes in harnessing merchant support for conciliation. But trade with Europe had improved, and many merchants had become convinced by the Boston Tea-Party that the time had come to teach the colonists a lesson. Petitions for conciliation were eventually extorted from Bristol, London, Norwich, Glasgow, Birmingham, Dudley, Liverpool, Manchester and Wolverhampton; but they were very moderate in tone, and all other attempts failed. Nor were the Rockinghams much comforted by the attitude of Chatham, who denounced the Declaratory Act of 1766 as the source of all the subsequent trouble. To the Rockinghams this was sacrilege of a high order, and any hope of a united Opposition melted away.

It was Chatham who took the initiative in proposing conciliation. On 20 January 1775 he moved for the removal of British troops from Boston, though he admitted that he would use force if the colonists tried to interfere with the Acts of Trade. When his motion was overwhelmingly defeated, he struck back with his Provisional Act for Reconciliation with America, asserting the subordination of the colonies to the Crown and Parliament, and the latter's right to legislate in imperial affairs as well as to maintain troops in the colonies, but denying Parliament's power to tax for revenue purposes. He also recognized the legality of the scheduled second Continental Congress so that it in turn might recognize the supreme authority of Parliament, and he predicted that Congress, as an act of affection towards the mother-country, would consider granting a permanent revenue to the King, of which Parliament would have the disposal. In return the grievances which had accumulated since 1763 would all be removed. In the mid-1760s Chatham's scheme might have stood some chance of success in America, but in 1775 there was no possibility of their being mollified by concessions over taxation. Indeed, men such as James Wilson and Thomas Jefferson were already repudiating all parliamentary authority, basing their case on natural rights, and asserting that the Crown, not Parliament, was the sole link between Britain and her colonies—the germ perhaps of twentieth-century 'dominion status', but a notion incomprehensible to Englishmen of 1775. Parliament at that stage was not even prepared to concede the right of taxation, and Chatham's measure was defeated by a large majority.

Rather surprisingly the next move came from the Government benches, where Dartmouth had even been prepared to contemplate Chatham's proposals as a starting-point. North at first showed a greater determination to stand firm, successfully moving for an address to the King declaring New England to be in a state of rebellion and asking for it to be reduced to obedience. Concurrently the forces were augmented and leave was given to bring in a bill restraining the trade of New England and excluding her from the Newfoundland fisheries. Then came a sudden change of front on North's part, consistent with that foolish mixture of firmness and clemency that had already done so much to worsen colonial relations. At one and the same time North wished to rally conservative support in the colonies and unite opinion in England. Instead of direct parliamentary taxation he proposed a requisition system in which Parliament would lay its demands before the colonial assemblies. If the colonists then taxed themselves to the satisfaction of Parliament, it would refrain from taxing them. The principle of the Declaratory Act would be preserved, and Parliament would merely forebear to exercise its rights. In effect North was espousing the Rockingham position, but—like Chatham—he was still confining himself to the issue of taxation, and thereby showing a woeful ignorance of contemporary American opinion. Despite a threatened revolt among his own followers, North's Conciliatory Propositions were carried by a large majority, the Rockinghams and Chathamites being hard-pressed to justify their votes against them. They are of some interest in that they represent the first major Government retreat since 1766 and contain the germ of a federal idea; but by the time they reached America the colonists were in arms.

Meanwhile, the Rockinghams, irritated at having had the initiative seized by Chatham and North, introduced a third plan, outlined in Burke's famous speech on conciliation of 22 March 1775. But not even Burke's superb oratory could lend credibility to his magnanimous principles. Unlike Chatham and North, he refused to contemplate the federal idea, and as before he preferred to side-step the question of right. Return to 1763, he claimed, and all would be well. The colonists in gratitude would provide funds for defence and for a civil list, and the mother-country would respond by repealing all the recent offensive acts. If North and Chatham had worn blinkers, Burke was completely blind. The question of right had been raised, and a return to 1763 was impossible. Not surprisingly the motion was lost by a majority of nearly two hundred votes. Outside Parliament only the City radicals showed any lingering sympathy for the colonists, and the outlook already seemed hopeless when, on 18 April 1775, was fired the shot heard round the world. Lexington and Concord, trivial clashes in themselves, provided the Americans with their first real martyrs and led to a fresh outburst of frenzied propaganda on both sides of the Atlantic. In America it was said that 'women in child-bed were driven naked into the street; old men, peaceably in their houses, were shot dead; innocent children were brained by blows from muskets'; while in England American soldiers were reported to rival the Indians in savagery and to have scalped dying British troops. Never before had propaganda played so vital a role in promoting war between nations, and never before had difficulties of communication contributed to much so the deteriorating situation that led remorselessly to war. Had the electric telegraph been invented in the eighteenth century, it is just possible that two peoples enjoying common traditions and common ideals might have been able to find at least a temporary solution to the vexed problem of imperial rule. As it was, any conciliatory move from either side was already overtaken by events before news of it could be transmitted across the Atlantic. Now the point of no-return had been reached. The Battle of Bunker Hill clearly indicated that the colonists were not the despicable rabble that Englishmen had envisaged; and once British troops had been forced to retreat in the face of American farmers, pride demanded total victory. The time for debate was over. Even Dartmouth and North had to abandon hope of localizing the conflict. North capitulated completely to the war party in the Cabinet, and Dartmouth sought in futile fashion to salve his conscience by refusing to attend Cabinet meetings on American affairs. As an ironical postscript to the last attempts at conciliation, the Olive Branch Petition from Congress was published in England on 24 August—the day after George III had published his Proclamation of Rebellion.

The reaction to the Proclamation was strikingly favourable. The leading merchant and manufacturing towns sent in loyal addresses—Manchester, Liverpool, Lancaster, Bradford, even Burke's Bristol—and the Irish House of Commons declared its allegiance to the Crown and its abhorrence of the American attitude. The vast majority of the politically conscious nation was clearly behind the Government. This made it all the more tragic that North, like Walpole before him, was singularly ill-suited to conduct a war and had no stomach for it. He was no more a tool of George III's than Walpole had been of George II's. Equally, he was no dominating, dynamic Pitt, but a capable and respected administrator who in time of peace could provide sensible conciliatory leadership and the minimum of co-ordination essential to the departmental system of government which he inherited and which was quite unfitted to the conduct of a major war. From the outset it was almost inevitable that George III would have to occupy the near-vacuum created by North's inadequacy, and endeavour to give some direction to the confused efforts of an undistinguished and divided Cabinet. Meanwhile North entered the war in a panic, ridiculously fearful of Opposition in Parliament, bemoaning City radical support of the rebellious colonists, and lamenting the defeatist attitudes of Howe, Clinton and Burgoyne in America and the inadequacy of Gage and Graves.

Early measures to support the British forces in America were at best feeble. Russian mercenaries failed to materialize, and five Irish regiments had to be sent instead—with results for Ireland that nobody foresaw. Additional troops were withdrawn from Minorca and Gibraltar, to be replaced—despite the usual Opposition protest—by Hanoverians, Gage and Graves were recalled, and a campaign launched against South Carolina. The Cabinet was restless, the great majority calling for more vigorous measures; and the general situation was strikingly reminiscent of that which had confronted Walpole in 1739–41. The only difference—and it was a difference of the first magnitude—was that the parliamentary Opposition was this time a subversive force within the nation. Sympathetically disposed towards the enemy, they could make little capital out of North's manifest inadequacy. Comforted to some extent by their obvious weakness, North reshuffled his Administration. Grafton, unable to accept war against the colonists, went over to Opposition, leaving Dartmouth free to adopt the somewhat cowardly solution of retreating to the office of Lord Privy Seal, without a seat in the Cabinet. The ineffectual Rochford resigned and Weymouth became Southern Secretary. Lord George Germain (formerly Sackville), who had long clamoured for more active measures and a chance to redeem himself from the disgrace of Minden, became Colonial Secretary in Dartmouth's place. Sandwich remained at the Admiralty, Suffolk as Northern Secretary and Gower as Lord President. This, apart from minor later changes, was the team that was to lose the war. All save North now wanted its vigorous prosecution, but the team lacked a leader, and George III was to prove no adequate substitute.

At first things went tolerably well. Britain raised twenty-three thousand German mercenaries and the American invasion of Canada proved abortive. North jumped at the opportunity to negotiate from a position of strength, and the Howe Peace Commission was despatched to America. But its terms were merely a reaffirmation of North's earlier conciliatory proposals, and its arrival was followed within a few weeks by the Declaration of Independence. Not only was full-scale war now inevitable, but the publication in the previous January of Tom Paine's *Common Sense* had destroyed the last vestige of faith in the King. Independence was seen as the only solution, and with Paine's rabid denunciation of George III the way was paved for the Americans to adopt the Rockingham legend in full and see the monarch in retrospect as the evil genius behind the various moves that had led to the disintegration of the

Empire—an interpretation that was to flourish on the King's enforced assumption of leadership as the war dragged on, and that was conveniently to ignore his wholly justifiable plea that he was merely 'fighting the battle of the legislature'. To a community that prided itself on its representative institutions a stand against royal tyranny was more congenial than one against parliamentary authority, especially when it could be synchronized with the claims of the Opposition in Britain.

During the ensuing eighteen months optimism at home gave way to increasing despair. The Carolina expedition was a failure, Boston had to be evacuated, France and Spain were supplying the rebels with war materials, and French naval preparations were reaching alarming proportions. Sandwich urgently demanded much greater expenditure on the navy, only to be met with the reluctance of North and the King, who feared that France might be further provoked and were foolishly opposed to incurring additional expense. The Ministry staggered on, placing its faith in some blind and ill-founded instinct that the colonists would soon be routed. Minor successes in the summer were counter-balanced by Washington's winter manoeuvres. Morale at home and the threatening international situation demanded a bold stroke, and Germain and Burgoyne conceived a master plan for the isolation of New England by an invasion of British forces from Canada (under Burgoyne) and a northwards thrust from Howe's forces in New York. But Howe foolishly delayed in order to shake American confidence by attacking Philadelphia, which he captured in July 1777. Momentary joy at this victory was dimmed by the awareness that Howe and Burgoyne had failed to link up, and in October came the disastrous surrender of Burgoyne at Saratoga, which was to change the whole course of the war.

After eighteen months of unsuccessful war, Walpole had been forced out of office; yet North, with an even worse record, had seemed in relatively little danger. Indeed, since 1775, the Opposition had been floundering as badly as the Government. Its members were mostly convinced that they and the Americans were fighting a common battle against a tyrannical King and a Parliament dominated by royal influence and guided by a 'double Cabinet' of men like William Eden (Under-Secretary of State until 1776 and then First Lord of Trade and Plantations), Charles Jenkinson (a Junior Lord of Treasury) and John Robinson (Secretary to the Treasury). As North, increasingly uncomfortable in a hostile Cabinet, tended more and more to rely on lesser men of this character—the civil servants of his day—the suspicions of the Rockinghams seemed confirmed, especially as those men became the main channel of communication between North and the King, thereby giving apparent substance to all Burke's fertile imaginings about the sinister influence of the 'King's Friends'. It was easy to see that their sympathy for America could lead them eventually to a frontal attack on the Crown, but this still lay in the future. For the moment they must of necessity concentrate on America, but here their position was essentially weak. Burke beseeched Rockingham to take the initiative, but Rockingham could think of nothing better than to secede with his followers from Parliament. Nor could Burke find consolation elsewhere. Even in the Bristol that had elected him with enthusiasm the previous year, less than half the corporation still favoured the Rockingham attitude and even these were unenthusiastic. By 1775 most merchants had forsaken the Americans to build up their trade with Europe and find additional consolation in the growing number of war contracts. Rockingham at least was realistic. In September 1775 he wrote to Burke:

> The generality of the people of England are now led away by the misrepresentations and arts of the Ministry, the Court and their abettors; so that the violent measures towards America are fairly adopted and countenanced by a majority of individuals of all ranks, professions or occupations in this country.

Resistance was useless; everyone was out of step but the Rockinghams, and their only hope of success was an American victory. For them patriotism had become the last refuge of the scoundrel. Burke was frantic. He tried to persuade Richmond and others with Irish interests to induce the Irish Commons to refuse supplies, but they were rightly suspicious of this wild plan. Bristol then proceeded to deal Burke a further blow by voting a loyal address to the King. Only in London was there any significant support for the colonists, and the wildness of the City radicals was as little palatable to the Rockinghams as it was to the rest of the nation and merely discredited all with American sympathies.

Within the ranks of the Opposition Shelburne was already adumbrating future policy by advocating the abandonment of arguments about the justice of the war, and concentration instead on attempts to limit the Influence of the Crown. As usual, he was ahead of his time. Meanwhile every attempt was made to ensure concerted action. Burke was in constant contact with Chatham and Shelburne, while Camden and Grafton were now on the periphery of the Opposition. By the end of 1775 the Opposition strategy had clarified. The war was unjust and America was not seeking independence. The struggle must therefore be ended and American liberties restored before France became involved. Burke's Bill for Quieting America, introduced in November 1775, showed that the Rockinghams were beginning to weaken. They could not bring themselves to abandon their one true love—the Declaratory Act; but they were now prepared to deny to Parliament the right to tax the colonists except to regulate commerce, and even then the colonies were to retain the ensuing revenue. Otherwise the coercive acts were to be repealed and a general amnesty granted. The bill was of course defeated, but it is interesting in that it closed the gap between the original positions of Rockingham and Chatham, even though the former was characteristically unprepared to admit as much. For the remainder of the session the Opposition could scarcely muster more than a score of votes.

If 1775 had been a bad year for the Opposition, the Declaration of Independence made nonsense of the arguments that they had used and left them without any tenable position during the 1776–7 session. Minor British victories were greeted as 'terrible news', and after a perfunctory appearance in Parliament most were content to retire to their country houses. As Sir George Savile confessed to Rockingham: 'We are not only patriots out of place, but patriots out of the opinion of the public.' In the course of 1777 the Rockinghams made their final change of front. Burke, in his letter to the Sheriffs of Bristol, showed himself prepared to concede American independence. Chatham, who could not bring himself to contemplate the disruption of the Empire which he considered largely his own handiwork, is rejected. All acts passed since 1763 must be repealed in the hope that the colonists would abandon their notion of independence, but if not, it must be recognized. Only then would the Rockinghams' return from the political wilderness become practicable; only then could the nation be rescued from the sinister machinations of the King. As a natural corollary to acceptance of independence the Rockinghams at last heeded Shelburne's advice and threw their whole weight behind demands for economical reform which were beginning to draw strength from the rising cost of the war. In April 1777 the King applied for a grant of £600,000 to pay arrears on the Civil List. Back to Parliament came the recently seceded Rockinghams, to attack the over-weening influence of the Crown, to demand particulars of recent expenditure, and to challenge the monarch with using his ill-gotten gains to corrupt Parliament. Considering the massive extent to which the country was behind King and Ministry, the Rockingham arguments were scarcely convincing. But many country gentlemen were at least prepared to listen where their purses were involved, and the Opposition managed to summon over one hundred votes in each of two divisions. Though still defeated by a majority of more than two to one, this was much better than they could hope to do over any issue connected with the war. More than ever they had to pray for British defeats, so that in retrospect their attitudes over America might seem to be justified, and war-weariness undermine North's position and give teeth to the incipient movement for economical reform. Their prayers were apparently answered when the news of Saratoga reached England. By an ironic coincidence Rockingham on that day penned his shortest ever letter to his party manager: 'My Dear Burke, my heart is at ease.'

The impact of Saratoga upon the political scene was four-fold. North authorized a series of secret negotiations with the American Commissioners in Paris, the Opposition launched a fresh attack on the Ministry, an attempt was made to convert the war into a purely naval one, and the terms of reference of the Carlisle Peace Commission embodied a new governmental approach to the problem of conciliation. The negotiations initiated by North and Eden—dangerously concealed from the rest of the Cabinet—sought to find out whether the Americans would settle for anything short of independence. Not only was the answer a clear-cut negative, but it was made obvious that if Britain tried to evade the issue she would soon find herself at war with France and Spain; and on 6 February 1778 Treaties of Amity and Commerce were duly signed between the colonists and France, who guaranteed support if Britain did not grant independence. Reluctantly North and the King were forced to recognize that a settlement could be reached only by a direct approach to Congress, and that the terms would have to be much more magnanimous than any hitherto envisaged.

Meanwhile North faced bitter dissension within the Cabinet, where some ministers were intent on disclaiming responsibility for an unsuccessful war policy, and others were trying to turn a confused situation to their own personal advantage. Germain, the obvious target for criticism, tried to throw all the blame for Saratoga on Burgoyne; Bathurst resented Howe's replacement by Clinton and threatened resignation; Suffolk was clamouring for the Order of the Garter; and Thurlow and Wedderburn were demanding legal promotion. North, unable to cope with both military disaster and factiousness within the Cabinet, fell into one of his periodic moods of despondency and strongly advised George III to modify his Ministry, preferably by calling on Chatham to assume the leadership. But when an indirect approach was made to that ailing and increasingly arrogant old statesman, he demanded a direct summons from the King and *carte blanche* in the formation of a new Ministry. This George III would not consider and the Ministry was forced to soldier on. Yet it was not the King who saved North, but the continuing inadequacy of the Opposition. At the opening of the 1777–8 session on 18 November (before the news of Saratoga had reached London) North's position seemed impregnable; and on the motion to adjourn for the Christmas recess attendance was so low and members so shaken by the defeat that they hesitated to commit themselves. Confidence was to some extent restored during the following weeks by the host of loyal addresses that poured in from all parts of the kingdom, and by the raising of public subscriptions in the face of the French threat. As patriotic fervour swept the nation, the Rockinghams began to hope that they might be swept into power with Chatham, whose name was on many lips. But Chatham gave Rockingham as short shrift as he had given the King, denouncing his acceptance of American independence and declaring that he could never again act with him. The City radicals added insult to injury by attacking the Declaratory Act as the source of all the troubles, and the Rockinghams were once more left in isolation, embittered further against both Chatham and the City. Yet within Parliament, where many country gentlemen were gravely alarmed by the ill-success of the war and by the imminence of the French threat, the Rockinghams were encouraged to mount a fresh attack on the unhappy North. When, on 2 February 1778, Charles James Fox[1] moved that no more men be sent out of the Kingdom —implying a virtual abandonment of the American war—the Opposition mustered 165 votes, their best performance for many years. Almost inevitably they were encouraged to overplay their hand, and fell into the trap that awaits all Oppositions in time of war. As they sought to score points, even at the expense of revealing England's military and naval unpreparedness to the French, and of hampering the war supplies, opinion swung sharply against them; and when, after news of the French treaty had been communicated to Parliament the Rockinghams at last formally adopted American independence as a policy, the division between the two main wings of the Opposition became ever more apparent. Chatham's dying speech in the Lords—when, as Burke said, 'he spit his last venom'— was a denunciation of Rockingham policy, and Shelburne, who inherited Chatham's following, was equally emphatic. All chance of a united Opposition was again destroyed.

Yet coming events were already beginning to cast their shadow. The Rockinghams came out strongly in favour of economical reform, where they could expect support from both Shelburne and the country gentlemen. In a series of thin Houses, characterized by significant abstentions

[1] Third son of Henry Fox, Lord Holland; entered Parliament in 1768 and at first followed in his father's footsteps by supporting the Court; but in 1774, largely for personal reasons, broke with North, adopted an increasingly liberal attitude over both American and domestic affairs, and became closely associated with the Rockinghams.

on the Government side, the Opposition forced North onto the defensive. In the Committee of Ways and Means on 9 March 1778 they even carried a tax of 25 per cent on the income of all placemen and pensioners, though North was able to have it rejected next day on the report by the slender margin of six votes. Fox, in advocating American independence on 10 April, linked economical reform with the American issue, portraying the breach with the colonists and the ensuing defeats as the outcome of the undue Influence of the Crown and the consequent political emasculation of Parliament. The country gentlemen might not yet be prepared to concede independence to America but, vexed by the misconduct and mounting expense of the war, they were prepared to listen to schemes for economy and reform. Thus Sir Philip Jennings Clerke was given leave to bring in a bill for excluding Government contractors from the Commons, and North was able to kill it on the second reading by only four votes. North survived this temporary crisis, and the Opposition was still too weak and disunited to be really effective; but it was only the King's repeated pleas that dissuaded North from resigning a position that he was finding increasingly unpalatable.

While the Opposition was seeking to undermine North in the Commons, ministers were debating the military significance of Saratoga and of imminent French entry into the war. Germain and the King were convinced that the American war must become primarily naval in character, but Sandwich was adamant that, with the new French threat in European waters, Britain could spare no extra ships for America. Nor would North, until the publication of the Franco-American treaty, consent to naval building, repairing and fitting, and by then American privateers were creating havoc in English and Irish waters. A series of inconclusive Cabinet debates produced only a decision to strike against the French West Indies; and this—combined with the necessity of maintaining an adequate fleet at home—meant the abandonment of an all-out naval war against America. Years of naval neglect were beginning to reap their harvest, and worse was yet to come.

In the new situation even George III was forced to concede that peace with America was desirable, if not essential. The result was the Carlisle Peace Commission, consisting of the Earl of Carlisle, Governor Johnstone and William Eden, and based on the principle that all acts of Parliament affecting America should be repealed and that the Commissioners should seek an acceptable foundation on which a new comprehensive act could be devised. Both Cabinet and Parliament gloomily conceded the necessity to treat the Americans as if they were in fact independent, though it was hoped that the settlement might reserve certain powers to Parliament. The ideal of the Commission was a common citizenship for Britain and the Empire, home rule for America in internal affairs and a negotiated treaty relationship as far as the common issues of trade and defence were concerned. The Crown would remain in charge of the military and naval forces in America, American debts to British merchants would be acknowledged, and loyalists would be restored to their estates. These proposed terms stopped short of independence, but the power to tax was surrendered, all civil officials in America were to be elected, and Congress would be recognized. In 1775 this might have been a possible solution, but the clock could not be put back. Secure in the knowledge of French support, Congress insisted either that independence immediately be recognized or that all British forces be withdrawn from America. The first British Empire was in ashes, but the terms of the Commission command attention because they contained the germ of a new imperial idea that was soon to be pursued by Shelburne in the eventual peace negotiations with America and by the younger Pitt in relation to Ireland.

During 1778–9 the war continued to go badly for Britain, largely because of naval unpreparedness and continued indecisive leadership. The Opposition again met with temporary success over Clerke's bill, and was encouraged to launch a full-scale attack on ministerial war policy. In a series of motions censuring the Admiralty for failing to provide adequate support for Admiral Keppel (significantly a Rockingham supporter), condemning the lack of naval preparation for war with France, criticizing the Ministry for failing to send reinforcements to Howe in New York, and demanding the resignation of Sandwich from the Admiralty, the Opposition managed at times to muster as many as 170 votes, and North's majority dropped as low as forty. But Rockingham and Shelburne remained suspect because of their sympathy towards the Americans, and sufficient country gentlemen continued to believe that the war was just to save North from the consequences of its ill-management. Yet continuing misfortune was by the winter of 1779–80 to involve the nation in a wave of protest that has been seen by some historians as comparable to the agitation which a decade later was to sweep France and engulf her in revolution. Though such an interpretation is untenable, there was indeed a real if temporary crisis, and the manifestations of tension were many and varied. Firstly, the petitioning movement of 1769–70 was re-born, with a much more widespread appeal, drawing its strength not from City radicalism but from discontent in the counties. Yorkshire, by far the largest county constituency, took the lead under the guidance of the Rev. Christopher Wyvill, a conservative parson whose programme of economical and parliamentary reform assumed, under the conditions of 1779–80, a spuriously radical guise. Secondly, the Volunteer Movement in Ireland, born of England's inability any longer to defend Irish shores, quickly turned to demanding Irish independence. Thirdly, the parliamentary Opposition mounted its greatest attack on North since 1770, based essentially on an extensive programme of economical reform, drawing on wide support in the country, and threatening the Ministry with total rout. Finally, the no-Popery riots of 1779 in Scotland (arising from North's proposals for mild relief for Roman Catholics) were followed by the much more serious Gordon Riots, which reduced London to chaos for a whole week.

These forces were sufficiently profound seriously to shake the Ministry, but they proceeded from no radical, still less revolutionary, ardour in the hearts of the British people. They were rather spontaneous manifestations of a sense of national frustration. A long, costly war was being gravely mismanaged, and the natural constitutional remedy was to oust those responsible for the mismanagement. Walpole had been driven out in 1742; Newcastle had felt obliged to resign in panic in 1756; yet North lingered on. He did so, not because the King was able to maintain him against the will of the people, but because he was not defeated in Parliament on any major motion; and this was above all due to the fact that sufficient independent members stood by him to enable him to survive. By 1779 the division between the two sides in Parliament had become so clear-cut that the defeat of North would bring in Rockingham and/or Shelburne. But the cure was worse than the disease, for both had always sympathized with the enemy and proclaimed from the start that it was an unjust war. This sat ill with country gentlemen who had long contributed through the land-tax to the defences of colonists who refused to assist themselves, and who rose in rebellion when attempts were made to coerce them into doing their duty. An Opposition whose members lit bonfires at the news of American victories was bound to be viewed with distaste by many independent members, and as long as any hope of victory over the colonists remained, North seemed preferable to his opponents; mismanagement of the war, however vexing, was preferable to selling out to the enemy. Nonetheless the frustration apparent both inside and outside Parliament was born of dissatisfaction with a system that seemed to produce only bunglers and traitors, and increasing support for some kind of reform became inevitable.

In these circumstances the Opposition's best strategy was obviously to synchronize their efforts in the Commons with the widespread extra-parliamentary agitation, but this proved a more delicate and difficult task than was at first realized. The petitioning movement which was launched by Wyvill in Yorkshire, and which was in due course to result in the delivery to the Commons of forty-one petitions between February and April 1780, arose from concern at the waste of public money and the high level of taxation, and expressed the view that the undue Influence of the Crown was in part responsible both for public indebtedness and for the corruption that sapped the strength of Administration. Thus far its interests, though spontaneously declared, conformed to those of most Opposition members. But the movement, following traditional 'Country' sentiments in its distaste for placemen and pensioners, sought further means of achieving the greater independence of the Commons than that of mere legislation against office-holders; it proposed also the elimination of many rotten-boroughs and the re-distribution of the available seats to the counties and to the metropolis. Although the Opposition applauded the country demands for economical reform (which would strike at the patronage of the Crown), parliamentary reform—striking also at the borough patronage of the aristocracy—was quite another matter. The radical Shelburne was prepared to follow Chatham in embracing not only a more equitable distribution of seats, but also the accompanying emphasis in the petitions on the need for more frequent Parliaments; but apart from Fox and Richmond, few Rockinghams were prepared to contemplate, still less support, such fundamental change. Many of the party were active in generally assisting the spread of county agitation, but apart from Fox's work on the Westminster Committee of Correspondence, Rockingham efforts were directed towards exclusive concentration on economical reform. Wyvill and his associates, however, had no intention of becoming the dupes of politicians, and their plans for a national meeting of deputies elected by local committees of correspondence, which might even supersede the moral authority of Parliament, were bound to create suspicion in the Commons. The Rockinghams appear to have been active in virtually all the county meetings which produced petitions, and to have provided the major initiative in approximately half of them. While they were well pleased with the petitions for economy that flowed in from twenty-six English and three Welsh counties, ten boroughs, and the cities of London and Westminster, they were unenthusiastic about the General Assembly of Deputies which duly assembled in London—especially when it endorsed the idea of a national association dedicated to parliamentary as well as economical reform—and were relieved to learn that only seventeen of the original forty-one committees were represented. Eventually, they were able to persuade Wyvill who, in the face of waning enthusiasm, came to appreciate that aristocratic backing might after all have some merit, to abandon the notion of annual Parliaments in favour of triennial ones; but in view of their failure to persuade the extra-parliamentary movements to concentrate exclusively on economical reform, they were happy enough to see it die a natural death when only ten counties, together with London, Westminster and Newcastle, could be induced to associate.

Within Parliament the reform movement began similarly by sweeping all before it, but lost momentum at the very moment when the Ministry looked doomed. The Opposition strategy was to condemn extravagance in every form, limit the Influence of the Crown, and censure American policy by abolishing the Secretaryship of State for the Colonies and the Board of Trade, thereby implying that America was already lost. On 8 February 1780 battle was joined; Shelburne introduced a scheme for reforming the public accounts and Savile presented the Yorkshire petition; three days later, without opposition, Burke introduced his Civil Establishment Bill; and when after a further ten days Savile moved more explicitly for an address to the King asking him to lay an account of all pensions before Parliament, North was again afraid to oppose outright, his amendment to exclude pensions on the Civil List and Secret Service Funds being carried by only two votes. On 9 March the Colonial Secretaryship was saved from abolition by a mere seven votes. Four days later the Board of Trade was abolished by a margin of eight, and Clerke's revived bill to exclude Government contractors from the House was subsequently allowed to pass both the committee stage and the third reading without a division. It appeared that nothing could save North, but the Opposition—elated by its success—went too far. Burke urged the abolition of separate treasuries within the royal household, in order to make the First Lord of the Treasury responsible for the whole Civil List, but between forty and fifty independents, uneasy at this interference with the royal prerogative, abstained from voting and allowed North to reject the proposal by 211 to 158. The remaining clauses of Burke's bill were then negatived without a division. On 6 April, however, John Dunning confidently moved his celebrated resolution, 'that the Influence of the Crown has increased, is increasing, and ought to be diminished'. In fact Government patronage had significantly decreased since 1760, in respect of both office-holders in the Commons and borough patronage; but Dunning based his case on emotional arguments, not statistical analysis, and his motion was carried in a very full and excited House by 233 to 215. So great indeed was the excitement and confusion that members proceeded to make nonsense of the grounds on which, a few days earlier, they had rejected Burke's proposal, by passing without a division a motion that the Commons was competent to reform the Civil List or any part of the public expenditure. A series of related resolutions followed in quick succession, as the Opposition flouted customary procedure in an attempt to press home its advantage before members could pause for reflection. But sanity soon returned as the country gentlemen realized that, in their eagerness to voice their alarm, they were on the point of overturning the Ministry. Passing general motions was one thing; inviting a Ministry composed of Rockingham, Fox and Shelburne was quite another. On a minor point Dunning's majority shrank to two, and on 10 April—a mere four days after his great victory—Crewe's bill was finally rejected by 224 to 195. North was successfully appealing from the Commons drunk to the Commons sober. On 24 April Dunning tried to regain the initiative by moving that there should be no dissolution of Parliament until steps had been taken to remedy the grievances complained of in the petitions of the people. This was too much. Many independents disliked the open challenge to the royal prerogative of dissolution, which smacked too much of the action of the Long Parliament in 1641, and others felt that specific motions of this nature would seal North's fate. As a result, forty members who had supported Dunning on 6 April now deserted him, sixteen voting for North and the remainder abstaining. The Government majority soared to fifty-one, Burke's Bill and subsequent motions relating to the petitions were rejected, and when Conway forlornly moved for conciliation with America the Opposition could muster only eighteen votes. On reflection the Commons had decided that bunglers were still preferable to traitors.

Concurrently North had to face an equally threatening challenge in Ireland, where the political and economic situation had been steadily deteriorating since the early 1770s. At first the skill at parliamentary management of the Lord-Lieutenant (Harcourt) and his secretary (Sir John Blaquiere) did much to minimize conflict, and even the Patriot leader, Henry Flood, was won over to Administration. But his place was quickly taken by that gifted orator, Henry Grattan, who was presented by the advent of the American war with a splendid opportunity to rally the forces of opposition. Ireland was already in a state of acute economic depression, the linen trade had declined dramatically since 1770, and the national debt had doubled in a decade. In these circumstances the closing of the American markets seemed to threaten bankruptcy, and the war was anyway unpopular in Ireland. Massive emigration to the colonies had created many personal bonds of sympathy between the Americans and the Irish, and the latter were increasingly conscious of the similarity between their own grievances and those of the colonists. North was well aware of the necessity for concession. Apart from the fact that he had no desire to face a second rebellion nearer home, he needed Irish troops and supplies for the American war, and with the cessation of colonial trade Ireland assumed greater importance as a market for English manufactures. In 1775 measures were therefore taken to boost Irish prosperity. The Newfoundland fisheries were opened to them, they were allowed to export clothing and equipment to Irish troops serving abroad, and—to revive the linen industry—a bounty was granted on the import of flax-seed. These concessions enabled Harcourt to get from the Irish Parliament a loyal address denouncing the Americans as rebels and pledging support for the war, and permission for four hundred Irish troops to serve in America, provided the cost was borne by Britain. But there was much forthright opposition to these gestures, as there was to the embargo placed by Britain in 1776 on the export of provisions from Ireland; and the defeat of two money bills in the Irish Commons persuaded Harcourt to dissolve Parliament and call a general election in 1776. Unfortunately the Lord-Lieutenant, who for some time had been on uneasy terms with his British colleagues, chose this moment to resign, and was succeeded by the feeble Earl of Buckinghamshire and his even more inadequate secretary, Richard Heron, neither of whom had any capacity for parliamentary management. Not only did Parliament become ever more difficult in the face of further economic decline, but military necessity after the entry of France into the war created the Volunteer movement, ostensibly to defend Irish shores against possible invasion, but in fact equally directed towards providing an outlet for the maturing political consciousness of the Irish people. The Volunteers were of course overwhelmingly Protestant, as were the growing demands for Irish liberties. But the need for Irish unity against Britain persuaded the Protestant ascendancy to look more kindly upon their Roman Catholic brethren than they had previously done. The penal laws, which the British authorities had anyway half-heartedly enforced, had been relaxed by the Irish Commons in the early 1770s, and in 1778 the major step was taken of granting Catholics the right to lease, inherit and bequeath land. It was perhaps this concession that produced significant Catholic support for the Volunteer movement, and for the 'non-importation' associations which the Protestants formed in the face of North's disinclination to grant further concessions. Here again the parallel with America was obvious.

This was the situation which North faced in Ireland during the troublesome winter of 1779–80. The Opposition had long been trying to turn it to their own advantage, and had been clamouring for trade concessions to the Irish, but North was loath to act for fear of alienating British merchant opinion. His hand was now forced. In the dying days of 1779 and the opening months of 1780 a series of measures gave the Irish all and more than they had sought. Indeed Ireland was admitted on equal terms to all areas of British trade save that of the East India Company's monopoly, thereby gaining concessions for which Scotland in 1707 had been obliged to give up its independent Parliament. But these concessions only encouraged the Irish to make further demands, and April 1780 saw North's authority as strongly challenged in Dublin as it was at Westminster. The culmination was Grattan's motion for Irish legislative independence on 19 April, but like Dunning's second motion it was doomed to fail, if only by 136 votes to ninety-seven. This was due partly to the belated success of the lethargic Buckinghamshire in rallying the parliamentary troops, but chiefly to a recognition on the part of the majority that the height of an unsuccessful war was a singularly inappropriate time to force a major constitutional crisis. Thus North was able to survive the challenge, though the debate on legislative independence made it clear that the issue was merely postponed, not abandoned.

If sober reflection had brought angered and frustrated parliamentary majorities in both England and Ireland back to support of North, the events of early June 1780 seemed to provide them with ample retrospective justification. Since the final collapse of Jacobitism in 1745 Roman Catholicism in England had ceased to be politically suspect, and the two most notable examples of the growing toleration were the Quebec Act of 1774, and the passage in 1778 of an act removing the impediments to the open practice of the Catholic religion and granting the same rights with regard to land-holding as were concurrently granted in Ireland. But the proposed extension of this act to Scotland provoked such rioting and general violence in the Lowlands that it had to be abandoned. This encouraged the eccentric and irresponsible Lord George Gordon to arouse opposition in England by the formation of a Protestant Association similar to that which had been established in Scotland. The result was a flood of petitions to Parliament, and a week of rioting in London from 2–9 June that reduced the city to chaos. Nearly five hundred people were killed or wounded, many houses were burnt, there was widespread looting, and Newgate prison was seized and its prisoners released. The almost total paralysis which seemed to afflict those responsible for the maintenance of law and order was apparently due to a mistaken belief that the troops, which were quickly called out, could not fire on the crowd until the Riot Act had been read, and the City magistrates were unwilling to sanction the reading of the act for fear of reprisals. Eventually the King and Privy Council recovered their nerve, and a royal proclamation provided the authority for the restoration of order. While the traditional latent anti-Catholicism of the masses, coupled perhaps with resentment at the religious and trade concessions recently granted to the Irish, partially explains the fury of the mob, it is clear that the riots were by no means exclusively religious in character. Many previously respectable working men took part, and wealthy rather than Roman Catholic districts suffered most. In some sense the riots were comparable to those of the 1760s, and the social and economic protest they embodied had been heightened by the national frustration that had swept the nation during the previous winter. North of course was the main beneficiary. The danger of flirting with extra-parliamentary forces had been convincingly demonstrated, the very idea of 'association' had been discredited, and the propertied classes rallied still further behind a minister who, however unimaginative and inadequate as a war leader, was at least moderate and safe. North also gained by the new wedge that was driven between the two wings of the Opposition. Shelburne's sympathies appeared to lie with the rioters, while Burke, Savile and many Rockinghams had long advocated wider toleration, and at the height of the disturbances Rockingham and Portland had attended the crucial Privy Council meeting, and the Marquis had even been prepared to hurry to Yorkshire if trouble should break out there. Indeed North was so impressed by the Rockinghams' eagerness to co-operate that he sought, in July 1780, to win their permanent adherence to Administration. But the possibility of coalition was frustrated by Rockingham's insistence on American independence, a full programme of economical reform, and the dismissal of Germain and Sandwich. After the successes of the previous weeks neither North nor the King was prepared to contemplate surrender on this scale, and the negotiations were abandoned. The news of British successes in the Carolinas and of increased support from the loyalists in America completed North's recovery and persuaded him to take full advantage of the swing of opinion in his favour by dissolving Parliament a year earlier than was necessary and attempting to consolidate his position. As usual, the Opposition was caught unawares by this premature dissolution and fared much worse than anyone would have predicted six months earlier. On balance North appears to have lost little more than half a dozen seats—scarcely a victory, but a welcome relief after the recent threats to his power. On paper his majority in the Commons was still more than one hundred, but as always the independents would decide the issue, and the last session of the previous Parliament had shown how apparently powerful majorities could disintegrate overnight.

At first North seemed safe enough. When the new Parliament assembled before Christmas, many independents were absent and the Ministry enjoyed comfortable working majorities. But when the House reassembled on 23 January 1781, even though the war news had continued to be better than hitherto, North was inclined to caution and unwilling to oppose the re-introduction of Burke's Civil Establishment Bill. Its defeat on the second reading by forty-three votes assuaged his fears, and thereafter the Ministry was clearly in the ascendant. During the summer of 1781 North was more at ease than for many years. Then suddenly the whole situation was transformed. On 25 November, two days before Parliament was due to assemble for the new session, the news of Cornwallis's surrender at Yorktown reached England, and it was clear that the American war was lost.[1] Since the Opposition was as little prepared for the news as the Ministry, the pre-Christmas session was relatively poorly attended, the Address in Reply being carried by a comfortable eighty-nine votes, and Lowther's motion that the war was now ineffectual being defeated by forty-one. But once the independents came up to town there was little chance that the Ministry could survive. North was eager for peace with America, as indeed were all the ministers save Germain; but the King would not yield, and no one was prepared to force his hand. During the Christmas recess Germain was dismissed, and North saw that his only slim hope was to concentrate the war effort against the Bourbon Powers and hope that success against them might enable England to salvage something from the American fiasco. But the new session, despite a vigorous rearguard action by the Ministry, extinguished that hope. In February two frontal attacks on Sandwich's administration of the navy were repelled by majorities of twenty-two and nineteen, but two successive motions asserting the impracticability of the continued war with America were respectively rejected by one and passed by nineteen. At last North had been defeated on the fundamental question of the war, and even George III had to concede that it must be abandoned. But, although independent support had swung against North and a handful of the Court and Treasury Party were wavering, the King still hoped to retain his first minister and avoid Rockingham by merely broadening the base of his Ministry. Some credence seemed momentarily to be given to his plan when on 8 and 15 March North was able to defeat two straight no-confidence motions by majorities of ten and nine, and it at least looked possible that the independents, having

---

[1] For a first-rate appraisal of British policy and strategy, see P. Mackesy, *The War for America, 1775–1783* (1964).

ended the war, might still baulk at the idea of accepting the Opposition. But it was not to be. North, well aware that single-figure majorities were no basis for a stable Administration, begged to resign; George III talked of abdication. Finally, the issue was forced when Thomas Grosvenor, country gentleman and member for Chester, indicated to North that he and a number of fellow-independents who up till then had supported the Ministry felt that they could no longer oppose the manifest will of the Commons. Even the King realized that this must mean defeat for North on the third no-confidence motion, scheduled for 20 March. At long last he accepted North's plea for relief, and before the debate could begin the premier was able to announce to a crowded House that he no longer held office. Members, expecting an all-night debate, were left stranded, and as North withdrew to his waiting coach he could not resist a characteristic quip at their expense: 'You see what it is to be in the secret.'

10

THE RETURN TO STABILITY: 1782–93

THE House of Commons which had been elected in 1780 was the most short-lived and politically fickle of the Hanoverian era. At the outset it had solidly supported North, only to turn against him in 1782. It then enabled the brief second Rockingham Administration to implement much of the policy advocated by the Opposition in the 1770s, and tentatively permitted Shelburne eight months of power before defeating him over the Peace Preliminaries. The notorious Fox–North coalition managed to command its support, even for some months after the King had driven it from office; yet before the premature dissolution of 1784 it had virtually surrendered to the younger Pitt.[1] The years between 1782 and 1784 were politically even more chaotic than 1742–6, 1754–7 and 1760–70. Once again clashes of personality were no less important an element in the instability than divisive issues of principle, and it was above all oscillations in independent opinion that initiated the series of political changes and ensured the final restoration of a stability reminiscent of the halcyon days of Sir Robert Walpole.

By 1782 the two sides in Parliament had become so clearly defined that the resignation of North inevitably meant more than merely the triumph of Rockingham. As the distraught George III lamented to his fallen minister on 27 March:

> At last the fatal day is come, which the misfortunes of the times and the sudden changes of sentiments of the House of Commons have drove me to, of changing the Ministry, and a more general removal of other persons than, I believe, ever was known before. I have to the last fought for individuals but the number I have saved except my Bedchamber is incredibly few.

Many of the Opposition had spent sixteen long years in the political wilderness, and the demands for office were understandably greater than

---

[1] Second son of Chatham; entered Parliament in 1781, at the age of only twenty-one, and became Prime Minister within three years.

they had been since the Whig triumph of 1714. So great indeed was the turnover of personnel, not only on the fall of North, but subsequently on those of Shelburne and of the Fox–North coalition, that one almost gains the impression of a two-party system at work. But such in fact was very far from the case, and the pattern of politics under Pitt was to prove remarkably similar to that under Walpole in the early part of the century.

It was not only the changes of personnel that distressed George III; the exigencies of an unsuccessful war also forced him to accept an abrupt change of policy. As early as 18 March Rockingham had warned Chancellor Thurlow that he would not accept office unless the King agreed in advance to independence for America and to significant measures of economical reform. Not unnaturally, George III preferred first to turn to Shelburne who, as the political heir of Chatham and the enemy of party, was politically more acceptable. But Shelburne, who had scarcely a dozen members of the Commons whom he could call his own, felt obliged to advise the King to approach Rockingham, whose followers in the lower House numbered almost a hundred and who was likely to be more able to command independent support. George III had therefore to accept Rockingham's terms, though his persistence in negotiating through Shelburne was to achieve retrospective significance on Rockingham's death four months later.

Perhaps the most striking index of Rockingham's political ineptitude was the composition of his Cabinet. Here he could count on the support of Lord John Cavendish, Lord Keppel, Fox, and in all probability the erratic and radical Duke of Richmond; but Camden and Ashburton (the former Dunning) were certain in the event of conflict to side with Shelburne, to whom (through Chatham) Grafton and Conway had long been gravitating. Rockingham's Cabinet was therefore equally divided between his own followers and those of Shelburne, and its final member, Thurlow, was a royal observer whose allegiance was bound to be dictated by the King. After sixteen years of political exile Rockingham had managed to devise an executive body in which he was effectively in a minority. Nor, in the light of the personalities involved, was the otherwise sensible division of the authority of the Secretaries of State between Home and Foreign affairs calculated to promote unity. Peace negotiations with the colonies fell within Shelburne's sphere, while Fox was responsible for negotiating with France. Their mutual antipathy made deadlock inevitable, and Rockingham's Administration was from the outset condemned to division on the most fundamental problem which it had to face.

For the moment, however, the Ministry applied itself to its committed programme with commendable alacrity and enthusiasm, priority understandably being given to the implementation of economical reform. Crewe's Act duly disenfranchised all revenue officers of the Crown, although in practice it affected few boroughs and even in these was of only minor significance. Clerke's Act disqualified Government contractors from sitting in the Commons, but the thirty-seven who had sat there in 1761 had shrunk by 1780 to a mere seventeen, and Pitt's later reform of the method of letting out Government contracts would anyway have achieved the desired results. But the major piece of legislation was the Civil Establishment Act—'Burke's foolish Bill' as William Eden aptly called it. Here misconception and doctrinaire hatred of royal Influence was at its height, as was also Burke's lack of administrative understanding. The Act was much less sweeping than the measure which Burke had advocated while in Opposition, and—doubtless to reassure the troubled ranks of the Court and Treasury party, whose support was essential to the new Ministry—many of the offices against which Burke had previously inveighed were left untouched. Nonetheless the Treasury was given complete control over all expenditure in the royal household, the pension list was severely limited (as was domestic as opposed to foreign secret service expenditure), and the payment of all Civil List expenses was to be made in a specified order, with salaries of ministers responsible for royal finance at the bottom of the list. Yet this elaborate scheme, the product of Burke's 'fertile, disordered and malignant' imagination, achieved surprisingly little. Partly this was because its basic assumption, that George III spent vast sums on corrupting members of Parliament, was unfounded; partly because Burke curiously ignored the considerable additional payments which were made every year to the Civil List for special purposes. In addition various specific offices were abolished. Most of these were sinecures like the Mastership of the Jewel Office or the Superintendentship of the King's Gardens and Waterworks, but lip-service was also paid to the supposed disintegration of the Empire by abolishing the Colonial Secretaryship and the Board of Trade and Plantations, both of which had to be restored later by Pitt. Finally, a separate act regulated the Paymaster's department, preventing the accumulation of huge balances for private investment by the holder of that office. The Ministry had substantially honoured its pledges, but the reforms did nothing to increase administrative efficiency, and little enough either to reduce expenditure or to limit the Influence of the Crown. In all these spheres the later work of Pitt was to be far more significant. As for parliamentary reform, there was no possibility that it would be formally advocated by a Cabinet presided over by Rockingham, even though Fox and Richmond were known to favour a modest redistribution of seats. When the young William Pitt, already connected with the reformers, moved for a committee of enquiry into the subject, he was defeated by 161 votes to 141; and a subsequent motion for shorter Parliaments, which he also supported, was rejected by the wider margin of eighty-eight votes. Having rejected the principle of reform, the Commons agreed to expunge from the journals all record of Wilke's expulsion and of proceedings relating to the vexed Middlesex election of 1768.

Meanwhile the Irish situation had been demanding attention. In February a huge Convention of Volunteers at Dungannon gave impressive backing to Grattan's renewed demands, and on 14 March his motion for legislative independence passed unopposed in the Irish Commons. Necessity thus reinforced the Rockinghams' known sympathies towards Ireland. The Declaratory Act of 1719 was repealed, and the Duke of Portland as the new Lord-Lieutenant of Ireland indicated to the Irish Parliament that George III was prepared to accept modification of Poynings's Law and a biennial mutiny bill. Though these concessions left some problems outstanding, they were sufficient for temporary appeasement and to gain additional Irish support in the dying stages of the war. It was indeed the termination of the war and the negotiations for an acceptable peace that posed the greatest threat to the stability of the new Ministry. At first sight the omens seemed far from auspicious. The previous year had seen not only the disaster of Yorktown and the loss of effective control of the Atlantic and the Caribbean, but the capture of Minorca and the siege of Gibraltar by the Spanish, the increased pressure of the Dutch fleet (Britain had declared war on Holland in 1780), growing hostility from the Armed Neutrality of the North, formed in 1780 to protest Britain's right of search on the high seas, and substantial losses in the West Indies. Yet the new Ministry soon found itself confronted by a set of circumstances calculated to encourage hopes of a more favourable peace than had recently seemed possible. In April 1782 Rodney's great victory over the French navy at the Battle of the Saints restored British control of the seas and saved the West Indies from further depredations. The Dutch showed less enthusiasm for the war after their fleet had been mauled in the somewhat indecisive clash off the Dogger Bank in 1781. Spain, uneasy at the effects that her support of rebel colonists might have upon her own empire, and conscious that her interests in north America (where she hoped to expand from her base in Louisiana) could not easily be reconciled with those of her colonial allies, was interested only in Gibraltar. Finally, France was in deep financial trouble and unwilling indefinitely to continue a conflict in which she stood to gain little but American good-will. Unhappily, a divided Ministry was in no position to take full advantage of this improvement in the international situation. Since responsibility for the negotiations was divided Shelburne despatched James Oswald to Paris for talks with Franklin and at the same time Fox sent Thomas Grenville to sound out Vergennes. But the fundamental difference of outlook between the two Secretaries of State made confusion inevitable. Shelburne was no more willing than Chatham had been to concede full independence to the colonists, and hoped by timely concessions to maintain some kind of co-operation in the important spheres of commerce and defence; but he had neither the patience nor the temperament to explain the subtleties of his policy to his Cabinet colleagues, who were anyway probably incapable of appreciating his breadth of vision. Fox, on the other hand, was intent on the immediate granting of unconditional independence, both as an article of faith and as a device for getting the remainder of the negotiations into his own hands as Foreign Secretary. But the clash between Fox and Shelburne went deeper than mere divergence over the issue of the peace. Fox had inherited a deep distrust of his rival from his father (who believed that he had been treated dishonestly by Shelburne in the 1760s), and almost from the creation of the Ministry was convinced that treachery was afoot. This belief thrived on Shelburne's disinclination to consult his colleagues, on his known favour with the King, and consequently on the conviction that 'the Administration was to consist of two parts, one belonging to the King, the other to the public'. In Fox's view, Shelburne's main object was to thwart the Rockinghams by reviving in modified form the 'system' supposedly in existence under North. Because of this, though ostensibly over the conduct of the peace negotiations, Fox had already determined upon resignation when Rockingham died suddenly on 1 July.

The death of Rockingham brought the first major breach in the ranks of his followers since 1766. At first Fox harboured hopes of succeeding to the Treasury, but yielded to the persuasion of his colleagues that it would be more expedient to urge the appointment of the dull and uncontroversial Duke of Portland. When George III exercised his undoubted right to offer the headship of the Ministry to Shelburne, Fox promptly resigned, to be followed by Portland, Lord John Cavendish, Burke and seven other lesser members of the Rockingham group. Since some twenty-five Rockinghams had been brought into major office in the previous March, this was anything but a convincing display of solidarity; and indeed over sixty members of the former Opposition to

North in the Commons now gave their allegiance to Shelburne—many more than the very limited personal following that he had brought with him into office. The split in the Rockingham ranks was basically due to Fox's curious failure to explain to his potential adherents the underlying conviction that prompted what appeared to most to be an irresponsible and precipitate action, founded largely on personal antipathy to Shelburne. Many of the Rockinghams were unwilling to challenge the King's prerogative of choosing his own first minister, more especially when it was difficult if not impossible to demonstrate that George III and Shelburne had sinister intentions, and that Rockingham policy had in any significant way been impeded. Once again, it appeared that Fox, the inveterate gambler, had miscalculated the odds.

If Fox's impetuosity and lack of political judgment had lost him the initiative, Shelburne's personal character and past history were no less instrumental in depriving him of any real chance of re-creating political stability. Saddled with the task of concluding an unpopular peace at the end of an unsuccessful war and after recent naval victories had raised false hopes, his position was anyway unenviable. In addition his known eagerness for further substantial instalments of economical reform, when even Edmund Burke considered that sufficient measures had been enacted, was unlikely to heal the breach within the ranks of the Court and Treasury party, many of whom appear to have followed North in the belief that the King would restore him as soon as peace had been concluded. Indeed the radical caste of Shelburne's thought on domestic no less than on imperial matters was beyond the understanding of many members, including those essentially conservative-minded independents who had been temporarily driven by the ill-success of the war along the path of moderate reform. But above all, few could forget Shelburne's earlier association with Bute, the suspicions of chicanery surrounding his intervention in East India Company affairs, or the reputation he had acquired for devious intrigue. The 'Jesuit of Berkeley Square' had undoubtedly a keen analytical mind and a breadth of vision equalled only by Chatham; but like Chatham he preferred to work alone, and lacked the capacity to inspire either trust or affection. Even those within his Cabinet who respected his manifest ability were soon protesting at his refusal to consult them and his arrogant use of ministerial power. He apparently shared the earlier belief of Carteret that royal support was in itself sufficient for political survival, and like Carteret he soon had to bow to reality. Keppel and Carlisle resigned early in 1783; Camden, Grafton and Temple were threatening to do so; and Richmond was refusing to attend Cabinet meetings. A few professional Government servants such as Dundas,

Henry, 2nd Duke of Newcastle

Leicester Square, 1750

Robinson and Jenkinson might be tentatively drawn by considerations of expediency towards Shelburne and the King, but the Ministry was clearly falling apart. If the Commons had been clearly divided into two sides at the time of North's fall, the division six months later was quadripartite, and the normal pattern of eighteenth-century politics had been temporarily shattered. In October 1782 William Eden estimated that Shelburne could count on some 140 votes, Fox on ninety, and North on 120. This left more than two hundred independents whose allegiance was unpredictable but who were bound to react unfavourably towards factiousness and irresponsibility. It was obvious that none of the three leaders could easily survive alone, and that a coalition of any two would be in a strong position. Even Shelburne could not deny the logic of the situation, and he permitted Dundas to approach North on his behalf, and Pitt to approach Fox. But Fox would not serve unless Shelburne resigned and Pitt would not continue in a Ministry that included North. Unwisely Shelburne tried to frighten North (whose sole concern was to provide for those followers who had stood by him) by suggesting the imminence of a Pitt–Fox coalition directed above all at North and his friends. As a result North was driven into the arms of Fox and the overthrow of Shelburne became virtually certain.

Meanwhile, Shelburne had announced a fairly sweeping programme of reform that owed much to the influence of radicals like Richard Price and Joseph Priestley. The national debt and the annual charge upon it were to be reduced by conversion of existing loans to lower rates of interest and by the re-establishment of an effective sinking fund; the revival of commerce was to be encouraged by the adoption of some of the free trade measures advocated by Adam Smith; substantial attacks on sinecures were envisaged and the whole Administration subjected to careful scrutiny on utilitarian grounds; and a significant instalment of parliamentary reform was to be implemented. Many of these proposals were as enlightened as they were far-reaching, but in advocating so radical a departure from previous policy Shelburne was misinterpreting the spirit of a House of Commons that already had absorbed enough innovatory legislation to exorcise the memory of North's inefficiency. In any case, the peace negotiations rather than domestic reform provided the occasion for Shelburne's defeat.

In retrospect Shelburne's vision of a north Atlantic community—of an Anglo-American partnership in commerce, foreign policy and defence—seems eminently sensible; in 1782 it could scarcely be other than a pipe dream, for it ran counter to all prevailing ideas. The Americans were still damned as rebels, to whom the cession of the lands between the

St Lawrence and the Ohio seemed not the creation of a market for British manufactures, but a humiliating surrender. Nor was there any enthusiasm for granting them fishing rights off Newfoundland or reciprocity of trade with Canada. Most Englishmen preferred to proscribe the Americans from any access to the Empire which they had ungraciously forsaken, and prejudice was to override reason in the assessment of Shelburne's settlement with the former colonists. In the end he had to secure rather more territory for Canada than he had envisaged and be content with a provision for future commercial negotiations; fishing rights were conceded to the Americans and the Mississippi area was to remain open to traders of all nations; American debts to Englishmen prior to 1775 were formally acknowledged, but the losses of loyalists were merely referred to individual states for attention. This was less generous towards America than Shelburne wished, but more so than most of his contemporaries had hoped. The Treaties with France, Spain and Holland were less controversial. There was a general restoration of conquests, French gains being limited to Tobago, Senegal, Gorée, St Pierre and Miquelon, a few Indian villages and fishing rights off Newfoundland; Britain gained Gambia and the satisfaction of knowing that effective French power in India was permanently stifled. Spain acquired Florida and Minorca, but Britain refused to surrender Gibraltar, recovered the Bahamas, and gained the concession of cutting log-wood in Honduras. Finally, the *status quo* was preserved between Britain and Holland, except that Britain obtained Negapatam and the important right to trade freely among the spice islands of the Dutch East Indies.

The peace terms may have appeared a sorry contrast to those of 1763 but, considering her indifferent record in the war, Britain had escaped relatively lightly. Nonetheless, even without the formation of the Fox–North coalition, passage through the Commons was unlikely to be easy; in the face of its serried ranks victory for Shelburne seemed well-nigh impossible. Though both North and Fox would doubtless have been happy to settle on similar terms, they challenged the peace preliminaries on 17 February 1783 and carried the day by 224 votes to 208. After a similar defeat four days later Shelburne handed his resignation to the King. The only surprise was that the majority against him was so small, solely because, despite significant continued Court and Treasury support for North, two-thirds of the independents present in the House voted for the preliminaries. Apparently their desire for peace outweighed their natural suspicion of Shelburne and their obvious disappointment at the actual terms.

To George III the union of Fox and North was a monstrous plot, and for more than five weeks he refused to accept the Duke of Portland, who had been designated as First Lord of the Treasury and nominal leader of the coalition. For the first and only time in the century a minister of the King had been forced out of office, not by a genuine swing of independent opinion, but as a result of a blatant deal between two factions. Considering the abuse which Fox and North had for years heaped upon each other's heads, it is not surprising that many besides the King regarded their alliance as hypocritical and unprincipled; and even though opinion both inside Parliament and out-of-doors was not to swing violently against them for a further twelve months, many pamphleteers and caricaturists already began to wax satirical at their expense. Yet the coalition was in a sense dictated by the prevailing political circumstances and by the characters of the principal participants. Fox and North may have differed bitterly over the American war and over the necessity for domestic reform, but the war was now over and sufficient economical reform had been implemented for Fox to be able to promise that he would not press for further measures. Neither he nor North trusted Shelburne and, despite their earlier political rivalry, neither was capable of bearing malice. There was now little enough to keep them apart and the desire of each to provide for his friends suggested alliance for mutual convenience. Fox was bound to be the dominant partner, but North had long since lost all personal political ambition and, perhaps because of his own supremely tolerant nature, appears to have underestimated the effect his conduct would have upon the King. For North the coalition was to be political suicide; for Fox it was to mark yet another stage in the relentless battle waged by the Rockinghams since the 1760s against the supposed endeavours of George III to tilt the balance of the constitution decisively in favour of monarchy. He was to end by claiming the right of the House of Commons to deprive the King of all choice in the appointment and dismissal of ministers.

Not unnaturally, George III did his utmost to avoid having his Closet stormed for the second time in twelve months. He strove unsuccessfully to detach North from Fox, sought in vain to persuade Pitt to form a Ministry, and threatened abdication. But in the end he had not only to accept the new Cabinet but to allow Portland *carte blanche* in the nomination to all junior ministerial posts. He was not even able to retain Thurlow as Chancellor, and among the Cabinet (Portland at the Treasury, Fox and North as Foreign and Home Secretaries, Stormont as Lord President, Carlisle as Lord Privy Seal, Keppel at the Admiralty, and Lord John Cavendish as Chancellor of the Exchequer) he could see only men who had reduced him to a cypher. He had furthermore to suffer the ignominy of witnessing Fox's increasing influence over the young Prince of Wales who had already offended his moral susceptibilities and who was well on the way to resuming the traditional political enmity between monarch and heir apparent. Little wonder that to George III Fox seemed to threaten all his deepest political and personal convictions. For the moment the King could only decline to exercise his undoubted prerogative of creating peers in favour of any friends of the coalition, but it is clear that he would not tolerate its continued existence for one day longer than was absolutely necessary.

It was 2 April 1783 before the new Ministry was formally admitted to office, and the remainder of that parliamentary session gave little enough hint of the crisis that lay ahead. Pitt, from the Opposition benches, brought forth resolutions for parliamentary reform which, despite Fox's support, were predictably defeated (although the adverse majority of almost two to one was mildly surprising) and the divergence of outlook between Fox and North was embarrassingly underlined. Minor reforms were effected in Administration, although the Ministry's reputation suffered somewhat from Burke's reinstatement in the Pay Office of two officials who had rightly been suspected of gross financial irregularities and who had also aided Fox's father to build up his fortune. Lord John Cavendish was rather unfairly criticized for having to raise a Government loan at short notice and on terms highly favourable to the subscribers, and aroused some hostility among the commercial community by the introduction of a receipts tax. Fox raised further doubts about the sincerity of his reforming zeal when he vigorously opposed the demands of the Irish Volunteers for parliamentary reform. To the Lord-Lieutenant he wrote:

> Immense concessions were made in the Duke of Portland's time, and those concessions were declared by an almost unanimous House of Commons to be sufficient. The account must be considered as having been closed on the day of that vote, and should never again be opened on any pretence whatever.

The coalition had survived its first session but, despite the known antagonism of the King, it had done nothing to strengthen itself within Parliament or out-of-doors.

During the summer the Ministry had its first serious confrontation with the King over the question of the establishment to be provided for the Prince of Wales when he came of age in August. Rather foolishly Fox committed himself to securing £100,000 a year for the Prince as well as the settlement of his existing debts. With some justification George III denounced this proposal as 'a shameful squandering of public money' and coming ill from men who had long been clamouring for economies; but he appeared on reflection to have decided that this was not a sufficiently important issue on which to force a breach with his ministers, and in the end agreed to contribute £50,000 annually from the Civil List which, together with the revenues from the Duchy of Cornwall, would give the Prince an annual income of some £62,000. Parliament was left to provide £30,000 for the settlement of the debts and a similar sum to set the Prince up in his new establishment. Fortunately, young George was persuaded to accept this compromise but, despite his declaration of filial submission, he was soon to make Carlton House the social centre of political opposition to his father.

If it had been American affairs that had initially condemned Fox to years of sterile Opposition, it was developments in India that drove him from the Government benches for virtually the remainder of his life. The many weaknesses of North's Regulating Act of 1773 had long since become obvious, and Warren Hastings had been left with the unenviable task of consolidating the East India Company's position in India in the face of a hostile majority on the Bengal Council. His methods may at times have been ruthless and authoritarian, but he was a realist battling against doctrinaire and prejudiced opponents. With trade disrupted by the Mahratta wars and by Hyder Ali's invasion of the Carnatic, the Company was once again in financial difficulties, and in 1781 two parliamentary committees—dominated respectively by Burke and Dundas—had been surveying the whole structure of British power in India. The American war had consumed most of the energies of successive ministers, but by 1783 it was no longer possible to ignore the financial, strategic and humanitarian implications of the existing system, and further governmental control over the Company became inevitable. Though the outcome was to be labelled 'Fox's India Bill', it was Edmund Burke who was its real author. Originally drawn to Indian affairs by a desire to aid his disreputable friends against Hastings, and basing many of his assumptions on the biased and vindictive evidence of Philip Francis, Burke had, by 1783, become completely fascinated with the subtleties of Indian civilization and utterly convinced that the sanctity of chartered rights must yield to the demands of justice and humanity. The most obvious solution might have been to transfer the vast powers of the Company to the Crown, something that Francis himself had advocated. But to one who had a pathological fear of royal Influence this was unthinkable. Burke's approach to India can be fully understood only in the light of his devotion to economical reform, and the resulting bill was in some sense the natural consequence of the thinking that had produced the Civil Establishment

Act of 1782. Responsibility for the government of all territorial possessions in India, together with the powers previously exercised by the Courts of Directors and Proprietors, were to be transferred to seven commissioners named in the bill, who were to hold office for four years in the first instance, and were to be removable only on an Address from either House of Parliament. The commercial business of the Company was to be entrusted to nine assistant commissioners, also to be named in the bill. This drastic invasion of the Company's rights was bound to provoke widespread protest, and the rigid subordination of the officials in India to the new authority at home—at a time when the real need was for the extension of the Governor-General's powers—was seriously open to criticism. But Burke and his colleagues showed themselves as politically obtuse as they were administratively naïve, for all of the sixteen new posts were given to supporters of the Ministry. Not unnaturally the opponents of the bill claimed that the assumption by the coalition of the whole vast patronage of the Company would make Fox even more powerful than the King—royal Influence would pale into insignificance beside that of 'Carlo Khan'.

Notwithstanding the hostile reaction in newspapers, pamphlets and prints, the Ministry's position in the Commons was still sufficiently secure to enable the eventual passage of the bill on 8 December by 208 votes to 102—though the usual absence of many independents before Christmas might have given Fox food for thought. But the political insensitivity of the ministers provided George III with the opportunity which he had been seeking since the previous April. Before he could venture with confidence to challenge the coalition he must have an issue on which to make a stand, a politician who would come forth in his defence and undertake the formation of a new Ministry, and a reasonable guarantee that the new leader would in time be able to command a working majority in the Commons. By early December these conditions were all fulfilled. Fox's India Bill had provided the issue, Pitt had conveyed through Lord Clarendon his willingness to serve, and Robinson had produced elaborate calculations to show that Pitt could expect to win increasing support and that a dissolution would be bound to consolidate his position. It remained for the King to determine the particular form which his intervention should take. The exercise of the royal veto, last used by Anne in 1708, was deemed impolitic, and the combination of dismissal coupled with an immediate dissolution too precipitate to guarantee success. On the advice of Temple and Thurlow, George III therefore decided to bring pressure to bear on the House of Lords to reject the bill, and on 11 December Temple was duly authorized by the

King to declare that 'whoever voted for the India Bill were not only not his friends, but he should consider them his enemies.' Six days later the Lords rejected the bill by a majority of nineteen, and on 18 December the ministers were dismissed.

There is no doubt that most members of the coalition believed that the King had over-reached himself and that no viable alternative Administration could be found. In the Commons, where the India Bill had passed by a majority of two to one, their position seemed impregnable; the earlier examples of Walpole, Carteret and North all appeared to support the view that no ministers could survive on the basis of royal support alone; and the initial reluctance of many to accept office was reminiscent of George II's abortive attempt to oust the Pelhams in February 1746. Although on 19 December Pitt became head of the Treasury, Temple Home Secretary, and Gower Lord President, the appointments stopped there; and the resignation two days later of Temple, terrified at the possibility of impeachment for his part in the crisis, suggested that the new Ministry might never be completed. Fox therefore felt confident in challenging the constitutional propriety of the King's actions and in strongly opposing any idea of dissolution—in order both to maintain his existing strength and to foster support from independents who would scarcely wax enthusiastic at the prospect of a premature and unnecessary outlay of substantial election expenses.

Yet a little reflection might have given the coalitionists pause. There were obvious dangers in declaring political war on a monarch whose Closet they had unceremoniously stormed a mere seven months earlier, especially when they had to make their stand on a bill that had appeared to smack of jobbery. Faced by hostility from the palace and out-of-doors, their only source of strength was the Commons, for which Fox in the ensuing months was to claim ultimate authority. But a two to one majority in a relatively thin house during the ministerial life of the coalition offered no guarantee of a permanent majority once it had been dismissed. Pitt now had all the advantages of patronage at his disposal, and many if not most of the Court and Treasury Party were likely to transfer their allegiance to him—especially those who had followed North after 1782, but were disinclined to repeat the performance once he had irrevocably offended the King. Pitt also had the magic of his name, a reputation for independence, and a parliamentary presence remarkable for a man of only twenty-four. No one was better suited to appeal against the factiousness to which politics had been reduced since 1782, and his avoidance of any division before the Christmas recess showed a shrewd appreciation of the admittedly delicate position in which he found himself.

Meanwhile, the Cabinet took final shape on 23 December. Thurlow returned to the Woolsack and Howe to the Admiralty, Sydney and Carmarthen assumed the Secretaryships of State, and Rutland became Lord Privy Seal. It was a singularly inexperienced body, but the more important junior ministers (Dundas as Treasurer of the Navy, William Grenville as Paymaster, Lloyd Kenyon as Attorney-General and Pepper Arden as Solicitor-General) provided useful support for Pitt in the Commons, and the later addition of Richmond (Master-General of the Ordnance) to the Cabinet gave it greater weight.

During the Christmas recess both sides were feverishly active in attempting to confirm their supporters and win adherents. Among the more prominent successes on Pitt's side were bargains with leading borough patrons such as the Duke of Newcastle (six seats), Edward Eliot (seven) and Sir James Lowther (nine); and by the end of the year John Robinson felt able—unjustifiably as events were to prove—to predict a workable majority for Pitt when Parliament reassembled. The coalitionists on the other hand could point to no gains, while the desertion of a number of Northites and the growing hostility in the country made their more experienced members increasingly less sanguine of making a successful stand. Nevertheless, when the Commons met again on 12 January, it quickly became obvious that Pitt was still in a minority, though only once in the ensuing eight weeks were his opponents able to defeat him by more than forty votes. Fox's tactics were of necessity dictated by circumstances. He vehemently opposed all suggestions of a dissolution, delayed the passage of the Mutiny Bill and the granting of supply in order to make dissolution more difficult, and encouraged a stream of motions and addresses to the King protesting at the unconstitutional manner in which the Ministry had come to power and at the iniquity of its continuing in the face of an adverse majority in the Commons. Pitt could respond only with a series of forward defensive strokes, his one attempt at constructive legislation being his India Bill, which he produced after careful consultation with the Company, and which was rejected by a mere eight votes. It might be thought that an immediate dissolution would have solved all his problems, but there were cogent reasons against so drastic a step. No Ministry in the eighteenth century had ever dissolved when it was in a minority; Pitt had no wish to appeal to the electorate while it could still be argued that he was a royal favourite incapable of commanding support in the existing Commons; by 25 January it was anyway too late to dissolve and assemble a new Parliament in time to prevent the lapsing of the Mutiny Act; Pitt could not afford to risk alienating independent opinion until every alternative to dissolution had been explored; every manifestation of support out-of-doors was bound to strengthen his hand; and in January arrangements for a general election were still far from complete.

Of these considerations, 'public opinion' and the attitude of the independents were perhaps the most important. During the spring of 1784 political activity in the country became ever more vehement in support of Pitt and the King. Over two hundred addresses flowed in to Westminster—more than had been produced by all the various contentious issues since the accession of George III. While this massive public vote of confidence in Pitt does not appear to have shaken the resolution of Fox's adherents to stand firm, a number of North's followers deserted and many more took the cautious part of abstaining, while the realization of the Foxites that all their efforts could produce only two or three counter-addresses in their favour did much to undermine their confidence. Independent opinion within the Commons was less clear-cut. Above all it was against a dissolution and warmly in favour of some form of agreement between Pitt and Fox that might end the factiousness of the times. In both January and February meetings of independents were held at the St Albans Tavern to co-ordinate activities and urge conciliation, but in the face of the politicians they were helpless. Fox refused to serve unless Pitt first resigned; Pitt declined to have North in his Cabinet, though he did not absolutely rule out the possibility of union with Fox. It is unlikely that Pitt was doing more than playing for time, for he confided crisply to Rutland: 'The independents are indefatigable for coalition, but as ineffectual as ever.' But if they could not make a Ministry, they could certainly break one, and Pitt was wise enough to gain their sympathies by appearing to be reasonable.

In a succession of divisions between 12 January and 8 March—dealing with the allegedly unconstitutional origin of the new Ministry, Pitt's India Bill, the Mutiny Bill and the granting of supply—the coalitionists' majorities, despite a few oscillations, showed a downward trend from fifty-nine to one. Pitt may perhaps have benefited from his outright denial that he knew of any secret influence accompanying the overthrow of the coalition, which may well have been construed by some to mean that he had not been privy to the King's actions. But there can be little doubt that the decisive factor in his final triumph was the growing conviction within the Commons and outside that Fox was improperly endeavouring to reduce the King to a mere figurehead, and that this would seriously upset the balance of the constitution. Even Fox baulked at indefinitely blocking the Mutiny Bill and supply, which alone might have enabled him to force the resignation of the Ministry; but the charges of irresponsibility levelled against him for merely delaying these measures suggests that his support would have melted away had he persisted. At bottom he failed to realize that only the gravest crisis, more particularly a mismanaged war, could persuade the Commons to risk a head-on collision with the King over the prerogative of choosing and dismissing ministers. He was living in Hanoverian, not Victorian, England.

The climax of the Opposition effort came on 8 March in the form of a remonstrance to the King deploring as detrimental to the constitution the maintenance of a Ministry to which the Commons had denied its confidence. When it was carried by a single vote, the coalitionists had to accept that their majority had reached vanishing point, the Mutiny Act was allowed to pass without opposition, and Parliament was duly dissolved on 24 March. The steady erosion of the coalitionists' majority appears to have been achieved less by defections among their own ranks than by the abstention of independents who had originally supported them. The ensuing general election, by far the most celebrated of the century, has since been the subject of much debate over the relative importance of patronage and 'public opinion' in determining its outcome. Pitt and the King were given a handsome majority of more than one hundred, gaining seventy seats instead of the sixty predicted by John Robinson, the most expert psephologist of his time. Certainly patronage played its part in this striking victory, although the £31,848 contributed from the Secret Service fund was significantly less than that expended on either of the two previous general elections. But the unprecedented impact of out-of-doors opinion becomes evident when one looks at the results in detail. Robinson had gravely over-estimated Government gains in close constituencies, where deals might in theory be arranged with borough patrons, and underestimated the gains in open ones where opinion, which he had no means of measuring, could be decisive. Again and again the coalitionists were forced to flee from counties and large towns to close boroughs, and in Yorkshire—former stronghold of Rockingham—the Foxites dared not even face a contest. Yet the number of 'Fox's martyrs' can easily be exaggerated. Although 163 members of the old Parliament failed to re-appear in the new one, only ninety-six of these were coalitionists, and almost half of them were 'North's martyrs' rather than Fox's; nor indeed had all the coalitionists sought re-election. Nonetheless the fact remains inescapable that public opinion, in so far as it could be expressed through the medium of an eighteenth-century general election, was overwhelmingly in favour of Pitt and the King.

Pitt's emergence to a position of dominance which, except for three brief years, he was to retain until his death in 1806 represented an extraordinary performance for a young man of only twenty-four years. Like his father in 1766, he had stepped forth in answer to a clear call from his sovereign, and for four months had withstood alone the full fury of one of the most talented parliamentary Oppositions of the century. The same unswerving confidence in his own abilities was to prove his greatest strength in the years ahead, but he had to serve a further twelve months' apprenticeship before he fully found his feet. Between the summer of 1784 and that of 1785 he was to suffer political defeat four times, and if thereafter his position was never seriously challenged it was because, unlike his father, he was quick to learn the facts of political life. Meanwhile his youth and inexperience, in the aftermath of victory, led him to oscillate curiously between arrogant self-assurance and nervous capitulation. The paradoxes of this brief phase of his career were pin-pointed by Daniel Pulteney in two letters to the Duke of Rutland. On 6 July 1784 he wrote:

> We conquer at present by numbers, and shall run no sort of risque this year at least; but I foresee what *may* happen if Pitt's Ministry is to be conducted on such a narrow system of public virtue.

On 13 August he struck a different note:

> It is the language very much at present among some of Pitt's country supporters in the House, that he is too full of *concession*.

At times therefore Pitt was inclined to share his father's contempt for party and for those techniques of parliamentary management that were so essential under eighteenth-century conditions; and he believed that the magic of his name and his reputation for disinterestedness entitled him almost as of right to support in the Commons. Yet on other occasions he seemed only too ready to surrender to Opposition, whether over his India Act, the jockey tax, the tax on coals, or his attempt to fund the Navy Bills. It was during this period of uncertainty that he was defeated over the Westminster scrutiny, parliamentary reform, the fortifications at Plymouth and Portsmouth, and the Irish commercial propositions.

One of the coalitionists' few notable successes in the general election had been at Westminster, where Charles James Fox had managed to defeat one of the Pittite candidates. But Pitt, with uncharacteristic pettiness, attempted to deprive Fox of the honour of representing so 'popular' a constituency by supporting for nine months a scrutiny of the votes and thereby preventing an official return. Almost inevitably, independent opinion eventually swung against him, and in the spring of 1785 he was forced ungraciously to concede victory to Fox. Independent concern for economy brought a further rebuff when the Duke of Richmond's plans to fortify the dockyards at Plymouth and Portsmouth—a sensible and necessary defence measure—were rejected by the casting vote of the Speaker after the Commons had divided equally. But of greater importance for the future was Pitt's defeat over parliamentary reform. He had already established his reputation as a reformer by his earlier motions of 1782 and 1783, and in March 1784 had indicated to Wyvill that his zeal for reform was unabated. When, in the following June, Alderman Sawbridge insisted prematurely on bringing forward a further motion, Pitt had felt obliged to support it even though many of his followers were in the majority of seventy-four which ensured its defeat. In accordance with a subsequent promise to Wyvill, he brought in his own bill on 18 April 1785, although in deference to the King's wishes he did so in his private capacity rather than as first minister. He proposed to abolish thirty-six close boroughs, with full compensation to their owners, and redistribute the seats to London and the counties; and at the same time enlarge the county electorate by enfranchising forty-shilling copyholders and some leaseholders. But the sting had long since gone out of radical agitation, and the measure was easily defeated by 248 votes to 174.

In Ireland the granting of legislative independence begun by the second Rockingham Ministry had been completed by the repeal of Poynings's Law by the Irish Parliament, and by the passage of a Renunciation Act under Shelburne which clearly stated that Ireland was bound only by Irish statutes and that no appeals could go from Irish to English Courts. This left the Lord-Lieutenant in the perilous position of being expected to promote policies favourable to British interests, yet dependent for success wholly upon his ability to manage the voluble and unpredictable Irish House of Commons. Fortunately, the Duke of Rutland and his secretary, Thomas Orde, were both able and conciliatory, but increasing economic distress soon brought requests for further trade concessions. In meeting these requests Pitt sought to follow the line which Shelburne had unsuccessfully adopted towards the American colonies—local home rule, coupled with an agreed policy over trade and defence. The propositions which he referred to the Irish Commons in February 1785 admitted Ireland to the colonial trade and equalized duties on commerce between Ireland and England; but in return the Irish were to contribute to the maintenance of the British navy. When these proposals were amended to ensure that a contribution would be made only when the Irish hereditary revenues exceeded £656,000 per annum, and then only in such manner as the Irish Parliament should direct, Pitt unwisely decided to submit the whole matter instead to the English Commons. In so doing he ran headlong into the unenlightened opposition of the English manufacturers, who clamoured that they could not hope to compete with cheap Irish labour, of the West Indian lobby who feared that the Irish would import foreign sugar, and of the East Indian Company who saw its monopoly threatened. The propaganda campaign against the proposals was led by Josiah Wedgwood and his Grand Chamber of Manufacturers, and petitions poured into Parliament from many ports and centres of industry. As a result the propositions were so mutilated that Fox, who had played no small part in their mutilation, was able hypocritically to accuse Pitt of violating the newly-won independence of the Irish Parliament; and when Irish resentment at the reduction of the concessions proved so widespread that the revised proposals passed their second reading in Dublin by only nineteen votes, Pitt deemed it expedient to bow before the storm rather than invite formal defeat. Thus a valuable and enlightened commercial measure was thwarted by a combination of petty jealousies, unwarranted fears and Opposition factiousness.

After these four defeats in 1785, Pitt never again persisted in a policy likely to prove unacceptable to the parliamentary classes. Because of this he has frequently been accused of insincerity, of forsaking his original liberal principles, and of subordinating everything to the desire to retain power. But these accusations ignore the fact that he was not a modern prime minister, independent of the Crown, and with a united party behind him. Like Walpole, Pelham and North, he was a characteristic product of the eighteenth-century political system. Even at the height of his power his 'friends' in the Commons rarely numbered more than fifty, and the friendship of many of these was dependent on his retaining office. He had risen to pre-eminence through royal and independent support, and his respect for the conventions of the time would no more allow him to dictate to George III than his common sense would permit him to flout the will of the independent majority in the Commons. He was a thorough-going pragmatist and an administrator of rare ability; and his practical work of post-war reconstruction was more important to him than any adherence to doctrinaire principles of political or commercial liberalism. The career of his arch-rival, Charles James Fox, was a constant reminder of the folly and sterility of refusing to face political reality.

The following eight years were the happiest and most productive of Pitt's life. Although no enemy to the Influence of the Crown, which after all had played its part in raising him to power, he believed passionately in efficient and economical administration. Ironically enough, his massive though gradual abolition of sinecures, substitution of salaries for fees, and general reorganization of the civil service did much more to reduce Influence than the more vaunted reforms of the second Rockingham Ministry; and his establishment of the Consolidated Fund, reorganization of the Civil List, and re-establishment of the Sinking Fund were financial reforms of lasting importance, as were at least some of his innovations in taxation. Since much of his most valuable work was carried out by administrative regulation rather than through the more spectacular agency of statutory legislation, it is all too easy to overlook its fundamental and far-reaching character, and to fail to give credit where credit was undoubtedly due. In the sphere of commerce his systematic lowering of duties, which began with the Commutation Act of 1784, seemed to establish him as the disciple of Adam Smith, as did his successful negotiation of a commercial treaty with France in 1786 which provided for reciprocal concessions by the two countries. But he was the successor of Walpole rather than the precursor of Huskisson, Peel and Gladstone, and was no doctrinaire advocate of free trade. Despite his occasional tributes to Adam Smith, his approach to commercial matters was essentially empirical, and the many other international commercial negotiations with which he was involved—none of which produced concrete results—were all along orthodox mercantilist lines. As so often in the eighteenth century, the influence of ideas upon policy was at best marginal.

Although the American colonies had been lost, the prevailing attitude in imperial affairs was by no means one of unrelieved pessimism, and Pitt turned his attention to the major problems of Indian and Canadian government. His India Act of 1784 represented the culmination of the trend towards greater control of the East India Company by the State that had begun with the parliamentary intervention of 1767 and endeavoured both to remedy the defects of previous legislation and avoid the errors of judgment that had made Fox's India Bill an act of political suicide. A Board of Control for India was established, consisting of six privy councillors appointed by the King; but, unlike Fox's commissioners, their tenure was not unaffected by changes of Ministry, and Indian patronage was left in the hands of the Company, subject to the royal power of veto or dismissal. The Board could issue orders to the directors and, in times of emergency, direct to the authorities in India, who in each province consisted of a Governor and three Councillors, with the Governor-General and Council at Calcutta empowered to dictate to the subordinate presidencies on questions of foreign policy.

Not until 1786 was the Governor-General at last given power to override his own Council, and Cornwallis was then able to accept the office without the fear that he might follow in the unhappy footsteps of Warren Hastings, whose return to England was followed by a seven-year impeachment and subjection to the sincere but almost paranoid attacks of Edmund Burke. Finally, an attempt was made to check the avarice of Company officials by making them declare their fortunes upon their return, and by holding them responsible to the English courts for any wrongs committed in India. Despite the vehement protests of Fox and Burke that tyranny in India was unchecked, and that the separation of government and patronage was impracticable, the Act provided the basis of Indian government until the powers of the Company were wholly taken over by the Crown in 1858.

Equally effective, at least as an interim measure, was Pitt's approach to the problem of the influx of American loyalists into Canada, which greatly swelled the number of British Protestants among a population that had hitherto been predominantly French and Roman Catholic. By the Canada Act of 1791 the two provinces of Upper and Lower Canada were created, each with an elective assembly; but executive power remained firmly with the Governor and his council, and the franchise was strictly limited. Although the settlement satisfied neither the French nor the British (especially the British minority in Lower Canada) it survived for almost fifty years, until union was effected and full responsible government introduced in accordance with the Durham Report of 1840. The vexed question of the slave trade also intermittently attracted Pitt's attention, especially after the formation of Granville Sharp's Abolitionist Society in 1787. Here Pitt was much influenced by the sincerity and eloquence of his friend, William Wilberforce, on whose behalf in May 1788 he introduced a motion for an enquiry into the slave trade. The only immediate concrete result was the passage of Sir William Dolben's act for mitigating some of the worst abuses, but it was gravely mutilated in the Lords as a result of the frantic opposition of the Liverpool merchants, who saw the continuance of the trade as essential to their own prosperity. Pitt continued to argue for abolition, but the French revolution soon ended all hope of reform, and not until 1807 were Fox and Grenville able at last to end British participation in the sordid traffic.

In foreign affairs Pitt's attitude was inevitably shaped in part, like those of Walpole and Pelham before him, by the conviction that peace was essential to the successful accomplishment of his domestic aims. But he had also to face the fact that, at the end of the American war, Britain was left in a position of far from splendid isolation. His commercial treaty with France was but one manifestation of his desire to reconcile old enemies, and his natural inclinations drew him towards Holland and Prussia, with whom Britain had earlier been on friendly terms. Here he was aided by the Dutch crisis of 1787, when the feud between the Stadtholder and the Republican party reached a crisis, with the French supporting the claims of the latter, and Prussia—because the Stadtholder had married the sister of Frederick William II—tempted to intervene on behalf of William V. Though reluctant to endanger the new *détente* with France, Pitt felt obliged to support the Stadtholder, and was ready with naval support when an insult to the Princess of Orange provoked the invasion of Holland by Prussian forces. But the Republican party collapsed in the face of armed resistance. France was unprepared to champion a lost cause, and Pitt was able to forge the defensive Triple Alliance between Britain, Prussia and Holland. While several of his Cabinet colleagues had favoured armed intervention, Pitt succeeded in restraining their ill-advised belligerence and thereby ended British isolation—though the strength of the new alliance was soon to be found less than he had hoped, and France, already convinced that she had been duped over the commercial treaty, became ever more certain that Britain was bent on her humiliation.

Pitt was also involved in two minor disputes with Spain and with Russia. Spain, in splendidly anachronistic fashion, still laid claim to the whole western coast of America, from Cape Horn to Alaska; and memories both of Jenkins's ear and of the Falkland Islands fiasco were revived when a small British settlement at Nootka Sound was attacked by the Spaniards in 1790. Again belligerent voices were raised both in the Cabinet and in the Commons, especially as the support of Holland and Prussia seemed assured. But France was too preoccupied with her revolutionary crisis to honour her obligations under the Family Compact, and Spain was quickly persuaded to agree to a peaceful settlement. Pitt's attempt to interfere in the affairs of eastern Europe had a less happy ending. In the late eighties Catherine the Great and Joseph II were at war with Turkey, but Austrian ambitions faded with the succession of the more pacific Leopold, and the way seemed open for possible mediation between Russia and Turkey. This was especially desired by Pitt and his fellow-ministers, who feared the spread of Russian power to the Mediterranean, and were anxious that Austria and Prussia should not draw too close to Catherine and leave Britain isolated against France. When Prussia urged her partners in the Triple Alliance to force Russia to the peace table, the more aggressive members of Pitt's Cabinet, especially the Duke of Leeds, favoured a strong line with Catherine, and the ultimatum of

March 1791 insisted that she restore all territory conquered from Turkey or face combined action by Britain and Russia. When Catherine refused to surrender Orchakov, a valuable base on the Black Sea, the Commons approved the augmentation of the navy and war seemed possible. But Prussia was already turning her eyes towards a possible further partition of Poland; and Pitt, increasingly aware that British and Prussian interests had little in common, baulked at the cost of intervention that seemed likely to achieve little. He therefore conceded Catherine's right to retain Orchakov, accepted the resignation of the embittered Leeds, and was relieved to see peace signed between Russia and Turkey a few months later. Though nettled by his failure to influence events, and embarrassed by his reversal of policy, he was too much of a realist to ignore the fact that the Triple Alliance was of value only against France, and that a significant role in eastern Europe was beyond Britain's reach.

During these years of peace Pitt's pre-eminence was temporarily threatened only by the brief Regency crisis of 1788–9. In November 1788 George III was stricken with a severe bout of what is now believed to have been porphyria, an hereditary malady the symptoms of which were indistinguishable from those of insanity. For the first time since 1784 the Foxite Opposition saw power within its grasp since, if the Prince of Wales were to become Regent, he could confidently be expected to oust Pitt and elevate his Carlton House cronies to ministerial office. Fox's second long period in the wilderness would be over. The Opposition therefore clamoured for an unfettered Regent, while Pitt and his followers, hoping for the King's speedy recovery, argued for temporary limitations upon the Regent's powers of appointing to office and creating peers. In the ensuing parliamentary debates, constitutional pedantry barely concealed the naked struggle for power, the Foxites suffering especially from their espousal of an attitude that by no stretch of the imagination could be called Whiggish. Once again out-of-doors opinion clearly favoured Pitt, but the issue was never finally decided. The recovery of the King in February 1789 shattered the hopes of Fox, and made Pitt seem more than ever irremovable.

During the first five years of his Ministry, Pitt had indeed come to enjoy authority on a scale which Walpole and Pelham had scarcely known. He had won the King's lasting gratitude by rescuing him from the clutches of the Fox–North coalition, and his growing self-assurance and extraordinary command of detail enabled him to dominate his colleagues and impose a degree of Cabinet solidarity that contrasted markedly with the system of departmental government which he had inherited. He was nonetheless wise enough not to command from his fellow-ministers an unquestioning submission on all matters, and permitted free votes on parliamentary reform, the abolition of the slave trade, the impeachment of Hastings, and the repeal of religious tests. But these were all on the periphery of politics, and when Pitt found himself in fundamental disagreement with a colleague he was more than ready to enforce resignation—as with Lord Sydney in 1789, the Duke of Leeds in 1791, and Thurlow in 1792. Within the Cabinet no less than in the House of Commons, Pitt knew when to yield and when to stand firm.

Meanwhile the Opposition floundered helplessly. Their suspicions of the King had been amply confirmed by the events of 1783–4, and Fox in particular could see Pitt in no other guise than as the instrument of George III's enlarged executive power, unconstitutionally foisted upon an unwilling House of Commons. But this was a sterile and—in view of the manifest popularity of both Pitt and the King—scarcely credible basis on which to found an Opposition, especially when Pitt's practical achievements and public attitudes entitled him to respect as an advocate of moderate reform. As always, the support of the Prince of Wales brought as much embarrassment as comfort to the Opposition, and their momentary display of solidarity during the Regency crisis could not conceal the aimlessness and lack of spirit within their ranks. Then came the sudden and traumatic impact of the French revolution, which was finally to split them asunder but leave Fox and his diminished band with a rejuvenated conviction in the rectitude of their cause.

The initial reactions in England to the fall of the Bastille on 14 July 1789 and the early stages of the revolution varied from enthusiastic support for the revolutionaries to cynical satisfaction at the humbling of the House of Bourbon. Fox and the radicals saw a new dawn of salvation for the French people, and most Englishmen appear to have hoped that France was at last belatedly following the English example of 1688. Only Edmund Burke, with his profound sense of history, had the vision to predict in his *Reflections on the Revolution in France* the corruption, anarchy and military dictatorship that lay ahead, or could appreciate the threat to established institutions throughout Europe that would be posed by the missionary zeal of the revolutionaries. In *The Rights of Man* Thomas Paine acutely analysed some of the weaknesses in Burke's argument, but as events unfolded across the Channel there could be little doubt where the sympathies of property-owning Englishmen would lie. No longer could Burke and Fox tread the same political path, and in a dramatic scene in the House of Commons on 6 May 1791 Burke bitterly declared their friendship at an end. But the breach within the ranks of the Opposition did not end there. The outbreak of war between

France and Austria, the overthrow of the monarchy, the September massacres, and the trial and execution of Louis XVI all confirmed the accuracy of Burke's predictions; and radical activity in England in the course of 1792 convinced many that the contagion could spread to England. When, on 1 February 1793, France declared war on Britain and Holland, there were relatively few among the more prominent aristocratic leaders of the Opposition who felt that they could support Fox's unabated enthusiasm for the French cause. To many, indeed, continued Opposition could scarcely avoid the stigma of disloyalty. Thus began a series of protracted negotiations which culminated in the conversion to Administration of twenty-three of Fox's more conservative colleagues, of whom the most prominent were the Duke of Portland, William Windham, Lord Fitzwilliam and Edmund Burke. Pitt's power was further consolidated, Fox was left with a handful of idealists and devoted personal friends. Meanwhile the nation summoned its energies for the last and most strenuous phase of the struggle against the traditional enemy, fortified by the growing conviction that more was at stake this time than mere dynastic interests or the hope of commercial gain.

II

THE FINAL CHALLENGE: 1793–1815

THE years between 1793 and 1815 constitute a watershed in English history comparable to the reigns of William III and Anne. In all areas other than that of international conflict they belong more properly—if only as a prologue—to the nineteenth rather than the eighteenth century. But the successful completion of the last and most dramatic phase of the traditional struggle against France—a struggle that was to acquire new dimensions in the Revolutionary and Napoleonic era—provides a fitting climax to the story of Britain's emergence as the predominant force in Europe.

For George III and indeed for most Englishmen the war from the beginning assumed something of the character of a crusade. With the French nation offering fraternal assistance to all peoples wishing to overthrow existing regimes, it could scarcely be otherwise. But William Pitt, who alone among the politicians of the war years achieved the status of a great national leader, was slow to appreciate the ideological nature of the French challenge and the problems inherent in facing a nation in arms. A few months before the outbreak of war he was confidently predicting a prolonged period of peace; and when events proved him wrong he continued to see the threat only in terms of British commercial and strategic interests in the Netherlands, the Baltic and the Mediterranean. Like his father, he was convinced that British effort should be concentrated in the naval and colonial spheres, although he was more willing from the outset to subsidize Britain's continental allies in the hope that they might be able to contain French power in Europe. But however limited his outlook he could count on the unwavering support of Parliament, the members of which saw their entire way of life threatened by the French contagion. Patriotism and self-interest were never more closely allied; Opposition, with its continuing enthusiasm for all things French, never more suspect. For the first time, domestic issues could be seen only in the light of external events, and the forces of the new defensive conservatism that rallied around Pitt regarded all reformers as subversive elements within the country. War and repression must go hand in hand. Burke's *Appeal from the New to the Old Whigs* had pointed the way to the union of the Portland Whigs with Pitt, who understandably abandoned his role of moderate reformer and dedicated the rest of his life to the defeat of France. No one who shared that dedication, whatever his earlier political beliefs, would be denied a share in Government; no one who rejected it could avoid obloquy.

Inevitably Pitt was to suffer at the hands of Whig historians, who retrospectively denounced his earlier liberalism as a mere sham, and portrayed the repressive legislation of the 1790s as both typical of the man and unwarranted by the circumstances. This was unjustified, for Pitt was above all a child of his times, whose earlier record of reform compares more than favourably with that of Fox, and whose repressive measures pale into insignificance when compared to the legislation passed during both World Wars of this century. The temporary popularity of Thomas Paine's *Rights of Man*, the fiery rhetoric of radical Dissenters such as Price and Priestley, the widespread working-class unrest during the depression years of 1793 and 1794, the resurgence of reforming groups such as the Society of Friends of the People, the Society for Constitutional Information, and especially the various Corresponding Societies (of which Thomas Hardy's London one was the most prominent) all created alarm among the property-owning classes in Parliament. Pitt was merely reflecting this fear when he suspended Habeas Corpus in 1794 (only the last in a long line of suspensions since the passage of the Habeas Corpus Amendment Act in 1679) and promoted the Treasonable Practices and Seditious Meetings Acts of 1795. By extending treason to encompass any criticism of King or Government, and by increasing the control of JPs over public meetings, these Acts undoubtedly restricted freedom of expression. But the Gordon riots had only recently emphasized the inadequacy of the machinery for quelling disorder, and in time of war the militia was apt to be needed elsewhere. The savagery of the sentences meted out in 1793 by the Scottish judges, especially Lord Braxfield, may have stifled radical movements north of the border; but the acquittal of Thomas Hardy and many others by English juries suggested that the laws needed strengthening, for the severity of the law seemed to most contemporaries the only bulwark against disaffection. On balance it appears that Pitt's measures were a relatively harmless product of unnceessary panic. The crisis was over by 1795, and there is little evidence of undue repression thereafter. Anti-reform societies, such as that of John Reeves, were becoming more numerous than their radical counterparts, and even the latter were disillusioned by events in France. What is more surprising is that the Acts of 1795 were allowed to remain on the statute books until the middle of the following century. Meanwhile, the defeat by 237 votes to ninety-one of Charles Grey's motion of 1797 in favour of parliamentary reform, and the ensuing secession from the Commons of the Foxites, showed how little support there was for reform. More formidable hindrances to individual and corporate liberty were the Combination Laws of 1799 and 1800, which were more industrial than political in character, and which gravely impeded the development of incipient trade unionism. The earlier radical societies had in large part carried on the traditions of the sixties and seventies; the combinations of workmen outlawed in 1799 and 1800 looked forward to the struggles of the nineteenth century. The Foxites seemed no more aware of the distinction than were the followers of Pitt.

Meanwhile the war with France was the centre of attention. An army of only thirteen thousand, even with the addition of the usual Hanoverian and Hessian mercenaries, seemed a puny force beside the 500,000 men whom—as a result of the *levée en masse*—the French were said to have under arms or in training. For the first time a nation was using enthusiastic amateurs in large numbers—men who could travel light, strike quickly and live off the land. But Pitt hoped for significant support from his allies, and by the summer of 1793 had agreed to subsidize Austria, Prussia, Sardinia, Spain and Naples on condition that they abandoned the unrealistic aim of a Bourbon restoration. At home inadequate recruiting, the lack of a commander-in-chief, and constant quarrels within the Cabinet all hampered the development of an efficient fighting machine. An expeditionary force under the Duke of York was hopefully dispatched to the Netherlands, but achieved little in the face of the usual jealousies and divisions that bedevilled allied military co-operation. By 1795 it had mournfully returned via Hanover to England, the Austrian Netherlands had been absorbed into France, and the United Provinces—under the title of the Batavian Republic—had become a French satellite. Prussia had quarrelled with Britain and, like Spain, withdrew from the conflict, while in 1796 Bonaparte assumed control of the French army in Italy, forced an armistice upon the Duke of Savoy, and drove the Austrians from the country. Half-hearted attempts to co-ordinate allied efforts with royalist uprisings in France had come to naught, and Pitt's vast outlay in subsidies seemed to have achieved nothing but confirmation of French superiority.

At sea, and in the colonial field, the prospect was a little brighter. Here again Britain was ill-prepared, the 110,000 sailors of 1783 having shrunk to a mere sixteen thousand. But there were 113 ships of the line in tolerable trim, the administration of the navy was infinitely superior to that of the army, and there were at least a few officers of real ability and experience. During 1794 a fleet under Sir John Jervis and a force of seven thousand men seized most of the French West Indies, although slave rebellions and yellow fever soon offset much of this success. Nearer home on the Glorious First of June the Channel fleet under Lord Howe defeated the Brest fleet when it ventured out of harbour to escort a much-needed convoy of grain ships from America; and in the Mediterranean Lord Howe, after gaining a temporary toe-hold on Toulon, blew up thirty-five French ships and sailed off to seize Corsica. When Holland was over-run the British took the Cape of Good Hope, Ceylon, Pondicherry, Trincomalee and various other Dutch possessions in the East Indies. But while these successes served to boost waning morale, they could scarcely counterbalance French domination in Europe.

After abortive efforts to seek peace—abortive because France was unwilling to surrender any of her conquests—Pitt braced himself for a renewed effort. When, in October 1796, the Spaniards re-entered the war on the French side, the French navy was augmented by that of Spain as well as by that of Holland, although the victory of Jervis off Cape St Vincent quickly disposed of the Spanish threat; and when, in April 1797, Bonaparte forced the Peace of Campo-Formio upon Austria, Britain stood alone. Moreover, the French were clearly thinking in terms of an invasion of Britain, of which the unsuccessful attempt to land forces in Ireland during the winter of 1797–8 seemed a sinister warning. Nor was Pitt's position made any easier by the financial crisis of 1797, when the Bank of England had to suspend cash payments, or by the naval mutinies at Spithead and the Nore. But the mutinies were quickly quelled, and the sailors given fresh heart by the promise of better wages, food and conditions of service. In October 1797 the Dutch invasion fleet was destroyed at Camperdown, and by Christmas the enemy navies were securely blockaded. The crisis was over and although when at the nadir of his fortunes Pitt had again sought peace—even at the cost of leaving the Netherlands in French hands—he accepted rejection as proof of France's determination to dominate Italy and Germany, and finally abandoned his original conception of a limited war. His new outlook was demonstrated by his introduction of a graduated income-tax, the granting of bounties to all militiamen willing to serve in Europe, and his initial approaches for the formation of the second coalition; its justification was Bonaparte's decision to abandon the idea of invading England and to embark instead upon his ill-fated Egyptian expedition. Not only did this constitute a threat to British naval and commercial interests in the Mediterranean and in the East; it awoke Austria to the possibility of a Franco-Turkish attack, and aroused Russian fears that her fleet might be bottled up in the Black Sea. Above all, it demonstrated to all Europe that French ambitions had become global.

Bonaparte's dream of conquest in the Near East was effectively shattered when Nelson, the greatest naval strategist of the war, destroyed the Toulon fleet at the Battle of the Nile in August 1798. His advance towards Syria was checked, with the aid of a naval squadron under Sir Sidney Smith, at Acre, leaving his army to return to Egypt while he made his way back to France to become First Consul at the end of 1799. Meanwhile Austria and Russia had re-entered the war and, with British naval support, had driven the French from Italy. But there the allied successes ended. An Anglo-Russian campaign in the Netherlands achieved nothing, Napoleon routed the Austrians at Marengo in June 1800 and six months later he defeated them again at Hohenlinden and forced them to accept the Treaty of Lunéville, by which they recognized the French satellite republics in Italy, Switzerland, the Rhineland and the Netherlands. Russia had meanwhile taken offence at the British capture of Malta, gone over to the side of France, and begun to organize a Northern League of armed neutrality against Britain. But by this time Pitt was no longer prime minister.

Ironically, it was not the declining fortunes of war but events in Ireland that led to Pitt's resignation on 14 March 1801. The Protestant ascendency, although temporarily mollified by North's commercial concessions and by the granting of legislative independence under Rockingham and Shelburne, soon came to regard these measures as inadequate. The failure of Pitt's commercial propositions hampered further economic development in a country bedevilled by poor natural resources, absentee landlords and intermittent senseless violence; and the divorce between executive and legislative power under the new constitution meant that the Irish Parliament was increasingly impatient of a Lord-Lieutenant and Chief Secretary who drew their authority from England. Henry Grattan, the silver-tongued Patriot leader, was even prepared to advocate parliamentary reform and Catholic emancipation in order to strengthen the hands of the Irish Commons in its battle with the executive, although many of his more conservative colleagues feared that this might lead to a social revolution that would strike at the roots of their own power. The parallel with earlier events in the American colonies was obvious. Naturally enough, the impact of the French Revolution enhanced these fears, bolstered the hopes of both Ulster

Presbyterians and southern Catholics that they might win full citizenship, heightened political consciousness through the formation of Wolfe Tone's United Irishmen in 1791, and forced the English Government—as always acutely conscious in time of war of Ireland's potential as a springboard for the invasion of England—to consider further concessions. The immediate results were Place and Pension Acts and a Catholic Relief Act of 1793 which gave the vote to Roman Catholics and empowered them to bear arms, sit on juries and even hold minor civil and military office. Pitt's ideas were in fact as liberal as and less self-interested than those of Grattan, but unhappily it was not he but Fox who commanded the sympathy of the Irish reformers, and in England he had to cope with the suspicions and prejudices of both King and country gentlemen. Nor was Pitt's situation eased when, as part of the bargain with the Portland Whigs, he sent the young hot-headed Earl Fitzwilliam to Ireland as Lord-Lieutenant. Fitzwilliam's tenure of office lasted a brief three months, but even before he had arrived in Dublin he had appealed to Grattan for support and hinted at widespread reform; and his dismissal of some of the existing ministers and known sympathy for emancipation soon had the country in an uproar. Since even Pitt was as yet unprepared to make a stand in defence of emancipation, Fitzwilliam was hastily recalled and the initiative in Ireland passed to the extremists. There followed in succession the unsuccessful French attempt at invasion, the savage coercion of Ulster and the rising of Wolfe Tone's United Irishmen in 1798. Although the rebellion was easily crushed, an unstable situation in Ireland would only invite further French aggression. By now Pitt was convinced that a combination of Catholic emancipation and union with England was the only solution, and his opinion was shared by the new Lord-Lieutenant, Lord Cornwallis. In the spring of 1800 the Irish Parliament was persuaded, by a majority of forty-three, to end its own life, and the Act of Union was accepted by the English legislature later in the same year. Traditionally the political suicide of Grattan's Parliament was attributed to an orgy of corruption on the part of the English Government, but the peerages, places and compensation for loss of private boroughs were only part of the story. Many of the Protestant ascendency realized that their long dominance was drawing to a close, and felt that their interests might be best served by ensuring that Catholic members were confined to a minority in the English Commons rather than allowed to command the Irish legislature. They therefore acquiesced in the abolition of the Irish Parliament, and in the addition of one hundred Irish members of the English House of Commons and twenty-eight Irish peers and four bishops to the House of Lords. The United Kingdom of Great Britain and Ireland had been created. But Catholic emancipation, which had been an implied part of the bargain, proved beyond the power of Pitt to grant. George III, taking his stand upon his Coronation oath, was adamant; Pitt's Cabinet colleagues were divided and hesitant; and the conservative back benchers in the Commons were deeply suspicious. As a man of honour, Pitt had no alternative to resignation; out of respect for the King, who had been driven by the controversy to a further brief breakdown, he promised never to revive the issue and to refrain from formal Opposition to the new Administration. Some of his fellow-ministers went out of office with him, some preferred to remain.

The King's choice as Pitt's successor was the Speaker of the House, Henry Addington, whose sudden elevation was reminiscent of that of Robert Harley a century earlier. Like Harley he had his finger on the pulse of the independent country gentlemen, whom he realized had become weary of war and of professional politicians and were, if only temporarily, reverting to type. They had little stomach for either parliamentary reform or Catholic emancipation, and had had enough of 'those confounded men of genius'. Like his father, Pitt had lost touch with the independents, who in 1784 had rallied to his support; and without the favour of the King his credentials had become suspect. It was a little ironical that he left behind him in office his brother, Chatham, and the former leader of the Fox–North coalition, the Duke of Portland. The wheel had gone full circle.

Addington, an amiable nonentity who quickly developed a taste for power, pressed on with negotiations for peace. Fortunately for him, the assassination of the Russian Tsar, combined with Nelson's destruction of the Danish fleet in Copenhagen harbour, shattered the Northern League; and by 1801 Arthur Wellesley had begun his brilliant military career by destroying the last vestiges of French power in India. Napoleon was ready for a brief breathing space, and the Peace of Amiens was duly signed in March 1802. Except for Trinidad and Ceylon, all overseas conquests were restored to France, Spain and Holland; and Malta was to be returned to the Knights of St John. France merely agreed to evacuate central and southern Italy, although by the Treaty of Lunéville she had already guaranteed to respect the independence of Holland, Switzerland and northern Italy. It is difficult to improve upon Sheridan's comment that it was a peace 'which all men are glad of, but no man could be proud of', although Pitt was magnanimous enough to commend it. But the accompanying reduction of taxation and expansion of trade were a welcome contrast to the economic recession of the closing years of the century, which had seen bad harvests, food shortages, bread riots, and depreciation in the value of the pound. The abolition of Pitt's income-tax, proposals for a drastic reduction in Government expenditure and a modest resumption of administrative reform were the prelude to a general election which strengthened the position of an Administration in which the not inconsiderable if unspectacular talents of Lord Liverpool (the former Charles Jenkinson), his son Lord Hawkesbury, and Spencer Perceval did something to offset the mediocrity of a leader who deserved the jibe that 'Pitt is to Addington as London is to Paddington'. But the situation was transformed when it became obvious that Napoleon's ambitions were unabated. He acquired Louisiana, Elba and Parma from Spain, assumed the presidency of the Cisalpine republic, annexed Piedmont to France, and blatantly intervened in the affairs of Holland and Switzerland. Faced with this fresh outburst of French expansionism, Britain refused to surrender Malta; and when it became evident that Napoleon was prepared to resume hostilities, the pacific Addington summoned up the courage to declare war on 17 May 1803. Whatever his modest merits as a peace-time minister, he manifestly lacked the stature to lead the nation against Napoleon, and all eyes turned again to Pitt, whom Canning had already apostrophized as 'the pilot who had weathered the storm'. For a year Addington delayed resignation, aided by Pitt's reluctance to enter into formal Opposition—a reluctance that split his impatient followers, driving Castlereagh over to Addington, and Lord Grenville and William Windham into the welcoming arms of Fox. But by May 1804 Pitt's sense of patriotism would no longer allow him to support Addington, and he accepted the premiership for the second time, acknowledging in the process the continuing influence of the King by confirming his earlier promise not to revive the issue of Catholic emancipation and by accepting a royal veto on the inclusion in his Ministry of Fox. The chance of an all-embracing coalition was thereby lost and the Foxites given a new lease of life by the acquisition of the Grenvillites (the combination thereafter laying sole claim to the title of 'Whigs'). Pitt's second Ministry was little more than the continuation of Addington's, with the addition of a few of his own friends; but once again Britain had a real leader.

The task facing Pitt was formidable. At home he no longer dominated the political scene as he had done during most of his first, long Ministry. The half-hearted support of the Addingtonians (Addington himself briefly joined the Ministry in 1805 but soon quarrelled with Pitt and resigned) could not compensate for the loss of the Grenvillites who, in conjunction with Fox, caused Pitt personal embarrassment by pushing for Catholic emancipation when he could do nothing but argue unconvincingly for postponement. Even worse, the Opposition was able, with the aid of the Addingtonians and the Speaker's casting vote, to secure the impeachment of Lord Melville (the former Henry Dundas), Pitt's oldest and closest political friend and adviser, for supposed malversation during his earlier tenure of the treasurership of the navy. While Melville had certainly been negligent, it was clear that in supporting his impeachment the Addingtonians were chiefly avenging themselves on Pitt for making Melville First Lord of the Admiralty in place of Lord St Vincent who, whatever his merits as a naval commander, had by his drastic economies left the navy ill-prepared for the resumption of the struggle with Napoleon. The impeachment failed, but the resurgence of political factiousness placed an additional strain upon a Prime Minister whose health was already beginning to fail.

Abroad the situation was perilous and the possibility of immediate decisive action negligible. The earlier conflict had shown that colonial conquests were of little use as long as France continued to dominate Europe and could use that domination to force the restoration of territory lost elsewhere. From the outset of his second Ministry Pitt fully acknowledged the fact that only a massive allied onslaught on the Continent could bring lasting success, but at that stage Russia, Austria and Prussia showed little enthusiasm for resuming the struggle. The only comfort was that Napoleon's position was equally problematic. His sole hope of ultimate victory lay in the successful invasion and conquest of Britain, but for this he needed command of the Channel and, even if Spain were to re-enter the war (as she did in 1805), it was far from clear that the combined Franco-Spanish naval forces would wrest naval supremacy from the British. All that Napoleon could do was push on with his plans for invasion, and by the summer of 1804 some one hundred thousand men and two thousand transports had been assembled at Boulogne; all that Pitt could do was strengthen the navy and seek European allies. Here he was aided by Napoleon's arrogant and obtuse behaviour. In March 1804 a French detachment seized the popular *émigré* duc d'Enghein in Baden and had him executed on a trumped-up charge of espionage, thereby shocking the consciences of most civilized Europeans; concurrently he extended his influence in Germany, blatantly redistributing territories and driving Russia on the first steps towards alliance with Britain; and in 1805, by having himself crowned King of Italy, he finally provoked a reluctant Austria into joining Britain and Russia. The Third coalition, which Sweden quickly joined, thus became a reality, although constructive action was hampered by indecision whether the main thrust should be made in northern or southern Europe, and by the continuing refusal of Prussia to be drawn into the conflict.

The only positive result of Pitt's creation of the coalition was that Napoleon was forced to abandon his planned invasion of Britain in order to use his troops against Austria and Russia. But unhappily he did this with devastating effect. An Austrian army under General Mack was smashed at Ulm on 7 October, Napoleon entered Vienna a few weeks later, a combined force of Austrians and Russians was annihilated at Austerlitz, and before the end of the year Austria was compelled to withdraw from the war by the Treaty of Pressburg. Meanwhile British spirits had been at least temporarily raised by her most decisive naval victory of the war. As long as invasion was still a possibility, the efforts of the Admiralty had been directed towards preventing the enemy fleets in Toulon, Brest, Rochefort, Cadiz and Ferrol from eluding their blockades. But Nelson remained convinced that the crucial theatre of war was the Mediterranean and, once the invasion danger was over, he was able to prove his point. On 21 October 1805, off Cape Trafalgar, he destroyed the main body of the French fleet under Villeneuve. Although the victory celebrations were muted by the news of Nelson's death in action, Trafalgar ended any possibility of Napoleon's reviving plans for invading England, made impossible French naval support for campaigns in Italy and, by convincingly demonstrating the importance of sea-power, pointed the way to the Peninsular campaign, in which the navy could facilitate the establishment and retention of a bridge-head in Europe.

The news of Trafalgar also boosted Pitt's waning morale, and at the Lord Mayor's banquet in the following month he made his shortest and most celebrated speech:

> I return you many thanks for the honour you have done me; but Europe is not to be saved by the exertions of any one man. England has saved herself by her exertions, and will, as I trust, save Europe by her example.

But these were the tired words of a man who had worn himself out in the service of his country. He was shattered by the humiliation of Austerlitz and on 23 January 1806 'his life departed like a candle burning out'. The loss of both Nelson and Pitt within a few months left the nation stunned and confused. Admittedly Pitt never achieved greatness as a war minister, yet many of the criticisms levelled against him seem unjust. If his military appointments lacked inspiration, the same could not be said of his naval ones, and the dearth of talent in the army left him little choice. Certainly he underestimated the nature and extent of the French threat, but so did virtually all his contemporaries in both England and Europe; and long before his death he acknowledged his mistake. The European coalitions which he so ardently supported invariably failed to live up to his expectations, and there frequently seemed precious little return for the vast sums which were poured out in subsidies. Yet there was no obvious alternative method of trying to contain Napoleon in Europe, and in the end the co-operation of the Allies, however spasmodic and rent by jealousies and prejudices, was to achieve its objective. Pitt's economic, financial and administrative reorganization, even if aided by the prosperity of a growing industrial nation, enabled England to act as the paymaster of Europe until victory was assured; and his superb single-mindedness and strength of character made him the only possible national leader during the first and most difficult half of the conflict. When he died most men felt, as did Charles James Fox, that something was missing from the world.

The last ten years of the war have their moments of drama, yet they somehow fail to capture the imagination. Jane Austen may perhaps be forgiven for ignoring the war in her novels, and it must have seemed as remote to most Englishmen as it apparently did to her. In part this was probably because of the lack of any leader who could even begin to serve as a symbol of national determination. Fox survived Pitt by little more than eighteen months, and was anyway irrelevant; Portland, Perceval and Liverpool, whatever their respective merits, could never inspire enthusiasm; Canning and Castlereagh, despite their great abilities, were too young, inexperienced and headstrong to command widespread support. Even in the military sphere the Duke of Wellington invited respect rather than affection, and no successor to Nelson was found among the naval commanders. In these circumstances the monarchy might have become a focal point for patriotic sentiment, but George III until 1810 was at best semi-senile, and after his permanent collapse the Prince Regent was a pathetic substitute for a king. Meanwhile society was disrupted by economic crisis and by the growing impact of industrialization. The eighteenth century was dead; the nineteenth was still in the throes of a long, difficult and somewhat dreary labour.

The Administrations which successively inherited the task of subduing Napoleon could at best boast a modest competence. The death of Pitt revealed the deep divisions within his Ministry, and the ill-feeling between his followers and those of Addington left the King with no option but to turn to Grenville and Fox, with Portland—whose memory could apparently no longer reach back to 1783—deploring the 'storming of the Closet'! But, apart from Grenville, Fox and Charles Grey, the resulting 'Ministry of all the Talents' scarcely deserved its name. Indeed, its proscription of the Pittites—especially Canning, Castlereagh and Perceval—left the more obvious talent on the Opposition benches. Its only claim to fame was the abolition of the slave trade in 1807, unhappily not carried until after Fox's death. While it must have occasioned Fox some satisfaction to force himself for the third time upon George III, that satisfaction must have been greatly diminished by the fact that Pitt was no longer there to witness it. Fox remains one of the most splendid failures of the eighteenth century—a man of tremendous talent, great personal charm, complete irresponsibility and pathetically poor political judgment. His only concrete achievement was his Libel Act of 1792, conceding a power to juries that he had joined in denying them twenty-one years earlier. With Wilkes and Fox as the 'friends of Liberty' it is scarcely surprising that the forces of conservatism enjoyed an overwhelming triumph.

After Fox's death Grenville was unwise enough to try to force the King's hand over further relief for Roman Catholics, and Portland was able to complete the last stage of his political transformation by standing forth to rescue George III from his 'thralldom'. If it were possible to describe Portland's Ministry in eighteenth-century terms, it might be called a combination of Old Whigs, Pittites and King's Friends, but such a description serves little purpose. The ministers were distinguishable from their opponents only in that they were more obviously dedicated to the whole-hearted prosecution of the war, and were prepared for the moment to postpone the issue of Catholic emancipation. As for the Whig Opposition, Grenville presided over the more conservative wing and Charles Grey over the rump of the Foxites. A general election, fought chiefly on the basis of 'no Popery' strengthened the Ministry's position; and on Portland's resignation in October 1809 (he died a few weeks later) Spencer Perceval assumed the premiership and merely added a few second-generation Pittites to the existing ministers. Approaches to Grenville and Grey foundered on their refusal to abandon Catholic emancipation. The only serious internal crisis which Perceval had to face was the final collapse of the King in December 1810, and the establishment of the Prince of Wales as Regent two months later. Not unnaturally the Whigs hoped that the promised land was in sight, and a complete change of Ministry was widely expected. But the Prince had long since abandoned his early flirtation with liberal causes and was as opposed as his father to further relief for Roman Catholics. When his position as Regent was made permanent in 1812 he made the gesture of offering a few places to Grenville and his friends, but they refused to be absorbed into the Ministry, and the 'reversionary interest' of the eighteenth century was at last laid to rest. In May 1812 Perceval achieved the unenviable distinction of being the first and only British prime minister to be assassinated and, after fruitless attempts to form a broadly-based coalition, Lord Liverpool began a premiership that was to last until 1827. The general pattern of the Ministry was preserved, but Canning—the first politician to revive and claim the title 'Tory'—remained with the Whigs on the Opposition benches.

Meanwhile the fortunes of war had begun to swing in Britain's favour, though only after further set-backs and some years of uncertainty. In 1806 Napoleon succeeded in goading Prussia into war, shattered her army at Jena on 1 October, and occupied Berlin a few weeks later. The following year he routed the Russians at Friedland, forced Alexander I to make peace, and then on a raft at Tilsit bewitched the unstable and ambitious Tsar into agreeing to a pact which ostensibly aimed at dividing the world between the two rulers but was in practice directed chiefly towards ruining Britain by closing all European ports to her commerce. Britain responded by seizing the Danish fleet in Copenhagen harbour, an act of aggression which was widely condemned both at home and abroad but which was necessary to forestall similar action by Napoleon. The winter of 1807–8 saw Britain again standing alone, with little apparent prospect of success. But fortunately the Emperor of the French (a title Napoleon had assumed in 1805) made his first serious mistake by attempting to extend his domination over the Iberian peninsula. In 1809 he had his brother Joseph made King of Spain, although his hope of capturing the Portuguese fleet was thwarted when the Portuguese regent sailed with it to Brazil. But the peoples of both Spain and Portugal refused to knuckle down under the French yoke. For the first time Napoleon found himself confronted not by the professional armies of his fellow-sovereigns, but by genuinely national uprisings; and Britain was at last provided with a coast-line along which she could infiltrate troops into Europe and with allies whose refreshing enthusiasm compensated for their dubious military capacity. In the summer of 1808 the Spaniards defeated a French force at Baylen, and Sir Arthur Wellesley gave Britain his first military victory at Vimiero. Yet before the year was out vast French armies had invaded Spain and captured Madrid; and only Sir John Moore's impudent diversionary sally into northern Spain prevented Napoleon from subjugating the south. Moore's subsequent masterly retreat to Corunna—he could scarcely be expected to face a French force that outnumbered his by ten to one—was a remarkable military feat, but did nothing to improve Britain's position. Indeed, it is difficult to know how the Peninsular campaign might have fared had not Napoleon been forced to withdraw in early 1809 in order to cope with a renewed challenge from Austria; and Britain's capacity to take advantage of the situation in Spain was anyway gravely hampered by the cumulative effects of the

Islington, 1780

Kew Gardens

economic warfare which Napoleon had initiated after the defeat of Prussia.

It was natural that Napoleon, well aware of Britain's economic strength should seek to strangle British commerce; and equally natural that Britain should use her command of the seas to thwart the Emperor's schemes. Economic warfare was the outcome of French inability to invade England, and of British inability to establish an effective bridge-head in Europe. Napoleon's Berlin decrees of November 1806 closed all European ports under his control to ships coming directly from Britain and her colonies; the British orders in council, authorized in March 1807, responded by ordering all neutral ships entering or leaving European ports to proceed by way of Britain in order to pay customs duties and purchase licences; and Napoleon's Milan decrees of November 1807 attempted to counter the British move by commanding the confiscation of all neutral vessels that passed through British ports. In the final analysis British naval supremacy and European need for British and colonial products were likely to undermine Napoleon's schemes, but in the meantime Britain suffered severe economic dislocation. In 1808 her exports declined sharply, grain imports disastrously, and high food prices and low wages produced much industrial unrest. European shortages persuaded Napoleon to relax his regulations in 1809, but the ensuing improvement in Britain's position compelled him to reinforce them in 1810. The resulting trade crisis of 1811 hit Britain when she was already reeling under the impact of inflation, bankruptcies and widespread industrial strife. But fortunately France was in equally poor shape, Napoleon was unable to press home his advantage and by 1812 the immediate crisis was over. Events in Spain and in Russia quickly ensured that it would not recur, but a belated and incidental by-product of the period of economic warfare was the unnecessary and irrelevant war between Britain and the United States, which reflected little credit on either side and achieved nothing. American expansionist aims on land were as little justified as British aggression on the high seas.

Integral to Napoleon's system of economic warfare were his domination of the Iberian peninsula and the continued co-operation of Russia. In endeavouring to ensure both he paved the way for his own downfall. In 1809 he was briefly diverted from his main objectives by the re-entry into the war of Austria, strengthened this time by the revulsion of the Austrian people against Napoleon's growing megalomania. But once again the Austrians were quickly crushed at Wagram and Britain failed to seize the opportunity to pour troops into Portugal and Spain, preferring instead the futile and disastrous expedition to Walcheren in the forlorn hope of capturing Antwerp and opening a second front against Napoleon. Nonetheless, in April 1809, Wellesley had returned to Portugal as Commander-in-Chief, with a relatively small force of twenty-five thousand men and a determination to wage a war of attrition against the French. While Napoleon was still preoccupied with Austria, Wellesley advanced into Spain and earned elevation to the peerage as Lord Wellington by defeating the French at the bloody battle of Talavera. But Spanish co-operation was erratic and ineffectual, and Wellington soon deemed it expedient to retreat to Portugal. Here he established an impregnable defensive position behind the lines of Torres Vedras, secure in the knowledge of adequate supplies by sea, and determined that the mobility of the French armies, which had for so long ensured their success, should be turned to their disadvantage. Living off the land, and lacking supply-lines and communications, they could remain stationary for only as long as the local resources of food could maintain them. Wellington ruthlessly trained his troops, built up a first-class staff and medical corps, and waited. For the first time Napoleon was to find himself pitted against an enemy whose genius for organization rivalled his own.

In September 1810 Masséna invaded Portugal with more than seventy thousand men. The British troops, numbering in all little more than a third of the French force, delayed the advance at Almeida and Cuidad Rodrigo, allowing time for the harvest to be collected. Then they retreated to Lisbon, scorching the earth as they withdrew. During a miserable winter Masséna camped outside the lines of Torres Vedras; and in the spring was forced to make his way back to Spain with a half-starved army, while Wellington harrassed him from the rear and peasant guerillas attacked on both flanks. The French lost twenty-five thousand men without fighting a single major engagement, and Napoleon had suffered the first significant military check to his ambitions. But the power of the French could not be broken overnight. Although they had been driven in ignominy from Portugal, they still retained the three great border fortresses of Badajoz, Almeida and Cuidad Rodrigo, and of these Wellington was able, in the course of 1811, to capture only the last. At home many doubted whether the war in the Peninsula could ever bring decisive victory, and in the face of economic dislocation and social unrest morale was tenuously maintained only by the news of colonial conquests in India, the East and West Indies, and the Cape of Good Hope, and by the knowledge of the upsurge of patriotism among the nations of Europe that had for so long been subject to Napoleon's arrogant demands. By the end of 1812 the prospect seemed dramatically brighter. Wellington had captured the two remaining fortresses, and had gained a major victory at Salamanca, the memory of which not even the subsequent retreat from Burgos could erase. But more important, Napoleon had lost patience with Alexander I's connivance at the entry of British ships into Russian ports, and decided to crush Russia once and for all. With an army of 700,000 men, almost half of which had been collected from the peoples whom he had subjugated, he began his invasion of Russia in the summer of 1812. By September he was in Moscow, having been momentarily halted only at Smolensk and by a bloody and indecisive engagement at Borodino. But, as in Spain, his opponents for the most part declined to fight pitched battles, laid waste the earth as they withdrew, and left the French isolated and starving. As the winter of 1812–13 approached Napoleon began his harrowing retreat; by the time that he reached Paris in early December he had lost half a million men.

Meanwhile Russia had joined in alliance with Britain and prepared to advance towards France. Heartened by the reverses in French fortunes, Prussia and Sweden quickly threw in their lot with Russia and, despite Napoleonic victories at Lutzen and Bautzen and abortive peace negotiations during the summer of 1813, the Allies stood firm and were joined in August by Austria. By this time Wellington had crushed the French at Vittoria, shattered the basis of their power in Spain, and was poised for the invasion of France itself. At Dresden in August Napoleon again managed to defeat his opponents in central Europe, but the ensuing three-day Battle of the Nations at Leipzig forced his retreat and, once the tide turned against him, his army was decimated by desertions. For the first time since 1793 French troops were compelled to withdraw behind the Rhine. At the end of 1813 Wellington invaded south-west France and pushed on towards Toulouse; concurrently the allied armies battled their way towards Paris from the north-east. On 31 March Paris capitulated; twelve days later Napoleon abdicated and his kingdom shrank to the tiny island of Elba. The Bourbon dynasty was forthwith restored in the person of Louis XVIII, and in the autumn of 1814 the Allies gathered at Vienna to settle the terms of peace.

Already in the previous May the astute Castlereagh had concluded the Treaty of Paris with France, by which her frontiers had been reduced to those of 1792, in return for which she regained all her lost colonial possessions except Tobago, St Lucia and Mauritius. Holland and Belgium were to be united, and a separate agreement with Holland permitted Britain to retain the Cape of Good Hope and the Guiana settlements. Castlereagh's over-all strategy was to promote stability in Europe by establishing Austria and Prussia as bulwarks against both France and Russia, ensure the maintenance of the Low Countries in friendly hands, and guarantee British commercial interests in the Mediterranean, the West Indies and India. He could therefore afford to return the East Indies to the Dutch, and even grant them £2,000,000 compensation for the loss of the Cape—on condition that the money was used to strengthen the Belgian frontier against France! But Castlereagh's plans looked like being frustrated at the Congress of Vienna by the determination of the Tsar to retain the whole of Poland and by Prussian eagerness to wrest most of Saxony from Austria. In the end a compromise settlement ensured that British interests by and large prevailed. But news of the rifts within the ranks of the Allies encouraged Napoleon to make one desperate attempt to recover his lost power and on 1 March 1815 he landed again on French soil. For the last time British subsidies were hastily guaranteed, and even more hastily Wellington left Vienna to assume command of the forces in the Netherlands. The four major Powers had each promised 150,000 men, but Wellington's army proved rather smaller and included little more than thirty thousand British troops. Prussia was quick to honour her obligations, but Russia and Austria were more dilatory. Napoleon, having checked the Prussians and showing an arrogant and ill-founded contempt for Wellington, endeavoured on 18 June to crush the main army at Waterloo. But Wellington withstood Napoleon's repeated assaults. By evening Blücher's Prussian troops were within earshot, Wellington was able to switch from defence to attack, the Prussians broke through on Napoleon's flank, and the French army dissolved in rout. Shortly afterwards Napoleon, deserted by his people, surrendered to the British and was sent to spend the last six years of his life in exile on St Helena. The only concrete results of his intervention were that the frontiers of France were further pushed back to those of 1790, an army of occupation was forced upon her for five years, and she was compelled to pay a war indemnity of 700,000,000 francs.

Had it not been for Britain there can be little doubt that Europe would have suffered for much longer the domination of Napoleon, yet in retrospect her ultimate success seems far from inevitable. At an individual level Pitt, Nelson and Wellington had made outstanding contributions; and Napoleon, by over-reaching himself, contributed even more. But neither inspired political leadership nor superior strategy had dictated the final outcome. This was above all the result of naval supremacy and economic strength. On these twin pillars Britain had stood firm against the might of Napoleon, and on these she would rest unchallenged for the remainder of the nineteenth century.

12

THE PATTERN OF POLITICS

BETWEEN the pattern of politics of the late 1780s and that of the late 1730s there were many obvious similarities. The King was still in a very real sense the head of the executive; the premiership of William Pitt had the same triple foundation as that of Sir Robert Walpole; the House of Commons was still basically composed of politicians, Court and Treasury Party, and independents; patronage was still an essential part of the political system; and the Opposition still basked in the favour of the Prince of Wales and—as the Regency crisis amply demonstrated—gambled upon the reversionary interest. Even though an Empire had been lost in the interim, many of the policies and attitudes of Pitt were strangely reminiscent of those of Walpole—the concern at the size of the national debt and the desire to reduce it through the establishment of a sinking fund, the systematic lowering of customs duties, even the readiness to withdraw in the face of determined opposition in the country or in Parliament. Yet the striking resemblances between the two eras could not conceal the fact that there had been many subtle changes, which had already wrought a partial transformation of the political scene, and which were further to modify it in the years of war that lay ahead. Central to an understanding of these changes is the disintegration of the chief political groupings of the early Hanoverian period, the growth of new divisive issues, the impact of the kingship of George III, new developments in the theory and practice of Opposition, and the rise to importance of extra-parliamentary agitation. All these find expression, at least partially, in the conceptions and misconceptions of the King on the one hand, and of the Rockingham–Foxite Whigs on the other.

Almost from the day of George III's accession the significance of that event has been debated. The orthodox Whig view—originating with Edmund Burke, and passing via Holland House from Lord Macaulay, Thomas Erskine May and both Trevelyans to more sophisticated modern exponents such as Sir Herbert Butterfield and W. R. Fryer—has been that the new King broke with existing constitutional practice by seeking, with the aid of a judicious amalgam of King's Friends and reinvigorated

Tories, to reassert the power of the Crown and, by assuming to himself control of patronage, reduce Parliament to little more than a cypher. The earlier 'Whig supremacy' was thereby ended, and American no less than English liberties placed at risk. The colonists preserved theirs by revolution and war, but in England the picture between 1760 and 1830 was one of almost unrelieved gloom; and only the constant vigilance of Rockingham Burke, Fox and their followers kept the torch of liberty alight, so that in the fullness of time it could be handed on to Russell, Grey, Palmerston and other nineteenth-century Whig stalwarts. From the opening years of George III's reign this attitude was challenged by those who, like the King himself, had been brought up in the Leicester House tradition. They saw no royal subversion of the constitution, but merely a legitimate attempt to reverse an unconstitutional cornering of power in the previous two reigns by the leading Whig families; and they applauded George III's efforts to vindicate his right to choose and dismiss his ministers. As early as 26 November 1760 the irrepressible Dodington was writing to Bute:

> During the last two reigns a set of undertakers have farmed the power of the Crown at a price certain under colour of making themselves responsible for the whole, have taken the sole direction of the Royal interest and influence into their own hands and applied it to their own creatures without consulting the Crown or leaving any room for the Royal nomination or direction.

This view came to be accepted by a few historians such as John Adolphus, John Wilson Croker and Albert von Ruville, and has been most cogently expressed in modern times by Sir Lewis Namier, Richard Pares and Romney Sedgwick.

Both the Whig interpretation and that of the so-called 'Tory critics' contain elements of truth, but both are based in part upon misconceptions and myths—in particular upon mistaken notions of the pattern of politics under the first two Georges, and upon failures to distinguish sufficiently between George III's motives and actions during the first three years of his reign and his attitudes thereafter. The Whig theory, even in its recent modified form, founders upon several points. Firstly, it is wrong in claiming that George III used the increasing patronage of the Crown to corrupt Parliament. Royal Influence decreased significantly during the first two decades of his reign, and there is no evidence to show that he left it any less—or for that matter any more—in the hands of his ministers than his predecessors had done. Of course, to most of the Rockingham Whigs, whose families had enjoyed preferment for half a century, but who now found themselves excluded from power, a system of patronage which had been highly acceptable when it had operated to their advantage became offensive when it was applied to their detriment. Secondly, the King's Friends were no new phenomenon. As a combination of Court and Treasury Party and a small number of Court Independents, they had existed at least since the days of Danby and Charles II, and had certainly flourished under the first two Georges. But with the Old Corps politicians in power between 1714 and 1760 they had never been required to declare their primary allegiance to the Crown. Support for the leading Whig families had conveniently been able to go hand in hand with support for the King, and conflicts of loyalties rarely arose. But George III ushered in his reign with a bewildering succession of Ministries, and with this kaleidoscopic series of changes the true allegiance of the King's Friends was thrown into bold relief. Had George II changed his ministers with the same rapidity, we should have heard of King's Friends much earlier, and doubtless they would have assumed the same sinister guise as in the pages of Edmund Burke. Thirdly, George III did not enjoy the support of a revived Tory party. By 1760, as we have already seen, the inveterate opposition of the Tories to all Administrations had been broken, and many had come round to support of the elder Pitt's war policy. With the accession of the new king they reappeared at Court after an absence of two generations, and a handful even accepted office. But in the course of the next few years they completely lost their separate identity. Contemporary analyses of the results of every general election from 1714 to 1761 include lists of some one hundred to a hundred and fifty Tories; from the election of 1768 onwards no Tories appear. A few gravitated towards the Court, some towards Chatham, some towards Grenville and some towards Rockingham; and the remainder continued their earlier policy of Country opposition. While Whiggery revived in recognizable form under George III, there was no revival of Toryism. Finally, George III was singularly scrupulous about his constitutional responsibilities towards his ministers—more so in fact than George II had been. There is no equivalent after 1760—not even Bute—to George II's use of Granville as 'minister behind the curtain' in 1744–6. Even Horace Walpole, no friend of George III's, admitted that once the King appointed his ministers he never interfered with them until the time came to consider their dismissal. This was certainly true during the 1760s. Of course he continually interfered with Lord North during the American crisis, but he had no option. North would not get on with the job, and someone had to take the lead. But as the King then pointed out, he was not seeking to enlarge the powers of the Crown, but merely fighting the battle of the legislature—struggling to maintain parliamentary supremacy over the colonies. For all these reasons, and many more, the Whig version is unacceptable. What of the Tory one?

Certainly George III believed that there had been a wicked cornering of power by his grandfather's ministers. Having been brought up at Leicester House he could scarcely be expected to believe otherwise. The supposed influence of Bolingbroke's *Patriot King* and of his mother ('George, be a King') belong to the Tory legend rather than the Whig one. Thus he came to the throne with ideas remarkably similar to those which had been expressed earlier by George II as Prince of Wales, and by Frederick in 1749–51. Hence his desire to get rid of the old ministers and, with the aid of Bute, eliminate parties and rule with the combined support of all his people. But in adopting this perverted version of his grandfather's reign he merely made a rod for his own back. Above all, he failed to realize that the Pitt–Newcastle coalition which he inherited was in fact his ideal. It was no oligarchical cabal of ministers, but the most broadly-based Administration of the century, successfully conducting a major war with the whole-hearted support of Parliament and the nation. Yet within two years George III had played his part in ousting the more prominent ministers, and in so doing unconsciously paved the way for the emergence of the Rockingham Whigs. Nonetheless it is only fair to acknowledge that he was quick to learn from his mistakes. No sooner had he realized the inadequacies of Bute than he was beseeching Newcastle, Hardwicke and Pitt to come back, but not unnaturally they had taken offence and were unwilling to make life easy either for the King or for his Scottish favourite. During the following seven years George III showed himself willing to turn to every shade of political opinion in his endeavour to find a Ministry that was personally congenial to him and capable of commanding support in the Commons. Here was no Machiavellian tyrant intent upon personal rule, but a rather pathetic young king looking ceaselessly for a strong man on whom he could depend. When one surveys his successive choices it is difficult not to feel sorry for him. Bute was a man of straw, Grenville an arrogant bully, Cumberland died almost immediately, Rockingham scarcely bothered to try, Chatham went mad and Grafton was more interested in the races at Newmarket and in wooing Nancy Parsons than in helping the King to withstand the pressures of the time. So George III went from one experiment to another, achieving in the process little but the creation of parties which had hitherto existed only in his imagination. In the ever-increasing sense of insecurity bred by the King's ministerial changes, politicians found it expedient to build up their bargaining power by developing their own connections, and the 1760s saw the emergence of the Bedford, Grenville,

Rockingham and Chathamite Whigs. Only when George III fortuitously came upon Lord North did he achieve the stability he so ardently desired, and it was ironical that in so doing he was returning to the practice of his grandfather. North was to be his Henry Pelham, the younger Pitt his Walpole. Indeed, the parallels between the two reigns, and the similarities between the fortunes of the two monarchs do not end there. George III was no more able to retain Bute in 1763 or Shelburne in 1783 than George II had been able to retain Granville in 1744; if George II had at one time or another to accept Pitt and bow temporarily to the Pelhams, his grandson several times had to accept Charles James Fox and in 1782 had to bow to King Rockingham; and both monarchs had to accept the loss of ministers who had proved incapable of conducting a major war. Indeed, one might be forgiven for wondering how George III ever came to be regarded as a more active and effective monarch than his predecessor since, in the last analysis, both had to work within the same framework of politics. In some ways George III had the easier task, for he was untroubled during the first two decades of his reign by any ambitious heir to the throne, the breach in the solidarity of the Old Corps after the death of Henry Pelham allowed him greater freedom of action, and he did not have to face the persistent opposition of a large body of Tories. But if he did not suffer from the same self-imposed limitations as the first two Georges, his absorption of Leicester House fantasies created new ones for him; and he was ill-equipped by temperament to cope with the challenges posed by the recalcitrance of the American colonists or by the ephemeral radicalism that periodically challenged his own views and those of his ministers. His greatest strength lay in the fact that he mirrored in his own outlook the hopes, fears and prejudices of the great majority of his politically conscious subjects, and this above all enabled him to achieve the greatest personal victory of his reign when he succeeded in 1783 in ousting the Fox–North coalition. Here was the only marked contrast between his political performance and that of his grandfather. When George II forced the resignation of the Pelhams in February 1746, he was unable to form his own Ministry and had to ask them to return. When George III dismissed Fox and North, Pitt was able to provide a viable alternative Administration and vindicate his action by appealing to the electorate. These two crises, with their contrasting outcomes, pinpoint a basic fact of eighteenth-century political life and indicate the parameters within which any contemporary sovereign was compelled to work. Across the decades an intermittent battle was waged between kings of varying political insight and politicians who, however much they might deny it, sought to impose themselves and their policies upon the monarch. The protagonists in this struggle were mostly reasonable men, or at least behaved reasonably for most of the time, and minor concessions by one side or the other normally avoided a head-on collision. But in 1746 and in 1783–4 there could be no compromise. In the first crisis the politicians emerged victorious, in the second the King. In neither case was the issue really decided on constitutional grounds, for the 'constitution' did not attempt precisely to define the powers of the Crown, and did not even recognize the existence of politicians or parties. It was therefore idle to debate whether George III or Charles James Fox was upholding or subverting the constitution. What mattered was which of the combatants appeared to most reasonable men to be behaving in such a manner as to facilitate the continued operation of that system of mixed government believed to be in the best interests of the parliamentary classes as a whole. In 1746 George II had failed to win support because he was trying to impose unacceptable ministers upon a House of Commons whose patience had already been sorely tried; in 1783–4 George III succeeded because his opponents, not content with having stormed the Closet, appeared intent upon reducing the monarch to a mere figure-head. The average Englishman might have been hard put to define in detail what he meant by a balanced constitution, but he was unprepared to accept a violent swing of the pendulum in the direction of either monarchy or aristocracy. Independent opinion in the Commons or (in 1784) in the electorate used as its yardstick something as vague as a sense of fair play. George II in 1746 and Fox in 1783–4 each pushed his luck too far. It was as simple as that.

As for the kingship of George III there seems little reason to quarrel with Namier's verdict that, to the best of his limited abilities, he carried on the system of government which he had inherited from his predecessors. Yet his initial motives and misconceptions gave a new look to politics during the first three years of his reign, he cannot be acquitted of all blame for the chronic instability of the 1760s, and he created during that decade suspicions and hostilities that were deep-seated and long-lived. Under the early Hanoverians the solidarity of the Old Corps and of the Tories had provided remarkable continuity on both Administration and Opposition benches in the House of Commons. Their gradual disintegration between 1754 and 1763 was merely hastened by the attitudes of the new King, but as a result politics became temporarily more atomized than hitherto—hence the growing tendency of politicians to hunt in packs and the brief high noon of connection. But of the various political groups which emerged, only one—the Rockingham Whigs—was to prove more ephemeral and develop ideas and practices which, regardless of their merits, were to colour political life for the remainder of the eighteenth century, and bequeath to the nineteenth a view of George III's reign that commanded general acceptance until the 1920s and still indeed has its adherents. Who were these Rockinghams, and what did they stand for?

In the eyes of Edmund Burke, only the Rockinghams lived up to his classic definition of party as 'a body of men united for promoting by their joint endeavours the national interest upon some particular principle in which they are all agreed'. By 1782 there may have been at least some truth in his claim, but it was scarcely tenable when he wrote the *Thoughts* in 1770, and still less so at the formation of the first Rockingham Ministry in 1765. Yet it is necessary to go back at least to 1762 in order to understand the Rockinghams since the first and most substantial element in their ranks was Newcastle and his friends—the rump of the Old Corps of Whigs from the previous reign.[1] Of the several original components of the Old Corps, some of the politicians gravitated after 1760 towards the Court and some towards other emerging political connections; and the Court and Treasury Party and many of the earlier Court independents were already assuming their new guise of King's Friends. But a solid rump of Old Corps politicians remained—the relatives and political followers of a loose confederation of great lords, of whom the most notable included Newcastle, Hardwicke, Devonshire, Richmond, Grafton, Albemarle and Ashburnham. To them was added a minority of former Court independents, who under the new stresses of the 1760s, decided that their primary allegiance was to the Old Whig leaders rather than to the King—men such as John White, William Plumer, William Whitmore and Andrew Archer. This point requires emphasizing, for Namier was inclined to under-estimate the extent to which Newcastle's following remained faithful to him after 1762, and John Brooke has argued[2] that it was not Rockingham but Lord North who inherited the personnel and principles of the Pelhams. Newcastle admittedly was bitterly disappointed that so many deserted him, and the Court and Treasury Party and some of the earlier Court independents were indeed eventually inherited by North in 1770. But George III's pin-pricking and tactless treatment of the Old Corps leaders between 1760 and 1763 undoubtedly did something to restore their waning solidarity. One has only to look at the divisions over the Peace Preliminaries in 1762 to realize the transformation that had been effected. Newcastle, Hardwicke

[1] See pp 179–80.
[2] *The Chatham Administration, 1766–68* (1956), p 219.

and Grafton spoke against the Ministry in the Lords, while the minority in the Commons reads like a roll-call of Old Whig families, including four Cavendishes, three Townshends, two Onslows, a Pelham, a Walpole, a Fitzroy. Not since Anne's reign had most of these families opposed an Administration, yet few had suffered directly under the new regime. Their numbers might be relatively small, but they resented the indignities to which George III had subjected the ministers of the previous reign. Their quarrel with the King was personal, not political, but personal loves and personal hatreds were still more important in politics than issues of principle. The King's striking of Devonshire's name from the list of Privy Councillors and his slaughter of the Pelhamite innocents did more to promote the rise of party than the crisis in the American colonies or the radicalism of the metropolis.

In 1765, then, the Rockinghams assumed power with their elder and more numerous wing deeply suspicious of the King and Bute. The younger men, including even Edmund Burke, did not yet share these suspicions, but by the termination of the Ministry twelve months later they had been converted. The key to that conversion was the crisis over the repeal of the Stamp Act, for the Rockinghams were convinced in retrospect that they had been double-crossed by the King and a further chapter was added to the Whig legend of George III. On balance, the evidence suggests that they were wrong, though since approximately one-third of the King's Friends voted against repeal, the reactions of the Rockinghams was understandable. George III had indeed been no more enthusiastic than most of his subjects at the prospect of having to repeal the Stamp Act, but when Lord Harcourt on 30 January 1766 urged him to make his sentiments known in order to thwart repeal, he retorted brusquely that 'he would never influence people in their parliamentary opinion, and he had promised to support his ministers'. His attitude is best summed up in his own memorandum on the subject:

> From the first I thought the modifying of the Stamp Act the wisest and most efficacious manner of proceeding, because any part remaining sufficiently ascertained the right of the Mother Country to tax the colonies; next it would show a desire to redress any grievances. But if the unhappy factions that divide the country would not permit this, in my opinion, equitable plan to be followed, I thought repeal infinitely more eligible than enforcing, which could only tend to widen the breach between this country and America. My language to all ever continued pointing out my wish for modification. On Friday, 6 Feb., Lord Rock. said to me that the two parties meant to push for repeal or enforce. I immediately answered that in that case I was for the former. He asked my permission to say so, which I freely gave. On Monday, 9 Feb., I saw Lord Strange and opened to him my opinion to the following effect, that modification was my constant, but if the

different parties were too wild to come to that, I clearly declared for repeal instead of enforcing. He said he agreed in both cases with me, but said it was currently reported that in all cases I was for repeal. I therefore authorized him to declare to whoever declared that to be my idea, the very words I now acquainted him with.

The origin of the subsequent confusion among the King's Friends is immediately apparent. The Rockinghams were oversimplifying the King's attitude by representing him as favouring repeal; Lord Strange (one of the leading King's Friends) was doing the same by portraying him as against repeal. It is not unreasonable to assume that most of the King's Friends, faced with this dilemma, voted as their consciences demanded. That they were clearly out of touch with their royal master is evident from the fact that Bute and Northington were concurrently making approaches to Bedford and Grenville without the King's knowledge. When as a result Bedford, through the Duke of York, suggested that George III formally declare in favour of modification rather than repeal he received the curt response: 'I do not think it constitutional for the Crown personally to interfere in measures which it has been thought proper to refer to the choice of Parliament.' The King's inner thoughts during these critical weeks for the Rockinghams had already been conveyed in an illuminating private letter to Bute on 10 January:

As to the talents or experience necessary to carry on the business of this nation [he wrote], we, I should imagine, look on the present set with the same eyes. But I own I should think I had great reason to complain if those of my friends that are still in office tried to overturn those I employ; for then they would be acting towards me the very part I have met with from all, that is making disturbance that they might profit by it. That conduct alone could make me think myself at liberty as a man of honour to be for ever detached from them; as to my friends differing from ministers where they think their honour and conscience requires it, that I not only think right, but am of opinion it is their duty to act so . . . I will now open my ideas with regard to this Ministry. Undoubtedly their still imbibing those strange ideas in government, that they adoptedw hilst in Opposition, cannot make me anxious for their continuance; but when I received them into my service, I promised them ample support. This I am as a man of honour obliged and will punctually act up to, for they have not rose in any one term that they made on first accepting; but should they find themselves unable to go on, then they quit me, not I them.

In this letter the King brings out the characteristic eighteenth-century distinction between the wickedness of 'formed Opposition' and the right of every individual to vote according to his conscience on a particular issue. The Rockinghams were correct in believing that George III had refused to order his friends to support repeal; they were wrong in thinking that he had deliberately encouraged them to oppose and undermine the Ministry.

Nonetheless the failure of their first Ministry left the Rockinghams wholly convinced that their earlier suspicions of the King were amply justified. It also left them with an American policy which, if born of internal stresses rather than any basic love of liberty, was to sustain them during the long years of Opposition; and with a deep abiding hatred of the elder Pitt, who had repeatedly refused to come to their aid and had added insult to injury by superseding them. It remained for Burke to weave these several threads into a coherent doctrine and to provide the Rockinghams with principles. In a sense these principles were but the elevation of their personal prejudices. They distrusted Bute, who was the great symbol of royal Influence; they became enthusiasts for economical reform, with Burke's *Thoughts* as their apostolic creed. They disliked George Grenville, who was the staunch advocate of American taxation; they became its prime opponents. They hated Chatham, who was the arch-enemy of party; they became its great apologists. If George III had brought passion into politics, the Rockinghams proved apt pupils. But even if they arrived at their principles in a curiously indirect manner, they came in the end sincerely to embrace those principles, and what they believed themselves to be was politically as important as what they in fact were. The Rockinghams cannot be dismissed as merely one of the many connections of the time. It was here that Burke's contribution was of peculiar importance. He had sufficient vision to realize that no connection on a family or territorial basis could ever hope to win political power. He therefore sought to graft popularity on to connection and thereby form party. The great irony was that in constantly urging the Rockinghams to sustain their support for the Americans, Burke was making them unpopular, not popular; but at least it gave them the appearance of consistency in supporting the liberties of *all* men against the threat implicit in the supposed 'system' of George III.

During their sixteen years of Opposition the Rockinghams did more than merely follow the pattern established in the first half of the century. Firstly, they inverted the earlier theoretical justification for Opposition. Instead of arguing that ministers held the King in thrall and that their sole aim was to rescue him from the clutches of an oligarchical cabal, they claimed that it was the King who held ministers in thrall, and that only the reduction of royal Influence and their own return to power could restore the balance of the constitution. In part this innovation in theory may have been induced by the absence of an adult Prince of Wales around whom the Rockinghams could rally; but it was also necessary to explain the downfall of their own Ministry in 1766 no less than justify an Opposition for which their political ancestry ill-equipped them. Secondly, they broke with the mainstream of past convention by upholding the idea of party, not denouncing it, and by completely abandoning the attitude that 'formed Oppposition' was wicked and irresponsible. They made no secret of the fact that they sought political power, and if and when their moment of triumph came they would impose a Ministry and a political programme upon an unwilling king. Hence the rigorous terms which Rockingham laid down when North invited coalition in 1780, and which Rockingham and the Fox–North coalition respectively forced upon George III in 1782 and 1783. Only thus could they gain revenge for the indignities and supposed treachery of 1762 and 1766. Finally, they accepted Burke's dictum that 'all Opposition is absolutely crippled if it can obtain no kind of support out-of-doors', and sought such support on an unprecedented scale. Occasionally in the first half of the century opponents of Administration had instituted propaganda campaigns in the country—as, for example, over the Excise Bill, the war with Spain and the Jew Bill—and had even flirted temporarily with mob activity in their attempts to unseat ministers or secure the repeal of unpopular legislation. But the Rockinghams were prepared to try to harness forces that had arisen spontaneously in the metropolis or in the country at large, and use them for their own political purposes. Even during their first brief period of political power, merchant support had helped determine their attitude towards America, and in the petitioning movements of both 1769–70 and 1779–80 they were very active. That they were not more successful was due largely to their own inflexibility and conservatism. Support for America might win merchant favour in 1765–6, but by the late seventies it had become, in the eyes of merchants no less than of other Englishmen, akin to disloyalty. Suspicion of becoming the tools of metropolitan radicals shattered the Rockingham alliance with the leaders of the petitioning movement of 1769–70, and although a common ardour for economical reform at first seemed to augur well for co-operation with Wyvill's more conservative movement of 1779–80, few Rockinghams other than Fox and Richmond could stomach the concurrent demand for parliamentary reform, still less the notion of an 'anti-parliament' envisaged by the Yorkshire Association. Much as they desired support out-of-doors, they would accept it only on their own terms, and as these increasingly involved confrontation with the King, a lasting alliance with extra-parliamentary forces was impossible. They did, however, initiate habits of action that were later briefly followed by Fox in organizing opposition to Pitt's Irish commercial propositions, and that were to be fully developed in the more favourable political climate of the nineteenth century.

The Rockinghams, then, had brought a new consistency and a new intensity to Opposition, and made it clear that the overthrow of North must involve the humbling of the King and the reduction of both his Influence and power. Only the continuing disasters and mounting expense of the American war, by forcing a reluctant majority of the House of Commons to desert North, gave them the opportunity to translate their ideas into practice, and their triumph was short-lived. A national crisis enabled both the second Rockingham Ministry and the Fox–North coalition temporarily to dictate to the King in a manner more appropriate to the nineteenth century than to the eighteenth; but the end of the war and the passage of token measures of economical reform cut the ground from under their feet, and the ultimate victory of Pitt and George III terminated the superficial and premature appearance of a two-party system and marked a return to the normal pattern of politics. Yet in the process trends of the future had been at least dimly adumbrated. The failure of Fox to vindicate his doctrine that ultimate authority rested in the Commons may have underlined the continuing importance of the monarchy and the survival of the system of mixed government; but the recourse of Pitt and the King to a general election suggested that the final word might lie with a body which had hitherto not been associated with the power to make or break Ministries or determine policy. Furthermore, the defeat of the coalitionists underscored the Rockinghams' earlier traumatic experiences of 1762 and 1766, and more than ever convinced the Foxite Whigs of the sinister motives and machinations of the King. The Whig legend had reached maturity, and the 'anti-monarchism' of Fox was to colour the remainder of his political life, especially his reaction to the French Revolution. Thus began his long crusade against Pitt, whom he could see only as the instrument of his own humiliation and the agent of royal tyranny. Though superficially the rivalry between Pitt and Fox might seem simply a repetition of that between Walpole and Pulteney fifty years earlier, the assumptions of the two pairs of protagonists were in many ways different. Walpole, when accused of having made himself a 'prime' minister, hotly denied the charge. North, in 1778, had conceded that 'in critical times it is necessary that there should be one directing minister who should plan the whole of the operations of Government', but only in order that he might plead his own inadequacy for the post and seek permission to resign. Pitt was unequivocal when, in 1803, he stated to Melville:

> His sentiments with regard to the absolute necessity there is in the conduct of the affairs of this country, that there should be an avowed and real Minister, possessing the chief weight in the council, and the principal place in the confidence of the King. In that respect there can be no rivality or division of power. That power must rest in the person generally called the First Minister, and that Minister ought . . . to be the person at the head of the finances.

Nor was recognition of the premiership the only index of the emerging conventions of true Cabinet Government. Walpole's attempts to impose a degree of discipline upon his ministerial colleagues had been intermittent and frequently ineffectual; North had hesitatingly adopted the principle of collective responsibility, but only because of his growing fear that if ministers did not hang together they would all hang separately; but Pitt, although prepared to allow free expression of opinion on some issues, had no hesitation in ousting rivals who would not follow his lead. He stood by his conviction that 'if it should come unfortunately to such a radical difference of opinion that no spirit of conciliation or concession can reconcile, the sentiments of the Minister must be allowed and understood to prevail'. When, in 1792, he forced a reluctant George III to dismiss Chancellor Thurlow, he established a landmark in the development of Cabinet solidarity, and by 1806 Castlereagh could ask with apparent surprise: 'Have not the members of the Cabinet always been considered by the country . . . both as individually and collectively responsible for the measures of government?' Nor did Fox suffer from the inhibitions that had prevented Pulteney and his associates from openly acknowledging their manifest practice of 'formed Opposition'. As frustrated ambition and hatred of the King and Pitt drove him to ever wilder extremes, he swore on oath in 1793 that 'there was no address at the moment Pitt could form he would not propose an amendment to, and divide the House upon'. In his view it was clearly the business of the Opposition to oppose, though as long as he lived any conception of 'His Majesty's Opposition' was unthinkable. Finally, Fox and his followers displayed in the 1780s a readiness to develop party organization on an unprecedented scale. In the general elections of 1784 and 1790 they attempted, though with only limited success, to appeal to the country at large in a manner that was distinct from Burke's earlier cultivation of out-of-doors support over particular issues. As yet they could not pretend to anything resembling a party programme, but their organization was centralized under the leadership of the Duke of Portland, with William Adam as their chief political manager; a general party fund and specific election funds were established by annual subscription; election campaigns were conducted from offices in Burlington House, with attention concentrated on those eighty or ninety constituencies where they might hope for success; and every effort was made to find suitable candidates for the available seats. Political clubs were even established in London and in the provinces, and in Parliament the faithful were more than ever before rallied by the party whips. They could not yet rival the Administration in organizational skills, and the futility of their fight against Pitt was bound to bring periodic disillusionment and dislocation of their efforts. Nor, until the French Revolution had decimated their ranks by driving the more conservative of them over to Administration, could they claim that ideological homogeneity that the Rockinghams had enjoyed in the 1770s. But their penchant for organization in the 1780s marked a further, if temporary, divergence from the politics of the past and pointed the way to the future.

One final development of the 1780s requires at least brief mention—the waning of those Country attitudes that for two centuries and more had been evident among the back-benchers in the House of Commons. Though they had been checked to some extent by the disintegration of the Tories after 1760, and by the patriotic rallying of the independents around North during the early years of the American war, they were quick to reappear over such issues as the Middlesex election, Grenville's Controverted Elections Act and the payment of Civil List debts; and the growth of the movements for economical and parliamentary reform gave them a new lease of life. If one takes as a general index of independent opinion the political behaviour of those among the eighty members for English counties who did not have aristocratic connections—and who may be assumed to represent the independent country gentlemen *par excellence*—a substantial majority in every Parliament from 1714 to 1784 maintained an attitude of general opposition to the Government of the day. But with the confirmation of the younger Pitt in power, Administration for the first time could count on more support from them than Opposition. It is a little ironical that at the very time when Fox and his followers were protesting most vehemently at the subservience of Parliament to the King, the most independent element in the Commons at long last showed signs of shedding its inveterate suspicion of executive power. In part this was probably the result of Pitt's commitment to cheap, efficient administration, in part a reaction against the extremism of the Foxites. But whatever the reason, it made more formidable than ever the task of the Opposition, especially when in the aftermath of the French Revolution Foxite views came increasingly to be equated with Jacobinism.

Considering the upsurge and volubility of extra-parliamentary opinion at the time of the dispute over the Middlesex election and during the crucial winter of 1779–80, the violence of the Gordon riots, and the expression of support in the electorate for Pitt and the King in 1784, it is tempting to believe that a new dimension was being added to British political life during the first twenty-five years of George III's reign. Some historians indeed have compared the supposed radicalism of the time to revolutionary activity in France and elsewhere in Europe, and have seen the beginning of a process that, despite a temporary setback during the conservative reaction after 1789, was to gather in momentum until it culminated in the reform movement of 1830–2 and wrought a fundamental change in the nature of Parliament itself. Such a view scarcely seems warranted. On the one hand it overlooks the fact that extra-parliamentary opinion, even if often artificially generated by Opposition politicians, had frequently been expressed in the first half of the century through the normal media of the Press, pamphlets, petitions, addresses and instructions to constituents; on the other hand it attaches to the movements of the sixties and seventies a homogeneity, a genuinely radical motivation, and a continuing influence that they did not possess. From Walpole to the younger Pitt, and from Pulteney to Charles James Fox, there were few prominent politicians who did not find it expedient at one time or another to appeal to the people, by whom they meant the politically active part of the nation or those whom Burke described as 'of adult age, not declining in life, of tolerable leisure for . . . discussions, and of some means of information, more or less, and who are above menial dependence'. But neither before nor after 1760 was the voice of the people meant to be superior to that of the House of Commons save when it suited the purposes of those who were temporarily heeding it. Burke, in his celebrated speech to the electors of Bristol in 1774 vehemently rejected the doctrine 'that a member of Parliament should be a delegate rather than a representative of his constituents', and upheld his right to vote according to his own independent judgment. Charles James Fox, before he began to court popularity out-of-doors, was equally explicit:

> I pay no regard whatever [he said] to the voice of the people; it is our duty to do what is proper, without considering what may be agreeable: their business is to chuse us; it is ours to act constitutionally and to maintain the independence of Parliament.

If his conversion to Opposition and the seeming plight of Lord North led Fox by 1780 to see the House of Commons as 'the most practical and expeditious means of declaring the sense of the people', the popular reaction against him in 1784 brought a return to his original view and a declaration that 'there were circumstances in which the people might err, and under such circumstances it becomes an act of duty to resist them'. Clearly, if these were the opinions of Opposition leaders, there was no new sense of obligation to extra-parliamentary opinion in the late eighteenth century, and the avenues through which it was expressed remained essentially the same as in Walpole's day, even though the volume and frequency of petitions and addresses may significantly have increased and their authors acted more independently of politicians than they had formerly done. Whether such opinion was genuinely radical is more difficult to assess. But despite the mob activities of the 'inferior set'—Wilkes's own description of his followers—of journeymen, apprentices, labourers, servants, small employers and petty tradesmen who clamoured for 'Wilkes and Liberty' in the 1760s and led the rioters of 1780 in violence directed as much against the wealthy as against Roman Catholics, the motives of the more prominent metropolitan leaders in the earlier movement were not very different from those of orthodox Country members of Parliament or from those of the independent freeholders who later flocked to Wyvill's standard. The great majority of those who advocated reform sought merely to restore the traditional independence of the House of Commons, not radically alter its composition. Economical and parliamentary reform were but different methods by which this objective might be achieved. The former aimed at reducing the *dependent* element in the House, and of course at curtailing Government expenditure; the latter sought to increase the *independent* element by abolishing at least a few close boroughs and increasing the representation of London and the counties. But the urge to achieve even these limited aims was born in the sixties of temporary economic depression, political instability, and the chicanery of Wilkes; and in the seventies of the national frustration accompanying the American war and the unacceptability of the parliamentary Opposition as an alternative Government. The modest measures of the second Rockingham Ministry were sufficient to quell the demand for parliamentary no less than economical reform, and by the mid-eighties it was difficult to believe that the perfection of the constitution had ever been challenged. The birth of a true radicalism had as its prerequisite a fundamental shift in the balance of economic power, which the Industrial Revolution—still in its infancy in 1780—alone could provide; and its ideological content was to be supplied, not by a rabble-rousing demagogue such as John Wilkes or a conservative parson such as Christopher Wyvill, but by revolutionaries across the Channel. Of course the radicals of the early nineteenth century cast a benevolent and grateful glance backwards to their supposed forbears, just as at least some of the men of the sixties and seventies acknowledged the commonwealthmen of the seventeenth century as their spiritual ancestors. At a literary level the radical tradition did indeed survive; in the world of practical politics there was little continuity. Before 1789 Pitt and Fox had more in common than either would have been prepared to admit, and the House of Commons still represented the major interests that were considered worthy of representation. Only in times of national crisis or of acute political instability were the voice of Parliament and the voice of the people likely to diverge.

After 1789 more fundamental changes in the pattern of politics began to appear, but they were both delayed and obscured by pre-occupation with the long struggle against France, and can be seen in perspective only from a vantage point well beyond 1815. Nor indeed has there been sufficient research into this much neglected period of English history to enable generalizations to be made with any real conviction. What does appear certain is that there was a much more marked and permanent decline in monarchical power than can legitimately be attributed to the era of the first two Georges. In part, of course, this was the natural corollary of George III's advancing years and recurrent breakdowns, culminating in 1810 in his permanent incapacity and the installation of the futile Prince of Wales as Regent; in part it was the inevitable outcome of the vastly increased activities and scope of government, which would have made it difficult for a younger, healthier and abler monarch than George III to keep sufficient grasp of detail to make his continued headship of the executive truly effective. Concurrently, the cumulative effects of economical and administrative reform were drastically if undramatically curtailing royal Influence. In 1780 there had still been some 180 office-holders in the House of Commons; by the 1820s there were only sixty or seventy. It seems likely that the number of boroughs under government control was also shrinking, those in private hands increasing, and significant borough empires—comparable only to that of Newcastle in mid-century—beginning to emerge. As the king receded from the forefront of the political stage, so the ranks of the Court and Treasury Party contracted, until many ministers protested that the resources of patronage had become insufficient for the maintenance of stable government. In time, conflicting economic interest and conflicting ideologies would breed at least temporary harmony within the ranks of each of the two main sets of opposing politicians and, as the Court and Treasury Party finally disappeared, enable them to reach down and, through the medium of Party, absorb the independents. Of the three basic types of member in the eighteenth-century House of Commons, only the politicians would survive; and when party discipline and organization became sufficiently developed they would be able to dictate to the sovereign as a matter of course—even if at the cost of acknowledging a degree of responsibility to a much-enlarged electorate that would have horrified both Burke and Fox. But in 1789, or indeed in 1815, all this lay in the future. Meanwhile the stimulus to the development of Party—considerable though it was as long as Pitt and Fox still lived—was checked by continuing divisions within the ranks of the politicians, the various factions between 1806 and 1815 being as numerous and as irreconcilable as they had been in the 1760s. It was checked too by the refusal of most independents to surrender to the demands of faction, and by their readiness to rally around any Government that was prepared to dedicate itself to the continuation of the struggle against Napoleon. The times did not favour Opposition, especially Opposition that could never quite shake off the reputation for revolutionary idealism that Fox had bequeathed to it, and that—like the Rockinghams thirty years earlier—could scarcely criticize the conduct of the war without appearing unpatriotic. The emergence of true parties must await the coming of peace, and even then polarization would be only partial and temporary.

Equally, if not more, significant for the future were developments outside Parliament, where industrialization and urbanization were leaving in their wake a host of unsolved political and social problems. Though the times were unpropitious to parliamentary reform, the industrial middle classes were already demanding a share in political power more commensurate with their growing economic power, and a working-class consciousness was beginning to emerge that at least in part saw the reform of Parliament as the essential pre-requisite to the achievement of even a modest degree of social justice. A genuine radicalism was emerging, and the suppression of the radical societies of the early 1790s could not conceal the growing dissatisfaction. The spread of literacy and the growth of the Press were bringing political awareness to a much greater audience than could be encompassed by Burke's conception of 'the people'. The landed aristocracy, who for so long had dominated English politics, would soon have to concede a share of power to the industrial middle classes, if only temporarily to preserve their own supremacy and delay the recognition of working-class demands. Nor was reform of Parliament the only issue in uneasy abeyance until the coming of peace. The years ahead would see not only the first Reform Act, but the repeal of the Test and Corporation Acts, Catholic Emancipation, and many other less dramatic but no less fundamental changes. Between 1789 and 1815 the normal pattern of eighteenth-century politics was continued only on sufferance and in increasingly attenuated form; already it contained within itself the seeds of its own destruction.

13

ECONOMIC AND SOCIAL DEVELOPMENT

ANY survey of economic and social history during the reign of George III must focus primarily upon the Industrial Revolution—its origins, its nature and its impact. Purists may of course argue that the use of 'revolution', with its implications of sudden, dramatic change and even discontinuity, is inappropriate to the context of economic growth; and they can point to the fact that historians cannot agree even on an approximate starting-point—1540, 1660, 1740, 1750 and 1780 have all been seen as significant dates. There has been much recent emphasis, particularly from historians of growth, on the need for precise definition, but none has been forthcoming. Yet the term 'industrial revolution' has been so universally accepted, and its more obvious characteristics so generally recognized, that it seems pedantic to quibble about its use. We may agree with Peter Mathias that 'the British economy in 1850 had become structurally more different compared with 1750 than 1750 was with 1650 or compared with structural changes coming in any previous century';[1] and with Max Hartwell that the 'essential character of the industrial revolution was the sustained increase in the rate of growth of total and *per capita* output at a rate which was revolutionary compared with what went before'.[2] Concentration upon statistics alone would suggest that W. W. Rostow's point of 'take-off into self-sustained growth' is not discernible before the 1780s, when total annual output is believed to have jumped to a level of nearly 2 per cent, output per head to almost 1 per cent, and both rates were maintained or exceeded thereafter. These increases to levels unknown in the pre-industrial world did not of course appear as if by magic. Phyllis Deane and W. A. Cole have detected a marked acceleration in the economy in the 1740s, which might have proved permanent but for the effects of the Seven Years' War, the post-war depression of the 1760s,

---

[1] P. Mathias, *The First Industrial Nation* (1969), p 2.
[2] R. M. Hartwell (ed.), *The Causes of the Industrial Revolution in England* (1967), p 8.

and the even more disruptive impact of the war with America. Furthermore, the pre-conditions for the industrial revolution were being established long before 1740, or indeed before the opening of the eighteenth century. There is much strength in Charles Wilson's argument that from 1660 'commercial enterprise, often closely allied with state power and aided by legislation and military or naval force, was changing the face of the old agrarian customary economy'.[1] This serves to remind us that a 'revolution' in commerce had taken place and one in agriculture had begun before George III ever came to the throne, and that both were prerequisites (though by no means the only ones) for the even more spectacular developments in industry.

But preoccupation with economic growth and quantification, valuable though it has been in encouraging the isolation and intensive study of the many relevant variables, has not so far produced any generally accepted interpretation, and in the process seems often to have been in danger of dehumanizing what was essentially a transformation of society no less than of economy. The earliest writers on the industrial revolution were undoubtedly naïve and subjective in seeing it as a cataclysmic change brought about largely by technological advance and the advent of *laissez-faire*, yet as social historians they at least showed an awareness that this was a vital chapter in the history of man. Economic analysis, with its emphasis on input, output, capital accumulation, investment and market expansion, can enrich our appreciation of the complexity of economic growth, but at the risk of ignoring the many intangibles in human conduct that can thwart the predictions of modern economists no less than they can invalidate their reconstructions of the past. It can lead Max Hartwell to one of the most succinct statements yet made in this controversial field:

> The turning point came in the eighties, when the mounting pressure of demand, both real and potential, created pressures on industry to further increase productivity. This resulted in a series of notable breakthroughs which so reduced the prices of industrial goods that not only was domestic demand greatly increased but English goods were cheap enough also to invade, even over tariff and transport barriers, the mass market of Europe. The industrial revolution had begun.

This is true enough, but to capture the many-faceted character of the movement one cannot do better than go back to the opening paragraphs of T. S. Ashton's classic essay which, because they combine the insight

---

[1] C. Wilson, *England's Apprenticeship, 1603–1763* (1965), p x.
[2] Hartwell, *op cit*, p 28.

of the economist with the humanity and broad perspective of the great historian, deserve quotation in full:[1]

> In the short span of years between the accession of George III and that of his son, William IV, the face of England changed. Areas that for centuries had been cultivated as open fields, or had lain untended as common pasture, were hedged or fenced; hamlets grew into populous towns; and chimney stacks rose to dwarf the ancient spires. Highroads were made—straighter, stronger, and wider than those evil communications that had corrupted the good manners of travellers in the days of Defoe. The North and Irish Seas, and the navigable reaches of the Mersey, Ouse, Trent, Severn, Thames, Forth and Clyde were joined together by threads of still water. In the North the first iron rails were laid down for the new locomotives, and steam packets began to ply on the estuaries and the narrow seas.
>
> Parallel changes took place in the structure of society. The number of people increased vastly, and the proportion of children and young people probably rose. The growth of new communities shifted the balance of population from the South and East to the North and Midlands; enterprising Scots headed a procession the end of which is not yet in sight; and a flood of unskilled, but vigorous, Irish poured in, not without effect on the health and ways of life of Englishmen. Men and women born and bred in the countryside came to live crowded together, earning their bread, no longer as families or groups of neighbours, but as units in the labour force of factories; work grew to be more specialized; new forms of skill were developed, and some old forms lost. Labour became more mobile, and higher standards of comfort were offered to those able and willing to move to centres of opportunity.
>
> At the same time fresh sources of raw materials were exploited, new markets were opened, and new methods of trade devised. Capital increased in volume and fluidity; the currency was set on a gold base; a banking system came into being. Many old privileges and monopolies were swept away, and legislative impediments to enterprise removed. The State came to play a less active, the individual and the voluntary association a more active, part in affairs. Ideas of innovation and progress undermined traditional sanctions: men began to look forward, rather than backward, and their thoughts as to the nature and purpose of social life were transformed.

The explanations of this remarkable phenomenon have been many and varied, with the principal emphasis being placed at one time on innovations and organization, and at others on increased demand (whether at home or abroad), rising population, greater availability and mobility of capital, agricultural improvement, the growth of *laissez-faire*, and the role of Protestant Dissent. The futility of seeking a single cause is now generally conceded, and it may well be that—as with so many fields of human endeavour—a completely satisfying explanation will never be found. The best one can do is outline the concatenation of

---

[1] *The Industrial Revolution* (1948), pp 1–2.

favourable circumstances which made possible a dramatic and permanent upswing in industrial output, attempt to identify the period at which that acceleration assumed proportions that in some sense could be called revolutionary, and assess the impact upon both the economy and contemporary society.

While conceding the essential continuity of economic development, and accepting the argument of Deane and Cole that industrial growth in the eighteenth century came in two main spurts (of which the first appeared roughly in 1745–60), there seems little that could be justifiably called 'revolutionary' before about 1780. Though Rostow's pre-conditions for take-off may have been partly met during the earlier period, and his required rise in the rate of productive investment from 5 to 10 per cent of the national income may not have come until after 1815, it is clear that from about 1780 onwards England was entering a new phase of industrial expansion that was both quantitatively and qualitatively distinct from any earlier achievement. It was then that activity in certain 'leading sectors', notably cotton and iron production and canal construction, reached unprecedented levels; that Cort's puddling and rolling processes 'revolutionized' the iron industry; and that the adaptation of Watt's engine to rotary motion added a new dimension to steam power. Large-scale factory organization became a substantial and permanent feature of industrial life, the relationship between employers and workers assumed a new guise, and the manifold problems of industrial society began to appear. Important as earlier developments may have been, they were dwarfed in significance by the changes after 1780, and not even the mammoth struggle against France could provide the disruption that had characterized the sixties and seventies. By 1815—indeed by 1830—England was still only partially urbanized and partially industrialized, but the contrast with 1780 was so striking that the scope and impact of the intervening changes were plain for all to see.

Perhaps the most obvious starting-point in the chain of causation is the population explosion of the late eigtheenth and early nineteenth centuries. As the examples of Ireland, India and China were later to show, an increase in population does not necessarily induce industrialization, or indeed any other form of economic expansion, though such expansion seldom takes place without prior population growth. In eighteenth-century England the connection was clear-cut, in that rising population both increased the demand for manufactured goods and provided an adequate labour force for producing them; though whether the demand for labour promoted population growth or industrialization was a response to increased numbers is uncertain. Cause and effect were probably inextricably interwoven. At all events, the stagnation believed to be characteristic of the earlier half of the century gave way to a rise in population of 7–9 per cent per decade from 1760 to 1800, and 10–15 per cent throughout the nineteenth century—with the peak of the upsurge coming in the 1820s and 1830s. By 1815 the population of England and Wales, estimated at approximately six and a half million in 1760, had leapt to some eleven million, and between 1760 and 1830 it more than doubled. But this spectacular rise was not uniform throughout the country. London, aided in the last decades by the beginning of a steep decline in its hitherto formidable death-rate, kept pace with the general increase and, together with the home counties, continued to attract migration from surrounding districts. But more impressive were the doubling of Birmingham's population between 1760 and 1800, and the trebling of those of Manchester and Liverpool. Already, between 1700 and 1750, the counties where industrialization was concentrated (Lancashire, Warwickshire, Staffordshire and the West Riding of Yorkshire) had grown more rapidly than elsewhere, and the acceleration of this growth after 1760 appears to have been due to natural increase in them and their immediate neighbours rather than to migration from more distant parts of the country. It is uncertain whether the rapid and sustained rise in population was due to a decline in the death-rate, an increase in the birth-rate or both; nor is it clear to what extent these changes were due to economic developments. Originally it was thought that improved medical facilities had played a major role by reducing the death-rate, and it is still acknowledged that the decline in epidemics after mid-century and (at least among the well-to-do) the introduction of vaccination were of considerable consequence. But medical historians have cast serious doubts upon the supposed improvements in health, emphasizing the lack of new drugs, the inadequacies of surgery and the deplorable conditions in hospitals, which may well have increased rather than diminished mortality. Great importance has come to be attached to the rising birth-rate which, outside London and especially in the north-west, may have been more marked than the limited evidence of parish registers suggests. Here economic factors loom large. Improved production in agriculture brought more and better food, and greater prosperity raised standards of housing and clothing. Earlier marriages and larger families were encouraged, especially by the increasing demand for child labour. It is also likely that these developments contributed more than medical factors to the declining death-rate. But whatever the causes of the rise in population, it provided an abundance of relatively cheap labour, for although money wages rose by about 25 per cent in the last third of the century, the cost-of-living also increased—from the 1790s faster than wages. It also intensified demand and held out the prospect of a mass market to those industries which had already begun significantly to expand in the first half of the century; and it encouraged investment in transport, housing, and urban improvements of every kind. Against the essential background of modest expansion from 1714 to 1745, and a sharp upswing in the economy from 1745 to 1760, the population explosion of the second half of the century helped to produce the greatly accelerated growth of the years after 1780.

The major role of agriculture was to feed the rapidly rising population, though landlords also continued to invest in industry and transport and the development of country banking facilitated the transfer of landed profits from the south and east for utilization in the industries of the north and Midlands. Marx's contention that enclosures wrought rural depopulation and provided manufacturers with an exploitable industrial proletariat is no longer tenable, though industry certainly provided jobs for many who might otherwise have faced starvation, and the interaction between industry and agriculture (further illustrated, for example, by the demand of the former for secondary agricultural products such as wool, tallow and hides) remained intimate and important. It is perhaps even more misleading to speak of a 'revolution' in agriculture than it is in industry, especially if one is dealing exclusively with the decades after 1760. Improvements in farming had been in evidence ever since the late middle ages, and the intensification of certain activities in the late eighteenth and early nineteenth centuries would scarcely have been possible without the widespread developments of the century before the accession of George III. Nor do we find much evidence of the application of science and technology to agriculture. Wooden tools persisted into the nineteenth century, the iron plough only gradually replaced the wooden one, Tull's seed drills and horse-drawn hoes were still little used, and Andrew Meikle's threshing machine of the 1780s was almost the only major improvement in the primitive methods of mowing and reaping—though the intermittent shortages of agricultural labour during the long wars with France tended for the first time to turn men's minds towards the employment of labour-saving machinery in farming. Interest in stock-breeding was intensified by the growing demand for meat, and the work of Bakewell and others in the first half of the century found its counterparts in that of John Ellman and the Colling brothers after 1780. But if anything was 'revolutionary' it was the dramatic increase in agricultural output. Corn production, which had risen little more than 15 per cent between 1700 and 1760, increased by 50 per cent between then and 1815; and though that of beef and dairy produce rose more slowly, the increase in the number of sheep was even greater. Output per head may have changed relatively little, but the over-all growth was sufficient in normal times to keep pace with the rise in population and thereby avoid the disaster that was later to overtake Ireland and many modern underdeveloped nations. Whereas adversity had been the spur to improvement in the first half of the century, rising demand and rising prices stimulated change after 1760. This time it was the turn of the heavier lands to progress and the chief instrument of improvement was that of enclosure, especially in the north, Wales, and part of the Midlands. Here the aim was not to save labour—indeed the size of the agricultural labour force actually rose—but to increase the yield per acre and the area under cultivation. Between 1760 and 1815 over 7,000,000 acres were enclosed by act alone—an average of more than 125,000 acres per year compared to the mere 7,300 from 1714 to 1760. Of the total land enclosed, approximately 1,500,000 acres had hitherto been waste and commons, and the most intensive activity was during 1760–75 and 1793–1815, both periods of rising agricultural prices. Only during the late seventies and mid-eighties did production appear temporarily to catch up with demand; otherwise corn prices rose more sharply than those of any other goods. Wheat, which had averaged some thirty to thirty-five shillings a quarter in the 1750s, reached fifty shillings by the early seventies, seventy-five to eighty shillings in the dearth years of 1795–6, 113–19 shillings in 1800–1, and 95–126 shillings in 1810–13. Indeed, between 1793 and 1815 there were only seven years when the price of wheat fell below seventy shillings, and that of barley and oats was similarly buoyant. There were of course substantial concurrent rises in rents and wages, but the accompanying time-lags ensured that the farming community enjoyed unprecedented prosperity—more than sufficient to offset the rising poor rates and high war taxation of the years after 1793, when land was in great demand and enclosures at their peak. Meanwhile England ceased to be an exporter of grain. Before 1793 years of plenty had seen net exports, those of dearth net imports; after that date imports rarely fell below 300,000 quarters, a year, and in times of scarcity could pass the million mark. But neither imports nor exports constituted more than a tiny fraction of total home consumption, which by 1815 exceeded 25,000,000 quarters. With remarkable success English agriculture had answered the challenge of the population explosion, and its continuing importance in the national economy is evidenced by the fact that even by 1815 it employed approximately one-third of the country's labour force and produced a similar proportion of the national income.

The initiative in expansion came chiefly from the greater landlords, in quest of higher rents. In some cases these rose as much as three times during the war years, and on average probably doubled—more than enough to counterbalance a wage increase that reached perhaps 75 per cent in the more prosperous areas and was frequently much lower. But most sections of the landed interest engaged in improvement, and many smaller farmers who would have been hard put to survive the depression of the thirties and forties, were able to profit from booming prices and even extend their holdings. Indeed, the decline in the number of small farmers seems to have been temporarily halted during these years, while the larger ones began to develop a certain solidarity and looked—unavailingly, as it turned out—to the Board of Agriculture, founded in 1793 under the chairmanship of Sir John Sinclair, to champion their interests. By 1815 the landed interest, hit badly by the falling prices of the previous two years, secured the passage of a new Corn Law which was much more protective than most of the earlier ones, though it had been foreshadowed by those of 1791 and 1804, which had been rendered largely inoperative by war shortages—not that war had impeded the advance of agriculture or in itself produced conditions of scarcity, which were chiefly the product of bad harvests combined with general inflation. Even Napoleon's blockade achieved little, and he was prepared at times to connive at the export of grain to England to relieve the worst effects of the glut in France. Finally, as far as labour was concerned, the demands of agriculture rose, though not enough to absorb the natural increase in rural population. In industrial counties the surplus was often quickly taken up, and at certain times during the war the better wages and opportunities in industry actually produced a dearth of agricultural labour. But in other areas, especially in the south and east, alternative employment was simply not available, and the ranks of the unemployed were swollen to a point where the intervention of the local authorities became essential.

The demand for the principal products of industry came from both home and abroad, but it is only the latter which, through the extant trade statistics, lends itself to even approximate quantification. Because of the demonstrable and dramatic increase after 1780 in the volume of foreign trade, it is tempting to see overseas demand as the dominant factor in the expansion of industry, especially since it also supplied considerable capital for investment. But although manufactures constituted perhaps 85 per cent of all domestic exports, only about one-third of Britain's industrial output went abroad. Home demand, even if it defies measurement, was clearly important. Nonetheless the trade figures both provide the best available index for the growth of the so-called 'export' industries, and give some idea of their expansion relative to one another. In general, after the boom of 1745–60, the sixties and seventies—embracing the early disputes and eventual war with the American colonies—were rather sluggish, and significant growth was not resumed until after 1780. Thereafter not even the French wars could stem the advance, and by the end of the century the annual increase in the volume of trade was some two and a half times that at the beginning. Imports, which had annually averaged £6,200,000 from 1714–23, and £10,700,000 from 1761–70, reached £30,000,000 by 1806–15; the figures for domestic exports during the same periods were respectively £4,800,000, £10,000,000 and £30,000,000; and for re-exports, £2,400,000, £4,500,000 and £70,500,000. Between the sixties and the last decade of the French wars imports had thus risen by 180 per cent, domestic exports by 200 per cent, re-exports by 133 per cent, and total trade by 180 per cent; and virtually all of these increases were concentrated in the decades after 1780. This illustrates beyond all doubt the importance of overseas trade in providing expanding markets and sources of raw materials, but equally significant were the varying fortunes of individual industries and the changes in geographical distribution. Among the textiles the value of woollen and worsted exports showed relatively little change, and by the end of the period had reverted to the £5,500,000 of the 1760s; silk actually dropped in value from £210,000 to £189,000; linen rose from £455,000 to £1,036,000, but had lost some of the momentum which it had shown in the first half of the century; cotton—the principal leading sector of the industrial revolution—showed a phenomenal leap from £227,000 to £15,840,000, a rise of nearly 7000 per cent. Otherwise, iron and steel exports more than doubled—from £594,000 to £1,304,000; those of coal showed a similar increase from £269,000 to £502,000; and the non-ferrous metals and manufactures rose modestly from £581,000 to £749,000. Nothing more vividly demonstrates that cotton and the industrial revolution were virtually synonymous, or that the domestic export trade was still relatively narrowly based upon a few commodities—cotton, wool, linen and metals. After four centuries wool had lost its dominant position, though it was still at least four times more important than any other export but cotton.

As far as the markets for exports and re-exports were concerned, the developments between the 1760s and 1806–15 confirmed the trends of the first half of the century. Europe continued as Britain's best customer but only by a small margin. The average value of exports to the

Continent increased from £8,200,000 to £19,900,000 (or 140 per cent), but its share of the total dropped further from 57 per cent to 49 per cent. Exports to the New World (defined as Canada, the mainland colonies and later the United States, the British and foreign West Indies, and Latin America) leapt from £3,400,000 to £17,100,000—a rise of 400 per cent—and by 1815 comprised 42 per cent of the total. Asia and Africa both showed modest increases. As a source of imports into Britain Europe had shown a similar decline. The annual average of £4,800,000 in the 1760s had risen by 1806–15 by only 65 per cent to £7,900,000; that for the New World by 270 per cent, from £3,900,000 to £14,400,000, a rise that of course reflected the spectacular increase in the import of raw cotton (from £250,000 in the sixties to £3,000,000 in 1806–15) and the burgeoning of re-exports. The latter also brought an increase in Asian imports from £1,500,000 to £4,800,000—a rise of 220 per cent.

From this maze of figures clearly emerges the growing importance of the colonial empire, the United States and the foreign possessions in the New World—both as sources of raw materials and as markets for manufactures. The over-all picture may somewhat exaggerate the expansion of the decades after 1780, for it tends to neglect the earlier growth of 1745–60 and appears in bold contrast to the stagnation and even decline of the sixties and seventies. According to Deane and Cole, the annual increase in the volume of net imports and domestic exports between 1700 and 1745 was little more than 0·5 per cent; between 1745 and 1760 it reached almost 4 per cent; and after 1780 it rose to 5 per cent and more. On the basis of these figures alone a case could be made for dating the industrial revolution from the mid-forties, and regarding the sixties and seventies as a temporary interruption. But the triumph of King Cotton and the abundance of supporting evidence from other quarters suggests that the expansion of 1745–60 was premature and that a sustained increase in output was not possible before the 1780s.

There is no comparable way of measuring the importance of home demand in the expanding export industries, but the excise series gives some indication of the order of rising consumption in the home ones. These show a rise of 190 per cent in paper production, 120 per cent in soap, 115 per cent in spirits, 75 per cent in candles, 50 per cent in beer, and 33 per cent in glass—all during a period when the population increased by no more than 70 per cent. Whether or not the apparent rise in reading, cleanliness and consumption of alcohol was matched by comparable demands for more food, better clothing, metal goods and pottery is uncertain but highly probable. From the fragmentary statistical evidence it would appear that between 1760 and 1793, at least in the industrial counties, real wages increased, and there are many contemporary references to greater consumption of wheaten bread, tea and sugar. But the demand from the working classes was severely curbed during the war years, when—except among the agricultural labourers—real wages tended to fall, food prices were often abnormally high, and there was a decided shift in distribution of income away from the wage earners. This suggests that middle- and upper-class demand, important throughout the century except perhaps during the agricultural depression of 1730–50, assumed even greater significance during the Revolutionary and Napoleonic wars, when the landed classes were at their most prosperous and both merchants and manufacturers were increasing in wealth. If one looks at the fluctuations in demand over the century as a whole, it might seem that from 1714 to 1745 it came from increasing prosperity in the north coupled with a modest expansion in overseas trade; from 1745 to 1760 real wages levelled off and the export market assumed the major significance; from 1760 to 1780 the stagnation of foreign trade was counterbalanced by the resumption of the rise in real wages; and from 1780 to 1815 the demand was provided partly by the upsurge in overseas commerce, partly (until 1793) by further wage increases, and partly (during the wars) by greater upper- and middle-class prosperity and the phenomenal increase in Government expenditure. One way and another there was sufficient demand to stimulate the earlier burst of industrial activity and, after 1780, to encourage an unprecedented acceleration.

A growing labour force and increased demand were unlikely to promote economic expansion unless there were sufficient capital to finance it. Here one must distinguish between the fixed capital needed for buildings and machinery, which could be substantial and involved long-term borrowing, and the variable capital required to cover such costs as raw materials, current stocks and credit to customers. As long as industry remained primarily labour-intensive and on a domestic basis, as was predominantly so until the 1780s with textiles and with the final product side of the metals, fixed capital was relatively unimportant, and the modest demands for variable capital could be met from the resources of local bankers or, more commonly, by mercantile credit. Spinning wheels, hand looms, knitting frames and nailing anvils were all inexpensive, and the cottage and forge remained the characteristic small units of production. Even Kay's flying shuttle and Hargreaves's spinning jenny could be used within the existing domestic system. Apart from the naval dockyards, which required by far the greatest concentration of labour and capital, only the extractive side of the metal industry at first needed much in the way of fixed investment, and its need increased as technological advances encouraged concentration around the principal coalfields and the integration of hitherto separately located processes. The earlier iron works, such as those of Abraham Darby at Coalbrookdale and of the Walker brothers near Sheffield, might be established with as little as a few hundred, or at most a few thousand, pounds; but their successful expansion required much more. Extensive capital was also needed by men with interests in many different facets of the iron industry, like the formidable Ambrose Crowley and a host of lesser men involved in copper, lead and tin. After the invention of Arkwright's water-frame in 1769 and Crompton's mule in 1779, the spinning side of textiles had to face similar problems, especially in cotton; and the earliest mills seem to have required an initial outlay of some £15,000. In the earlier part of the century the proportion of fixed capital in most industries was probably as little as 5–10 per cent of the total need; after 1780 it may in some cases have been as much as 50 per cent.

Substantial savings were available for investment in the eighteenth century, as the riotous speculation of the South Sea Bubble had early demonstrated. From mid-century onward, revenue from land rose steadily and, from the 1790s, dramatically; the profits of commerce especially from the trans-Atlantic trade, expanded rapidly in the forties and fifties and again after 1780; and the drain of wealth from India alone between 1783 and 1792 has been calculated at more than £17,000,000. But industry was excluded by the Bubble Act from joint-stock enterprise, and businesses had therefore to be conducted on an individual, family or partnership basis. In seeking capital, industrialists had many rivals, and in the early stages of growth their competitive position was not very strong. Land was traditionally the most popular and respectable form of investment, though the drying-up of the land market in the course of the century greatly limited the opportunities for new investors. Nonetheless, great sums were spent on agricultural improvement, especially on enclosures, and the greater availability of mortgages at relatively low interest rates consumed much capital. Transport, whether in the form of improved river navigation, canals or turnpike roads, was an essential concomitant of industrialization, but competed with it in the capital market, as did housing and the various other forms of social expenditure connected with growing urbanization. Savings were also squandered in travel, notably on the Grand Tour, and on many different kinds of conspicuous consumption. But since the great eras in the building of stately homes were concentrated in the early eighteenth and early nineteenth centuries, the intervening decades must have released capital for investment elsewhere. The greatest demand for money came of course from the Government and its need to finance war on an unprecedented scale. The national debt, which had reached £132,600,000 by the end of the Seven Years' War in 1763, rose to £231,800,000 by 1783, and during the long wars with France between 1793 and 1815 leapt from £242,900,000 to £744,900,000. Moreover, some two-thirds of the debt had been in Dutch hands for most of the century, but this proportion was drastically reduced after 1783 and the British capital to replace it was being sought at the time when industrial demands were reaching new levels. The total expenditure of over £1,000,000,000 on war alone between 1793 and 1815 could scarcely have been achieved without severely limiting the funds that might otherwise have been available for industrial expansion, though the most desperate shortage appears to have been in those areas of social expenditure which were essential for mitigating the harmful effects of over-rapid industrialization and urbanization.

Despite these competing demands, the leaders of industry did not complain at being hampered by shortage of capital, though in more favourable circumstances the rate of expansion may have been even greater than it was. Most businesses began on a relatively small scale, relied much upon short-term credit, and financed expansion by ploughing back profits. When Darby's merchant partners from Bristol helped to finance his iron-works they were setting a pattern that was to be widely followed, and commercial profits seem the most likely single source of early industrial investment. Landed profits were also highly relevant to the early stages of the metal industry, where individual landowners played a major role in developing mineral resources on their properties, though later they tended to lease out the rights. The precise sources of fixed capital in the era of rapid expansion remain somewhat obscure, especially since banks were notoriously averse to long-term lending; though short-term loans could often be indefinitely extended and since some £20,000,000 is said to have been invested in building and machinery in the cotton and metal industries by the opening of the nineteenth century it seems clear that the problem was far from insoluble. The low prevailing rates of interest, accorded great significance by Ashton, may have been less important than he thought. The usury laws imposed an upper limit of 5 per cent except for Government stocks; this level was rarely reached save in time of war, in the middle decades of the century the rate was frequently as low as 3½ per cent; and credit was generally cheap in the eighties and early nineties. But for most industries, in contrast to building, transport and enclosures, the cost of credit was not a major part of annual expenditure, and marginal movements in the rates were therefore of little consequence. Perhaps the chief significance of the low rates was the indication that capital was readily available.

One can be more explicit about the supply of variable capital, where mobility was as important as general availability. Here the role of banking assumed ever great importance, though it was never perhaps quite as vital to industry as it was to other contemporary forms of economic expansion. The Bank of England was of course not directly concerned with the needs of industry, but confined its activities to the issue of notes, government business, and the provision of the usual facilities for the great trading companies and the more substantial London merchants; though as other forms of banking proliferated and the whole sprawling edifice became more vulnerable to financial panic, the Bank became generally important as a lender of last resort and as the anchor of the entire system. Of the London private banks, the West End ones, such as Coutts's and Hoare's, dealt almost exclusively with the landed aristocracy and the wealthier gentry, but those in the City (whose number increased from thirty to sixty in the second half of the century) provided direct services to the merchant and industrial community by discounting bills of exchange and advancing short-term credit. After 1770 their influence became still more important as they turned increasingly to acting as agents for the growing army of country banks, thus greatly facilitating the flow of bills of exchange between London and the provinces. But these country banks were most directly involved with industry, and their growth in number from a mere twelve in 1750 to perhaps seven hundred by 1815 is an impressive index of the economic expansion in the wake of which they flourished and which they in turn stimulated. Most country bankers were primarily engaged in other activities. Some were clothiers, some iron-masters, some mine-owners, some brewers, some merchants, some tax-receivers, some solicitors and some mere cattle drovers. But all had accumulated savings and sought profit by lending them to those in need. They discounted bills of exchange, supplied bills that could be discounted by their London agents, created currency, extended credit, and came gradually to act as deposit bankers. Their position could be highly vulnerable, and at times of financial crisis many went bankrupt. Most therefore were neither willing nor able to advance long-term credit, and since nearly all of them confined their activity to a single locality, they were little able to cope with transfers of bills, credit or money between the provinces. It was to provide greater mobility of capital and credit that the bill-brokers were born, and by the early nineteenth century they were playing a dominant role in facilitating the flow between agriculture and industry, especially in making available the landed profits of East Anglia and the south-west for investment in the industrial concerns of the Midlands and north. With the aid of this complex and often fragile mechanism a significant proportion of the nation's wealth—perhaps by 1815 as much as 7 per cent—was being channelled into industry.

For maximum utilization of the resources of capital, labour and raw materials, major advances in technology and organization were essential to clear bottle-necks that would otherwise have impeded advance. Here perhaps one comes closest to the traditional picture of the industrial revolution, though its lines were less clear-cut than was once believed and, as in agriculture, some of its former great figures have shrunk in stature. Nevertheless, improved machinery, the discovery of new sources of power, the growth of factory organization on a large scale, and the increasing tendency towards concentration of industrial processes were all vital ingredients of expansion. It was the cotton industry that provided the most spectacular changes, but the technological impact was first felt in the extractive side of the metals. By the beginning of the eighteenth century the problem of smelting lead, copper and tin with coal had already been solved, and most of the reverberatory furnaces were gradually moving from the main sources of ore in Anglesey, Cornwall, Derbyshire and North Wales to the coalfields of South Wales and the Midlands. After 1760 the spread of Darby's process for producing pig-iron by smelting ore with coke similarly freed the blast furances from their dependence on the woodlands for fuel. But even after the furnace owners began to re-locate themselves on the coalfields, the continued use of charcoal for converting pig into bar iron prevented the forges from following suit. Not until Henry Cort invented the puddling process and the rolling mill in 1784 were the forges able to join the furnaces, and integrated iron works become concentrated in Staffordshire, south Yorkshire, South Wales and the Clyde region. Thereafter the iron industry expanded on a vast scale, with metal replacing timber and stone in many areas of construction, and cast-iron (which could be produced in its final form direct from the blast furnace or re-heated pig iron) barely keeping up with demand. But apart from castings the final product side of the metal industry relied on the bar iron from the major works, and continued on a predominantly domestic basis in cottages, workshops and forges concentrated chiefly in Birmingham and Sheffield.

Meanwhile an even greater innovation was taking place in the cotton industry. The invention in 1733 of John Kay's flying shuttle, which enabled a single weaver to double the width of woven cloth, but which was not put into general use until after 1760, merely accentuated the bottle-neck in spinning. The first significant break-through came with

James Hargreaves's spinning-jenny of 1766, which made possible the spinning of many threads by one pair of hands, and of which within twenty years some twenty thousand were in operation. But the resulting soft yarn could be used only for weft, and it was Richard Arkwright's water-frame of 1768 that first produced a coarse yarn suitable for the warp. Both were surpassed in importance by Samuel Crompton's mule of 1779 which, as its name implies, combined some of the features of each, ensured a strong, fine yarn that could be used for warp as well as weft, and was easily adaptable to the making of other textiles, especially muslins. The inventions of Arkwright and Crompton both required more than human power, and the use of water at first brought about the dispersal of the early cotton mills and factories among many remote villages. But with the advent of steam power in 1785 concentration quickly developed in a series of cotton towns stretching from Stockport to Preston, and with their centre of gravity in Manchester, which by the turn of the century had more than fifty cotton mills. As factory spinning developed, the demand for weaving grew apace, and the late eighties and early nineties saw the brief golden age of the hand-loom weavers. But a power-loom was invented as early as 1784 by Edmund Cartwright, though it required many improvements before it could be used in factory production. As late as 1813, ninety-nine out of a hundred looms were still operated by hand, but thereafter the change to power-driven machinery was very rapid, and the sorry story of the struggle of the hand-loom weavers to compete with the machines was beginning to unfold. By 1815 the larger cotton mills were employing between 1000 and 1500 operatives and, since Arkwright's patent of 1775, carding had been carried out by cylinders on the same premises as spinning. Most of the above developments in the cotton industry were applicable to the manufacture of other textiles, but their adoption was much slower, as was the change to factory production.

Central to the advances in both cotton and the metals was the advent of steam power, undoubtedly the most important technical innovation of the early industrial revolution. Newcomen's atmospheric steam-engine of 1708 had been widely used for pumping out mines, and perhaps a hundred were in use in Cornwall and Northumberland by the mid-seventies. But it was large, expensive and slow-working, and its power was limited by its confinement to reciprocating motion. The general substitution in industry of steam power for that of water was left to a mathematical instrument maker, James Watt, whose interest was aroused when repairing a model of Newcomen's engine at Glasgow University, where he discussed his ideas with Joseph Black and other interested professors. In 1765 Watt conceived the notion of introducing a separate condenser, which could be kept permanently cool and thus avoid the loss of energy in the cylinder caused by the sudden changes of temperature inherent in the alternate injection and condensation of the steam. But while the principle was sound, its effective implementation required greater precision in metal-working than could be provided in Scotland. Although Watt, in partnership with John Roebuck, took out a patent in 1769, it was not until Roebuck transferred his share to Matthew Boulton, and Watt moved to Birmingham in 1774, that the real advances were made. At Boulton's Soho works skilled craftsmen could produce the necessary valves and other delicate parts of the engine, especially an accurately bored cylinder, for which they could draw upon Wilkinson's recent device for boring cannon. The new steam-engine was duly patented in 1775. Watt had thus drawn upon the resources of many men in perfecting his invention, which quadrupled the efficiency of Newcomen's engine, and which was quickly adopted for pumping in the Cornish mines, and for raising water to turn the wheels which operated the bellows, hammers, and rolling mills of the iron industry. Yet Watt was curiously hesitant about carrying his ideas further. He resisted the development of high pressure engines and was reluctant to adapt steam power to transport on road, river and rail. Here a host of others like Richard Trevethick made much faster progress, even though hampered by Watt's patent, which did not expire until 1800. But Boulton was at least able to bully Watt into considering the obvious advantages of rotary action over a single reciprocating stroke, and a succession of developments in the 1780s finally produced the rotative engine that was to revolutionize production in both cotton and metal industries and vitally affect every form of enterprise where machinery was used.

Though Watt deserves his niche in the industrial revolution's hall of fame, the evolution of steam power well illustrates the complexity of the innovatory process and the many individual contributions that were integral parts of a single major advance. In every field of activity the relatively few names which were handed down to posterity represent only a random selection from those who, in Ashton's words, 'had the wit and resource to devise new instruments of production and new methods of administering industry'. The remarkable spread of innovation can be seen from the statistics for patents granted in England. The annual average did not reach double figures until the 1750s; but from 1760 it climbed in successive decades from 22·1 to 26·4, to 47·7, to 64·7, to 92·4, and finally in 1810–20 to 122·7. It is tempting to see this apparent passion for invention as the application to industry of the discoveries born of the scientific revolution of the previous century, but in most cases the men who innovated knew little of physics and less of chemistry. Not until the mid-nineteenth century did science make its major impact, and meanwhile progress was largely the work of gifted amateurs and skilled craftsmen, whose horizons were limited and whose pragmatic approach was directed towards the solution of particular problems often only of immediate and local significance. Perhaps the most important development, apart from the introduction of steam power, was the increasing use of iron machinery in virtually all forms of industry, which was largely made possible by the transfer of exacting skills hitherto employed on soft metals in the production of scientific instruments, watches, clocks and mechanical toys to the creation of precision engineering in iron. The modern fitter came of a marriage between blacksmith and watch-maker, who together created the engineering industry which, harnessed to steam power, transformed the economic and social life of the nation.

As with inventors, so with entrepreneurs. Among the great organizers were men like Ambrose Crowley (iron), Samuel Oldknow (cotton), Josiah Wedgwood (pottery), Thomas Cubitt (building), Coke of Holkham (agriculture), Samuel Whitbread (brewing) and the Duke of Bridgewater (canals); yet these were only the tip of the iceberg. For the most part they were not themselves the instruments of technological innovation, but rather provided the capital and the enterprise to turn to economic advantage the discoveries of others. They were prepared to risk their money and dedicate their time to the many problems inherent in the new forms of industry. They provided raw materials (maintaining where necessary agents abroad), imposed uniform standards of quality, elaborated codes of discipline for the workers in their factories, arranged transport facilities at both ends of the manufacturing process, and supervised the marketing of their products. They came from every walk of life. Arkwright, one-time barber, became the greatest of the cotton spinners; Samuel Walker forsook school-teaching to dominate the northern iron industry; early promoters of engineering, such as Joseph Clement and Henry Maudslay, had been trained as blacksmiths and carpenters; and in agriculture and canal transport the leading figures were landed aristocrats. In so far as any one category of people predominated it was the Protestant nonconformists, especially Quakers and Unitarians; and the family groups that were active in the political life of the country found their counterparts in the world of industry, where ties of kinship proved remarkably strong and were often essential to the provision of the necessary capital. The prototype of the eighteenth-century entrepreneur was perhaps Ambrose Crowley, who already by 1700 was the most substantial iron-master in Europe. Originally a Quaker, he became an Anglican and Tory member of Parliament, and from his house at Greenwich managed to supervise the production of bar-iron, a nail factory, forges and a slitting-mill in Sunderland, warehouses in London and across the Midlands, and a modest fleet of ships to provide transport between his varied enterprises. More attractive, as became his choice of industry, was Josiah Wedgwood, whose pottery works at Etruria were established in 1769. His many activities included the provision of a village for his workers and support for the development of local transport; and by careful training and increased division of labour, he combined skilled craftsmanship with a limited use of power-driven machinery. Though he managed in the process to amass a fortune, he also introduced a note of elegance into an industrial world the general aspect of which was already becoming more than a little bleak.

It is always difficult to explain a sudden and widespread flowering of talent in any field of human activity, and the inventive and organizing genius of so many eighteenth-century Britons cannot be attributed to any single factor. The challenge of increased demand, the availability of ample resources of men, money and materials, and the existence of specific problems of production all doubtless encouraged enterprise and innovation. Just as the foundation of the Royal Society in 1660 reflected the rise of scientific curiosity, so the Society of Arts of 1754 recognized the growing interest in industrial technology, and the establishment in 1785 of the Grand Chamber of Manufacturers under the chairmanship of Wedgwood expressed at least the temporary solidarity of outlook of the entrepreneurs. But these were all manifestations of the changing climate of opinion, not stimuli. It is true that the education provided by the Scottish universities and by the Dissenting Academies was much more inclined towards scientific and technological instruction than that of the traditional English schools and universities (though the contrast was not as great as was once believed) and that many of the more celebrated figures of the industrial revolution were products of the former institutions. But it is easy to exaggerate the connection between innovation and educational training, and many significant inventions came from men with little formal education. Even the very obvious relationship between industrial activity and Protestant Dissent must be handled with care. There was nothing in the theology of either Protestantism or Dissent that induced a penchant for invention or a capitalist ideology; generations of Protestant sects in Scandinavia, Germany and even Scotland continued to eke out a precarious living from the soil; and the Catholic provinces of the Netherlands industrialized before their northern Protestant neighbours. Nonetheless, the legal exclusion of nonconformists from the English universities and from civil and military office seriously limited their choice of career, and undoubtedly helped to direct their attention towards commerce and industry, for which their educational system equipped them reasonably well. The accent which they placed upon seriousness of purpose, probity, thrift, energy and personal abstinence was as important to pioneering in industry as that of their Puritan predecessors had been in the founding of infant colonies across the Atlantic. It was therefore not surprising that Quakers abounded in iron-making, brewing and banking, and Unitarians in cotton-spinning; or that Newcomen was a Baptist, Watt a Presbyterian and Roebuck an Independent. The nonconformist sense of social alienation from the establishment, in itself a source of solidarity, was also of inestimable value in forging the groups which helped by their combined efforts to nourish infant industry.

Whether the inventors and entrepreneurs were a natural by-product of a new era of individualism and *laissez-faire* is as much a matter for speculation as the role of Government in the promotion of industrial progress. The writings of Adam Smith and the early Utilitarians were scarcely a decisive factor in determining official policy before 1815, and the impediments to the pursuit of individual self-interest were by no means as widespread as they seemed to suggest. The commercial expansion which was one of the essential prerequisites of industrialization was admittedly carried out under a highly protectionist policy, and the wars of the eighteenth century were fought partly, though by no means exclusively, for economic reasons, frequently resulted in the acquisition of new markets and sources of raw materials, and provided a limited stimulus to technological innovation. Thus far the Government might be said, at least indirectly, to have encouraged industry and opened the way for individual enterprise. The patent system and a few prizes for particular inventions contributed very modestly to the same end, though patents could inhibit as well as stimulate inventiveness. But it is doubtful whether support from the Government was a crucial factor in the emergence of large-scale industry. For the most part it remained curiously aloof from the process of industrialization, and showed even less concern for the major social problems that resulted. It made little attempt, compared to modern governments, to provide capital or attract investment from abroad; it ignored the intolerable strain imposed upon local authorities by the transformation that was sweeping the country; it impeded corporate activity by the Bubble Act, and placed restrictions upon the expansion of banking; and its greater interest in enhancing the profits of the landed classes than in providing cheap bread for industrial workers was made clear by the increasingly protectionist trend of the Corn Laws. But if such legislation, in conjunction with the Acts of Trade and Navigation, provided ammunition for the advocates of *laissez-faire*, Britain, by comparison with most contemporary European nations, was relatively free from tiresome and anachronistic restrictions. The Government did not unduly hinder industrial advance, but neither did it actively promote it; nor, presumably, would the exponents of individualism have wished it to do so.

It was no more directly involved with the final aspect of the industrial revolution that demands attention—the provision of adequate transport facilities. Clearly the carriage of raw materials, food and finished products (especially bulky commodities such as coal, iron, timber, stone, bricks, salt and clay) required more efficient and cheaper transport than was possible on the pitiful roads of mid-eighteenth-century England. Fortunately the plentiful supply of coal and mineral ores which fed industrial growth was matched by a convenient network of rivers. These, together with a long coast-line, suggested water transport as the most obvious form of improvement for a small, sea-girt nation, and already by the 1720s one hundred miles of river navigation were in use. But it was the era of canal-building, concentrated in the early fifties and between 1788 and 1795 (when cheap credit facilitated the raising of the substantial necessary capital), that really transformed the transport system. The first industrial canal in England linked St Helens with the Mersey, but it was that of the Duke of Bridgewater, opened in 1761, engineered by James Brindley, and running from the Duke's colliery at Worsley to Manchester, that first caught the public imagination. By the seventies trunk canals were beginning to link the great waterways—the Mersey with the Severn, the Severn with the Thames, and the Trent with the Mersey. By these means, and even more by the Grand Junction Canal of 1805, London was connected with the industrial Midlands, whose local canal system opened the way for Birmingham to emerge as one of the greatest of industrial centres. The cost was considerable—by 1815 perhaps as much as £20,000,000 had been invested—but it was far exceeded by the reduction in transport costs. With few exceptions the capital was privately raised, the users had to pay tolls, and the Government confined its assistance to facilitating the necessary private Acts and according the canal companies the benefits of incorporation. But the immediate advantages encouraged ample investment from local landowners, merchants and industrialists, and the hope of profit attracted support on more than a purely local basis. The canals not only facilitated the progress of industrialization. They provided employment, brought prosperity to hitherto relatively backward areas, helped to break down parochial attitudes, and provided useful training for a new generation of engineers, of whom Brindley was only the most celebrated.

Road improvement was less spectacular but of real importance, and here again the role of the Government was chiefly confined to the creation of turnpike trusts through private acts. Indeed the Government seemed directly interested only in roads of potential military importance, which merely served to make independent country gentlemen suspect that great highways might serve to undermine their constitutional liberties. Hence, despite the growth of turnpikes in the late seventeenth and early eighteenth centuries, the tendency until about 1750 was to restrict the traffic on existing roads rather than develop a network adequate to the rapidly changing needs of the country. But thereafter the forces of progress triumphed and, as with canals, the periods of greatest activity were those of cheap credit—the early fifties and the early nineties. Here the great names were those of John Metcalf, Thomas Telford[1] and John MacAdam, who together transformed the roads of England in the second half of the eighteenth century. Pack-horses gave way to waggons, high-speed coaches halved the travelling time between the south and Scotland, and the Royal Mail provided a more efficient channel for business and private communications. A revolution in transport had been effected and even if, because of the local and private character of both road and canal development, it sometimes engendered corruption and its efforts were often ill-integrated, it reflected the restless energy of industrial Britain, helped to cut costs and enhance profits, and shattered for all time the relative isolation in which so many pre-industrial Englishmen had lived out their lives.

These achievements represent one of the great triumphs of human ingenuity and enterprise, and the bald statistics of expansion in agriculture, trade and industry scarcely convey the energy, initiative, skill and determination that went into making the advances possible. Given the sharp up-swing in population, only the industrial revolution could have avoided the disasters that later overtook many nations which had to face a similar situation without adequate human and material resources to cope with it. There seems little doubt that all classes of society generally enjoyed rising incomes between 1760 and 1793, and if some suffered a decline between then and 1815 it was due not to industrialization but to war-

[1] The most distinguished civil engineer of his day. His many spectacular feats included the building of the Caledonian Canal, the Shropshire Union Aquaduct, and the Menai Bridge.

time disruption and inflation and to high food prices born of an abnormal number of bad seasons. The prolonged debate on whether industrialization brought amelioration or deterioration of living standards has been as vitriolic and tiresome[1] as that over the direction in which the gentry were moving between 1540 and 1640, and the paucity and inconclusive nature of the statistical evidence may well deprive both optimists and pessimists of ultimate proven victory. What does seem incontrovertible is that without industrialization the poorer orders of society would have faced a bleaker age than that ushered in by the slag-heaps, chimney-stacks and polluted air of industrial Britain. Nor should we forget that by 1815 the transformation was still very far from complete. Even by 1821 (apart from London) only Glasgow, Liverpool, Manchester and Birmingham could boast populations of more than 100,000; and only Bristol, Sheffield and Norwich (scarcely a new industrial centre) more than 50,000. Most industrial undertakings were still very moderate in size, many factories employed only a few hundred workers, and—except in cotton-spinning and iron production—most manufacturing was still conducted on a predominantly domestic basis. Yet the various developments which have been outlined in the preceding pages had as profound an effect upon society as they had upon the economy, and their qualitative no less than the quantitative effects deserve consideration.

In the first place, the landlords (especially during the Revolutionary and Napoleonic wars) enjoyed unprecedented prosperity, of which renewed zeal in the building of stately homes was merely the most obvious outward sign. The accumulated agricultural improvements of the century, rising food prices, and the increase in yields and in the areas under cultivation were all able to support substantial rises in rents, and those landowners who spread their activities to commerce, industry and transport could further augment their incomes. The ranks of landed society continued to be swelled by an increasing number of newcomers who had made their fortune in trade or industry and who chose to follow the traditional pattern of buying social respectability through the acquisition of country estates. But it was the gentry rather than the aristocracy who absorbed them. Despite the younger Pitt's great expansion of the peerage, virtually all the recipients of his favour were substantial landowners or had achieved high office in the army, navy, diplomacy or the law; and the infusion of new wealth into the aristocracy came mostly through the marriage of the daughters of merchants or industrialists to a declining number

[1] For a convenient summary see J. E. Williams, 'The British Standard of Living, 1750–1850', in *Economic History Review*, 1966.

of impoverished peers. The ambitions of the fathers, partly because of the scarcity and high price of land, were largely confined to joining the ranks of the gentry—as with Abraham Darby, Matthew Boulton, Samuel Whitbread and Jedediah Strutt. At the very time when the landed aristocracy seemed most in danger of becoming a caste, membership of the gentry was even more fluid than in the past; and while their ranks were being constantly augmented, their younger sons were leaving in ever greater numbers to enter the professions, trade or industry. This was particularly important in helping to prevent a head-on collision between the ambitions of the landed interest as a whole and the incipient demands of an increasingly conscious 'middle class' for a share in political power more commensurate with their new-found economic strength. Freeholders and tenant farmers also shared in the general agricultural prosperity, the number of smallholders probably increased rather than decreased after 1760, and many certainly bought or rented additional land and extended their farming activities.

The growth of wealth among those who led the expansion in trade and industry needs no emphasis, though the stories of individual inventors and entrepreneurs did not always have happy endings. Henry Cort was involved in the embezzlements of his partner's father and had to end his days on a small government pension; Edmund Cartwright's cotton factory failed, as had Thomas Lombe's silk factory a few decades earlier; and many smaller men who dabbled in country banking severely burnt their fingers. But these were the exceptions. At the other end of the spectrum Wedgwood made half a million pounds, the elder Peel could afford to employ 15,000 workers and set his son on the road to a most distinguished political career, and Arkwright could joke about living long enough to be able to pay off the national debt. Not the least important aspect of their great wealth and the activities which it financed was the rise to prominence of the north and the west Midlands, which since Anglo-Saxon days had been over-shadowed by the more prosperous and populous south and east. One of the basic conflicts of nineteenth-century Britain, that of north against south, of industry against agriculture, was already dimly adumbrated, and its social, economic and political repercussions at least vaguely perceived. In time it would lead to a recrudescence of party strife on a scale unknown since the days of Anne.

What of the working classes? There were so many local variations and short-term fluctuations in their fortunes that it is impossible to generalize about quantitative changes in their standards of living. Between 1760 and 1790 it would appear that most sections of the working population enjoyed some improvement in real wages, the smallest increases going to the agricultural labourers of the south and west, the greatest to the industrial workers of the north and Midlands. During the ensuing war years, prices tended to outstrip wages in the upward climb, and it may be that only agricultural workers in areas where their employers had to compete with industry really improved their position. But if others, at least when prices were highest, may intermittently have lost ground, it was not because of industrialization but because of war-time inflation coupled with an abnormal run of bad harvests in 1792–3, 1795–6, 1799–1800 and 1808–12. Indeed, it seems likely that after 1760, increased demand for female and child labour brought higher family incomes than had yet been known. Moreover, although there were brief periods of severe unemployment, these had been characteristic of the pre-industrial age, when permanent underemployment in both agriculture and industry had added to the general distress. Factory wages were more regular as well as higher than those of the past. There was less emphasis on keeping wages down, and a growing conviction that higher payments could improve the quality of labour and, in conjunction with mechanization, enhance rather than reduce profits. The prospect of being able to rise significantly above the subsistence level also encouraged many labourers to develop more regular habits of work and thereby achieve a real increase in spending power.

But real wages and standards of living are not necessarily synonymous. Most members of the working classes by 1815 could afford better food, better clothing and even better housing than their ancestors of 1714. But it would be both idle and foolish to ignore the monotony, squalor, ill-health, long hours and harsh treatment that were too often an integral part of the factory system; or the smoke, grime and generally insanitary conditions of the new rising towns. For many the quality of life must have deteriorated sadly, though the contrast with the past was probably not as great to them as it seemed to the earliest historians of the industrial revolution. The labourer of the first half of the century may have led a more leisurely existence in a less distressing environment, but the lot of cottagers, squatters and the urban poor had been far from idyllic. Nor were conditions in the factories much worse than those which had prevailed, and indeed still prevailed, in domestic industry. Indeed, in many ways the factories at first merely carried on existing traditions. Husbands, wives and children who had toiled together in cottage and workshop transferred their activities to the mine and the factory, where family discipline for long continued to be an important part of the new organization of production. For large families child labour had always been the only alternative to poor relief. All this does not mean that the conditions of life and work in early industrial England were not appalling; merely that the undoubted deterioration was not as drastic or sudden as might at first sight appear, and that—given the fact of the population explosion—it was the price that had to be paid for survival.

Perhaps the most psychologically devastating effect of the industrial revolution was to make the relationship between employer and employee much less personal, and determined almost entirely on a cash basis. The earlier agricultural society had seen a certain mutual respect and understanding between master and servant, and families had been able to supplement their admittedly meagre incomes from their small holdings, grazing rights and craft workshops. Now they were much more completely at the mercy of fluctuating demands for labour and often pitifully alone in an unfamiliar world. The casual habits of the countryside were replaced by the severe discipline and regular work of the factory, and as family organization increasingly gave way to the harsh direction of foremen and managers the new conditions seemed ever more intolerable. While the Government appeared for the most part indifferent to their fate, and the Evangelicals exhorted them to placid acceptance of the station to which the Almighty in his wisdom had called them, the workers began to evolve their own institutions for helping them to adapt to the facts of industrial society. The artisans—that aristocracy of the early labour movement who had provided so much support for the earlier ephemeral radicalism of the sixties and seventies—were more than ready to accept the advantages of industrialization, but sought to strengthen their bargaining power by further developing their radical ideology and organization in clubs and societies throughout the country and by taking the lead in the early development of trade unions. The main body of the working classes looked to friendly societies, which were recognized by law in 1793, and which were more reminiscent of the old guilds than characteristic of the incipient trade unions, to express their solidarity—especially when the Combination Laws of 1799 and 1800 temporarily and partially hampered the development of corporate organization among workers. These friendly societies not only advocated self-discipline, but developed rudimentary schemes for providing benefits for those smitten by sickness, accident or unemployment, and were frequently encouraged and even actively supported by many factory owners. The growing acceptance by the working classes of the doctrine of self-help, further evidenced by the appearance of savings banks and co-operative ventures of various kinds, might seem an index of their gullibility, but it also enabled them to maintain something of the dignity of labour and a degree of independence in an era that threatened to reduce them to mere cyphers in an impersonal world.

At the bottom of the social pyramid remained the poor, perhaps—except in times of real dearth—not so numerous as in the past, but because of the changing structure of society less able to rely upon individual charity and compassion. It was in the south that poverty was most extensive, and neither Gilbert's Act of 1792, which permitted parishes to form unions for the creation of workhouses, nor the Speenhamland system of 1795, whereby the Berkshire magistrates authorized the supplementation of agricultural wages by poor-law allowances based upon the price of bread and the size of families, brought much amelioration. Supplementation, which was quickly adopted by other countries, served only to keep wages low and to restrict the mobility of labour. The humanitarian efforts of the Evangelicals were initially directed more towards the abolition of slavery and the slave-trade, and towards missionary activity abroad, than they were towards the manifest social problems of their own country; and although various philanthropic societies were founded, their combined efforts were insignificant. The Sunday Schools of Robert Raikes and the educational experiments of Hannah More in providing a rudimentary education for the children of the poor were directed mainly towards the inculcation of the virtues of obedience, industry and thrift. The notion of the 'deserving' poor was in decline, and the ruthless attitude later to be demonstrated in the 'reform' of the Poor Law of 1834 was already in evidence. The problem of poverty, like those of conditions in factory, mine and city, was a legacy to the generations after 1815.

Within forty years Britain had achieved a position in Europe of economic no less than political primacy. Sudden changes are almost invariably painful, and many people on both sides of the Channel bore the scars of her dual success. Perhaps the worst evils of industrialization were due primarily to the fact that the transformation had been wrought during decades when the nation and the Government were almost continuously preoccupied with meeting the military challenge from France, and had little time or inclination to survey the social and human problems that everywhere cried out for attention. After 1815 successive waves of protest, coupled with a slowly awakening social conscience, brought those problems clearly into focus and in time led to their solution. Meanwhile what is perhaps most surprising is the relative absence of resistance to change, apart from the burst of machine-breaking by the Luddites in 1811–13. The general acceptance of the new society may have been the outcome of despair, but it may also have reflected recognition that, however depressing the conditions of life and work, the labouring classes were less close to the margin of subsistence than they had been in the past, and at least from time to time glimpsed a vision of better times ahead. Despite their spectacular growth in numbers they had managed to survive, life expectancy was rising, and a working-class no less than a middle-class consciousness was beginning to emerge. On balance they might have believed, and even been justified in believing, that they had a modest stake in the 'age of improvement'.

14

RELIGIOUS, INTELLECTUAL AND CULTURAL LIFE

THE religious no less than the political and economic developments of the years between 1760 and 1815 support the view that long reigns can begin and end in different worlds. In 1760 most people who regarded themselves as practising Christians wore their religion comfortably and unostentatiously, whether they were Anglicans, Protestant nonconformists or Roman Catholics; the vitality and sense of personal conviction as well as the intolerance of the seventeenth century had almost completely disappeared; and, except for the Methodists and a handful of individual clerics within the Established Church, enthusiasm in any shape or form was suspect and strictly unfashionable. Yet by 1815 this earlier rational, urbane approach to religion was yielding to the growing fervour and pressure of the Methodists, who by then could claim over 200,000 orthodox converts and a significant number among their various splinter groups, and to the more restrained enthusiasm of a substantial body of Evangelicals within the Anglican fold which was not only helping to change the Established Church from within, but had acquired a voice in political circles that could demand and obtain reform both at home and abroad. In his personal piety as in so many other ways George III reflected the spirit of his age, and by the time of his death in 1820 many of his subjects had undergone a depth of religious experience and acquired habits of sobriety which, sixty years earlier, would have marked them out as at least mildly idiosyncratic. The 'fathers of the Victorians' were busy spreading the light, impelled perhaps by their growing conviction that God was an Englishman. Men—and women—were proud to proclaim a sense of mission and display an egocentric earnestness of purpose that in the mid-eighteenth century would have been regarded as immature and slightly nauseating.

For the most part the acceptance of enthusiasm in religion was a by-product of the reaction against the French Revolution, which seemed to most Englishmen a salutary warning against the uncritical worship of reason. It was therefore understandable that the Evangelical movement, the major impact of which was scarcely felt before the 1790s, should find the prevailing climate of opinion much more favourable than John Wesley and his associates had done fifty years earlier. That Wesley had been able to make himself and his movement socially acceptable was due partly to the temperament and personality of the man himself, partly to the fact that he was fulfilling a need which the Established Church saw fit to ignore, and partly to the recognition that Methodism was a conservative rather than a disruptive influence. Until his death in 1791 Wesley dominated his followers in true patriarchal fashion. His views may have been challenged and his feelings hurt by the frequent scurrility of those within his ranks who deplored his refusal to accept the Calvinist doctrine of predestination. But such was his energy, authority and capacity for organization that he was able to prevent secession from the Church of England and the disintegration into diverse sects that were to become features of the movement in the early nineteenth century. Meanwhile he carried religion to the hearts of the working classes in the new urban centres of industrial England, where parochial organization either did not exist or was hopelessly inadequate, and the continued neglect of which the prevalence of pluralism and non-residence within the Anglican Church made inevitable. In politics Wesley himself was an arch-conservative, rivalling Edmund Burke and Blackstone in his veneration for the English constitution, deploring the insubordination of the American colonists, and exhorting his followers to accept their designated place in the social structure. Long before the French Revolution it was noticed that Methodist working men showed little inclination to join in those radical agitations that intermittently alarmed the governing classes, and the first Sir Robert Peel was but one of many who acknowledged their usefulness and sense of responsibility in maintaining discipline on the factory floor. After 1789 Methodism was widely accepted as a major counter-revolutionary force. Yet there was a sense in which the celebrated epigram of Dr J. N. Figgis, that 'political liberty was the child of the Reformation, but not of the reformers' is applicable to Wesley and the Methodists. Wesley himself was no more a democrat than Luther or Calvin had been, but his beliefs and the organization which he evolved could be turned to ends which he would profoundly have disapproved. Equality before God and the availability of salvation for all could easily be translated into terms of social and political equality; and the system of classes, each with its leader, holding weekly meetings and acknowledging responsibility to a steward and ultimately to the annual conference, could easily be adapted to the purposes of incipient trade unionism and political societies. Although Wesley remained a staunch Anglican, his organization was scarcely compatible with the episcopal structure of the Established Church, and his ordination of presbyters for the American mission in the 1780s further emphasized his anomalous position. By 1797 the New Methodists had been founded by Alexander Kilham, to be followed in 1810 by the Primitive Methodists under Hugh Bourne and William Clowes. These groups did not share Wesley's social and political views, and many of their members became associated with the radicalism of the early nineteenth century. But although it is possible to exaggerate the role of Methodism as 'the opiate of the masses' it remained for the most part a significant conservative influence on working-class society at a time when that society was being subjected to a barrage of radical ideas; and not a few of its members, after the style of earlier dissenting sects, sought through industry and frugality to make their way into the increasingly respectable ranks of the middle classes.

The moral earnestness and personal piety which characterized the Methodists were shared by the Evangelicals, who also appealed to the hearts and consciences of men but who, because of the changed attitude towards enthusiasm, were able directly to influence the Established Church and the upper and middle ranks of society. Except through the medium of personal benevolence their contact with the working classes was comparatively slight, but elsewhere they helped to awaken a social conscience that was directed at first towards missionary activity in the Empire and a reformation of manners at home; and ultimately—though not for the most part until after 1815—towards some of the more pressing social problems of industrial society. Among the more prominent Evangelical clergy were Henry Venn, Vicar of Huddersfield from 1759 to 1771, and from then until his death in 1797 Rector of Yelling in Cambridgeshire; his son, John Venn, Rector of Clapham from 1792 to 1813 and the chief spiritual adviser of the so-called Clapham Sect; John Newton, former master of a slaving ship, eventually Rector of St Mary Woolnoth in London, and described on his tombstone as 'servant of the slaves of Africa'; Isaac Milner, resident of Queens' College, Cambridge, and later Dean of Carlisle; and Charles Simeon, Fellow of King's College, Cambridge and the movement's outstanding preacher. But equally important was the band of influential laymen who comprised the main body of the Clapham Sect and included William Wilberforce, personal friend and political ally of the younger Pitt; Henry Thornton, wealthy banker; Zachary Macaulay, London merchant and father of the historian; James Stephen, lawyer, Master in Chancery and

Under-Secretary for the Colonies; and Lord Teignmouth, Governor-General of India from 1793 to 1798. The Evangelicals could even boast a Prime Minister in Spencer Perceval and a future Colonial Secretary in Lord Glenelg; and when they won over Hannah More from the fashionable world of literary society they acquired the services of the most formidable, tireless and tiresome woman of the age. Before 1815 their principal and most successful efforts were concentrated upon improving the lot of native peoples within the Empire. Their greatest triumph was of course their contribution to the abolition of the slave trade, with which was associated their establishment of a non-slave colony in Sierra Leone in 1791 and the foundation of the African Association. They also showed a keen interest in promoting missionary enterprise, playing a major role in the foundations of the Church Missionary Society in 1799 and the British and Foreign Bible Society in 1804, and persuading Parliament to agree to the appointment of a bishop and three archdeacons in India. Indeed theirs was one of the dominating influences in the evolution of British colonial policy in the early nineteenth century. Whether that influence was on balance beneficial may be open to question. Too often—as for example in both South Africa and New Zealand—the parent missionary societies quarrelled with the missionaries on the spot, and both were arrogant and tactless in their approach to the natives, to the colonial governments and to the settlers in the colonies. At home too the sanctimonious self-righteousness of Hannah More and many of her fellow-workers made them less attractive and probably less effective as reformers than many earlier and later humanitarians. Nor indeed did their emphasis on a reformation of manners suggest any real appreciation of current problems. They succeeded in inculcating a new sense of responsibility and a new seriousness of purpose among many members of the governing classes, and through the medium of rudimentary education—especially in the Sunday schools which Robert Raikes did so much to develop—reinforced the Methodist emphasis on frugality and self-discipline. But for the most part the Proclamation Society of 1787 for improving moral standards, and the later Society for the Suppression of Vice were unpleasantly reminiscent of the Puritanism of the previous century and foreshadowed the hypocrisy of Victorian England. In so far as the Evangelicals contributed to the cause of social reform, they did so by arousing in others a conscience which they themselves appeared to lack. But in preparing the way they served a useful enough function, and some of their more important achievements were as gradual and unspectacular as those of the younger Pitt in the sphere of administrative reform. The Church of England was being quietly transformed from within. Pluralism and non-residence were on the wane, political influence in clerical preferments was becoming the exception rather than the rule, and pastoral duties were being taken much more seriously. The anti-intellectualism and rigid Calvinism of most of the Evangelicals restricted both their horizons and their effectiveness, but like the Methodists they were a significant counter-revolutionary force during the years of the long struggle against France. Not unnaturally they invited much hostile comment from radicals such as Thomas Paine, William Cobbett and Jeremy Bentham; yet like the Methodists they left a legacy that was taken up and adapted by later social and political reformers—although this legacy understandably proved more attractive to middle-class than to working-class movements. Their use of magazines, tracts, public meetings and voluntary societies became a common feature of Victorian life.

The reaction against natural and rational religion was in some sense part of a wider movement in the realm of general ideas that can most conveniently be called Romanticism. In political theory this represented a rejection of those trends of thought embodied in natural morality and natural law, with its derivative system of natural rights. We have already seen how these notions commanded general acceptance in the first half of the eighteenth century, and during the reign of George III they reached their fullest practical expressions in the American and French Revolutions. Notwithstanding the onslaughts of David Hume and the French Utilitarians, the majority of political writers continued to proclaim their belief that there was a natural order of things in the world, designed by a reasonable God for the guidance of mankind, and that the laws of this natural order were discernible by human reason and constituted an immutable standard for testing the ideas, behaviour and institutions of men. The theory of an original contract as the instrument by which men in the state of nature created government for the more effective protection of their inalienable rights, and the consequent justification of resistance when government ceased to respect those rights, were as central to the American Declaration of Independence and the French Declaration of the Rights of Man as they had been to the writings of John Locke. But in the French context Locke's philosophy lost something of its historical and conservative quality and assumed a much more radical guise. Moreover, its essentially individualistic character was challenged by the collectivist beliefs of Jean Jacques Rousseau that the nation was the source of all sovereignty and that the law was an expression of the will of the community. As the French Revolution progressed, Rousseau's influence came increasingly to the fore and, except in economic thought, individualism was thereafter on the defensive in England no less than on the Continent. The natural rights philosophy was doomed to an early demise, and Tom Paine's self-allocated task was to provide its swan-song.

The decline of belief in the omnicompetent power of deductive reason was one facet of the concurrent growth of a cult of sensibility, of which the most prominent aspect was perhaps the transformation which took place in the idea of Nature, which came to be described in emotional rather than rational terms. The *cogito ergo sum* of Descartes became the *je sens, donc je suis* of Rousseau. Hume may already have suggested that man could not live by reason alone, but it was Rousseau who first most cogently expressed the Romantic view that appeal to sentiment went deeper than appeal to reason, and who emphasized the primitive and emotional character of man. His vision of the noble savage, defiled by the imposition of civilization, and his belief in the necessity of restoring a primitive community bound by basic moral sentiments and guided by a new common will was close to the heart of Romanticism. With Rousseau, as with Byron and Shelley, it could be radical and revolutionary, but in England as in Germany it became more often associated with the forces of conservatism. Through Burke, who hated abstract reason and the arid dogmatism of the *philosophes*, it was linked with tradition and reverence for existing institutions as embodying the accumulated wisdom of our ancestors, although Burke was peculiarly blind to their accumulated ignorance and prejudice. Similar views were expressed by the Lake Poets—especially Samuel Taylor Coleridge—after their disillusionment with the anarchy and despotism resulting from the French Revolution; and in Europe Romanticism gave an emotional appeal to the monarchical restorations after 1815, to the temporary revival in France of the outmoded doctrine of the Divine Right of Kings, and to the birth of the Napoleonic legend and the cult of Bonapartism.

Two other aspects of eighteenth-century rationalism—the belief in the perfectibility of the written constitution and faith in cosmopolitanism—also reached their peak in this period and were in turn discredited. Englishmen had had a surfeit of constitution-making in the seventeenth century, and were thereafter mature enough to remain aloof. But the Americans produced a document that seemed to them the embodiment of human reason and they are still reluctant to acknowledge its manifest shortcomings; and the French indulged in an orgy of experiment which rather discredited paper constitutions, except in the eyes of a few nineteenth-century European liberals. Cosmopolitanism, itself a partial by-product of theories of natural law and natural rights, went into decline with those doctrines. Although the French, unable to appeal to the non-existent rights of Frenchmen, had initially addressed themselves to the rights of man, force of circumstance soon impelled them towards a more nationalistic outlook, and reaction against Napoleonic domination contributed towards the emergence of the nationalist ideal in many other parts of Europe—especially in Italy and Germany. Moreover, the assertion of universal inalienable rights seemed to many an invitation to universal revolution, and conservative thinkers turned instead to emphasizing the individuality of nations and the possibility that the differing institutions of many nations could all be equally in harmony with nature. In so arguing they evolved three new conceptions, all of which became part of the Romantic reaction against the rule of reason.

Firstly, the meaning of Nature underwent yet another change, in the course of which it came increasingly to be identified with History. Rousseau's association of the natural with the primitive was rejected, and the true nature of a thing was held to be revealed, not in its primitive state, but by its full maturity. As with Aristotle, the end rather than the beginning came to be of fundamental importance, and the historic process claimed increasing attention. The eighteenth-century belief in the virtue of stability was yielding to the nineteenth-century faith in progress.

Closely associated with this revised concept of Nature, and with the waning of individualism, was the emergence of the organic theory of the State, adumbrated by Rousseau and eloquently propounded by Burke. The State was now seen, not as the creation of an artificial and rational contract, but as springing organically from the life and history of a people; and the individual was consigned to his allotted place in the hierarchical order of society. In England this highly conservative approach to politics was boosted by the biological theories of Darwin, and achieved its fullest expression in the writings of Herbert Spencer. Meanwhile its acceptance drove reforming theorists to find a new philosophical basis for liberalism, which was provided by the Utilitarianism of Jeremy Bentham and James Mill. All laws and institutions were measured against the yardstick of utility, and judged by the extent to which they contributed towards fulfilling the mathematically meaningless, but emotionally appealing 'greatest happiness of the greatest number'.

The third and final concept evolved by the conservative philosophers was that of historic rights, most notably expressed by the German jurist, Savigny. Law was seen as the natural moral product of a people, deriving organically from its past and present life. Like Bentham, Savigny attached great importance to the legislator; unlike Bentham, he believed that the function of the legislator was not to make law but, through historical research, to discover what the law was. While admitting that rights were founded in nature, he identified nature with history, and asserted that the institutions of any nation were the crystallization of its traditions. Nationalism and evolutionary reform were thus reconciled, and the study of history assumed a new importance, not only for a better undertanding of the present, but even for predicting the future.

In England as on the Continent many of these trends of thought were not fully developed until after 1815, and before then their influence in the world of practical politics was at its best marginal. Yet during the long reign of George III the philosophical basis of a new conservatism was laid, the direction of radical speculation was permanently changed, and in economic thought the former mercantilist beliefs were challenged by the growing faith in *laissez-faire*. Between 1765 and 1769 Sir William Blackstone, the first Vinerian Professor of Law at the University of Oxford, published his four volumes of lectures under the title of *Commentaries on the Law of England*. Blackstone, the most eminent antiquarian lawyer since Sir Edward Coke, was a man of great learning; but he was obsessed with the supposed perfection of the English constitution and, in expounding its nature, he lacked the critical and analytical power of Hume and the genuine historical insight of Montesquieu or Burke. He venerated where he could not readily comprehend, and his particular brand of conservatism, which did not even reflect the bluff, honest prejudice of Dr Johnson, could reinforce the reactionary sentiments of those who after 1789 feared the spread of revolution to England, but had little to contribute to the mainstream of nineteenth-century conservative thought. Here it was Edmund Burke who was the true guide.

Burke is not an easy man to understand, for he operated at three quite different levels. As a private individual he was warm-hearted and generous, for ever worrying over, and providing for, his disreputable relatives and assorted lame-ducks; as a practising politician he was prejudiced, self-interested and capable of deceit; as a political philosopher—though he would have rejected the title—he showed a profound insight into the springs of human action, and a common sense and humanity that were expressed in prose that has seldom been equalled in the annals of political disquisition. It is easy enough to expose the weakness of his argument in relation to specific issues. His assessment of the contemporary English political scene was perverse and superficial; his solution to the imperial problem was to pretend that it did not exist; his charges against Warren Hastings were based largely on the paranoid imaginings of Philip Francis and completely ignored the realities which Hastings had to face; and in denouncing the French Revolution he laid himself open to Tom Paine's jibe that 'he pities the plumage, but forgets the dying bird'. Too often before 1782 his writings were directed largely towards proving that only the Rockingham Whigs were fit to rule Britain; too often he merited Goldsmith's rebuke that he 'narrow'd his mind, and to party gave up what was meant for mankind'. Yet however questionable his motives and however dubious his selection and interpretation of evidence might sometimes have been, few men could move with greater ease from the specific to the general, from a mass of detail to the basic political principles which lay behind it. Although he was the greatest Whig apologist of the century, and although over America, Ireland and India he consistently adopted a liberal point of view, his instincts were always profoundly conservative, and the horrors of the French Revolution merely brought that conservatism into sharper focus; although he was avowedly hostile to the early politics of the Romantic movement—in particular the doctrines of Rousseau and William Godwin—his exaltation of emotion and imagination over reason made him a true Romantic, and his outlook and principles were inherited by Coleridge, Wordsworth and Disraeli.

Burke's Romantic Conservatism led him to react violently against abstract reason and the associated system of natural rights. The social contract was 'at best a confusion of judicial with civil principles', and he passionately detested all metaphysical speculation. 'One sure symptom of an ill-conducted State' he wrote, 'is the propensity of the people to resort to theories.' To Burke political philosophy was merely generalizing from experience, and his sense of history—'the known march of the ordinary providence of God'—made him value what was old because it had reached maturity and embodied the wisdom of past ages. No one more clearly appreciated that the State was not the creation of a moment, but the result of slow organic growth; no one more earnestly and sincerely stressed the need for continuity. 'In what we improve, we are never wholly new; and in what we retain we are never wholly obsolete.' Yet he could see that 'when the reason of old establishments is gone, it is absurd to preserve nothing but the burden of them', and openly assert that 'a disposition to preserve and an ability to improve, taken together, would be my standard of a statesman'. It has been said that Burke protested against natural rights in the name of expediency, and that in so doing he adopted an attitude that was in essence Utilitarian. But, unlike Bentham, he was no democrat, and his Utilitarianism must be seen in the light of his deep religious conviction, his emphasis on the need for prudence, and his devotion to an hierarchical order of society—all qualities singularly lacking in Bentham and his followers. Burke saw religion as 'the basis of civil society, and the source of all good and all comfort'; to him 'man is a religious animal; atheism is against not only our nature but our instincts'. Prudence was 'not only the first in rank of the virtues, political and moral, but she is the director, the regulator, the standard of them all'. His Platonic faith in a natural aristocracy, which he was too ready to identify with the leaders of the Rockingham Whigs, led him to distrust the voice of the people save when that voice echoed his own sentiments. He might argue that 'in all disputes between the people and their rulers, the prescription is at least upon a par in favour of the people', and that 'I reverently look up to the opinion of the people and with an awe that is almost superstitious'; but in the last analysis he believed that 'we are not to go to school to them to learn the principles of law and government . . . as to the details of particular measures, or to any schemes of general policy, they have neither enough of speculation in the closet, nor of experience in business, to decide upon it'. He might hotly deny his subservience to the aristocracy—'I have no vulgar admiration, nor any vulgar antipathy towards them; I hold their order in cold and decent respect'—but the egalitarian doctrines of the French Revolution brought out his most passionate and celebrated defence of the hierarchical system. 'Never, never more shall we behold that generous loyalty to rank and sex, that proud submission, that dignified obedience, which kept alive, even in servitude itself, the spirit of an exalted freedom.'

In the decades after 1789 it was natural that Burke's ideas should command general acceptance among the governing classes of Britain. Yet the radical tradition, far from withering away, gained new strength and moved along new paths. Even as early as the 1760s writers began to query Blackstone's worship of the constitution, and to show greater respect for legislators who might change and improve the law than for lawyers who merely expounded and revered it. Most radical thinkers were at first backward rather than forward looking, and like their contemporaries in the world of practical politics, were intent primarily upon restoring a mythical golden past. But John Cartwright's *Take your Choice* advocated sweeping changes that adumbrated the programme of the Chartists seventy years later, and with Joseph Priestley's *Essay on the First Principles of Government* radical thought began to assume a new guise. Priestley still paid lip-service to ideas of natural rights, but his basic approach was expediential and utilitarian, and he optimistically looked forward to a new society made possible by the removal of hampering Government restrictions and the consequent release of individual energy—political, economic and religious—on a scale hitherto unknown. The way was clearly pointed to Jeremy Bentham and Adam Smith. In 1776

Bentham in his *Fragments on Government* fairly joined issue with Blackstone, denouncing the law as anachronistic, incomprehensible and repressive; and his later *Principles of Morals and Legislation* announced his faith in the achievement of an ideal society through the agency of legislation designed to achieve the greatest happiness of the greatest number. No bolder contrast could be imagined than that between Burke's reverence for the past and Bentham's contempt for it, or between Burke's intuitive appreciation of the organic nature of society and Bentham's doctrinaire determination to build anew on the basis of the felicific calculus. The Utilitarianism of Bentham and his followers was not a system of political philosophy but a congeries of assorted and ill-related ideas—a series of jig-saw pieces which could not themselves form a coherent pattern, but many of which could be used to complete other pictures. Few subsequent writers on political or economic thought have not pilfered Bentham's do-it-yourself kit for enlightened legislators, but in the short term his chief importance lay in the fact that his yardstick of utility could prove a powerful solvent of archaic laws and institutions. He was thus a useful antidote to Burke in an age when the dividing line between moderate conservatism and unthinking reaction was perilously thin. It is doubtful whether he had as much influence on reform as once was thought, and that influence was anyway not to be felt until after 1815. Meanwhile in England radical theory and natural rights had permanently parted company.

More influential than Bentham and much more representative of his age was Adam Smith, whose *Wealth of Nations* (1776) remains one of the seminal works of modern times. In rejecting the basic tenets of mercantilism and demanding the removal of all government restraints upon individual economic enterprise, Smith was scarcely adopting a novel or revolutionary attitude. In some sense religious liberty was the parent of economic as well as political liberty, and for many decades Protestant nonconformists had argued against State control of economic life as firmly as they had advocated the removal of their political disabilities and the granting of full religious toleration; and Sir Dudley North, David Hume, Josiah Tucker and the French Physiocrats had all argued against artificial restrictions upon commerce. But with Smith the elements of a rugged economic individualism were woven into a coherent system which provided a seemingly convincing apologia for the entrepreneurs of the new industrial age. The State, in his view, should be confined to the spheres of defence, justice, and the erection and maintenance of necessary public works and institutions. The improvement of society must be left to the natural instincts of economic man, and each individual, in pursuing his own economic self-interest would in some mysterious undefined manner promote the general happiness of all. The way was prepared for repeal of the Acts of Trade and Navigation, the repeal of the Corn Laws, and the adoption of complete free trade. It is easy to sympathize with Smith's impatience at unenlightened and misinformed governmental regulation, and with his passionate desire to release the creative impulses of men; it is easy, too, to criticize his naïve belief that unrestricted economic freedom could bring nothing but benefit to mankind. Even early nineteenth-century Englishmen could see that economic *laissez-faire* left in its wake social problems of such a magnitude that they could be solved only through the medium of State intervention; and before *laissez-faire* reached its peak in the 1840s much social reform had found its way into the statute-books. Smith, like virtually all his contemporaries, was bedevilled by the conviction that man and nature (however that elusive word might be defined) were somehow in harmony. But even before the eighteenth century was over T. R. Malthus had delivered the first blast against its incorrigible optimism in his *Essay on the Principle of Population as it Affects the Future Improvement of Society.* Food, he argued, increased arithmetically, while population increased in geometrical ratio. Rising production therefore could never keep pace with the rise in population, and the majority of mankind were condemned to eternal misery. For the supposed harmony between man and nature was substituted a basic conflict—a doctrine which in the fullness of time was to be given its biological certificate by Charles Darwin, and become immortalized in the pages of Jack London. This, of course, was an over-reaction, which earned for political economy the title of 'the dismal science'. Meanwhile Smith remained the chief apostle of the new economic liberalism, and his notions were as welcome to the captains of rising industry as those of Locke had been a century earlier to the architects of the Glorious Revolution. It remains only to add that, had neither writer ever existed, it is unlikely that the course of English history would have differed in any essential respect.

In literature and the arts the dominant theme was the emergence of the many-faceted Romantic ideal, which found occasional expression even in the early decades of George III's reign, but the full flowering of which had to await the traumatic impact of the French Revolution. As far back as 1756 Burke, in his *Philosophical Inquiry into the Origins of our Ideas on the Sublime and Beautiful*, had queried the comfortable rationalism of the age by pointing out that man could be profoundly stirred by experiences which were irrational, unpleasing, even horrifying. Within each of us was Rousseau's 'noble savage' struggling to get out. This fascination with the inner workings of the human mind affected many of the leading poets of the period, most notably William Cowper, with his persistent melancholia and masochistic religious convictions; William Blake who, apart from the demented power of his prophetic works, sought in savagely symbolic terms to condemn the new industrial society against which his tortured, radical soul rebelled; and Samuel Taylor Coleridge, whose subsequent addiction to opium both heightened and confused the fertile and sensitive imagination that had conceived *Kubla Khan*, *Christabel*, and *The Rime of the Ancient Mariner*. Yet other poets, as for example Thomas Gray in his later years, turned their attention to half-forgotten myths and legends; and James Macpherson and Thomas Chatterton even went so far as to fabricate works by imaginery medieval bards. The rising fashion for exotic writing extended to prose as well as poetry, and produced a spate of Gothic novels, of which the more successful were Horace Walpole's *Castle of Otranto*, William Beckford's *Vathek*, Ann Radcliffe's *The Mysteries of Udolpho*, Matthew Lewis's *The Monk*, and—by far the most distinguished—Mary Wollstonecraft's *Frankenstein*. But these flights of fancy enjoyed only a brief popularity, and it was left to Sir Walter Scott, who had already established himself as a writer of ballads by 1815, to express in his Waverley novels a romantic dedication to the past that was to inaugurate a new tradition in British prose.

Concurrently the Romantic poets abandoned themselves to an uninhibited adoration of nature, the publication in 1798 of the *Lyrical Ballads* of Wordsworth and Coleridge opening the most glorious age of English poetry. Enthusiasm had invaded the world of literature no less than that of religion. The conventional language and metres of the Augustans were finally rejected, and a new honesty, intensity and depth of feeling were everywhere appearing. The Lake Poets in particular—although Robert Southey was but a pale imitation of Wordsworth and Coleridge—typified the ubiquitous spirit of restlessness and freedom, welcoming the French Revolution with naïve exuberance and, in their subsequent disillusionment, moving towards a position of Tory radicalism that made them an intellectual link between Burke and Disraeli. North of the border the same impassioned feelings moved Robert Burns to his greatest and most unaffected work, and after 1815 John Keats and Percy Bysshe Shelley were to achieve heights of lyrical expression unsurpassed before or since.

In prose writing, apart from the early romances of Scott, there were no comparable developments. Laurence Sterne's *Tristram Shandy* and *Sentimental Journey* appeared in the 1760s, thereby bringing to a close a period in which the English novel first achieved real literary status. But despite their sophisticated brilliance and the elements of fantasy which they contained, they were as artificial and contrived—although in a very different manner—as the mannered comedies of Oliver Goldsmith and Richard Brinsley Sheridan, the gently ironical but somehow superficial novels of Fanny Burney, or even the majestic prose of Edward Gibbon's *Decline and Fall of the Roman Empire*. Even the greatest novelist of the age, Jane Austen, was apparently as immune to the influence of Romanticism as she was to the impacts of the French wars or the industrial revolution. *Northanger Abbey* was avowedly written with the object of satirizing the more bizarre Gothic mysteries of her day, and nothing could be further removed from the Romantic tradition than *Pride and Prejudice* or *Sense and Sensibility*. Yet, within the strictly circumscribed limits of her own upper middle-class experience, Jane Austen's acute powers of observation, fine sense of proportion and exquisite irony allowed her to incapsulate a particular segment of English life with a verisimilitude that had eluded even the most gifted of her predecessors.

In painting, the long reign of George III witnessed a flowering of talent only marginally less remarkable than that in literature, and of which the founding of the Royal Academy in 1768 was the early and formal recognition. If writers as a class had first achieved a modest degree of financial security under the early Hanoverians, artists were quick to follow. The chief driving force in the revival of British painting was Sir Joshua Reynolds, who preserved the classical style but showed a candour and freshness in his delineation of character and a sense of the dramatic and heroic that was reflected in lesser manner by the new school of history painters, of whom the most successful was Benjamin West. Less intellectually impressive, but more imaginative, sensitive and lyrical were the portraits of Thomas Gainsborough; while the greater simplicity, clarity and vivacity of George Romney's work showed perhaps the first hints of the Romantic influence. But it was in landscape painting that the latter made its real impact—not so much in George Stubbs's somewhat stylized addiction to rural scenes and animal painting, but in the intensity, sense of movement and unrestrained naturalism that characterized the work of J. M. W. Turner and John Constable who, with their subtle use of colonr, brought a new spontaneity and warmth to British art.

In music no composer of real distinction arose; while in architecture the century (if one includes the years up to 1815) drew to a splendid close without any dramatic change in direction and without bequeathing any lasting tradition to an architecturally sterile future. Horace Walpole's passing taste for neo-Gothicism produced the turreted extravagance of Strawberry Hill, the younger William Beckford similarly married his literary and architectural interests by persuading James Wyatt to abandon his classical style and design the extraordinary Gothic abbey at Fonthill, and the Brighton Pavilion (built for the Prince of Wales) mingled medievalism with Chinoiserie. But these aberrations represented the lunatic fringe of Romanticism, which otherwise had little immediate impact except perhaps for a passing fashion for mock Tudor and the occasional intrusion of exotic elements into the parks and gardens of the eccentric few. The main-stream of English architecture continued to follow the Palladian tradition, as modified by the classical leanings of the Adam brothers (whose equal dedication to interior decoration produced a new pattern of integrated elegance), and the preoccupation with the gay and picturesque which characterized the work of John Nash and lent a more light-hearted air to many Regency buildings than would hitherto have been acceptable. The formal dignity of the earlier part of the century was maintained, as was the fine sense of proportion; but the ornamentation which in Regency England seemed merely to enhance the classical simplicity behind it was soon to become an end in itself. The appearance of the suburban villa and even the semi-detached house was already heralding the emergence of middle-class values and tastes, and by 1815 the age of elegance was drawing to a close.

CONCLUSION

SUPERFICIALLY the eighteenth century may seem to lack the great issues which dominated that which preceded it and that which came after, and to those living in the last third of the twentieth century its conventions and values can appear alien and misguided. Most writers tend to look askance at the 'corruption' of the age and deplore the apparently adamantine resistance to change of the ruling classes of Hanoverian England; and it is not surprising that admiration is usually reserved for those who were for the most part political failures—Bolingbroke, Burke, Rockingham, Shelburne, even the great Chatham—or that the years after 1815 are hailed with relief and enthusiasm as 'the age of reform'. Yet few periods of English history have witnessed so impressive a variety of outstanding achievements or provided so rich a cultural heritage. The question marks which had everywhere stood against Britain's future in 1714 had been almost completely erased by men of rare enterprise and sturdy common sense.

Not the least achievement was the manner in which successive Kings and generations of politicians wrestled with the problems and paradoxes inherent in the system of mixed government which they had inherited, and achieved sufficient stability to withstand minor domestic and major foreign threats, permit a modest record of reform, and allow the gradual evolution of the several elements of modern Cabinet Government. Concurrently, Britain had emerged supreme in Europe, and was well on the way to becoming the workshop of the world without losing her position in the vanguard of agricultural progress. She had successfully coped with a virtual doubling of her population without significant social unrest or undue repression; and, if she had lost one Empire, the spread of her power in India, the conquest of Canada, the acquisition of a foothold in South Africa, and the beginnings of the colonization of Australia (even if through the dubious medium of transportation) paved the way for the development of a new, more extensive, and more liberal imperial design. Scotland, notwithstanding her temporary flirtations with Jacobitism, had been reconciled to a union of which she had originally been profoundly distrustful; and although the Irish problem remained intractable, the incorporation of Ireland within the United Kingdom at least inaugurated a new phase of constructive thinking. Above all, society had remained highly fluid, the old conflict between the monied and landed interests had died a natural death, and a readiness to tolerate and even welcome the new captains of industry augured well for continued economic progress and political cohesion. In 1714 France, despite her military failures, had seemed the more powerful nation; by 1815 she had been through national bankruptcy, revolution, dictatorship and decisive military defeat, while Britain had been able to finance the struggle against her ancient rival without more than temporary checks to her own prosperity.

Most Englishmen in 1815 could face the future with infinitely greater confidence than their forbears of a century before. Landed proprietors, merchants and industrialists might all look anxiously over their shoulders at the signs of growing working-class discontent, devout Anglicans might view with alarm the continuing claims of Protestant nonconformists and Roman Catholics for full political rights, and the demands of a new generation of radicals seemed a much more sinister threat to the establishment than those which had been presented by the carefree demagogy of John Wilkes or the nostalgic 'country' programme of Christopher Wyvill. The social problems arising from industrialization had of necessity been pushed into the background during the long years of war, and had now squarely to be faced in exacerbated form. But the political, social, economic and religious structure of Hanoverian England was sufficiently strong and flexible to bend to the winds of change without breaking. In 1828 the Test and Corporation Acts would be repealed, in 1829 Catholic Emancipation would be granted, and in 1832 the House of Commons would reform itself. Only then would the era which had opened in 1688 draw to its peaceful close, and in a very real sense 1832 marked the end rather than the beginning of a phase of reform that had its roots firmly planted in the rich and fertile soil of Hanoverian England. An oligarchy which could ensure a hundred years of internal peace, establish an undisputed hegemony in Europe, acquire an Empire, preside over quiet revolutions in agriculture, industry and religion, and agree to share its power when the national interest so required, is deserving of respect, even of admiration. It is not clear that Britain has since been so well served by her rulers.

APPENDIX A

Duration of Parliaments

Date of Assembly	*Date of Dismissal*
12 NOV. 1713	15 JAN. 1715
17 MAR. 1715	10 MAR. 1722
10 MAY 1722	5 AUG. 1727
28 NOV. 1727	17 APR. 1734
13 JUN. 1734	27 APR. 1741
25 JUN. 1741	18 JUN. 1747
13 AUG. 1747	8 APR. 1754
31 MAY 1754	20 MAR. 1761
19 MAY 1761	11 MAR. 1768
10 MAY 1768	30 SEP. 1774
29 NOV. 1774	1 SEP. 1780
31 OCT. 1780	25 MAR. 1784
18 MAY 1784	11 JUN. 1790
10 AUG. 1790	20 MAY 1796
12 JUL. 1796	29 JUN. 1802
31 AUG. 1802	24 OCT. 1806
13 DEC. 1806	29 APR. 1807
22 JUN. 1807	29 SEP. 1812
24 NOV. 1812	10 JUN. 1818

APPENDIX B

Principal Office-holders

Conventional title of Ministry	*First Lord of Treasury*	*Sec. of State (S); Home Sec. from 1782*	*Sec. of State (N); Foreign Sec. from 1782*	*Other important Ministers*
1714–21 Stanhope	OCT. 1714: Halifax MAY 1715: Carlisle OCT. 1715: Walpole APR. 1717: Stanhope MAR. 1718: Sunderland	SEP. 1714: Townshend DEC. 1716: Stanhope APR. 1717: Sunderland MAR. 1718: Stanhope FEB. 1721: Townshend	SEP. 1714: Stanhope JUN. 1716: Methuen APR. 1717: Addison MAR. 1718: Craggs MAR. 1721: Carteret	MAR. 1718–FEB. 1719: Sunderland (Lord President of Council)
1721–42 Walpole	APR. 1721: Walpole	JUN. 1730: Harrington	APR. 1724: Newcastle	FEB. 1737–NOV. 1756: Hardwicke (Lord Chancellor)
1742–44 Carteret	FEB. 1742: Wilmington AUG. 1743: H. Pelham	FEB. 1742: Carteret		
1744–46 Pelham		NOV. 1744: Harrington		
1746 Bath	FEB. 1746: Bath	FEB. 1746: Granville	FEB. 1746: Granville	
1746–54 Pelham	FEB. 1746: H. Pelham	FEB. 1746: Harrington OCT. 1746: Chesterfield FEB. 1748: Newcastle	FEB. 1746: Newcastle JUL. 1748: Bedford JUN. 1751: Holderness	
1754–56 Newcastle	MAR. 1754: Newcastle	MAR. 1754: Holderness	MAR. 1754: Robinson NOV. 1755: H. Fox	
1756–57 Pitt–Devonshire	NOV. 1756: Devonshire		DEC. 1756: W. Pitt	
1757–61 Pitt–Newcastle	JUN. 1757: Newcastle	MAR. 1761: Bute	JUN. 1757: W. Pitt	
1761–63 Bute	MAY 1762: Bute	MAY 1762: G. Grenville OCT. 1762: Halifax	OCT. 1761: Egremont	
1763–65 Grenville	APR. 1763: G. Grenville	SEP. 1763: Sandwich	SEP. 1763: Halifax	
1765–66 Rockingham	JUL. 1765: Rockingham	JUL. 1765: Grafton MAY 1766: Conway	JUL. 1765: Conway MAY 1766: Richmond	

1766–68	Chatham	AUG. 1766: Grafton	JAN. 1768: Weymouth	JUL. 1766: Shelburne	JUL. 1766–OCT. 1768: Chatham (Lord Privy Seal)
1768–70	Grafton		OCT. 1768: Rochford	OCT. 1768: Weymouth	
1770–82	North	JAN. 1770: North	DEC. 1770: Sandwich JAN. 1771: Halifax JUN. 1771: Suffolk OCT. 1779: Stormont	DEC. 1770: Rochford NOV. 1775: Weymouth NOV. 1779: Hillsborough	JAN. 1778–APR. 1783: Thurlow (Lord Chancellor)
1782	Rockingham	MAR. 1782: Rockingham	MAR. 1782: Shelburne	MAR. 1782: C. J. Fox	
1782–83	Shelburne	JUL. 1782: Shelburne	JUL. 1782: Sydney	JUL. 1782: Grantham	
1783	Fox–North	APR. 1783: Portland	APR. 1783: North	APR. 1783: C. J. Fox	
1783–1801	Pitt	DEC. 1783: W. Pitt	DEC. 1783: Temple DEC. 1783: Sydney JUN. 1789: W. W. Grenville JUN. 1791: H. Dundas JUL. 1794: Portland	DEC. 1783: Temple DEC. 1783: Leeds JUN. 1791: Grenville FEB. 1801: Hawkesbury	DEC. 1783–APR. 1792: Thurlow (Lord Chancellor)
1801–04	Addington	MAR. 1801: H. Addington	JUL. 1801: Pelham AUG. 1803: C. P. Yorke		
1804–06	Pitt	MAY 1804: W. Pitt	MAY 1804: Hawkesbury	MAY 1804: Harrowby JAN. 1805: Mulgrave	
1806–07	All the Talents	FEB. 1806: Grenville	FEB. 1806: Spencer	FEB. 1806: C. J. Fox SEP. 1806: Howick	
1807–09	Portland	MAR. 1807: Portland	MAR. 1807: Hawkesbury	MAR. 1807: G. Canning	
1809–12	Perceval	OCT. 1809: S. Perceval	NOV. 1809: R. Ryder	OCT. 1809: Bathurst DEC. 1809: Wellesley MAR. 1812: Castlereagh	
1812–	Liverpool	JUN. 1812: Liverpool	JUN. 1812: Sidmouth		

BOOKS FOR FURTHER READING

The reader whose interest has been stimulated rather than destroyed by the foregoing pages will find no more entertaining and instructive way of pursuing that interest than by dipping into the pages of the voluminous memoirs and letters of Horace Walpole and memoirs of Lord Hervey. Much of the spirit of the period can also be captured from the novels of Swift, Fielding, Richardson, Smollett, Sterne and Scott, and from the poetry of Pope, Collins, Gray, Wordsworth and Coleridge. No serious student can afford to ignore the seminal writings of Hume, Burke and Adam Smith, and no one with a zest for life should fail, through James Boswell, to strike up an acquaintance with the formidable Dr Johnson. The correspondence of George III and of many of the leading politicians of the age are also readily available. Of modern works, the following are among the more useful, although for serious guidance reference must be had to more extensive bibliographies.

Econ.H.R. = *Economic History Review*
E.H.R. = *English Historical Review*
H.J. = *Historical Journal*
J.Econ.H. = *Journal of Economic History*
T.R.H.S. = *Transactions of the Royal Historical Society*

1. GENERAL

Aspinall, A., and Smith, E. A. (ed.), *English Historical Documents, 1783–1832*, Eyre & Spottiswoode, (1959)

Briggs, A., *The Age of Improvement*, Longman, (1959)

Horn, D. B., and Ransome, M., *English Historical Documents, 1715–83*, Eyre and Spottiswoode, (1957)

Jarrett, D., *Britain, 1688–1815*, Longman, (1965)

Marshall, D., *Eighteenth Century England*, Longman, (1962)

Mitchison, R., (ed.), *Essays in Eighteenth Century History*, Longman, (1966)

Watson, J. S., *The Reign of George III*, Oxford University Press, (1960)

Whiteman, A., Bromley, J. S., and Dickson, P. G. M., (ed.), *Statesmen, Scholars and Merchants: Essays in Eighteenth Century History presented to Dame Lucy Sutherland*, Oxford University Press, (1973)

Williams, B., *The Whig Supremacy*, Oxford University Press, (rev. ed. 1962)

2. BIOGRAPHIES

Brooke, J., *King George III*, Constable, (1973)
Chenevix-Trench, C., *Portrait of a Patriot: John Wilkes*, Blackwood, (1962)
Chenevix-Trench, C., *George II: a Biography*, Allen Lane, (1973).
Derry, J. W., *William Pitt*, Batsford, (1962)
Derry, J. W., *Charles James Fox*, Batsford, (1973)
Dickinson, H. T., *Bolingbroke*, Constable, (1970)
Ehrman, J., *The Younger Pitt: the Years of Acclaim*, Constable, (1969)
Gray, D., *Spencer Perceval*, Manchester University Press, (1963)
Halsband, R., *Lord Hervey: Eighteenth Century Courtier*, Oxford University Press, (1973)
Namier, Sir L., and Brooke, J., *Charles Townshend*, Macmillan (1964)
Oman, C., *Nelson*, Sphere Books (1967)
Plumb, J. H., *Sir Robert Walpole: the Making of a Statesman*, Barrie & Jenkins, (1956)
Plumb, J. H., *Sir Robert Walpole: the King's Minister*, Barrie & Jenkins, (1961)
Williams, B., *Life of William Pitt, Earl of Chatham*, 2 vols., F. Cass, (1913)
Williams, B., *Stanhope*, Oxford University Press, (1932)

3. POLITICAL AND CONSTITUTIONAL

(*a*) *Books*

Barnes, D. G., *George III and William Pitt, 1783–1806*, F. Cass, (1939)
Black, E. C., *The Association, 1769–93*, Harvard University Press, (1963)
Brooke, J., *The Chatham Administration, 1766–8*, Macmillan, (1956)
Butterfield, H., *George III, Lord North and the People, 1779–80*, Bell, (1949)
Butterfield, H., *George III and the Historians*, Collins, (1957)
Cannon, J., *The Fox–North Coalition: Crisis of the Constitution*, Cambridge University Press, (1970)
Christie, I. R., *The End of North's Ministry, 1780–2*, Macmillan, (1958)
Christie, I. R., *Wilkes, Wyvill and Reform*, Macmillan, (1962)
Christie, I. R., *Myth and Reality in Eighteenth Century England*, Macmillan, (1970)
Dickinson, H. T., *Walpole and the Whig Supremacy*, University of London Press, (1973)
Foord, A., *His Majesty's Opposition, 1714–1830*, Oxford University Press (1964)
Ginter, D. E., *Whig Organization in the General Election of 1790*, University of California Press, (1967)
Gunn, J. A. W., *Factions no More*, F. Cass, (1972)
Guttridge, G. H., *English Whiggism and the American Revolution*, University of California Press, (1942)
Hibbert, C., *King Mob*, Longman, (1958)
Kemp, B., *King and Commons, 1660–1832*, Macmillan, (1957)
Langford, P., *The First Rockingham Administration, 1765–6*, Oxford University Press, (1973)
Mitchell, L. G., *Charles James Fox and the Disintegration of the Whig Party, 1782–94*, Oxford University Press, (1970)
Namier, Sir L., *The Structure of Politics at the Accession of George III*, Macmillan, (rev. ed. 1957)
Namier, Sir L., *England in the Age of the American Revolution*, Macmillan, (rev. ed. 1961)
Namier, Sir L., *Crossroads of Power*, Hamish Hamilton, (1963)

Namier, Sir L., and Brooke, J., *History of Parliament: the House of Commons, 1754–90*, 3 vols., H.M.S.O., (1964)
Norris, J., *Shelburne and Reform*, Macmillan, (1963)
O'Gorman, F., *The Whig Party and the French Revolution*, Macmillan, (1967)
Owen, J. B., *The Rise of the Pelhams*, Methuen, (1957)
Pares, R., *George III and the Politicians*, Oxford University Press, (1953)
Plumb, J. H., *The Growth of Political Stability in England, 1675–1725*, Macmillan, (1967)
Roberts, M., *The Whig Party, 1807–12*, F. Cass, (1939)
Rudé, G., *Wilkes and Liberty*, Oxford University Press, (1962)
Sedgwick, R., *History of Parliament: the House of Commons, 1715–54*, 2 vols., H.M.S.O., (1970)
Smith, R. A., *Eighteenth Century Politics, Patrons and Place-Hunters*, Holt, Rinehart & Winston, (1972)
Sutherland, L. S., *The East India Company in Eighteenth Century Politics*, Oxford University Press, (1952)
Thomas, P. D. G., *The House of Commons in the Eighteenth Century*, Oxford University Press, (1971)
Thomson, M. A., *Constitutional History of England, 1640–1801*, Methuen, (1938)
Williams, E. N., *The Eighteenth Century Constitution*, Cambridge University Press, (1960)

(*b*) *Articles of Special Importance*
Foord, A., 'The Waning of the Influence of the Crown', *E.H.R.* 1947
Fryer, W. R., 'King George III: his Political Career and Conduct', *Renaissance and Modern Studies* 1962
George, D. M., 'Fox's Martyrs: the General Election of 1784', *T.R.H.S.* 1939
Newman, A. N., 'Leicester House Politics, 1748–61', *E.H.R.* 1961
Pares, R., 'Limited Monarchy in the Eighteenth Century', Historical Association Pamphlet, 1957
Phillips, N. C., 'Burke and the County Movement', *E.H.R.* 1961
Reitan, E. A., 'The Civil List in Eighteenth Century British Politics', *H.J.* 1966
Rudé, G., 'The Gordon Riots', *T.R.H.S.* 1956
Sutherland, L. S., 'Burke and the First Rockingham Ministry', *E.H.R.* 1932
Sutherland, L. S., 'The City of London in Eighteenth Century Politics', in *Essays presented to Sir Lewis Namier*, ed. R. Pares and A. J. P. Taylor, Macmillan, (1956)

4. SOCIAL AND ECONOMIC
(*a*) Books
Ashton, T. S., *The Industrial Revolution, 1760–1830*, Oxford University Press, (1948)
Ashton, T. S., *An Economic History of England: the Eighteenth Century*, Methuen, (1953)
Ashton, T. S., *Economic Fluctuations in England, 1700–1800*, Oxford University Press (1959)
Bagwell, P. S., *The Transport Revolution from 1770*, Batsford, (1973)
Bovill, E. W., *English Country Life, 1780–1830*, Oxford University Press, (1962)
Carswell, J., *The South Sea Bubble*, Barrie & Jenkins, (1960)
Carus-Wilson, E. M. (ed.), *Essays in Economic History*, 3 vols., E. Arnold, (1954–62)
Chambers, J. D., and Mingay, G. E., *The Agricultural Revolution, 1750–1850*, (1966)

Davis, R., *The Rise of the British Shipping Industry in the Seventeenth and Eighteenth Centuries*, David & Charles, (1962)
Deane, P., *The First Industrial Revolution*, Cambridge University Press, (1965)
Deane, P., and Cole, W. A., *British Economic Growth, 1688–1959*, Cambridge University Press, (1967)
Dickson, P. G. M., *The Financial Revolution in England, 1688–1756*, Macmillan (1967)
Flinn, M. W., *The Origins of the Industrial Revolution*, Longman, (1966)
George, M. D., *London Life in the Eighteenth Century*, Penguin, (1925)
Hartwell, R. M. (ed.), *The Causes of the Industrial Revolution*, Methuen, (1967)
Hobsbawm, E. J., *Industry and Empire*, Weidenfeld & Nicolson, (1968)
Hughes, E., *North Country Life in the Eighteenth Century*, 2 vols., Oxford University Press, (1952–65)
Jones, E. L. (ed.), *Agricultural and Economic Growth in England, 1650–1815*, Methuen, (1967)
Jones, E. L., and Mingay, G. E., *Land, Labour and Population in the Industrial Revolution*, E. Arnold, (1967)
Marshall, D., *The English Poor in the Eighteenth Century*, Routledge, (1941)
Marshall, D., *English People in the Eighteenth Century*, Longman, (1956)
Mathias, P., *The First Industrial Nation*, Methuen, (1969)
Minchinton, W., (ed.,) *The Growth of English Overseas Trade in the Seventeenth and Eighteenth Centuries*, Methuen, (1970)
Mingay, G. E., *English Landed Society in the Eighteenth Century*, Routledge, (1963)
Mingay, G. E., *Enclosure and the Small Farmer in the Age of the Industrial Revolution*, Macmillan, (1968)
Mitchell, B. R., and Deane, P., *Abstract of British Historical Statistics*, Cambridge University Press, (1962)
Pares, R., *A West Indian Fortune*, Longman, (1950)
Perkin, H., *The Origins of Modern English Society, 1780–1880*, Routledge, (1969)
Pressnell, L. S., *Country Banking in the Industrial Revolution*, Oxford University Press, (1956)
Pressnell, L. S., (ed.), *Studies in the Industrial Revolution*, University of London Press, (1960)
Pollard, S., *The Genesis of Modern Management*, E. Arnold, (1965)
Shelton, W. J., *English Hunger and Industrial Disorders*, Macmillan, (1973)
Sutherland, L. S., *A London Merchant, 1665–1774*, F. Cass, (1933)
Thompson, E. P., *The Making of the English Working Class*, Gollancz, (1963)
Williams, E. N., *Life in Georgian England*, Batsford, (1962)
Wilson, C. H., *Anglo-Dutch Commerce and Finance in the Eighteenth Century*, Cambridge University Press, (1941)
Wilson, C. H., *England's Apprenticeship, 1603–1763*, Longman, (1965)

(*b*) *Articles of Special Importance*

Chambers, J. D., 'Enclosure and Labour Supply in the Industrial Revolution', *Econ.H.R.* 1953
Coats, A. W., 'Changing Attitudes to Labour in the mid-Eighteenth Century', *Econ.H.R.* 1958
Davis, R., 'English Foreign Trade, 1700–70', *E.H.R.* 1962
Habakkuk, H. J., 'English Landownership, 1680–1740', *Econ.H.R.* 1940
Habakkuk, H. J., 'Marriage Settlements in the Eighteenth Century', *T.R.H.S.* 1950

Habakkuk, H. J., 'The Long-Term Rate of Interest and the Price of Land in the Eighteenth Century', *Econ.H.R.* 1952

Habakkuk, H. J., 'English Population in the Eighteenth Century', *Econ.H.R.* 1953

Hartwell, R. M., 'The Rising Standard of Living in England, 1800–50', *Econ.H.R.* 1961

Hartwell, R. M., 'The Industrial Revolution', Historical Association Pamphlet, 1965

Hobsbawm, E. J., 'The British Standard of Living, 1790–1850', *Econ.H.R.* 1957

Hobsbawm, E. J., and Hartwell, R. M., 'The Standard of Living during the Industrial Revolution: a Discussion', *Econ.H.R.* 1963

John, A. H., 'War and the English Economy, 1700–83', *Econ.H.R.* 1955

John, A. H., 'Aspects of Economic Growth in the First Half of the Eighteenth Century', *Economica* 1966

Krause, J. T., 'Some Neglected Factors in the Industrial Revolution', *J.Econ.Hist.* 1959

Mingay, G. E. 'The Agricultural Depression, 1730–50', *Econ.H.R.* 1956

Perkins, H., 'Social Causes of the Industrial Revolution', *T.R.H.S.* 1968

Pollard, S., 'Investment and Consumption in the Industrial Revolution', *Econ.H.R.* 1958

Pollard, S., 'Factory Discipline in the Industrial Revolution', *Econ.H.R.* 1963

Pollard, S., 'Fixed Capital in the Industrial Revolution', *J.Econ.Hist.* 1964

Pressnell, L. S., 'Public Monies and the Development of English Banking', *Econ.H.R.* 1955

Taylor, A. J., 'Progress and Poverty in Britain, 1780–1850', *History* 1960

Wilson, C. H., 'The Entrepreneur in the Industrial Revolution', *History* 1957

Wilson, C. H., 'Mercantilism', Historical Association Pamphlet, 1958

Wrigley, E. A., 'The Supply of Raw Materials in the Industrial Revolution', *Econ.H.R.* 1962

Wrigley, E. A., 'London's Importance, 1650–1750', *Past and Present* 1967

5. FOREIGN AND IMPERIAL

Bailyn, B., *The Sociological Origins of the American Revolution*, Harvard University Press, (1967)

Christie, I. R., *Crisis of Empire*, E. Arnold, (1966)

Donoughue, B., *British Politics and the American Revolution, 1773–5*, (1964)

Gipson, L. H., *The Coming of the Revolution, 1763–75*, Harper & Row, (1954)

Harlow, V. T., *The Founding of the Second British Empire*, 2 vols., Longman, (1952–64)

Horn, D. B., *The British Diplomatic Service, 1689–1789*, Oxford University Press, (1961)

Horn, D. B., *Great Britain and Europe in the Eighteenth Century*, Oxford University Press, (1967)

Mackesy, P., *War in the Mediterranean, 1803–10*, Longman, (1957)

Mackesy, P., *The War for America, 1775–83*, Longman, (1964)

Marshall, P. J., *Problems of Empire: Britain and India, 1757–1813*, Allen & Unwin, (1968)

Miller, J. C., *The Origins of the American Revolution*, Stanford University Press, (1943)

Olsen, A. G., and Brown, R. M., (ed.), *Anglo-American Relations, 1675–1775*, Rutgess University Press, (1970)

Pares, R., *War and and Trade in the West Indies*, F. Cass (1936)
Ritcheson, C. R., *British Politics and the American Revolution*, University of Oklahoma Press, (1945)
Robson, E., *The American Revolution*, Batchworth, (1955)
Wright, E., *Causes and Consequences of the American Revolution*, Quadrangle Books, (1966)

6. RELIGIOUS, INTELLECTUAL AND CULTURAL

Bennett, G. V., and Walsh, J. D., (ed.), *Essays in Modern Church History*, Black, (1966)
Brailsford, H. N., *Shelley, Godwin and their Circle*, Oxford University Press, (1951)
Brinton, C., *The Political Ideas of the English Romanticists*, Oxford University Press, (1926)
Brown, F. K., *Fathers of the Victorians*, Cambridge University Press, (1961)
Butt, J. E., *The Augustan Age*, Hutchinson, (1950)
Butterfield, H., *The Origins of Modern Science, 1300–1800*, G. Bell, (1949)
Carpenter, S. C., *Eighteenth Century Church and People*, J. Murray, (1959)
Clifford, J. L., (ed.), *Man versus Society in Eighteenth Century Britain: Six Points of View*, Cambridge University Press, (1968)
Coomer, D., *English Dissent under the Hanoverians*, Epworth Press, (1946)
Dobrée, B., *English Literature in the Early Eighteenth Century*, Oxford University Press, (1959)
Gill, F. C., *The Romantic Movement and Methodism*, Epworth Press, (1954)
Halévy, E., *The Growth of Philosophical Radicalism*, Faber, (1934)
Harris, R. W., *Romanticism and the Social Order, 1780–1830*, Blandford Press, (1969)
Hennell, M., *John Venn and the Clapham Sect*, Lutt Press, (1958)
Howse, E. M., *Saints and Politics*, University of Toronto Press, (1952)
Hussey, C., *English Country Houses, 1760–1830*, 2 vols., Country Life Ltd., (1956–8)
Jones, M. G., *The Charity School Movement*, Cambridge University Press, (1938)
Klingender, F. D., *Art and the Industrial Revolution*, Adams & D., (1947)
Knox, R., *Enthusiasm*, Oxford University Press, (1950)
Mack, M. P., *Jeremy Bentham: an Odyssey of Ideas, 1748–92*, Heinemann Ed., (1962)
Renwick, W. L., *English Literature, 1793–1815*, Oxford University Press, (1963)
Robbins, C., *The Eighteenth Century Commonwealthman*, Atheneum N.Y., (1959)
Stromberg, R. N., *Religious Liberalism in Eighteenth Century England*, Oxford University Press, (1954)
Summerson, J. W., *Architecture in Britain, 1530–1830*, Penguin, (1953)
Sykes, N., *Church and State in England in the Eighteenth Century*, Archon, (1932)
Sykes, N., *From Sheldon to Secker: Aspects of Church History, 1660–1768*, Cambridge University Press, (1959).
Wardroper, J., *Kings, Lords and Wicked Libellers: Satire and Protest, 1760–1837*, J. Murray, (1973)
Warner, W. J., *The Wesleyan Movement in the Industrial Revolution*, Longman, (1930)
Waterhouse, E., *Painting in Britain, 1530–1790*, Penguin, (1957)
Whinney, M., *Sculpture in Britain, 1530–1830*, Penguin, (1964)
Willey, B., *The Eighteenth Century Background*, Chatto, (1949)

INDEX

The eighteenth century, 1714-1815.